Judicial Review in Greater China

This book examines the judicial review systems in the four areas of Greater China – China, Taiwan, Hong Kong, and Macau – and uncovers judicial review activities of the apex courts of each region. It provides a comparative assessment of judicial activism and deference. The development of modern judicial review is one of the key elements of the twentieth century's legal heritage. By enforcing the principles of constitutionalism, the rule of law, and human rights protection, many courts have been vested with unprecedented powers and have played an essential role in supervising the exercise of government power through constitutional and administrative review. This work investigates the most up-to-date aspects of judicial review in Greater China and reflects on the modern theory regarding the judicialization of politics in different political regimes: democratic, authoritarian, and hybrid. The volume collects all substantive judicial review decisions delivered in the past twenty years by the four apex courts: the China's Supreme People's Court, the Taiwan Constitutional Court, the Court of Final Appeal of Hong Kong, and the Court of Final Appeal of Macau. This comprehensive dataset includes some 800 judicial review decisions, presenting a comprehensive resource of fundamental baseline data for evaluating judicial review in Greater China. The book will be an invaluable companion for scholars and researchers working in the areas of Comparative Public Law, Comparative Constitutional Law, Constitutional Politics, and Asian Studies.

Shiling Xiao is a lecturer in Public Law at the University of Manchester, UK.

Globalization: Law and Policy

Globalization: Law and Policy builds an integrated body of scholarship that critically addresses key issues and theoretical debates in comparative and transnational law and the principles governance and policy on which they are developed. Volumes in the series focus on the consequential effects of globalization, including emerging frameworks and processes for the internationalization, legal harmonization, juridification, and democratization of law among increasingly connected political, economic, religious, cultural, ethnic, and other functionally differentiated governance communities. Legal systems, their harmonization and incorporation in other governance orders, and their relationship to globalization are taking on new importance within a coordinated network of domestic legal orders, the legal orders of groups of states, and the governance frameworks of non-state actors. These legal orders engage a number of important actors, sources, principles, and tribunals-including multinational corporations as governance entities, contract and surveillance as forms of governance that substitute for traditional law, sovereign wealth funds and other new forms of state activity, hybrid supra national entities like the World Bank and the International Monetary Fund, and international tribunals with autonomous jurisdiction, including the International Criminal Court, the World Trade Organization, and regional human rights courts. The effects have been profound, especially with respect to the role of states, and especially of developed states as their long time position in global affairs undergoes significant transformation. Comparative and transnational law serve as natural nexus points for vigorous and sometimes interdisciplinary approaches to the study of state and non-state law systems, along with their linkages and interactions. The series is intended as a resource for scholars, students, policy makers, and civil society actors, and includes a balance of theoretical and policy studies in single-authored volumes and collections of original essays.

Larry Catá Backer is the W. Richard and Mary Eshelman Faculty Scholar, Professor of Law and International Affairs at the Pennsylvania State University. Previously he served as Executive Director of the Comparative and International Law Center at the University of Tulsa. He has published widely on comparative and transnational law.

Also in the series:

Hostile Business and the Sovereign State
Privatized Governance, State Security and International Law
Michael J. Strauss

Legal and Rhetorical Foundations of Economic Globalization
An Atlas of Ritual Sacrifice in Late-Capitalism
Keren Wang

Armed Conflict and Human Rights Law
Protecting Civilians and International Humanitarian Law
Daniel Ivo Odon

Business, Compliance and Human Rights Law
The Effectiveness of Transnational Private Regulations for Vulnerable Stakeholders
Gabriel Webber Ziero

The United Nations Convention on the Law of the Sea
A System of Regulation
Edited by Kristina Siig, Birgit Feldtmann and Fenella M.W. Billing

Judicial Review in Greater China
Activism and Deference of Four Apex Courts
Shiling Xiao

For more information about this series, please visit:
www.routledge.com/Globalization-Law-and-Policy/book-series/GLOBLP

Judicial Review in Greater China

Activism and Deference of Four Apex Courts

Shiling Xiao

Routledge
Taylor & Francis Group
LONDON AND NEW YORK

First published 2025
by Routledge
4 Park Square, Milton Park, Abingdon, Oxon OX14 4RN

and by Routledge
605 Third Avenue, New York, NY 10158

Routledge is an imprint of the Taylor & Francis Group, an informa business

British Library Cataloguing-in-Publication Data
A catalogue record for this book is available from the British Library

Library of Congress Cataloging-in-Publication Data
Names: Xiao, Shiling, author.
Title: Judicial review in Greater China : activism and deference of four apex courts / Shiling Xiao.
Description: Abingdon, Oxon [UK] ; New York, NY : Routledge, 2025. | Series: Globalization: law and policy | Includes bibliographical references and index.
Identifiers: LCCN 2025001471 | ISBN 9781032767895 (hardback) | ISBN 9781032773407 (paperback) | ISBN 9781003482536 (ebook)
Subjects: LCSH: Judicial review of administrative acts–China. | Judicial review of administrative acts–Taiwan. | Judicial review of administrative acts–China–Hong Kong. | Judicial review of administrative acts–China–Macau (Special Administrative Region) | Constitutional courts–China. | Constitutional courts–Taiwan. | Constitutional courts–China–Hong Kong. | Constitutional courts–China–Macau (Special Administrative Region)
Classification: LCC KNQ2790 .X53 2025 | DDC 347.51/0352–dc23/eng/20250114
LC record available at https://lccn.loc.gov/2025001471

ISBN: 978-1-032-76789-5 (hbk)
ISBN: 978-1-032-77340-7 (pbk)
ISBN: 978-1-003-48253-6 (ebk)

DOI: 10.4324/9781003482536

Typeset in Galliard
by Deanta Global Publishing Services, Chennai, India

Contents

Acknowledgments

This monograph, adapted from my PhD thesis completed at the University of Hong Kong, has been further refined and updated during my work at the City University of Hong Kong and the University of Manchester. It would not have been possible without the guidance, encouragement, and support of many individuals, to whom I am deeply grateful.

First and foremost, my deep gratitude goes to my PhD supervisor, Professor Simon N. M. Young. His unwavering support, insightful guidance, and belief in my work have been invaluable. His mentorship served as a map, guiding me through the dense and complex jungle of PhD research. Most importantly, his encouragement sustained me throughout my PhD journey and the development of this manuscript.

I am also sincerely thankful to Professors Albert Chen, Eric Ip, Scott Veitch, Po Jen Yap, Alec Stone Sweet, Wen-Chang Chang, and Professor and Grand Justice Te-Chung Tang. As members of my PhD qualification panel, viva committee, and my public law teachers, they offered thoughtful and insightful feedback that significantly shaped both my thesis and this monograph.

To my colleagues at the City University of Hong Kong and the University of Manchester, particularly Professors Chunyan Ding, Guobin Zhu, Robert Thomas, Javier Garcia Oliva, John Picton, Luke Graham, and Guy Baldwin, I owe heartfelt thanks. Thanks also go to Professor Jeroen Kloet Geronimo. Their support and encouragement eased my transition to new academic environments, allowing me precious time to focus on refining this manuscript. I always feel privileged and lucky to work with them.

To my friends and PhD peers at the University of Hong Kong – Yi Tang, Yang Lin, Han Zhu, Guanhong Chen, and Ye Feng – their companionship and support enriched my academic experience. Many ideas were crystallized in our chats at cha chaan teng. Special thanks must go out to my dear friends Greg Wong and Xueji Su for their encouragement during the most challenging moments.

To Professor Larry Backer, Anna Gallagher, and Alison Kirk. It is absolutely a pleasure to work with them and I am grateful for their support and assistant at every stage of this project.

Finally, to my parents, sisters, niece, and nephew, I express my deepest appreciation. Their unwavering love and faith in me have been my greatest motivation. This book is as much a testament to their support as it is to my own efforts.

Abbreviations

ALL	Administrative Litigation Law of China
AND	Administrative normative document
BORO	Hong Kong Bill of Rights Ordinance
CAL	Code of Administrative Litigation of Macau
CAP	Code of Administrative Procedure of Macau
CCPA	Constitutional Court Procedure Act of Taiwan
CIPA	Constitutional Interpretation Procedure Act of Taiwan
CLC	Constitution and Law Committee of the NPC
CRC	Convention on the Rights of Child
CSSA	Comprehensive Social Security Assistance of Hong Kong
ECtHR	European Court of Human Rights
GFCC	German Federal Constitutional Court
HKBL	Basic Law of Hong Kong Special Administrative Region
HKSAR	Hong Kong Special Administrative Region
ICCPR	International Covenant on Civil and Political Rights
ICESCR	International Covenant on Economic, Social and Cultural Rights
LAC	Legislative Affairs Commission of the NPCSC
LC	Law Committee of the NPC
LegCo	Legislative Council of the Hong Kong
MBL	Basic Law of Macau
MSAR	Macau Special Administrative Region
NPC	National People's Congress of China
NPCSC	Standing Committee of the NPC
NSL	National Security Law of Hong Kong
PRC	People's Republic of China
SCC	Supreme Court of Canada
SPC	Supreme People's Court of China
TCC	Taiwan Constitutional Court
TUI	Court of Final Appeal of Macau (Tribunal de Última Instância de Macau)
UKSC	Supreme Court of the United Kingdom
UNHCR	United Nations High Commission for Refugees
USSC	Supreme Court of the United States
WWII	Second World War

Figures

Tables

1 Introduction

Greater China usually refers to four geographic areas comprising of China (Mainland), Taiwan, Hong Kong, and Macau, which are strikingly similar in terms of their culture, history, ethnicity, and demography. However, as elaborated below, they are lined up at different points on the political spectrum. China, being an authoritarian regime, is on one end of the political spectrum, with Taiwan on the other end as it is a democratic regime, and Hong Kong and Macau, being hybrid regimes, somewhere in the middle (Figure 1.1).

This book investigates the judicial review competence and activity of four apex courts in Greater China, being the Supreme People's Court in China (SPC), the Taiwan Constitutional Courts (TCC), the Court of Final Appeal of Hong Kong (CFA), and the Court of Final Appeal of Macau (*Tribunal de Última Instância de Macau*, TUI).

By comparing the judicial review jurisdictions conferred on the four apex courts and examining approximately 800 judicial review decisions delivered by them between 1999 and 2019, this book reveals that the TCC and the CFA have converged on active and assertive judicial review, and the SPC and the TUI have converged on a more timid and deferential approach to judicial review (Figure 1.2). The TCC and CFA have exhibited a high level of judicial activism. They were confident and fearless in striking down legislation and government actions and have frequently applied the standards of proportionality and equality protection rigorously. Through judicial review, the TCC and the CFA have positively influenced government policy, protected people's rights,

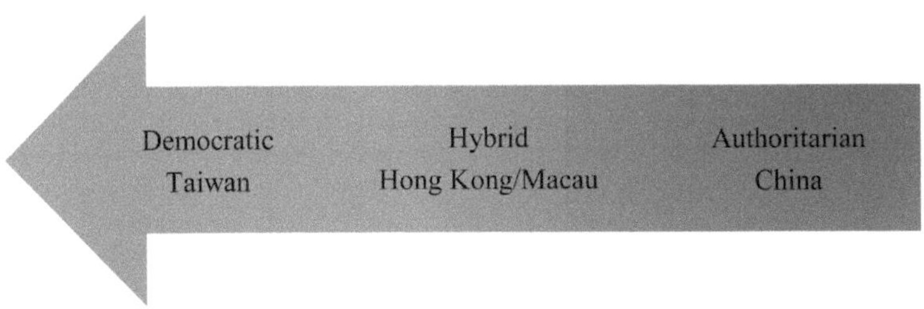

Figure 1.1 Political Spectrum of Greater China.

DOI: 10.4324/9781003482536-1

Figure 1.2 Spectrum of Judicial Activism and Deference of the Four Apex Courts in Greater China.

Source: Author.

safeguarded the rule of law, and refined local legal landscapes. Conversely, the TUI has displayed a deferential approach, reminiscent of the SPC, a supreme court in an authoritarian regime. They were either incompetent or unwilling to review legislation and administrative rules. They granted substantial leeway to their governments in reviewing concrete administrative decisions. Despite these four geographic areas sharing almost identical culture, history, ethnicity, language, and demography, two opposite trends have emerged in relation to judicial review of government power. It is particularly striking that judicial review in Hong Kong and Macau, two hybrid regimes with nearly identical constitutional orders, have developed in two opposite directions, showing judicial review in hybrid regimes is indeterminate, fluid, and dynamic in the sense that they can trend toward the democratic or authoritarian ends.

What explains the convergence and divergence in judicial activism/deference among the four apex courts in Greater China? The phenomenon of global expansion of judicial power is explained through expanding literature providing various accounts. The classic comparative judicial review studies, focusing on countries who are the "usual suspects" of comparative studies,[1] emphasized the relationship between modern democracies and judicial review that more established and vibrant democracies can host more activist courts and stronger judicial review.[2] Martin Shapiro suggested that active judicial review was both

1 Ran Hirschl, *Comparative Matters: The Renaissance of Comparative Constitutional Law* (OUP 2014) 192.

2 Democracy, by definition, is typically associated with fragmentation of power and implies political competitiveness. No matter the variousness of Alec Stone Sweet's incomplete contracting theory, Ginsburg's insurance model of judicial review, or Hirschl's hegemonic preservation theory, they all were built on democracy and fragmentation of power. Stone Sweet stated that a constitution could be conceived as a contract between political elites who jointly negotiate the constitutional framework of a state. In establishing a democracy, the contracting parties know that they will compete with each other for office, through elections. They want to restrict the opponents who could be in power through elections. This is realized, in part, by constitutional rights and constitutional review. Alec Stone Sweet, *Governing with Judges: Constitutional Politics in Europe* (OUP 2000); Alec Stone Sweet and Jud Matthew, *Proportionality Balancing and*

a prerequisite and a by-product of a viable democratic government.[3] Ran Hirschl asserted that "more democracy equals more courts".[4] Tom Ginsburg stated that "judicial review is more likely in cultures where judges are associated with the liberal ideal of limited government".[5] On the other hand, studies of judicial review practiced in semi- and authoritarian regimes asserted that these regimes could not host an active and assertive judicial review. For example, Ginsburg stated, "Compared to autocratic regimes, this means that courts [of democratic regimes] have more room in which to work".[6] Björn Dressel asserted that "more established and vibrant democracies seem to host more activist courts; in semi- and authoritarian settings judges are far less assertive",[7] and "the proliferation and growing assertiveness of judicial and quasi-judicial agencies are expressions of a universal modernization that embraces the rule of law and separation of powers as constructs of viable democratic government".[8]

If the democratic theories are adequate to explain the judicial review activity in Greater China, why does the spectrum of judicial review activism/deference

Constitutional Governance: A Comparative and Global Approach (OUP 2019). Ginsburg suggested that judicial review was a form of political insurance that mitigates the risk of electoral loss. As democracy increases electoral uncertainty, no party can predict with confidence that it will maintain power indefinitely. It makes sense that parties that believe they could lose power in elections agree to adopt judicial review as a forum to challenge government action. A polity is more likely to adopt judicial review where each party's power is pretty even. Tom Ginsburg, *Judicial Review in New Democracies: Constitutional Courts in Asian Cases* (CUP 2003). Hirschl offered another political account called "hegemonic preservation". When a ruling party foresees itself losing power, it may initiate a constitutional entrenchment of rights and judicial review to transfer power to the courts. It assumes that empowering courts is a way of ensuring its policy preferences are preserved. Ran Hirschl, *Towards Juristocracy: The Origins and Consequences of the New Constitutionalism* (Harvard University Press 2004). Besides political competition, modern democracy connotes respecting human rights and the rule of law. Bills of rights and independent judicial bodies to which any individual can bring a constitutional complaint are basic characteristics of modern constitutionalism. Ginsburg stated: "Constitutional review in this account is a dependent variable with demand for rights as the key independent variable." Tom Ginsburg, 'The Global Spread of Constitutional Review' in Keith E. Whittington, R. Daniel Kelemen, and Gregory A. Caldeira (eds) *The Oxford Handbook of Law and Politics* (OUP 2008) 88.

3 Martin Shapiro, 'The Success of Judicial Review' in Sally J. Kenney, William M. Reisinger, and John C. Reitz (eds) *Constitutional Dialogues in Comparative Perspective* (Palgrave Macmillan 1999).

4 Ran Hirschl, 'The Judicialization of Politics' in Keith E. Whittington, R. Daniel Kelemen, and Gregory A. Caldeira (eds) *The Oxford Handbook of Law and Politics* (OUP 2008) 135.

5 Ginsburg, 'The Global Spread of Constitutional Review' (n 2) 88.

6 Tom Ginsburg, 'The Judicialization of Administrative Governance: Causes, Consequence and Limits' in Tom Ginsburg and Albert H. Y. Chen (eds) *Administrative Law and Governance in Asia* (Routledge 2009) 7.

7 Björn Dressel (ed), *The Judicialization of Politics in Asia* (Routledge 2012) 8.

8 *Ibid.*, 4.

of the four apex courts not mirror the political spectrum? Several prominent scholars have analyzed the judicial review practices in Greater China, identifying institutional, political, and historical factors that shape the different trajectories among the apex courts. Po Jen Yap and Chien-Chih Lin suggested that a fragmentation of power and an independent judiciary are two institutional explanations for the TCC's and CFA's convergence on structure proportionality and constitutional remedies. Eric Ip suggested transaction costs may account for the difference in the CFA's and the TUI's constitutional review evolutionary path. The factional infight inside Hong Kong's ruling elites and formidable popular resistance to its initiatives disable the government from credibly threatening the CFA, reinforcing the demand for judicial review of unpopular policies. In contrast, Macau has a higher level of executive-legislative harmony, minimal civil unrest, and very weak pressure to democratization. The Macau government could pre-empt and discourage the TUI from engaging in any active judicial review. Albert Chen and PY Lo suggested the legal traditions that already existed in Hong Kong and Macau at the time of their respective handovers explained the divergence between the CFA and the TUI.

In addition to these factors, this book also suggests the judges' educational background and the foreign legal knowledge and jurisprudence they brought to the courts impact judicial review activities, resulting in the convergence and divergence of judicial review in Greater China. Many judges on the TCC and the CFA obtained their legal education in Western countries, particularly in Germany, the US (for TCC judges), and the UK (for CFA judges). This educational experience and legal knowledge they obtained have significantly informed their decisions and reasoning, reflecting on the pervasive references to and citations of foreign laws and precedents. The TCC judges frequently referred to and discussed German and American public law decisions and jurisprudence in their separate opinions,[9] and the CFA has extensively used comparative law, especially authorities from the UK, Canada, Australia, and the ECtHR,[10] leading them to align more closely with the judicial review in liberal democracies. Additionally, on the CFA, overseas non-permanent judges have played an additional and essential role in maintaining Hong Kong's judicial review in line with common law jurisprudence.

By contrast, in Macau, three out of four TUI judges sitting on the bench between 1999 and 2019 were born in Mainland China, and two judges obtained their first law degree in China and two in Portugal. Chinese and

9 Wen-Chen Chang (張文貞), 'An Empirical Study on the Reference of Foreign Laws and Precedents by Constitutional Court Interpretations: The Study-Abroad Backgrounds as the Key (司法院大法官解釋引用外國法及判決之實證研究—大法官留學背景作為引用的關鍵因素)' in Yun-Chien Chang (張永健) (ed) *Empirical Studies of the Judicial System 2011* (2011司法制度實證研究) (The Institutum Iurisprudentiae Academia Sinica 2013) 66–73.

10 Sir Anthony Mason, 'The Common Law' in Simon N. M. Young and Yash Ghai (eds), *Hong Kong's Court of Final Appeal: The Development of the Law in China's Hong Kong* (CUP 2014) 347–348.

Portuguese influence is overt and profound in the TUI's decisions and has led the court to a deferential and cautious stance in judicial review. In politically sensitive cases of constitutional importance, the TUI readily invokes Chinese law, Chinese courts' decisions, and Chinese scholars' opinions. It is worthy highlighting that, despite the same constitutional arrangement and even more enormous pressure imposed on Hong Kong by Beijing, Chinese laws hold little leverage on the CFA's judicial review. The CFA has been steadfastly guarding the expertise and authorities of Hong Kong's courts in interpreting and applying laws following the common law approach. In China, nearly all senior judges of the SPC are trained domestically, and they have rarely cited foreign laws, precedents, or scholarship.[11] But this does not mean that China completely isolates itself from foreign legal systems. Chinese judges are well-informed and sometimes embrace foreign laws. Nevertheless, these foreign doctrines are adjusted to accommodate China's political and legal environment, where judicial review power is seriously restrained.[12] For example, doctrines like proportionality, which are robust in other jurisdictions, have been weakened when applied within China.

Four Regimes in Greater China and One Political Spectrum

Authoritarian China. The Chinese Communist Party (CCP) established the People's Republic of China (PRC) on 1 October 1949 in the aftermath of the costly full-scale civil war. Since then, the CCP has been the single ruling party in China and "an integral and vital part of the state's constitutional, political and legal systems".[13] Since its establishment, the PRC has enacted four constitutions in 1954, 1975, 1978, and 1982, respectively. The constitution of 1982, subject to five amendments, is the one currently in force. The one-party rule and CCP's leadership have been enshrined in the Preamble of the PRC Constitutions since 1954. In 2018, CCP's leadership was even written into the body content of the Constitution. Article 1 of the PRC Constitution stipulates that "the CCP's leadership is a defining feature of socialism with Chinese characteristics". There are political parties in China, but plural political competition is impermissible under the CCP's rule.[14] Those political parties participate in politics through the system of multi-party cooperation and

11 Zhihang Zheng (郑智航), 'Domestic Application of Foreign Laws and Precedents (外国法与案例在本国司法中的运用)' (2014) 2 *Global Law Review* (环球法律评论) 105, 118–122.

12 Shiling Xiao, 'State-Centric Proportionality Analysis in Chinese Administrative Litigation' (2023) 21 *International Journal of Constitutional Law* 461, 474–479.

13 Albert H. Y. Chen, 'Constitutions, Constitutional Practice and Constitutionalism in East Asia' in Christoph Antons (ed) *Routledge Handbook of Asian Law* (Routledge 2019) 89.

14 Li-Ann Thio, 'Varieties of Constitutionalism in Asia' (2021) *Asia Journal of Comparative Law* 1, 15.

political consultation under the leadership of the CCP.[15] Democracy with the changeover of political parties through competitive elections has not been established in China.

After the end of the Cultural Revolution, China has been implementing the policy of "reform and openness" since 1978. The economic growth of China is a big miracle, and people's economic life has changed dramatically. The CCP wields legitimacy through economic development. At the same time, China has moved a long way from a totalitarian control system, by which the party-state controlled the social and economic domains and all aspects of people's lives.[16] Nonetheless, the CCP's rule remains authoritarian and still exerts a high level of control over politics, the economy, and people's lives, including freedom of speech and religion. The CCP has almost total control over the people's congresses and the people's governments at all levels. Although the law requires the representatives of people's congresses to be elected directly or indirectly by people, in practice, candidatures of higher-level people's congresses are nominated and selected by CCP organs behind the scenes.[17] The main government officials are appointed by the people's congresses, and most are CCP members. The state organs, military, and congresses are submissive and subject to directives of the CCP.[18]

President Xi Jinping stressed that "[n]o organization or individual has the power to overstep the Constitution and law".[19] However, the supremacy of the party persists, overshadowing the principle of the rule of law.[20] An illustrative instance is the removal of presidential term limits by amending the constitution in 2018.[21] Consequently, Xi Jinping, as the leader of the Chinese CCP, commenced his third term in 2023 and could potentially extend his tenure beyond.

In 2014, the CCP Central Committee claimed that "the socialist legal system with Chinese characteristics has formed".[22] Hualing Fu suggests that

15 The Preamble of the Constitution of PRC (中华人民共和国宪法). References to the Constitution of the PRC in this book will be to the PRC Constitution 2018, unless otherwise indicated.

16 Randall Peerenboom, *China's Long March Toward Rule of Law* (CUP 2002) 47.

17 Albert H. Y. Chen, 'Pathways of Western Liberal Constitutional Development in Asia: A Comparative Study of Five Major Nations' (2010) *International Journal of Constitutional Law* 849, 878.

18 Xin He, 'The Party's Leadership as a Living Constitution in China', in Tom Ginsburg and Alberto Simpser (eds), *Constitutions in Authoritarian Regimes* (CUP 2013) 245–264.

19 'Xi Stresses Importance of Constitution' *Xinhuanet*, available at www.xinhuanet.com/english/2018-02/25/c_136998465.htm, accessed 10 October 2021.

20 Thio, 'Varieties of Constitutionalism in Asia' (n 14) 16.

21 Constitution of the PRC (n 15), art 79(1).

22 'CCP Central Committee Decision Concerning Several Major Issues in Comprehensively Advancing Governance According to Law' (中共中央关于全面推进依法治国若干重大问题的决定), available at www.gov.cn/zhengce/2014-10/28/content_2771946.htm, accessed 29 July 2024.

China's legal system is a dual legal system under the CCP's governance. The private law system has become "professionalized, institutionalized, and semi-autonomous".[23] Chinese contract law, property law, investment law, company law, and many others have facilitated social and economic development and attracted foreign investment. The civil law system and its enforcement are largely fair, predictable, and authoritative.[24] Chinese courts have developed their ability to absorb and internalize political commands and factors in political concerns through their judicial discretion in civil litigation.[25]

Laws and legal rules are useful tools for the CPP's authoritarian rule. This instrumental function of laws is more discernible in the fields of administrative law and criminal law. Many political offenses in criminal law are often used and abused to repress social activists, human rights lawyers, and religious and ethnic dissidents. But laws are not the only tools, nor the most efficient and effective ones, given the fact that laws are stable and formal with relatively strict legislative processes. The CPP is adept at using extra-legal tools to achieve its governing purposes. For instance, the CCP issued a series of Five-Year Plans, which mapped out the goals and directions for the national economic and social development. The anti-corruption campaign carried out since 2012, following the conclusion of the 18th CCP National Congress,[26] along with the project of "Hunting Fox",[27] is another example of the CCP's powerful and extra-legal rule model, by which Xi Jinping redesigned China's political structure and rewrote China's political rules. The mass internment in Xinjiang is an extra-legal method to crack down on religious and ethnic dissent.

As far as human rights protection in China are concerned, there is a duality as well. For 40 years, China has achieved substantial progress in the realization and improvement of people's lives. According to the World Bank's statistics, more than 800 million people have been lifted out of poverty since China began to open up and reform.[28] There have also been significant achievements in access to health, education, and other services over the same period.[29] The CCP often proclaims these achievements in domestic and international propaganda. Nonetheless, the long-term and increasingly strict control over media, religion, and ethnic affairs, and repression of human rights defenders and pro-

23 Hualing Fu, 'Duality and China's Struggle for Legal Autonomy' (2019) *China Perspectives* 1, 6.
24 *Ibid.*
25 *Ibid.*, 7.
26 'Xi Pledges "Sweeping Victory" in Anti-Corruption' *Xinhua News* (18 October 2017), available at www.xinhuanet.com/english/2017-10/18/c_136688762.htm, accessed 29 July 2024.
27 "Hunting Fox" is an anti-corruption campaign launched by China in 2014. It aims to arrest people who commit corruption and flee China.
28 The World Bank in China, available at www.worldbank.org/en/country/china/overview#1, accessed 29 July 2024.
29 *Ibid.*

democracy activists are the stinging stains on China's human rights record. Human rights, in particular civil and political rights, take a back seat to the CCP's agenda of political control, economic growth, and maintaining social stability.

Democratic Taiwan. Before 1949, the Kuomintang was the political party ruling China. Due to its defeat by the CCP in the civil war on the mainland, the Kuomintang retreated to Taiwan and moved the Government of the Republic of China to Taiwan. In Taiwan, the Kuomintang started authoritarian rule with martial law, which persisted for more than 30 years until the late 1980s, when the Kuomintang began an incremental democratization process.[30] First, it acquiesced to the establishment of the Democratic Progressive Party, an opposition party, in 1986.[31] The following year, it lifted the Martial Law Decree. After three decades of democratization, Taiwan is now one of the most recognizable Asian constitutional democracies,[32] featuring stable competitive elections and advanced protection for human rights and civil liberties.

There have been peaceful changeovers of governmental power and free electoral competition for the president and legislature in Taiwan. The first legislative election was held in 1992, and the first direct presidential election in 1996.[33] The Kuomintang lost the presidential election and handed over the power to the Democratic Progressive Party in 2000 for the first time, with Chen Shui-bian becoming president. In 2008, Kuomintang regained power with its leader Ma Ying-jeou elected as president (2008–2016). In 2016, the Democratic Progressive Party was back in power, and Tsai Ing-Wen (2016–2024) and Lai Ching-Te (2024–) were elected as presidents. According to the Economist Intelligence Unit's Democracy Index, Taiwan was 10th among 167 areas in 2023, the most democratic area in Asia.[34]

The Constitution of the Republic of China, which was enacted in 1947, has undergone seven amendments, in 1991, 1992, 1994, 1997, 1999, 2000, and 2005, respectively.[35] After democratization, the constitution is fully effective and regulates the behavior of political actors.[36] Taiwan establishes a five-power government system according to the teaching of Sun Yat-sen. The central government is comprising of five branches. Besides the traditional legislative,

30 Chen, 'Pathways of Western Liberal Constitutional Development in Asia' (n 17) 876.
31 Po Jen Yap, *Courts and Democracies in Asia* (CUP 2017) 94.
32 Jiunn-Rong Yeh and Wen-Chen Chang, 'The Emergence of East Asian Constitutionalism: Features in Comparison' (2011) 59 *American Journal of Comparative Law* 805, 807.
33 Jiunn-Rong Yeh and Wen-Chen Chang, 'A Decade of Changing Constitutionalism in Taiwan: Transitional and Transnational Perspectives' in Albert H. Y. Chen (ed) *Constitutionalism in Asia in the Early Twenty-First Century* (CUP 2014) 142.
34 Economist Intelligence Unit, *Democracy Index 2023*, available at www.eiu.com/n/campaigns/democracy-index-2023/, accessed 20 September 2024.
35 The Amendment to the Constitutional of Taiwan (1999) was invalidated by the TCC through Interpretation No. 499.
36 Chen, 'Constitutions, Constitutional Practice and Constitutionalism in East Asia' (n 13) 80.

executive, and judicial branches, Taiwan also established the Examination Yuan, to administer the selection of candidates for the bureaucracies, and the Control Yuan, to supervise the integrity and efficiency of the government.[37] Although the five-branch system is considered complex and inefficient,[38] five powers under this system could achieve the effect of checks and balances to a large extent.

Prior to democratization, tight restrictions were imposed on people's civil and political rights, while the governmental power was not properly regulated, resulting in the so-called "era of White Terror".[39] In the transition from authoritarianism to democracy, Taiwan took steps to enhance the regulation of the government's power and expressed a deep commitment to human rights protection. To address the transitional justice issues, Taiwan established the Compensation Foundation for Improper Verdicts on Sedition and Communist Espionage in 1999 and has compensated over 10,000 victims.[40] Despite the fact that Taiwan is not a United Nations member and that its instruments of accession and ratification were rejected by the United Nations, it still enacted the Implementation Acts for six international human rights treaties, including the International Covenant on Civil and Political Rights (ICCPR) and the International Covenant on Economic, Social and Cultural Rights (ICESCR).[41] These Implementation Acts make all rights enshrined in the international human rights treaties directly applicable to Taiwan.[42] Notably, in 2019, Taiwan became the first area in Asia that legalized same-sex marriage. In a nutshell, Taiwan is a vibrant Asian democracy with commitments to human rights and the rule of law.

Hybrid Regimes in Hong Kong and Macau. In 1842, the Qing Empire in China lost the First Opium War and was forced to enter the Treaty of Nanking which ceded Hong Kong Island to the British Empire. Later, the Kowloon Peninsula was added to the colony of Hong Kong through the Convention of Peking in 1860. The New Territories, comprising a larger portion of the mainland, were leased to Britain for 99 years in 1898. Under British colonial governance, Hong Kong evolved into a vital British outpost, thriving as a major trading port and financial center. Its strategic location made it a hub

37 Jiunn-Rong Yeh, *The Constitution of Taiwan: A Contextual Analysis* (Hart 2016) 53.

38 *Ibid.*, 56.

39 Randal Peerenboom and Weitseng Chen, 'Developing the Rule of Law' in Bruce Gilley and Larry Diamond (eds) *Political Change in China: Comparisons with Taiwan* (Lynne Rienner Publisher 2008) 138.

40 Weitseng Chen, 'Twins of Opposites: Why China Will Not Follow Taiwan's Model of Rule of Law Transition toward Democracy' (2018) 66 *American Journal of Comparative Law* 481, 497.

41 The other four treaties are the Convention on Elimination of All Forms of Discrimination against Women, the Convention on the Rights of Child, the Convention on the Rights of Persons with Disabilities, and the International Convention on the Elimination of All Forms of Racial Discrimination.

42 Yeh and Chang, 'A Decade of Changing Constitutionalism in Taiwan' (n 33) 143.

for commerce, connecting East and West. The end of colonial rule came on 1 July 1997 when China resumed its sovereignty over Hong Kong. The Basic Law of Hong Kong (HKBL), the mini-constitution of Hong Kong, came into force on the same day.

The One Country Two Systems (OCTS) principle, enshrined in the preamble of the HKBL, is a fundamental principle of Hong Kong's governance and relationship with Beijing. Under this principle, Hong Kong, as a special administrative region of China (HKSAR), exercises a high degree of autonomy and enjoys executive, legislative, and independent judicial power.[43] The previous capitalist system and way of life remain unchanged in Hong Kong for 50 years, and the laws previously in force are maintained except for those which Beijing declares to be inconsistent with the HKBL.[44] More importantly, the HKBL contains democratic elements and potentially leads Hong Kong to a democratic society under China's authoritarian reign. Articles 45 and 68 of the HKBL specify universal suffrage to be the ultimate approach to electing the Chief Executive and legislative councilors. As a matter of fact, however, the HKBL does not lead Hong Kong to establish a democratic regime. Instead, it constitutes the roots of Hong Kong's hybrid regime.[45]

Elections in Hong Kong are flawed and far from democratic. The head of the executive branch, the Chief Executive of the HKSAR, is elected by an Election Committee and appointed by Beijing.[46] According to Hong Kong's latest electoral system designed by the National People's Congress (NPC) and its Standing Committee (NPCSC) in Beijing in March 2021, the Election Committee is comprised of 1500 members from five sectors,[47] which are dominated by pro-Beijing members.[48] In the 2021 election overhaul, the subsectors that are traditionally pro-democracy were either reduced or eliminated. For example, 117 seats for District Councilors were removed, and the seats for Social Welfare; Sports, Entertainment, Culture, and Publishing; Education; and Medical and Health Services were halved, from 60 to 30. Conversely, pro-Beijing subsectors were either newly introduced or significantly expanded. Notable additions include Representatives of Hong Kong Members of Relevant

43 HKBL, art 2.

44 HKBL, arts 5 and 8. In February 1997, the NPCSC adopted all the laws previously in force in Hong Kong, save for 24 ordinances which it found inconsistent with the HKBL. This means that over 600 ordinances that were previously in force continue to apply in Hong Kong. Elsie Leung, 'The Continuity of Hong Kong's Legal System', Speech at the Asia-Pacific Society, Oxford University on 4 March 2001, para 14, available at www.doj.gov.hk/en/archive/sa_by_sec_2001.html, accessed 20 February 2022.

45 Julius Yam, 'Approaching the Legitimacy Paradox in Hong Kong: Lessons for Hybrid Regime Courts' (2020) 46 *Law and Society Inquiry* 153, 158.

46 HKBL, art 45 and Annex I.

47 HKBL Annex I: Method for the Selection of the Chief Executive of the Hong Kong Special Administrative Region, art 2 (30 March 2021).

48 *Ibid.*, art 3.

National Organizations (110 seats), Grassroots Associations (60 seats), and Association of Chinese Fellow Townsmen (60 seats).[49]

The election of the Legislative Council is not totally democratic. Before the electoral overhaul in 2021, half of the seats (35 seats) used to be elected through universal suffrage.[50] Under the new electoral arrangement, only 20 out of 90 seats are elected via direct universal suffrage. The remaining seats are returned from indirect elections by the Election Committee (40 seats) and functional constituencies (30 seats).[51] Both the Election Committee and functional constituencies have a close tie with Beijing. Eventually, the Legislative Council election in 2021 resulted in only one non-pro-establishment candidate being elected.[52] After enacting the National Security Law (NSL) for Hong Kong in June 2020, Beijing introduced a new requirement that those governing Hong Kong need to be patriots.[53] To implement this requirement and ensure that only patriots govern Hong Kong, the HKSAR Government set up a Candidate Eligibility Review Committee.[54] Seven members of the committee are empowered to disqualify unpatriotic candidates from running for the elections of Chief Executive, Legislative Council members, and district council members. To obtain approval from the committee, candidates' records and past behaviors must prove that they do not oppose the political order that Beijing defines and wants. The electoral overhaul further drags Hong Kong away from the progress toward democracy.

49 *Ibid.*

50 From 1998 to 2012, Hong Kong LegCo was comprised of 60 members. The number of LegCo members returned by geographic constituencies (direct election) increased from 20 in the first term (1998–2000) to 24 in the second term (2000–2004) and reached 30 in the Third and Fourth terms (2004–2012). Decision of the National People's Congress on the Method for the Formation of the First Government and the First Legislative Council of the Hong Kong Special Administrative Region, para. 6 (4 April 1990); HKBL Annex II, art 1 (4 April 1990); Decision of the Standing Committee of the National People's Congress on Issues Relating to the Methods for Selecting the Chief Executive of the Hong Kong Special Administrative Region in the Year 2007 and for Forming the Legislative Council of the Hong Kong Special Administrative Region in the Year 2008 (26 April 2004).

51 HKBL Annex II: Method for the Formation of the Legislative Council of the Hong Kong Special Administrative Region and Its Voting Procedures, art 1 (30 March 2021).

52 '"Patriots" Election: Hong Kong's Sole Non-Establishment Lawmaker-Elect Says He Felt "Lonely" Until He Met New Colleagues' *Hong Kong Free Press* (21 December 2021), available at https://hongkongfp.com/2021/12/21/patriots-election-hong-kongs-sole-non-establishment-lawmaker-elect-says-he-felt-lonely-until-he-met-new-colleagues/, accessed 19 January 2022.

53 '"Patriots Governing Hong Kong" Essence of "One Country, Two Systems": Senior Chinese Official' *Xinhuanet* (23 February 2021), available at www.xinhuanet.com/english/2021-02/23/c_139761790.htm, accessed 11 October 2021.

54 'Chief Executive Appoints Candidate Eligibility Review Committee Members' *Hong Kong Government Press Releases* (6 July 2021), available at www.info.gov.hk/gia/general/202107/06/P2021070600318.htm?fontSize=1, accessed 11 October 2021.

Despite the undemocratic elections, Hong Kong is still recognized as an area with a well-established rule of law. Even after Beijing foisted the NSL on this city in 2020, Hong Kong still retains a good record of rule of law – 23rd in 2023.[55] As far as human rights and freedoms are concerned, Hong Kong has a good reputation. A wide range of human rights and freedoms are enshrined in the HKBL and the Hong Kong Bill of Rights Ordinance (BORO), which was enacted in 1991 to implement the ICCPR.[56] A total of 15 United Nations human rights treaties apply to Hong Kong.[57] Before the NSL came into force in 2020, Hong Kong people's right to peaceful assembly, freedom of expression, and other political and civil rights were generally respected.[58]

Located across the Lingding Channel from Hong Kong, Macau Special Administrative Region (MSAR) was established on 20 December 1999, when China resumed its sovereignty over Macau, concluding more than four centuries of Portuguese rule.[59] In 1557, Portuguese merchants and sailors were authorized by China's Ming Emperor to establish a settlement on the peninsula as a reward for defeating pirate fleets on China's southern coast. [60] Over time, the Portuguese gained control over Macau through a series of invasions, suppressions, and agreements with the Chinese Ming and Qing Empires, formalized by the Treaty of Peking in 1887.[61] Macau served as a crucial trading post, facilitating cultural and economic exchanges between Europe and Asia.

Similar to Hong Kong, Macau operates as a hybrid political regime with a limited electoral franchise and certain civil liberties.[62] The Basic Law of Macau (MBL) mirrored the HKBL.[63] OCTS is the cardinal principle of the MBL,[64]

55 World Justice Project, *Rule of Law Index 2023*, available at https://worldjusticeproject.org/rule-of-law-index/downloads/WJPIndex2023.pdf, accessed 20 September 2024.

56 For the detailed history of the BORO and the relationship between BORO, the Basic Law and the Covenant, see Johannes Chan and Chin Leng Lim, *Law of the Hong Kong Constitution* (Sweet and Maxwell 2015) 16.009–16.127.

57 The Rights of the Individual, available at www.cmab.gov.hk/en/issues/human.htm, accessed 12 October 2021.

58 Mathew Y. H. Wong and others, 'Democracy, Constitutional Framework, and Human Rights: A Comparison of Monaco, Tonga, Hong Kong, and Singapore' (2021) 64 *International Journal of Law, Crime and Justice* 1, 6.

59 Jason Buhi, *Global Constitutional Narratives of Autonomous Regions: The Constitutional History of Macau* (Routledge 2020).

60 Paul Cardinal, 'Macau: Transformation of an Historic Autonomy', in Yash Ghai and Sophia Woodman (eds), *Practising Self-Government: A Comparative Study of Autonomous Regions* (CUP 2013) 384–385.

61 Zhihui He (何志辉), *A New Study on the Legal History of Macau* (澳门法制史新编) (Social Sciences Literature Press 社会科学文献出版社 2019) 124–125.

62 Zhidong Hao, *Macau: History and Society* (2nd edn, HKU Press 2020) 48; Ying-Ho Kwong, 'Ruling Coalition Restructuring under Macao's Hybrid Regime' (2017) 17 *China Review* 111, 112.

63 Eric C. Ip, *Hybrid Constitutionalism: The Politics of Constitutional Review in the Chinese Special Administrative Regions* (CUP 2019) 105.

64 The Preamble of the MBL.

and Macau exercises a high degree of autonomy and enjoys legislative, executive, and judicial power, including final adjudication.[65] The previous capitalist system and way of life remain unchanged for 50 years and the laws previously in force are maintained except for those which Beijing declares to be inconsistent with the MBL.[66]

In Macau, the Chief Executive is not directly elected by its citizens but is chosen by an Election Committee and appointed by Beijing, mirroring Hong Kong's Chief Executive election system.[67] The Election Committee of Macau expanded to 400 from 300 members in 2012.[68] The members are drawn from various sectors of society and are divided into four sectors.[69] The Election Committee is also dominated by elites who are loyal to Beijing. Each Election Committee member can only nominate one candidate for the office of Chief Executive.[70] To run for office, a candidate must be nominated by at least 66 Election Committee members.[71] Since the handover, Macau has held six Chief Executive elections, only the first Chief Executive election in 1999 being contested. In the other elections of 2004, 2009, 2014, 2019, and 2024, there was only one candidate running for the Chief Executive "election".

The last Legislative Assembly of colonial Macau formed in 1996 continued operating as the first Legislative Assembly of the MSAR under the "through train" arrangement.[72] The Legislative Assembly comprised 23 seats (the first term) and increased to 27 seats (the second term), 29 seats (the third and fourth terms)[73] and 33 seats (the fifth term and after).[74] Under the electoral system after 2013, fewer than half of the seats are directly elected (14 seats) by universal suffrage. Twelve seats are indirectly elected by social and economic sectoral constituencies and seven seats are appointed by the Chief Executive.[75] Since the handover, Macau has held six Legislative Assembly elections. The

65 *Ibid.*, art 2.

66 *Ibid.*, arts 5 and 8.

67 MBL, art 47 and Annex I.

68 Amendment to MBL Annex I: Method for the Selection of the Chief Executive of the Macau Special Administrative Region, art 1 (30 June 2012).

69 *Ibid.*

70 *Ibid.*, art 2.

71 *Ibid.*

72 The "through train" arrangement would have been applied to Hong Kong. However, Beijing claimed that the last colonial Legislative Council formed according to Christopher Patten's reform was inconsistent with the Basic Law promulgated in 1990. Lo Shiu-Hing and Yu Wing-Yat, 'The Politics of Electoral Reform in Hong Kong' (2001) 39(2) *Commonwealth & Comparative Politics* 98, 105. China established a Provisional Legislative Council for Hong Kong in December 1996 which operated until 1998 when the first Legislative Council of Hong Kong was founded.

73 MBL Annex II: Method for the Formation of the Legislative Assembly of the Macau Special Administrative Region, art 1 (31 March 1993).

74 Amendment to MBL Annex II: Method for the Formation of the Legislative Assembly of the Macau Special Administrative Region, art 1 (30 June 2012).

75 *Ibid.*

great majority of seats were taken by pro-Beijing lawmakers in each election. Pro-democracy lawmakers merely obtained two (from 2001 to 2017) or three seats (2017–2021), and all returned from the direct election.[76] In the 2021 Legislative Assembly election, all candidates from pro-democracy camps were disqualified for running the election on the grounds that they failed to uphold the MBL and bear allegiance to the MSAR.[77] The fact behind these disqualification decisions was these democrats organized and participated in protests and assemblies in memory of the Tiananmen Square military crackdown, and some organized and participated in assemblies in memory of Liu Xiaobo and Charter 08.[78] Unlike the HKBL, the MBL does not contain a vision for universal suffrage. Even though the HKBL mentions universal suffrage, Hong Kong has not made much progress in this kind.[79] There is even less chance for Macau to have a popularly elected Chief Executive and Legislative Assembly in the future.

Despite its small territory and limited natural materials, Macau has thrived economically, mainly due to the gambling-related tourism industry.[80] Its casino industry has experienced rapid growth since 2002 when the Macau government liberalized this sector and introduced six big casino operators.[81] According to Chapter III of the MBL, people in Macau enjoy a wide range of fundamental rights and freedoms. International treaties also play an important role in rights protection in Macau.[82] Although Portugal had not extended the

76 The two pro-democracy political parties that won some seats through direct elections were the New Macau Association (新澳門學社) and its splinter party – New Democratic Macau Association (澳門社區發展新動力). The New Macau Association held two seats from 2001 to 2017 and one seat from 2017 to 2021. The New Democratic Macau Association won two seats in the 2017 election.

77 '澳门立法会候选人遭集体DQ,「爱国爱澳」面临重新定义' BBC, 14 July 2021, www.bbc.com/zhongwen/trad/chinese-news-57811700, accessed 4 October 2024.

78 Case 113/2021, pages 191, 204–209 (31 July 2021). Liu Xiaobo is one of China's prominent dissidents and the most well-known human rights activists and political prisoners. He was arrested and sentenced to jail in December 2008 for the crime of inciting subversion of state power. His crime was to publicize his criticisms of the Chinese government and to be one of main drafters of Charter 08, a manifesto calling for democracy, respect for human rights, and the rule of law. Liu Xiaobo was awarded the Nobel Peace Prize on 8 October 2010, but he was absent from the ceremony and was represented by an empty chair. On 13 July 2017, Liu Xiaobo died from liver cancer. Jean-Philippe Beja, Fu Hualing, and Eva Pils (eds), *Liu Xiaobo, Charter 08 and the Challenges of Political Reform in China* (Hong Kong University Press, 2012).

79 Hao (n 62) 49.

80 Macau poised to become richest place on the planet by 2020, *South China Morning Post* (8 August 2018) , available at www.scmp.com/news/hong-kong/hong-kong-economy/article/2158708/macau-poised-become-richest-place-planet-2020, accessed 13 October 2021.

81 Sonny Shiu-Hing Lo and Eric King-Man Chong, 'Casino Interests, Fujian Tongxianghui and Electoral Politics in Macao' (2016) 46 *Journal of Contemporary Asia* 286, 291.

82 Simon N. M. Young, 'Fundamental Rights and the Basic Laws of the Hong Kong and Macau Special Administrative Regions' in Jorge Oliveira and Paulo Cardinal (eds) *One Country Two Systems, Three Legal Orders - Perspectives of Evolution* (Springer 2009) 683.

ICCPR and ICESCR to Macau, China agreed to apply them to Macau after the handover.[83] They are entrenched in the MBL.[84]

In summary, the four areas of Greater China are lined up at different points on one political spectrum. At the authoritarian end of the spectrum is China, at the democratic end is Taiwan, and Hong Kong and Macau are hybrid regimes in the middle. However, after careful investigation, this book reveals that the judicial review in the four areas does not mirror their respective level of democracy. Instead, Taiwan and Hong Kong converged on active and assertive judicial review, while China and Macau converged on timid and deferential judicial review.

Contributions of This Book

This book represents the first-ever comprehensive study of the judicial review competence and activity of the four apex courts in Greater China. These apex courts are an essential part of the political and legal structure of each regime. They are at the center of the storm of judicialization of politics, and their activity largely reflects the activeness and assertiveness of judicial review in each area. This book compares the scope of judicial review and examines a complete set of judicial review decisions delivered by the four apex courts from 1999 to 2019, which contributes to a better understanding of judicial review in Greater China, broadening the empirical and theoretical base of the development of judicial review in different types of political regimes. Specifically, this book contributes to comparative public law and theory from four aspects.

Jurisdictionally. This book focuses on judicial review in Greater China, an appealing area in East Asia for comparative studies. It enriches the jurisdictional sphere of comparative public law. For the first time, this book details China's and Macau's judicial review mechanisms and practices, providing a comprehensive account of these systems. It is appealing to researchers and students who are interested in public law in Greater China and East Asia.

Substantively. This book presents a complete picture of judicial review in Greater China by exhaustively examining substantive judicial review cases decided by the apex courts in the four areas from 1999 to 2019. In contrast to a small range of selected cases included in the existing scholarship, a complete set of judicial review decisions illuminates judicial review activism and deference and reduces the possibility that the research will lead to misleading findings based on an abridged picture. These data organized into tables and figures and case analyses with considerable detail will be of substantial use to political science and legal scholars who are interested in public law in one or more of these jurisdictions.

83 Yash Ghai, 'The Basic Law of the Special Administrative Region of Macau: Some Reflections' (2000) 49 *International and Comparative Law Quarterly* 183, 189.

84 MBL, art 40.

Theoretically. This book investigates judicial review in Greater China and adds nuances to the dominant comparative public law theories concerning the interrelationship between judicial empowerment and liberal constitutionalism to confront the simplistic assertion that non-democratic regimes host less active and assertive courts and judicial review. This sparks new reflections among political science and legal scholars on the paths taken by semi- and authoritarian regimes.

Methodologically. This book applies a metric system designed for gauging judicial activism and deference. This system comprises three key indicators: the jurisdiction of judicial review, the standard of judicial review, and the intensity of judicial review.[85] Through these indicators, the framework effectively captures the competence of the court and its inclination toward either activism or deference in the realm of judicial review.[86] This metric system would extend its applicability beyond Greater China, offering a valuable tool for researchers to assess judicial activism and deference. The main body of this book delves into the three indicators and compares the judicial activism and deference of the four apex courts. Therefore, an elaboration of the metric system facilitates a smoother comprehension of the book for readers.

The first indicator is *the jurisdiction of judicial review*. It investigates the scope of government actions subject to judicial review. A broad jurisdiction of judicial review increases the possibilities of a more active court, because the court has more opportunities to check the government actions. A court with narrow jurisdiction in judicial review can hardly be an active one.

This book categorizes the jurisdiction of judicial review into three types according to the decision-making power: judicial review of primary legislation, judicial review of administrative rules, and judicial review of concrete executive

85 The three indicators are inspired by Professor Albert Chen's "degree of judicialization" and Professor Cora Chan's "framework for measuring deference in rights reasoning". Professor Chen lists three factors that he thinks affect the degree of judicialization of administrative law. They are: "(1) To what extent is litigation used by citizens and businesses to challenge administrative actions affecting their rights or interests? (2) To what extent are the courts active in reviewing and striking down administrative actions, or to what extent are they deferential to the administration? (3) To what extent do the courts engage in judicial activism in determining controversial political issues or intervening in matters of social, economic and other policies and shaping such policies, or to what extent do they practice judicial restraint?" See Albert H. Y. Chen, 'Conclusion: Reflections on Administrative Law and Judicialized Governance in East and Southeast Asia' in Tom Ginsburg and Albert H. Y. Chen (eds) *Administrative Law and Governance in Asia* (Routledge 2009) 362. Professor Chan proposes a framework for measuring judicial deference in human rights cases. The framework ranks four strategies of exercising deference, including "rights definition, standard of justification, burden of justification and cogency of arguments." See Cora Chan, 'A Preliminary Framework for Measuring Deference in Rights Reasoning' (2016) 14 *International Journal of Constitutional Law* 851.

86 Activism and deference of judicial review can also be measured through outcome of review, the ratio of successful challenges, and whether the courts take remedial measure to save unconstitutional or illegal actions. These indicators are considered by this book, but they are not main indicators because the outcome of judicial review depends on many objective factors.

decisions.[87] Judicial review of primary legislation is often considered a significant dimension of judicial power because primary legislation is usually enacted by popularly elected legislators through deliberative processes and contains important substance. They are the most formal and influential method of rule-making and normally lie at the top of the hierarchy of domestic legal systems beneath the constitution.[88] Administrative rules, as the name suggests, are promulgated by administrative authorities. They are an essential source of law in domestic legal systems. In many jurisdictions, the volume of administrative rules far exceeds comparable measures of primary legislation.[89] Although administrative rules vary from state to state, they can be divided into two groups: hard rules and soft rules.[90] Hard rules are legislative in character. They are binding, general, prospective, and usually created with statutory authorization. Soft rules are made by administrative agencies without express statutory authorization, aiming to provide general and prospective guidance about the law and means of complying with it.[91] Judicial review of administrative rules in this book includes scrutiny of hard rules and soft rules. Concrete executive acts are actions and decisions the governments take to implement legislation and fulfill administrative functions and duties. In general, when they review primary legislation and administrative rules, judges experience greater pressure, and their rulings have a more far-reaching impact on domestic legal systems, politics and people's rights. By contrast, the influence of concrete executive acts is usually more confined, as they are one-off in nature and made to a particular person or a particular group of people. Judicial review of legislation and administrative rules usually displays a higher degree of judicial activism and influence.

The second indicator is *the standards of judicial review*. Whereas the jurisdiction of judicial review is an objective institutional factor that determines the space for active judicial review, the standards of review, and the intensity of review, which will be discussed below, indicate courts' subjective willingness

87 Government acts amenable to judicial review can be categorized in accordance with different criteria. Based on the content, government acts are divided into categories, such as political, economic and finance, defense, housing and community amenities, health, and education. Based on the interests at stake, they are divided into public order and national security, environmental protection, and human rights. Much research on judicial review has been done on the dimensions of the content of government decisions and interests at stake. The dearth of research on judicial power based on the division of decision-making power is surprising.

88 Roscoe Pound commented that the legislation is the outcome of "long and patient study by experts, careful consideration by conferences or congresses or associations, press discussion in which public opinion is focused upon all important details, and hearings before legislative committees". Roscoe Pound, 'Common Law and Legislation' (1908) 21 *Harvard Law Review* 383, 383–384.

89 Kevin M. Stack, 'Rulemaking Regimes in the Modern State' in Peter Cane and others (eds), *The Oxford Handbook of Comparative Administrative Law* (OUP 2021) 555.

90 Peter Cane, *Controlling Administrative Power: An Historical Comparison* (CUP 2016) 269.

91 *Ibid.*

to execute intrusive scrutiny. Courts and legal scholars have developed various standards of judicial review, such as ultra vires, procedural impropriety, unreasonableness, proportionality, equal protection, and legitimate expectations. Different standards of review provide distinct argumentation frameworks that structure the courts to read the facts of cases and make their decisions. Some standards of review enable the courts to scrutinize government acts more deeply and intensively than others. An intrusive standard of review increases the possibility of a more liberal and rights-friendly outcome.[92] A deferential standard of review will make it easier and quicker for the courts to uphold impugned government actions. A settled consensus in the comparative constitutional law literature holds that "[a] court that chooses only to use a deferential standard of review will never be a liberal one".[93]

The standards of review can be roughly divided into two groups. The first group of standards focuses on the procedure and formality of decision-making, such as procedural impropriety and the requirement of being "provided by law". In general, these standards of review are less intrusive. Yeong-Chin Su, Grand Justice of the TCC, said that when judges strike down government actions on these grounds, they feel less pressured and such decisions usually cause less controversy, because these standards are basic requirements of legitimate governance and are related to some fundamental legal rationality.[94] Lord Irvine also observed that the scrutiny of decision-making process has usually and traditionally involved

> Something akin to the application of a set of rules. If the rules are broken, the conduct will be condemned. But if the rules are obeyed…the decision will be upheld, usually irrespective of the overall merits of the policy. In some cases much may turn – or at least appear to turn – on the form in which a decision is expressed rather than its substance.[95]

The second group of standards of review, including proportionality, unreasonableness, and equal protection, focuses on the substance and merits of government actions. They are considered more intrusive than the first group

92 Po Jen Yap and Chien-chih Lin, *Constitutional Convergence in East Asia* (CUP 2022) 12. The outcome of judicial review is determined by many factors, including objective factors such as the facts of the case, harm to people's rights, or harm to public interests. The courts should not ignore them and make decisions according to their own preference. This is one of the reasons that the research does not include the outcome of judicial review as an indicator of the court's activeness and assertiveness.

93 *Ibid.*

94 Yeong-Chin Su, David S. Law and Aharon Barak, 'Forum: Constitutional Adjudication in Comparative Perspectives' in Yen-Tu Su (蘇彥圖) (ed) *Constitutional Interpretation: Theory and Practice Volume 10* (憲法解釋之理論與實務第十輯) (Institutum Iurisprudentiae Academic Sinica 2020) 26–27.

95 Lord Irvine, 'The Development of Human Rights in Britain under an Incorporated Convention on Human Rights' (1998) *Public Law* 221, 235.

of standards.[96] When courts deploy these standards to scrutinize government actions, they need more power, trust, confidence, and determination because they appear to make decisions in place of the legislature or executive authorities.[97]

The third indicator is *the intensity of review*, which means the deference, respect, latitude, or leeway of the courts when they review the government actions. It is not easy to measure the intensity of review as there is no standardized metric system for measuring judicial review intensity and assertiveness. This book will assess the intensity of judicial review in various aspects.

- The intensity of judicial review is revealed by different approaches to legal interpretation, especially human rights and their limitations provisions. A generous approach to rights interpretation is more likely to lead to rights-friendly outcomes. Courts that tend to interpret human rights' scope narrowly and interpret restrictions on rights broadly can hardly be liberal ones.
- The intensity of judicial review can be gauged by assessing the intensity with which the courts apply a particular standard. Over time, some standards of review, including proportionality and unreasonableness, have developed variable intensity of review and now operate on a sliding scale.[98] Take proportionality as an example. According to its original understanding, proportionality requires that the authorities adopt the least intrusive means among the viable means that promote legitimate aims.[99] The courts have developed deferential approaches to proportionality, such as "a reasonable relationship of proportionality between the means employed and the aim sought to be realized"[100] and the "manifestly without reasonable foundation" standard.[101] The higher levels of intensity the court adopts, the less deference the court accords to the legislature and executive authorities.
- In cases concerning equal protection, the intensity of review is revealed by the court's choice between formal or substantive equality review. Substantive equality review requires the government to take active, positive, and beneficial measures responsive to those who are disadvantaged, in

96 Li-Ann Thio, 'Courts and Judicial Review' in Peter Cane and others (eds) *The Oxford Handbook of Comparative Administrative Law* (OUP 2021) 723–724.

97 Su, Law and Barak (n 94) 28.

98 Harry Woolf and others, *De Smith's Judicial Review* (7th edn, Sweet and Maxwell 2013) 635; Cora Chan, 'Proportionality and Invariable Baseline Intensity of Review' (2013) 33 *Legal Studies* 1; Margit Cohn, 'Legal Transplant Chronicles: The Evolution of Unreasonableness and Proportionality Review of the Administration in the United Kingdom' (2010) 58 *American Journal of Comparative Law* 583.

99 Aharon Barak, *Proportionality: Constitutional Rights and Their Limitation* (CUP 2012) 317; Robert Alexy, 'Constitutional Rights and Proportionality' (2014) 22 *Journal for Constitutional Theory and Philosophy of Law* 51, 52.

100 *James v United Kingdom* (1986) 8 EHRR 123, [50].

101 *Hysan Development Co Ltd v Town Planning Board* (2016) 19 HKCFAR 372, [120]-[122].

need, and ignored.[102] It establishes a higher standard of review than formal equality, a requirement of "like cases must be treated alike, unlike cases must not be treated alike".

Structure of the Book

This book is organized as follows. Chapter 2 compares the judicial review competence of the four apex courts from two perspectives – legal basis and power dynamics. Statutory laws and case laws constitute the legal foundation of courts' judicial review power. At the same time, the four apex courts' judicial review power is not static. Instead, it evolves (either through expansion or contraction) due to the power dynamics between the courts and other branches of government. Chapter 2 reveals that the judicial review jurisdictions of the CFA and TUI, two apex courts in hybrid regimes, are wide, covering primary legislation, administrative rules, as well as concrete executive acts. The TCC has jurisdiction over primary legislation and administrative rules, but no jurisdiction over concrete executive action. The jurisdiction of the SPC's judicial review is the narrowest. Its central terrain of judicial review is concrete administrative decisions. Primary legislation and administrative rules of high rank have always been excluded from judicial scrutiny in China.

In contrast to the power on paper, the actual exercise of judicial review power by the four apex courts shows a very different picture. The TCC and the CFA were much more active than the SPC and the TUI in reviewing primary legislation and administrative rules. The SPC and the TUI were either unable or unwilling to review legislation. Their main terrain of judicial review rests on concrete executive actions. If saying review of legislation symbolizes a relatively high level of judicial interference, then the statistics indicate the TCC and the CFA are more interferential and intrusive than the SPC and the TUI.

Chapters 3 to 5 closely examine the standards and intensity of judicial review deployed in decisions delivered by the four apex courts between 1999 and 2019. As discussed above, these decisions are categorized into three groups: decisions against primary legislation, decisions against administrative rules, and decisions against concrete executive acts. Each chapter examines one category of judicial review decisions. Chapters 3 to 5 will present various standards of judicial review adopted by the four apex courts in their decisions, including proportionality, the principle of equality, prescribed by law, due process, legitimate expectation, ultra vires, and others. Additionally, Chapters 3 to 5 will also examine the intensity of judicial review of the four apex courts, comprehensively presenting and systematically comparing judicial activism and deference among the four apex courts. These chapters reveal a convergence between the TCC and the CFA on active and intrusive judicial review and a

102 Sandra Fredman, 'Substantive Equality Revisited' (2016) 14 *International Journal of Constitutional Law* 712.

convergence between the SPC and the TUI on a more timid and deferential approach to judicial review.

Chapter 6 suggests that judges' education background and the foreign legal knowledge and jurisprudence they brought to the courts impact judicial review activities, resulting in the convergence and divergence of judicial review in Greater China. Chapter 7 is a concise conclusion of this book.

2 Judicial Review Competences of Courts in Greater China

Introduction

This chapter compares the judicial review competence of courts in Greater China, with a focus on the apex court in each area. Generally speaking, the broader the jurisdiction of judicial review, the more opportunities the courts have to scrutinize the exercise of power by other branches of government. This chapter explores the jurisdiction of judicial review in each area of Greater China from two perspectives – legal basis and power dynamics. Statutory laws and case laws constitute the legal basis of the courts' competence in judicial review. But this competence in judicial review is not static. Instead, it evolves – either expanding or contracting – based on the shifting power dynamics between the courts and other branches of government.

It is striking that the jurisdictions of judicial review of the CFA and the TUI, two apex courts of hybrid regimes, are the widest among the four apex courts, covering primary legislation, administrative rules, as well as concrete executive acts. The TCC enjoys jurisdiction over primary legislation and administrative rules, excluding concrete executive actions, which fall within the purview of Taiwan's administrative courts. The SPC has the narrowest judicial review jurisdiction of the four courts. Its review is limited to administrative actions and administrative rules of low rank.

China does not embrace judicial constitutional review. The Chinese courts are prohibited from reviewing the constitutionality of legislative and administrative actions, and they are not even allowed to apply the Constitution as the basis for their decisions.[1] The constitutional review power is vested solely in the NPC and NPCSC – the highest organ of state power in China.[2] Scrutinizing

1 Alec Stone Sweet and Jud Matthew, *Proportionality Balancing and Constitutional Governance: A Comparative and Global Approach* (OUP 2019) 145–146.

2 Constitution of the PRC (中华人民共和国宪法), arts 62, 67. Article 62 of the Constitution of the PRC provides that "The NPC exercises the following functions and powers: (1) to amend the Constitution; (2) to supervise the enforcement of the Constitution". Article 67 of the Constitution of the PRC provides that "The NPCSC exercises the following functions and powers: (1) to interpret the Constitution and supervise its enforcement…; (7) to revoke administrative

DOI: 10.4324/9781003482536-2

concrete executive acts is the central purview of the Chinese judicial review. It was only in 2014 that Chinese courts were expressly granted the authority to review administrative rules,[3] but this power comes with significant limitations. It is confined to administrative normative documents,[4] which are administrative rules of the lowest level in the Chinese legal system. Even then, their review is a weak form of review, meaning that courts cannot invalidate illegal administrative rules outright. Instead, they can only disapply these rules in specific cases where the claimant has been successful.[5] These challenged administrative rules remain in effect and are applicable in other cases until being repealed by administrative authorities.[6]

Taiwan has established a centralized model of judicial review, under which the TCC and Taiwan's administrative courts are specialized courts for reviewing government actions. The constitutional review power is vested exclusively in the TCC, which is one of the oldest constitutional courts in Asia and delivered its first decision on 6 January 1949.[7] The TCC's constitutional review competence has gradually expanded since the late 1980s, when Taiwan started its democratic transition.[8] It now has the power to review legislation and administrative rules and to invalidate them if found unconstitutional.[9] It also adjudicates matters relating to the impeachment of the president or the vice president, and the dissolution of unconstitutional political parties.[10] Concrete administrative decisions still fall outside the TCC's purview. The power to review concrete executive actions is vested in Taiwan's administrative courts.[11]

regulations, decisions and orders formulated by the State Council that are in conflict with the Constitution or laws; (8) to revoke local regulations and resolutions formulated by the state organs of power in provinces, autonomous regions and cities directly under central government jurisdiction that are in conflict with the Constitution, laws, or administrative regulations".

3 Administrative Litigation Law (ALL) (行政诉讼法), art 53. The ALL was enacted in 1989 and has been amended in 2014 and 2017. References to the ALL in this book will be to the ALL of 2017, unless otherwise indicated.

4 *Ibid.*, art 53(2).

5 The Interpretation of the SPC on the Application of the Administrative Litigation Law (SPC ALL Interpretation of 2018) (最高人民法院关于适用《中华人民共和国行政诉讼法》的解释), art 149(1) (2018).

6 *Ibid.*, art 149(2).

7 J.Y. Interpretation No. 1.

8 Tom Ginsburg, *Judicial Review in New Democracies: Constitutional Courts in Asian Cases* (CUP 2003) 123; Chien-Chil Lin, 'The Judicialization of Politics in Taiwan' (2016) *Asian Journal of Law and Society* 299, 302.

9 Constitution of Taiwan (中華民國憲法), arts 78, 172.

10 Amendment to the Constitutional of Taiwan, art 5 (2005).

11 Administrative Litigation Act (行政訴訟法), art 13; The introduction of Taiwan's administrative courts, available at https://tpa.judicial.gov.tw/tw/cp-1758-52436-1fdd2-021.html, accessed 7 October 2024. The ordinary courts in Taiwan can also review administrative rules when adjudicating cases.

After the British handover of Hong Kong to China in July 1997, Hong Kong retained the previous common law legal systems and traditions, including judicial review.[12] The CFA, the new apex court of this region, seized the opportunity of its first major case, *Ng Ka Ling v Director of Immigration* (1999), to claim that the courts of Hong Kong have the power of constitutionally reviewing the compliance of laws with the HKBL.[13] The jurisdiction of Hong Kong courts' judicial review is wide, covering ordinances (primary legislation of this area), administrative rules, and executive decisions. However, the courts of Hong Kong do not enjoy the final and unchallengeable authority to interpret the HKBL.[14] The power of final interpretation of the HKBL is reserved to the NPCSC due to the OCTS and the power clash between Hong Kong and Beijing.[15]

The development of constitutional review in Macau was not smooth going. Immediately after the Portuguese handover of Macau to China in December 1999, the TUI declared that the legal system of the MSAR did not provide any appeal mechanism for reviewing the compliance of laws with the MBL.[16] In 2006, the TUI changed its stance and affirmed that the courts of this region were competent to interpret the MBL and constitutionally review the laws.[17] Inheriting Portuguese legal systems, Macau retains two proceedings for reviewing administrative rules – concrete review and abstract review.[18] In concrete review, illegal rules are disapplied only to successful claimants, while abstract review aims to strike down and remove illegal administrative rules from the legal system. Additionally, concrete administrative decisions are subject to courts' supervision in Macau.

Judicial review competence delimited by law represents one facet of the broader legal landscape, but the actual exercise of judicial review power warrants attention too. This chapter collects and compares the judicial review statistics of the four apex courts from 1999 to 2019, presenting an overview of their respective judicial review activity. The statistics show that the TCC and the CFA were far more active than the SPC and the TUI in reviewing primary legislation and administrative rules. The primary terrain of SPC's and the TUI's judicial review was concrete executive actions, which generally have a more limited impact without altering broader legal standards or policies. These

12 HKBL, art 8.

13 (1999) 2 HKCFAR 4, 25G-H.

14 Xiaonan Yang, 'Two Interpreters of the Basic Law: The Court of Final Appeal and the Standing Committee of the National People's Congress' in Simon N. M. Young and Yash Ghai (eds), *Hong Kong's Court of Final Appeal: The Development of the Law in China's Hong Kong* (CUP 2014) 69.

15 Simon N. M. Young, 'Constitutional Rights in Hong Kong's Court of Final Appeal' (2012) *Chinese (Taiwan) Yearbook of International Law and Affairs* 67, 68.

16 Case 1/2000, page 3; Case 2/2000, page 2.

17 Case 9/2006, page 3; Case 28/2006, pages 28–31.

18 Code of Administrative Litigation (CAL) (行政訴訟法典), arts 88–93.

overall statistics already demonstrate the SPC's and TUI's judicial activism and influence are far more constrained in contrast to the TCC and the CFA.

This chapter encompasses seven parts. Following this introductory part, from Part 2 to Part 5, each part details one of the four judicial review schemes across Greater China. Part 6 exhibits an overview of judicial review activity of the four apex courts between 1999 and 2019. Part 7 concludes this chapter.

China's Judicial Review Scheme

No Judicial Constitutional Review in China

When applying the orthodox precept of constitutional review to China, many lawyers and scholars might conclude that constitutional review does not exist in China because Chinese courts are deprived of the power to interpret the Constitution and to constitutionally review actions of other branches of government.[19] However, China does have established constitutional review and China's legal system that divides rules into higher laws and lower laws upholds an inherent need to ensure the lower laws do not contradict the higher laws, particularly the Constitution. China's constitutional review model is unique. It is not the courts but the NPC and NPCSC – the highest legislature – that are entitled to the power of supervising the enforcement of the Constitution, interpreting the Constitution, and striking down unconstitutional statutes, regulations, and resolutions.[20]

The NPC and the NPCSC Monopolize Constitutional Review Power

Before unfolding the NPC's and the NPCSC's constitutional review power, a short note on the Chinese legal system and the hierarchical ranking of legal sources may assist in this understanding (Figure 2.1). Chinese legal system includes formal and informal legal sources.[21] Formal legal sources are composed of the Constitution, statutes (*falv*), regulations (*fagui*), and rules (*guizhang*). In public law, informal legal sources mainly refer to administrative normative documents (*xingzheng guifanxing wenjian*) issued by executive authorities. The legal force rank of these legal sources is constructed as follows:

19 Guobin Zhu, 'Constitutional Review in China: An Unaccomplished Project or a Mirage' (2010) 43 *Suffolk University Law Review* 625, 625.

20 Constitution of the PRC (n 2), arts 62, 67.

21 Minutes of the Symposiums of the Supreme People's Court concerning Application of Laws in Adjudicating Administrative Cases (Minutes 2004) (关于审理行政案件适用法律规范问题的座谈纪要) s 1 (2004).

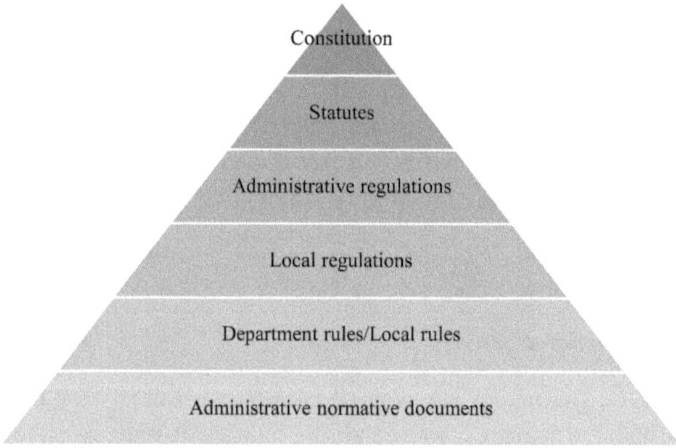

Figure 2.1 The Hierarchical Ranking of Chinese Legal Sources.
Source: Author.

- The Constitution is at the apex of the pyramid of the legal system of China. It is the fundamental law of the country and has supreme legal authority.[22] All statutes, regulations, and rules must be consistent with the Constitution.[23]
- Statutes are primary legislation enacted by the NPC or the NPCSC. They are usually titled as an "act" or "law" and have higher legal authority than regulations and rules.[24]
- Administrative regulations, promulgated by the State Council, have higher legal authority than local regulations and all rules.[25]
- Local regulations promulgated by local people's congresses and its standing committees have higher legal authority than local rules.[26]
- There are two kinds of rules: local rules promulgated by local governments and department rules issued by the departments of the State Council.[27] They have equal legal force.[28]
- Executive authorities can promulgate administrative normative documents. Administrative normative documents have general binding force.[29] They

22 The preamble of the Constitution of the PRC (n 2).
23 Law on Legislation (立法法), art 98. References to the Law on Legislation in this book will be to the Law on Legislation of 2023, unless otherwise indicated.
24 *Ibid.*, art 99(1).
25 *Ibid.*, art 99(2).
26 *Ibid.*, art 100(1).
27 *Ibid.*, arts 91, 93.
28 *Ibid.*, art 102.
29 Notice of the State Council General Office on Strengthening the Formulation, Supervision and Management of Administrative Normative Documents (国务院办公厅关于加强行政规范性文件制定和监督管理工作的通知) (2018), para 1.

are normally titled as an "announcement", "plan", "instruction", "order", "opinion", and "notice".[30]

The NPC and the NPCSC, as both statute-makers and guardians of the Constitution, are responsible for ensuring the constitutionality of statutes enacted by themselves. This responsibility is fulfilled through pre-emptive scrutiny of legislative bills, allowing them to review and address potential constitutional issues before the laws are enacted. In other words, constitutional review of statutes is a self-control of NPC and NPCSC.[31] The Law Committee (LC) under the NPC, established according to the Constitution of the PRC in 1983, was created to discharge the duty of reviewing the constitutionality of legislative bills.[32] In 2018, the Constitution of the PRC created a new committee, the Constitution and Law Committee (CLC), in place of the LC.[33] This new committee is granted more power than the LC. In addition to reviewing legislative bills, the CLC has the power and duties to promote the enforcement of the Constitution, interpret the constitution, carry out constitutional review, enhance the constitutional supervision, and coordinate constitutional propaganda.[34] The CLC is the first institute to be explicitly granted the power of constitutional review in China. However, the working procedures for the CLC, particularly the procedures for constitutional interpretation and constitutional review, are not promulgated yet.[35] Specific rules and guidelines are called for.[36]

As for regulations, rules, and other policy documents, the NPCSC reviews them through a procedure called filing and review, or *bei'an shencha* in Chinese.[37] *Bei'an* means "filing" and "recording", and *shencha* means "examination" and "review". Filing and review was first created in 1979, when the people's congresses at the provincial level were empowered to enact local

30 Regulations on Handling of Official Documents by Party and Governmental Organs (党政机关公文处理工作条例) (2012), art 8.

31 Björn Ahl, 'Judicialization in Authoritarian Regimes: The Expansion of Powers of the Chinese Supreme People's Court' (2019) 17 *International Journal of Constitutional Law* 252, 257.

32 Law on Legislation (n 23), arts 18, 22, 31 (2000).

33 Constitution of the PRC (n 2), art 70(1).

34 Decision of the Standing Committee of the National People's Congress on Matters concerning the Duties of the Committee of Constitution and Law of the National People's Congress (全国人民代表大会常务委员会关于全国人民代表大会宪法和法律委员会职责问题的决定) (2018).

35 There might be some internal working instructions and rules, but they are not open to the public yet. Wenhao Yu (于文豪), 'The Implementation of Constitutionality Review Duty by the Constitution and Law Committee' (宪法和法律委员会合宪性审查职责的展开) (2018) 6 *China Legal Science* (中国法学) 43, 49–54.

36 Dayuan Han (韩大元), 'From NPC Law Committee to NPC Constitution and Law Committee: The Transformation of System and Function' (从法律委员会到宪法和法律委员会:体制与功能的转型) (2018) 4 *Journal of Eastern University of Political Science and Law* (华东政法大学学报) 6, 11.

37 Law on Legislation (n 23), ch 5.

regulations,[38] potentially resulting in conflicts and inconsistency between the local regulations and national statutes, which necessitated the maintenance of the consistency of the legal system. The duty of reviewing regulations was first assigned to the general office of the NPCSC and later reallocated to the special committees of the NPC.[39] In 2000, the Law on Legislation entitled the Legislative Affairs Commission (LAC), which is under the control of NPCSC, to conduct filing and review.[40] In the same year, the NPCSC promulgated a set of filing and review procedure rules,[41] which was replaced by the *Working Measures for the Filing and Review of Regulations and Judicial Interpretations* in 2019 (Filing and Reviewing Work Measures).[42] Over the years, the LAC has developed distinct ways to launch review proceedings, including (1) review after recording, (2) review upon a request, and (3) targeted review.[43]

Reviewing regulations after recording is the oldest constitutional review method that has been adopted since the late 1970s.[44] The regulation-makers should submit regulations to the NPCSC for record.[45] However, for a long time, regulations were not reviewed after being filed for record.[46] Not until 2019 did the Filing and Reviewing Work Measures stipulate that "every legislation must be submitted for recording, every legislation must be reviewed, every mistake must be corrected".[47] Per this requirement, the LAC must scrutinize all regulations filed for recording.

A review of regulations can be initiated upon requests from state institutions and individuals.[48] While the LAC is obliged to launch a review when requested

38 Organic Law of the Local People's Congresses and Local People's Governments (中华人民共和国地方各级人民代表大会和地方各级人民政府组织法), art 6.

39 Zheng Liu (刘政), *The Historical Footprint of People's Congress Scheme* (人民代表大会制度的历史足迹) (China Democracy Legal System Publishing House 2014) 216.

40 Law on Legislation (n 23), art 91 (2000).

41 Work Procedure Relative to Filing and Review of Administrative Regulations, Local Regulations, Autonomous Regulations and Specific Regulations, and Regulations of Special Economic Zones (行政法规、地方性法规、自治条例, 和单行条例、经济特区法规备案审查工作程序) (2000)

42 Working Measures for the Filing and Review of Regulations and Judicial Interpretations (法规、司法解释备案审查工作办法) (2019).

43 *Ibid.*, art 18.

44 There are different types of regulations enacted by various institutions in the Chinese legal system, including administrative regulations, local regulations, autonomous regulations and specific regulations, and regulations of special economic zones. Because all regulations are subject to filing and review and to avoid lengthy and wordy expression, unless otherwise specified, regulation in this paper refers to all types of regulation.

45 Law on Legislation (n 23), art 89 (2000).

46 Lei Zheng (郑磊), 'Development and Evolution of Filing and Review and Rule of Law' (备案审查与法治体系的复调变迁) (2022) 6 *Journal of Chinese University of Political Science and Law* (中国政法大学学报) 73, 77.

47 Filing and Reviewing Work Measures (n 42), art 4.

48 Law on Legislation (n 23), art 110; Filing and Reviewing Work Measures (n 42), arts 21–22.

by certain state institutions,[49] requests from individuals do not automatically trigger a review.[50] Prior to 2012, state institutions rarely made such requests,[51] and the LAC tended to reject review requests from individuals,[52] resulting in a very limited number of review cases. Only after 2012 did the LAC become responsive to citizens' requests for reviews.[53]

Targeted review is a new review model recognized by the Filing and Reviewing Work Measures in 2019[54] and later enshrined in the Law on Legislation in 2023.[55] It aims to examine all regulations, rules, and policies in certain targeted fields. Differing from the two forgoing review procedures, the LAC launches targeted reviews on its own initiative rather than subsequent to filing for record or upon requests. Over the past decade, the LAC carried out many rounds of targeted reviews of sub-statutory legislation, covering regulations, rules, and administrative normative documents. These reviews encompassed various thematic domains, including administrative punishment and administrative coercion in 2011, election-related legislation in 2016, environmental protection and traffic safety legislation in 2018, food and drug safety legislation in 2019, as well as wild animal protection, the improvement of business environment, Covid controlling, Civil Code, and food and drug safety in 2020. Each round of targeted review identified a certain number of sub-statutory legislations that were inconsistent with statutes and the Constitution.

When the LAC finds any regulation, rule, and policy inconsistent with the Constitution or any superior laws, they will communicate with the regulation-makers or give a written opinion suggesting amending or repealing the regulation.[56] Suppose a regulation-maker declines to amend or repeal the unconstitutional regulation. The LAC can suggest the NPCSC repeal the regulation.[57] According to Article 51 of the Filing and Reviewing Work Measures, the LAC authorities should disclose their reviewing work to the public by appropriate means.[58] Since 2018, the LAC has consistently disclosed its annual

49 Law on Legislation (n 23), art 110(1). Upon the request of the following institutions, the LAC must initiate review proceedings: the State Council, the Central Military Commission, the National Supervisory Commission, the Supreme People's Court, the Supreme People's Procuratorate, and the standing committees of people's congresses at the provincial level.

50 Law on Legislation (n 23), art 110(2).

51 Yan Lin (林彦), 'Two Dilemmas of the Operation of the Review System of Regulation' (法规审查制度运行的双重悖论), (2018) 4 *Peking University Law Journal* (中外法学) 937, 940.

52 *Ibid.*, at 937, 940–943; Zheng (n 46), at 78–80.

53 See the LAC annual reports on filing and review work from 2017 to 2023. Available at https://npcobserver.com/recording-review/, accessed 7 October 2024.

54 Filing and Reviewing Work Measures (n 42), art 25.

55 Law on Legislation (n 23), art 116.

56 Filing and Reviewing Work Measures (n 42), arts 40–41.

57 *Ibid.*, art 44.

58 *Ibid.*, art 51. Prior to the issue of Filing and Reviewing Work Measures, the constitutional review results were only disclosed to the institutions and individuals who requested the review.

filing and review work report,[59] which has considerably enhanced the transparency of Chinese filing and review.

In Filing and Review Work Report 2020, the LAC for the first time disclosed constitutional review cases.[60] This is considered a breakthrough in Chinese constitutional review.[61] Chinese scholars were surprised as they expected it would take a long time for the LAC to make unconstitutional cases public.[62] One of the cases involved reviewing a local regulation that required ethnic schools to use ethnic languages in teaching and learning. The LAC considered it inconsistent with Article 19 of the PRC Constitution, which provides "The state shall promote the Mandarin used nationwide".

Not Justiciable Constitution

The Chinese courts are not only prohibited from constitutionally reviewing government actions, but they are also prevented from referring to and making decisions based on Constitution provisions.[63] Despite the political commitment "the state respects and protects human rights" written into the Constitution in 2004 and the fact that Chapter 2 of the PRC Constitution contains a series of individual rights and freedoms,[64] these constitutional guarantees are not effectively enforceable through the courts.[65]

Chinese courts have attempted to judicialize the Constitution but eventually failed. *Qi Yuling v Chen Xiaoqi et al* (2001) is often cited as China's first constitutional case equivalent to the United States' *Marbury v Madison*.[66] Qi and Chen were classmates. In their college entrance examinations in 1990, Qi did well but Chen did not. Chen "stole" Qi's exam result and opportunity to go to college by falsifying photographs and identity documents. After three years, Chen graduated and got a job in a local bank, which was an expected

59 n 53.

60 The LAC Filing and Review Work Report 2020 (全国人民代表大会常务委员会法制工作委员会关于2020年备案审查工作情况的报告) <www.npc.gov.cn/npc/c30834/202101/239178b5d03944c7b453ddc6bdd7c087.shtml> accessed 25 March 2021.

61 Ying Liang (梁鹰), 'Comments on File and Check Work Report 2020' (2020年备案审查工作情况报告评述) (2021) 2 *China Law Review* (中国法律评论) 171, 175.

62 'Announced unconstitutional cases for the first time in four years, constitutionality review "runs fast"' (四年来首次公布"不合宪"案例，合宪性审查"小步快跑") *infzm* (南方周末) (25 February 2021) <www.infzm.com/content/201828> accessed 25 March 2021.

63 Notice of the Supreme People's Court on Specifications for Making Civil Judgments by People's Courts and the Sample of Civil Judgments (最高人民法院关于印发〈人民法院民事裁判文书制作规范〉<民事诉讼文书样式>的通知) (28 June 2016).

64 Constitution of the PRC (n 2), art 33(3).

65 Tom Ginsburg and Alberto Simpser, 'Introduction: Constitutions in Authoritarian Regimes' in Tom Ginsburg and Alberto Simpser (eds), *Constitutions in Authoritarian Regimes* (CUP 2014) 7.

66 *Marbury v Madison*, 5 U.S. 137, 1803; Robert J Morris, 'China's Marbury: Qi Yuling v Chen Xiaoqi – The Once and Future Trial of Both Education & Constitutionalization.' (2010) *Tsinghua China Law Review* 274, 275.

consequence of her education. Years later, Qi discovered the ruse and brought a case before the court. She claimed that Chen, by stealing her name and identity, infringed on her right to education. As a constitutional right was involved and claimed, the High Court of Shandong Province was unsure of what law to apply and how to apply it. It requested the SPC for advice. The SPC issued a Reply (*dafu*), in which it applied the Constitution provisions and held that Chen infringed upon Qi's right to education and was liable for the damage.[67]

The SPC's Reply sparked heated debate among Chinese scholars and was widely reported by the media. Songyou Huang, the presiding judge of the First Civil Tribunal of the SPC, who was responsible for the Reply, commented that the courts at each level should gradually be equipped with the power of constitutional review that their American counterparts enjoy.[68]

However, some officials criticized the SPC's Reply for purporting to interpret the Constitution in place of the NPCSC. They considered such action a threat to the people's congress system and the CCP's leadership.[69] The CCP Central Political Legal Committee mounted an investigation into the *Qi Yuling* case and decided to prohibit the courts from applying Constitution provisions in their adjudications.[70] In a decision made in December 2008, the SPC stated that the Reply to the *Qi Yuling* case was "no longer applicable", which formally repealed the Reply.[71] This decision marked the death of hope for the applicability of the PRC Constitution in judicial decision-making. In 2016, the SPC issued judgment-drafting specifications for Chinese judges, expressly requiring judge not to cite Constitution provisions as the basis of their decisions.[72]

Judicial Review of Concrete Executive Actions

The Administrative Litigation Law (ALL), enacted on 4 April 1989 and effective as of 1 October 1990,[73] was a milestone in the development of Chinese judicial review. Before this enactment, people could challenge only a very

67 SPC Gazette (2001).

68 Songyou Huang (黄松有), 'Talking about the Justiciability of Constitution and Its Significance from the Point of View of Today's Reply of the People's Supreme Court' (宪法司法化及其意义——从最高人民法院今天的一个《批复》谈起), *People's Court Daily Legal Times* (人民法院报报法制时代周刊) (13 August 2001).

69 Qianfan Zhang, 'A Constitution with Constitutionalism? The Paths of Constitutional Development in China' (2010) 8 *International Journal of Constitutional Law* 950, 962.

70 Ahl (n 31) 260.

71 Decision of the SPC on the Annulment of Some Judicial Interpretations Issued before the End of 2007 (最高人民法院关于废止2007年底以前发布的有关司法解释(第7批)的决定) (18 December 2007).

72 n 63.

73 ALL (n 3).

limited range of executive actions in civil tribunals of the courts.[74] After the ALL, thousands of administrative tribunals were established within the people's courts at all levels, and the scope of executive actions subject to judicial review was significantly expanded.[75] Each year, thousands of complaints against executive actions have been petitioned to the administrative tribunals.[76]

Chinese administrative law divides executive acts into two categories, namely "abstract acts" and "concrete acts".[77] This division is central to an understanding of Chinese administrative law and judicial review.[78] An abstract executive act, which is also called a general executive act, refers to executive authorities' rule-making activity, such as promulgating administrative regulations, rules, and administrative normative documents.[79] A concrete executive act is performed in relation to a particular person in a particular circumstance and usually takes the form of grant, confirmation, permission, certification, exemption, or punishment.[80]

Judicial review in China primarily focuses on concrete executive acts, with the vast majority of these acts being subject to courts' scrutiny. Individuals, organizations or legal persons can file a petition to courts when they believe an executive act infringes on their rights and interests.[81] However, there are still categories of actions explicitly excluded from judicial review by the ALL and the SPC's judicial interpretations. These include actions related to public security and national security, mediation and arbitration decisions, administrative guidance, and internal executive acts (such as disciplinary decisions).[82]

Judicial Review of Administrative Rules

Abstract executive actions (or administrative rules) had long been excluded from judicial review until 2014 when the ALL explicitly empowered people to challenge administrative rules of low rank. Judicial review of administrative rules has gone through three stages with an incremental expansion of judicial review power. In the first stage, between 1989 and 2000, the courts were completely excluded from reviewing any administrative rules. Article 5 of the

74 Tom Ginsburg, 'Administrative Law and the Judicial Control of Agents in Authoritarian Regimes' in Tom Ginsburg and Tamir Moustafa (eds), *Rule by Law: The Politics of Courts in Authoritarian Regimes* (CUP 2008) 67.

75 The first administrative tribunal was set up within of Miluo County People's Court in Hunan Province in 1986. The SPC established its administrative tribunal in 1988.

76 Ginsburg, 'Administrative Law and the Judicial Control of Agents in Authoritarian Regimes' (n 74) 67.

77 Albert H. Y. Chen, *An Introduction to the Legal System of the People's Republic of China* (4th edn, LexisNexis 2011) 334.

78 Jianfu Chen, *Chinese Law: Context and Transformation* (Brill 2016) 223.

79 *Ibid.*, 224.

80 *Ibid.*

81 ALL (n 3), art 2.

82 *Ibid.*, art 13; SPC ALL Interpretation of 2018 (n 5), arts 1–2.

ALL of 1989 provided that "The people's courts hear administrative cases and review the legality of *concrete* administrative acts". Further, Article 12(2) expressly required the courts to dismiss any petitions against administrative regulations, rules, as well as decisions and orders of general application made by the administrative.

In 2000, the SPC issued the Interpretation on Several Issues Regarding the Implementation of the ALL. Article 62(2) of this judicial interpretation provided that when adjudicating administrative cases, the courts may apply lawful and valid rules and administrative normative documents. Some scholars argued that by this provision, the SPC empowered the courts to review the legality of rules and administrative normative documents.[83] This marks the second stage of judicial review of administrative rules, although this empowerment was veiled and ambiguous. But the SPC reaffirmed the courts' power of this kind in more explicit words after the *Luoyang Seed* case in 2004.

The facts of this case are simple enough: the plaintiff entered into a contract with the defendant, a seed retailer. The defendant breached the contract by selling the seeds to others. The case came to the Intermediate Court of Luoyang City in 2003. The core dispute of the case was how to determine the compensation to be paid to the plaintiff. The plaintiff argued that the damages should be calculated based on the market price in accordance with the Seed Law enacted by the NPCSC. However, the defendant claimed that the damages should be calculated based on a government guidance price, according to Article 26 of the Regulation on Crop Seeds of Henan Province promulgated by the Standing Committee of the People's Congress of Henan Province. Li Huijuan, the presiding judge, decided the case in favor of the plaintiff and applied the Seed Law. She took one more step and declared that Article 26 of the Regulation was invalid as it contradicted the Seed Law. This declaration resulted in trouble for her. The leaders of the People's Congress of Henan Province reacted furiously, claiming that the court had wrongfully and unlawfully reviewed the local regulation, undermining the people's congress system and encroaching on power of local people's congresses.[84] The Intermediate Court of Luoyang City removed Judge Li Huijuan and the vice-head of the civil tribunal from their posts as demanded by the People's Congress of Henan Province.[85] This event sparked fierce controversy nationwide. The SPC, on the request from the High Court of Henan Province, made a Reply, in which it stated that when a law of inferior rank conflicted with a law of superior rank, the court should apply the law of superior rank.[86] This

83 Jun Yu (于军) and Wen Zhang (张文), 'A Survey of the Effectiveness of Power of Judicial Review of Administrative Normative Documents' (行政规范性文件司法审查权的实效性分析) (2016) 2 *Chinese Journal of Law* (法学研究) 42, 44.

84 Keith Hand, 'Resolving Constitutional Dispute in Contemporary China' (2011) 7 *University of Pennsylvania East Asia Law Review* 51, 109–110.

85 *Ibid.*, 110.

86 *Ibid.*

Reply indicated that Judge Li's choice of law and decision were correct, but she should not have declared the local regulation invalid.

Immediately after the *Luoyang Seed* case, the SPC organized a symposium on the applicable laws in administrative adjudication and issued the Minutes of the Symposium of the Supreme People's Court concerning the Application of Laws in Adjudicating Administrative Cases (Minutes 2004).[87] The SPC required the courts to suspend trials and seek an opinion from superior agencies when they were confronted with conflicts between legal norms and unable to decide which one ought to be applied.[88] Additionally, the SPC expressly stated:

> According to relevant provisions of the Administrative Litigation Law and the Law on Legislation, people's courts should adjudicate administrative litigation cases according to statutes, administrative regulations, local regulations, autonomy regulations, and specific regulations, and in reference to rules. *When referring to rules, [the courts] should judge the legality of the rules and only apply legal and valid rules ...*
>
> Administrative normative documents are not formal sources of law. They are not legally binding for the people's courts. However, *if people's courts, after examination, consider that an administrative normative document is lawful, valid, reasonable and proportionate and constitutes the legal basis of the impugned specific administrative decision, they should confirm its validity*. The people's courts may comment, in the reasoning section of their judgments, on the legality, validity, reasonableness, or appropriateness of administrative normative documents.[89] [Emphasis added]

This opinion is revealing in two respects. First, the SPC explicitly affirmed that the courts can scrutinize rules and administrative normative documents. They can check the legality, reasonableness and proportionality of administrative normative documents, and for rules, they can review their legality. Second, whether or not to review rules and administrative normative documents is entirely in the discretion of the court. This means that parties involved in administrative litigation do not possess the right to request a review of these documents.

In 2014, the NPCSC amended the ALL, marking the third stage of judicial review of administrative rules. This amendment removed the word "concrete" from Article 5 of the ALL of 1989. The court now can "scrutinize the legality of executive acts", including abstract executive acts.[90] Moreover, Article 53(1)

87 Minutes 2004 (n 21).
88 *Ibid.*, s 2
89 *Ibid.*, s 1.
90 ALL (n 3), art 6.

expressly entitles people to the right to challenge the legality of administrative normative documents before the courts.[91]

Nonetheless, the right to challenge administrative normative documents is subject to various restrictions. First, citizens *cannot* mount a challenge against administrative regulations and rules. Administrative regulation is still beyond the courts' jurisdiction. The courts still maintain the sole discretion in regard to the review of rules.[92] Second, the right to petition for a review of an administrative normative document cannot be pursued independently; instead, it must be filed concurrently with a lawsuit against a specific executive action.[93] In other words, judicial review against administrative normative documents takes the form of concrete review, rather than abstract review. Moreover, the contested executive decisions must be made according to the impugned administrative normative documents.[94] Third, the courts can only reject the application of illegal administrative normative documents and they lack the authority to strike them down.[95] But the courts should recommend the rule-makers amend or repeal the illegal documents.[96] The disposition recommendations, along with their decisions, should also be reported to superior courts for record.[97] In practice, the courts send their disposition recommendations to their superior courts *before* rendering decisions. This preemptive action aims to seek informal endorsements from superior courts to forestall the overturning of decisions on appeals.[98] Although this practice may improve the consistency in judicial review of administrative normative documents, it undermines courts' independent judgment.[99] Lastly, it is unclear from the laws whether

91 *Ibid.*, art 53(1); Wei Cui, Jie Cheng, and Dominika Wiesner, 'Judicial Review of Government Actions in China' (2019) 1 *China Perspectives* 35, 41.

92 Yunsheng Chen (陈运生), 'The Initiation Requirements of Incidental Review of Normative Documents – An Empirical Examination Based on 1738 Judicial Decisions' (规范性文件附带审查的启动要件 – 基于1738份裁判文书样本的实证考察) (2019) *Legal Science* (法学) 165, 169.

93 ALL (n 3), art 53(1).

94 Guohua Wang (王国华) and Qingqing Yi (易清清), 'Empirical Study of Judicial Review Administrative Normative Instrument: A Study Based on 947 Judgements' (行政规范性文件附带审查的实证分析 – 以947份裁判文书为样本) (2019) *Law and Modernisation* (法治现代化研究) 28, 40–42.

95 Article 64 of the ALL provides: "The people's court in the hearing of administrative cases, after determining that a normative document is not legal, in accordance with Article 53 of this Law, they cannot use the normative document as the basis for determining the legality of administrative actions".

96 SPC ALL Interpretation of 2018 (n 5), art 149.

97 *Ibid.*, art 150. If the administrative normative documents are enacted by the State Council or the provincial governments, the disposition recommendations must be sent to the State Council and the SPC.

98 Chao Lu (卢超), 'Judicial Predicament and Cohesive Function of Normative Documents Incidental Review' (规范性文件附带审查的司法困境及其枢纽功能) (2020) 3 *Journal of Comparative Law* (比较法研究) 127, 133.

99 *Ibid.*

the courts can review the reasonableness and proportionality of administrative normative documents. The Minute 2004 empowered the courts to review the legality, validity, reasonableness and proportionality of administrative normative documents. But Article 53(1) of the ALL and Article 148 of the SPC ALL Interpretation of 2018 only mention "illegality", without mentioning "unreasonableness" or "disproportionality". A literal interpretation of these provisions could render a constrained judicial review of administrative rules, excluding a substantive review of the rules and administrative normative documents.[100]

In summary, Chinese courts are constitutionally barred from reviewing the constitutionality of government actions. This power is monopolized by the NPC and the NPCSC – China's highest legislature. The courts' primary judicial review authority lies in reviewing administrative decisions. Additionally, Chinese courts can scrutinize administrative rules, but their jurisdiction is limited to lower-ranked rules within the hierarchy of the Chinese legal system. This restricted jurisdiction hampers the courts' potential to serve as a check on government power, leaving individuals with few avenues for judicial recourse against government.

Taiwan's Judicial Review Scheme

Taiwan's judicial review is constructed based on a centralized model. Judicial review power is principally vested in the TCC and administrative courts. The TCC exclusively exercises the constitutional review power. It was established in 1948 and is one of the oldest constitutional courts in Asia.[101] It has the power to review primary legislation and administrative rules and can invalidate them if found unconstitutional. The TCC also has jurisdiction over constitutional amendments and impeaches the president of Taiwan. However, administrative decisions have long been excluded from the TCC's purview. The power to review executive actions is vested in administrative courts.[102]

Gradual Expansion of Judicial Power of the TCC

In Taiwan's legal system, statutes (*falv*) are primary legislation enacted by the Legislative Yuan and promulgated by the President.[103] The executive authorities have the power to promulgate regulations (*mingling*), which is either delegated by the Legislative Yuan or based on their administrative

100 Haibo He (何海波), 'Court's Collateral Review of Normative Document' (论法院对规范性文件的附带审查) (2021) *China Legal Science* (中国法学) 139, 158.

101 Jiunn-Rong Yeh and Wen-Chen Chang, 'An Evolving Court with Changing Functions: The Constitutional Court and Judicial Review in Taiwan' in Albert H.Y. Chen and Andrew Harding (eds), *Constitutional Courts in Asia: A Comparative Perspective* (CUP 2018) 110.

102 Administrative Litigation Act (n 11), art 13.

103 Central Regulation Standard Act (中央法規標準法), arts 2, 4.

powers.[104] Additionally, the executive authorities can also issue administrative rules (*xingzheng guize*), which are internal directives that do not have direct external legal effects.[105] These administrative rules guide the internal functioning of administrative agencies but do not affect individuals or entities outside the government directly. A statute is usually titled as an "act" or "code", and a regulation is usually titled as a "regulation", "enforcement rule", or "standard".[106] Both statutes and regulations are the most important sources of law.

Articles 78 and 171 of the Constitution of Taiwan empower the TCC to interpret the Constitution, unify legal interpretation,[107] and constitutionally review statutes.[108] The TCC has exercised these powers for over seven decades and experienced changes over time.[109] During the authoritarian period (1948–1987), the TCC was largely a handmaiden of the KMT.[110] The majority of interpretations rendered by the TCC during this period were unifying legal interpretation, instead of reviewing the constitutionality of laws.[111] The TCC's ability to supervise government power in favor of individual rights was ineffective.[112] The situation has changed remarkably since the late 1980s when Taiwan started its democratic transition, with the constitutional review power being consolidated and expanded through constitutional amendments, statutory revision, and its own decisions.[113]

The 1992 Taiwan Constitutional Amendment empowered the TCC to dissolve unconstitutional political parties whose goals or activities endanger the existence of Taiwan and the free and democratic constitutional order of this region.[114] The 1997 Taiwan Constitutional Amendment enhanced the TCC's independence by excluding the Executive Yuan from eliminating or reducing the annual budget proposed by the Judicial Yuan (J.Y.).[115] Although this amendment did not directly expand the TCC judicial power, it made such development more likely, as active and consequential judicial review occurs more frequently when the judiciary is more independent.[116] The 2005 Taiwan Constitutional Amendment conferred the power on the TCC to adjudicate

104 *Ibid.*, arts 3, 7.
105 Administrative Procedure Act (行政程序法), art 159.
106 The translation is in accordance with the Table of Standard of English translation of Laws approved by the Executive Yuan in 2013, available at www.ey.gov.tw/Page/4F152FEBB9602003, accessed 7 October 2024.
107 Constitution of Taiwan (n 9), art 78.
108 *Ibid.*, art. 171.
109 Lin (n 8) 302.
110 Po Jen Yap, *Courts and Democracies in Asia* (CUP 2017) 95.
111 Yeh and Chang (n 101) 114.
112 *Ibid.*,129–130.
113 Lin (n 8) 302–304.
114 Amendment to the Constitutional of Taiwan, art 13 (1992).
115 Amendment to the Constitutional of Taiwan, art 5 (1997).
116 Lin (n 8) 302.

motions to impeach the president and vice president.[117] Transferring this power from the National Assembly to the TCC suggests the expansion of judicial power at the expense of the legislature. To date, however, the TCC has not heard cases of presidential impeachment or dissolution of unconstitutional political parties.

The TCC's constitutional review power has been expanded through amending relevant statutes. The Council of Grand Justices Act promulgated in 1958 contained the rules regulating the power and jurisdiction of the TCC, as well as the procedure for constitution review.[118] It comprised only 20 provisions, which were inadequate for complicated constitutional review proceedings. In the next 70 years, this Act was amended twice. The first amendment was enacting the Constitutional Interpretation Procedure Act (CIPA) in 1993. The CIPA detailed the procedural rules for constitutional review and expanded the TCC's power by providing the TCC with more opportunities to intervene in law-making and policy-making. Article 5 of this Act enabled the minority of the Legislative Yuan (one-third) to challenge the constitutionality of laws. This means the legislature could more easily file a petition with the TCC for constitutional review. Additionally, the CIPA lowered the vote threshold for issuing interpretations from three-quarters to two-thirds.[119] The preceding high threshold was once an obstacle for the TCC to exercise meaningful constitutional supervision.[120] Due to these changes, the TCC could exercise its power more efficiently and effectively.

The second significant amendment was passing the Constitutional Court Procedure Act (CCPA) in 2019, which took effect on 4 January 2022. The CCPA conferred new power on the TCC to hear constitutional complaints, which enabled the TCC to review final court decisions.[121] People who allege that their constitutional rights have been violated by the final judicial decisions can file a petition to the TCC for a judgment declaring the judicial decision unconstitutional. This new constitutional complaint procedure was migrated from Germany,[122] where constitutional complaints have contributed to the high standing of the Federal Constitutional Court and the rising constitutional consciousness among its people.[123] For Taiwan, this new procedure is

117 Amendment to the Constitutional of Taiwan, art 5 (2005).

118 Yeh and Chang (n 101) 113.

119 Constitutional Interpretation Procedure Act (CIPA) (司法院大法官審理案件法), art 14.

120 Jiunn-Rong Yeh, 'Democracy-Driven Transformation to Regulatory State' in Tom Ginsburg and Albert H. Y. Chen (eds), *Administrative Law and Governance in Asia: Comparative Perspectives* (Routledge 2008) 129.

121 Constitutional Court Procedure Act (CCPA) (憲法訴訟法), art 59.

122 *Judicial Yuan Research Project on Introducing Constitutional Complaints to the Draft of the CIPA Amendment: Final Report* (司法院大法官審理案件法修正草案引進裁判憲法訴願制度專題研究計劃：期末報告) (31 July 2018), available at www.judicial.gov.tw/tw/cp-1535-57148-1d27d-1.html, accessed 30 July 2024.

123 Albert H. Y. Chen, 'The Global Expansion of Constitutional Judicial Review: Some Historical and Comparative Perspectives' 9 (1 January 2013), Available at SSRN: https://ssrn.com/abstract=2210340 or http://dx.doi.org/10.2139/ssrn.2210340.

important as it is capable of leading to stronger judicial protection of people's rights and freedoms.[124] The infringements of individual rights are not only from legislation and executive action that enforces laws but can be from the court's application of laws.[125] Through the constitutional complaint procedure, people can question the application of laws by courts.

Additionally, the CCPA expands the TCC's constitutional review power by further decreasing the threshold for constitutional petition by the members of Legislative Yuan from one-third to one-fourth and by lowering the threshold for rendering judgment, from two-thirds (10 out of 15 Grand Justices) to a majority of the Grand Justices.[126] These changes further increased the opportunity for the TCC to review the legislations and more efficiently.

Lastly, the TCC expanded its constitutional review power through its own interpretations. In Interpretation No. 371 (1995), the TCC nullified Article 5 of the CIPA and entitled judges of courts at all levels to file a petition with the TCC for constitutional review.[127] According to the impugned provision, only judges from the Supreme Court and Supreme Administrative Court could petition the TCC when they suspect the law to be applied is unconstitutional. The TCC emphasized:

> The power to interpret a statute's constitutionality and to invalidate it rests exclusively with the grand justice of the Judicial Yuan ... The Constitution is the final authority in this country, so judges are obliged to apply the Constitution in the first place. Regardless of appellate jurisdiction, judges of each level of courts should be allowed to petition this Court for constitutional interpretation, if they have reasonable grounds to regard a statute to be applied as unconstitutional.[128]

Constitutional Review of Administrative Rules by the TCC

Article 172 of the Constitution of Taiwan stipulates that regulations conflicting with the Constitution of Taiwan or with statutes are null and void. But the Constitution does not specify which institution could check the compliance of a regulation with the Constitution and statutes. The Council of Grand Justices Act, the CIPA, and the CCPA address this gap by explicitly designating the TCC as the authority to review administrative rules for their constitutional and statutory compliance.[129] In Interpretation No. 210 (1986), the TCC struck down Article 27 of the Enforcement Rules of the Act of Encouragement of

124 Wen-Chen Chang, 'Back into the Political? Rethinking Judicial, Legal, and Transnational Constitutionalism' (2019) *International Journal of Constitutional Law* 453, 457.

125 *Judicial Yuan Research Project* (n 122) 6.

126 CCPA (n 121), arts 30, 49.

127 J.Y. Interpretation No. 371, [2].

128 *Ibid.*

129 Wen-Chen Chang (張文貞), 'Judicial Review of Administrative Rules and Regulations: Focusing on Reviewing Decisions of the Supreme Administrative Court" (行政命令的司法審查—以最高行政法院判決為中心) in Yen-Tu Su (蘇彥圖) (ed) Constitutional

Investment on the grounds that it was inconsistent with the enabling statute and hence violated the basic principle of taxation by law under Article 19 of the Constitution of Taiwan.[130] In this case, the TCC established a principle – a regulation is unconstitutional if it contravenes its enabling statute.[131] Therefore, the TCC transformed a "compliance with statutes" issue of an administrative rule into a "compliance with the Constitution" issue.[132]

The TCC would also strike down an administrative rule when the enabling statute was unclear in authorizing delegation. It is the enabling statute that is flawed, but the TCC declares the administrative rules unconstitutional rather than the enabling statute itself. In Interpretation No. 313 (1993), the TCC overturned Article 46 of the Rules Governing the Management of the Business of Civil Aviation because the authorization provided by the enabling statute was unclear. The TCC emphasized that, in accordance with Article 23 of the Constitution of Taiwan, any provision that limits individual rights by imposing administrative fines must be provided by statutes, including specific conditions and the amount of the fine. When the legislature authorizes the promulgation of regulations to supplement statutes with enforcement details, the content and scope of such authorization must be concrete and clear to ensure that the regulation complies with Article 23 of the Constitution of Taiwan.[133]

Taiwan's Administrative Courts and Administrative Litigation

Taiwan's administrative courts are specific courts for hearing challenges against administrative decisions.[134] The Administrative Litigation Act explicitly states that the purpose of administrative litigation is to protect people's rights and interests and ensure that all executive authorities exercise their power in accordance with laws.[135] Taiwan's administrative court system comprises three levels. The Supreme Administrative Court is the final instance and focuses on questions of law. Below it are three High Administrative Courts in Taipei, Taichung, and Kaohsiung. They are trial courts of ordinary cases at first instance. The administrative divisions of district courts handle simple administrative litigation, such as traffic cases or petitions for relief from detention.[136] The final decisions delivered by administrative courts are still subject to review by the TCC. This book focuses on the judicial review done by the apex court in each area. Judicial review carried out by Taiwan's administrative courts is not the focus of this study.

Interpretation: Theory and Practice Volume 10 (憲法解釋之理論與實務第十輯) (Institutum Iurisprudentiae Academic Sinica 2020).

130 J.Y. Interpretation No. 210, [2].

131 Chang (n 129) 279.

132 *Ibid.*

133 J.Y. Interpretations No. 313, [1].

134 Administrative Litigation Act (n 11), art 13.

135 *Ibid.*, art 1.

136 *Ibid.*, arts 229–237.

In summary, the TCC holds constitutional review jurisdiction over the statutes, administrative rules, and final court decisions. It also enjoys the power to impeach the president and the vice president and dissolve unconstitutional political parties whose goals or activities endanger the existence and the free and democratic constitutional order of Taiwan. However, concrete administrative decisions are not subject to constitutional review by the TCC.

Hong Kong's Judicial Review Scheme

Hong Kong retained the common law legal systems and traditions, including judicial review, after the British handover of this region to China on 1 July 1997. The jurisdiction of Hong Kong courts' judicial review is wide, covering primary legislation, administrative rules, and administrative decisions. The CFA, the apex court of this region, seized the opportunity of its first major case to claim the courts of Hong Kong have the power of constitutional review.[137] However, the courts of Hong Kong do not enjoy the final and unchallengeable authority to interpret the HKBL, the mini-constitution of this region.[138] The power of the final interpretation of the HKBL is reserved for the NPCSC in Beijing.[139]

Courts and Constitutional Review in Hong Kong

Judicial review in Hong Kong embraces two interrelated meaning.[140] Judicial review in a narrow sense is the British notion of review of administrative decisions, through which the court determines legality but does not second-guess the merits of administrative decisions.[141] Additionally, judicial review in Hong Kong also embraces constitutional review in which the courts scrutinize the compatibility of legislative and executive actions with the HKBL and the BORO, which was enacted in 1991 to make the ICCPR enforceable in

137 Eric C. Ip, *Hybrid Constitutionalism: The Politics of Constitutional Review in the Chinese Special Administrative Regions* (CUP 2019) 121.

138 Xiaonan Yang, 'Two Interpreters of the Basic Law: The Court of Final Appeal and the Standing Committee of the National People's Congress' in Simon N. M. Young and Yash Ghai (eds), *Hong Kong's Court of Final Appeal: The Development of the Law in China's Hong Kong* (CUP 2014) 69.

139 Simon N. M. Young, 'Constitutional Rights in Hong Kong's Court of Final Appeal' (2012) *Chinese (Taiwan) Yearbook of International Law and Affairs* 67, 68.

140 Johannes Chan, 'Administrative Law, Politics, and Governance' in Tom Ginsburg and Albert H. Y. Chen (eds), *Administrative Law and Governance in Asia: Comparative Perspectives* (Routledge 2008) 148.

141 The Department of Justice of Hong Kong, *The Judge over Your Shoulder: A Guide to Judicial Review for Administrators* (3rd edn, 2019) 1.

Hong Kong.[142] Both types of judicial review are conducted by ordinary courts of Hong Kong.

After the handover, the Legislative Council becomes the sole legislature of the HKSAR and enacts laws for Hong Kong, which are known as ordinances.[143] Besides ordinances, there are plenty of administrative rules, including subsidiary legislation. Subsidiary legislation in Hong Kong refers to "any proclamation, rule, regulation, order, resolution, notice, rule of court, bylaw or other instrument made under or by virtue of any ordinance and which is having legislative effect".[144] They are detailed rules and regulations providing technical or procedural details necessary for the enforcement of ordinances.[145] They are considered important, taking into account their quantity and extensive interference with people's rights and freedoms.[146] As far as the executive power is concerned, the HKBL empowers the government and the Chief Executive to exercise a series of executive powers, such as carrying out administrative affairs, making administrative decisions, promulgating policy, and drafting and introducing bills, motions, and subordinate legislation.[147]

Constitutional review in Hong Kong has historical roots dating back to the colonial era. During this period, the courts in colonial Hong Kong were vested with constitutional review power according to the provisions outlined in the Letters Patent and the Royal Instructions, which served as Hong Kong's constitution.[148] After the BORO was introduced to Hong Kong in 1990, the courts heard a larger number of cases involving challenges to the compatibility of legislation and executive actions with the constitutional guarantees enshrined in the BORO.[149]

The HKBL contains several key provisions that form the foundation of Hong Kong's constitutional review.[150] Article 2 of the HKBL authorizes Hong Kong to "exercise a high degree of autonomy and enjoy executive, legislative

142 Yash Ghai, *Hong Kong's New Constitutional Order: The Resumption of Chinese Sovereignty and the Basic Law* 250 (HKU Press 1999).

143 HKBL, arts 66, 73. Before the handover, the governor of Hong Kong possessed plenary legislative power to make laws for colonial Hong Kong. *Secretary for Justice v Lau Kwok Fai and Another* (2005) 8 HKCFAR 304, [38].

144 Interpretation and General Clauses Ordinance (Cap 1), s 3.

145 Peter Wesley-Smith, *Constitutional and Administrative Law in Hong Kong* (Longman Asia Ltd 1994) 163.

146 Yu Gu, *Hong Kong's Legislature under China's Sovereignty: 1998–2013* (Brill Nijhoff 2016) 98.

147 HKBL, arts 48 and 62.

148 Norman Miners, *The Government and Politics of Hong Kong* (5th edn, OUP 1995) ch. 5; Wesley-Smith (n 145) ch. 2.

149 Yash Ghai, 'Litigating the Basic Law: Jurisdiction, Interpretation and Procedure' in Johannes Chan, Hualing Fu and Yash Ghai (eds), *Hong Kong's Constitutional Debate: Conflict Over Interpretation* (HKU Press 2000) 14.

150 Albert H. Y. Chen and P. Y. Lo, 'The Constitutional Orders of "One Country, Two Systems": A Comparative Study of the Visible and Invisible Bases of Constitutional Review and Proportionality Analysis in the Chinese Special Administrative Regions of Hong Kong and

and independent judicial power, including that of final adjudication". Article 11(2) stipulates that the laws enacted by the legislature of Hong Kong must not contravene the HKBL. Chapter III of the HKBL provides for a series of fundamental rights. Article 19 of the HKBL provides that Hong Kong courts have jurisdiction over all cases in this region. Article 158 of the HKBL equips Hong Kong courts with competence to interpret the HKBL on their own in adjudicating cases.

After the handover, the CFA seized the opportunity of its first major case to claim the courts of Hong Kong have the power of constitutional review.[151] In *Ng Ka Ling v Director of Immigration* (1999), the CFA made a daring and significant judgment,[152] acknowledging that the courts of Hong Kong "undoubtedly have the jurisdiction to examine whether legislation enacted by the legislature of this Region or acts of the executive authorities of the Region are consistent with the HKBL and, if found to be inconsistent, to hold them to be invalid".[153]

Ng Ka Ling was about the abode right of Mainland China-born children of Hong Kong permanent residents. Article 24 (3) of the HKBL entitles permanent residents to the right of abode in Hong Kong, and Article 24(2) sets out six categories of permanent citizens. Ng Ka Ling belonged to the third category: those of Chinese nationality born outside of Hong Kong to the first and second categories of permanent citizens. In July 1997, the Provisional Legislative Council passed Immigration (Amendment) (No. 3) Ordinance 1997, which provided that for Mainland China-born children of Hong Kong permanent residents, permanent residency could only be established and the right of abode could only be exercised by affixing one-way permits, which were issued on the quota basis and determined by the Mainland authorities.[154] Subsequent to this ordinance, the rights of abode of the Mainland China-born children of Hong Kong permanent residents were qualified by one-way permits. By contrast, the right of abode of the same category of permanent residents who were residents outside Mainland would not be so qualified.[155] The CFA stated that:

> In exercising their judicial power conferred by the Basic Law, the courts of the Region have a duty to enforce and interpret that Law...The exercise of this jurisdiction is a matter of obligation, not of discretion so

Macau' in Rosalind Dixon and Adrienne Stone (eds), *The Invisible Constitution in Comparative Perspective* (CUP 2018) 235–236.

151 Ip (n 137) 121.

152 Simon N. M. Young, 'Human Rights' in Simon N. M. Young and Yash Ghai (eds), *Hong Kong's Court of Final Appeal: The Development of the Law in China's Hong Kong* (CUP 2014) 415.

153 *Ng Ka Ling and Others v Director of Immigration* (1999) 2 HKCFAR 4, 25G–H.

154 *Ibid.*, 34C–J.

155 *Ibid.*, 34G–J.

> that if inconsistency is established, the courts are bound to hold that a law or executive act is invalid at least to the extent of the inconsistency. Although this has not been questioned, it is right that we should take this opportunity of stating it unequivocally. In exercising this jurisdiction, the courts perform their constitutional role under the Basic Law of acting as a constitutional check on the executive and legislative branches of government to ensure that they act in accordance with the Basic Law.[156]

This statement confirmed Hong Kong courts' power of constitutional review against legislation and executive authorities' actions. Elsie Leung, the then Secretary of Justice of the HKSAR, agreed with the CFA's opinion that the "mini-constitution – the Basic Law – enables litigants to challenge legislation, and government administrative action, on the basis that it is unconstitutional".[157]

Besides confirmation of the competence of reviewing of local laws, the CFA took a further step, stating that the courts of Hong Kong had power to review the compliance of the legislative acts of the NPC and the NPCSC with the HKBL:

> What has been controversial is the jurisdiction of the courts of the Region to examine whether any legislative acts of the National People's Congress or its Standing Committee ... are consistent with the Basic Law and to declare them to be invalid if found to be inconsistent. In our view, the courts of the Region do have this jurisdiction and indeed the duty to declare invalidity if inconsistency is found. It is right that we should take this opportunity of stating so unequivocally.[158]

Nevertheless, this bold statement eventually became regrettable.

Final Interpretation of the Basic Law by the NPCSC

Shortly after *Ng Ka Ling*, it became known that the CFA's final adjudication did not include the final power of interpreting the HKBL and the ultimate power of interpreting the HKBL belonged to the NPCSC.[159]

The Central Government criticized the CFA's opinion on constitutionally reviewing the NPC's and the NPCSC's legislation as an unacceptable challenge to the authority of Beijing.[160] The Hong Kong Government requested

156 *Ibid.*, 25G–J.
157 Elsie Leung, 'The Continuity of Hong Kong's Legal System', Speech at the Asia-Pacific Society, Oxford University on 4 March 2001, para 28, available at www.doj.gov.hk/en/archive/sa_by_sec_2001.html, accessed 20 February 2022.
158 *Ng Ka Ling* (n 153) 26A–B.
159 Chan, 'Administrative Law, Politics, and Governance' (n 140) 145.
160 Frank Ching, 'Judgment Call' (1999) *Far Eastern Economic Review* 21.

the CFA to "clarify" its opinion. On 26 February 1999, the CFA issued a clarification – *Ng Ka Ling v Director of Immigration (2)* – in which the CFA stated that:

> The Court's judgment on 29 January 1999 did not question the authority of the Standing Committee to make an interpretation under Article 158 which would have to be followed by the courts of the Region. The Court accepts that it cannot question that authority. Nor did the Court's judgment question, and the Court accepts that it cannot question, the authority of the National People's Congress or the Standing Committee to do any act which is in accordance with the provisions of the Basic Law and the procedure therein.[161]

In this clarification, nonetheless, the CFA refrained from addressing its competence to scrutinize actions of the NPC or the NPCSC that it deemed incompatible with the HKBL. The storm of *Ng Ka Ling* did not stop at this point. The Hong Kong Government was concerned about the societal and economic consequence of granting the right of abode automatically to all Mainland-born children of Hong Kong permanent residents. On 26 June 1999, six months after the CFA handed down *Ng Ka Ling* decision, the Hong Kong Government successfully acquired an interpretation of the HKBL from the NPCSC, which reversed the CFA's decision.[162] The NPCSC expressly stated that the CFA's understanding of Articles 22(4) and 24(2)(3) of the HKBL was not in conformity with the original legislative intent and should be struck down.[163]

The clarification of the CFA and the ensuing interpretation by the NPCSC sparked heated debate and caused frustration among Hong Kong citizens, judges, politicians, lawyers and academics.[164] The critics saw the interpretation as undermining judicial independence, the power of final adjudication of local courts, and the rule of law of Hong Kong.[165] It started a practice that the NPCSC bypasses the CFA and interprets the Basic Law proactively or at the request of the Government of Hong Kong. According to Article 158 of the HKBL, it is the CFA that should seek an interpretation of the Basic Law from

161 (1999) 2 HKCFAR 141, 142C–E.

162 Interpretation by the Standing Committee of the National People's Congress Regarding Paragraph 4 in Article 22 and Category (3) of Paragraph 2 in Article 24 of the Basic Law of the Hong Kong Special Administrative Region of the People's Republic of China (全国人民代表大会常务委员会关于《中华人民共和国香港特别行政区基本法》第二十二条第四款和第二十四条第二款第(三)项的解释) (1996).

163 *Ibid.*

164 Yash Ghai, 'The NPC Interpretation and Its Consequence' in Johannes Cham, Hualing Fu and Yash Ghai (eds), *Hong Kong's Constitutional Debate: Conflict Over Interpretation* (HKU Press 2000) 199.

165 *Ibid.*

the NPCSC if the relevant provision to be interpreted concerns the affairs which are the responsibility of the Central Government or concerns the relationship between the Central Authorities and the Region. The NPCSC interpretation after *Ng Kai Ling* was a product of the Chief Executive's request, instead of the CFA's request. The NPCSC has issued five interpretations of the HKBL so far. Two interpretations were at the request of the Hong Kong Government. Only one was at the request of the CFA. The NPCSC issued two interpretations of the HKBL even without any request from Hong Kong. On 3 December 1999, in *Lau Kong Yung and Others v Director of Immigration*, the CFA unanimously held that the NPCSC's interpretation was binding on the courts of Hong Kong and was effective retroactively to the date that the HKBL entered into force.[166]

Although the NPCSC has the ultimate power of interpreting the HKBL, the courts of Hong Kong are still the prime institutes for interpreting and applying the Basic Law. In 2007, Chief Justice Li remarked:

> The courts continue to face many challenging issues in judicial review cases. Questions relating to the proper interpretation of the Basic Law, the construction of statutes and common law principles arise in these cases. As far as the Basic Law is concerned, many articles of the Basic Law have been considered in court decisions since 1997 … It is not an exaggeration to say that the phenomenon of judicial review has redefined the legal landscape. Further, the availability and use of judicial review has had a significant impact on the conduct of the business of government and has exercised a considerable influence on public debate on many issues.[167]

Judicial Review in a Narrow Common Law Sense

As mentioned above, judicial review in a narrow sense is the British notion of review of any exercise, or any refusal to exercise, any public decision-making powers. It is a means by which the courts supervise whether executive authorities exercise their powers and carry out their duties legally. High Court Ordinance and the Rules of the High Court provide the judicial review procedural rules. Judicial reviews in Hong Kong are brought before the Court of First Instance of the High Court when the leave for judicial review is granted.[168] Where leave is granted and judicial review is substantively determined by the Court of First Instance, the parties, if dissatisfied with the decision, may

166 (1999) 2 HKCFAR 300, 323B–324E.

167 'Chief Justice Speech at the Ceremonial Opening of the Legal Year 2007', 8 January 2007, available at www.info.gov.hk/gia/general/200701/08/P200701080120.htm, accessed 19 February 2022.

168 High Court Ordinance (cap 4) s 21K (3); The Rules of the High Court (cap 4A) O 53, r 3(1).

appeal to the Court of Appeal.[169] In exceptional cases, appeals may go directly to the CFA if a point of law of great general or public importance is involved, which is the leapfrog procedure.[170]

Macau's Judicial Review Scheme

Judicial review in Macau has received less attention in the literature than that in Taiwan and Hong Kong. As a matter of fact, the jurisdiction of judicial review in Macau is broad, covering primary legislation, administrative rules, and concrete executive decisions. But unlike the CFA, which assertively claimed the constitutional review power, the TUI showed a more timid and restrained attitude at the beginning and later experienced a significant shift in its stance on whether Macau courts have the authority to carry out constitutional review.

Dillydallying TUI: Development of Constitutional Review

Before detailing the development of Macau's judicial review scheme after the handover, it is helpful to briefly review the distribution of legislative and executive powers in Macau. The Legislative Assembly is the sole legislature of the MSAR, and the statutes enacted by the Legislative Assembly are known as "laws". In the period of Portuguese colonial rule, the Legislative Assembly shared legislative power with the Governor of Macau.[171] The decrees promulgated by the governor had the same legal effect as the laws enacted by the Legislative Assembly.[172] Some decrees continue to apply after the handover. The Chief Executive of the MSAR enjoys a wide range of executive power. Besides generic power of enforcing the laws and administrative measures, he enjoys the power to promulgate administrative rules, including administrative regulations, executive orders and dispatch.[173]

169 High Court Ordinance (cap 4) s 13(2); The Rules of the High Court (cap 4A) O 59, r 1(1).

170 Hong Kong Court of Final Appeal Ordinance (cap 484) Div 2, s 27C. The leapfrog procedure was first used in *Town Planning Board v Society for Protection of the Harbour Ltd*, where the respondent challenged the applicant's draft plan about the proposed reclamation in Wan Chai North. *Town Planning Board v Society for the Protection of the Harbour Ltd* (2004) 7 HKCFAR 1, [21].

171 Organic Statute of Macau (澳門組織章程), art 5 (1976).

172 Yu Wang (王禹), 'The Discussion of Source of Law in Macau Special Administrative Region' (澳門特別行政區的法律淵源探討) (2014) 20 *Academic Journal of "One Country Two Systems"* ("一國兩制"研究) 13, 17.

173 Administrative regulation and executive orders are concepts introduced to Macau from the Chinese legal system after the handover. These did not exist in colonial Macau, where the governor had the power to issue *despachos* and *portaria*. Post-handover, the MBL empowers the Chief Executive to issue administrative regulations and executive orders, with no mention of *despachos* or *portaria*. However, after the handover, the Chief Executive continues issuing despachos. While executive orders are new in theory, in practice, they have replaced *portaria* that were previously issued by the colonial governor. Administrative regulations generally cover provisions on certain types of matters and have legislative characteristics,

An Unfortunate Kick-Off

Macau courts in the colonial era were vested with constitutional review power. Article 41(1) of the Organic Statute of Macau provided that the courts would not apply any laws that were in breach of the Portuguese Constitution or the Organic Statute of Macau.[174] The *recurso de amparo* (the writ of protection) was introduced to Macau through Article 17 of the Basic Law of Judiciary Organization in 1991.[175] According to this provision, people could appeal to the High Court of Justice on the grounds that judgments rendered by lower courts or executive actions taken by the government had violated their fundamental rights and freedoms. After the handover, the MBL replaced the Organic Statute of Macau, becoming the mini-constitution of Macau. The new Basic Law of Judiciary Organization that came into force after the handover abolished *amparo* by removing relevant provisions.

Like the HKBL, the MBL guarantees Macau enjoys a high level of autonomy and also contains provisions offering a constitutional foundation for constitutional review within this region.[176] Article 8 of the MBL provides that the laws previously in force are preserved, except for those that contravene the MBL and are subject to amendment by the Legislative Assembly.[177] Article 19 of the MBL stipulates that Macau courts have jurisdiction over all cases in this region. Chapter III of the MBL contains a series of fundamental rights. Article 143 of the MBL empowers the courts to interpret the MBL in adjudicating cases. Despite the similarities between the MBL and HKBL, the implementation of constitutional review in Macau has taken a notably different path from Hong Kong. In Hong Kong, courts have assertively claimed the power of constitutional review and actively engaged in protecting fundamental rights and ensuring the supremacy of the HKBL in legal matters. In contrast, the TUI

while executive orders and *despachos* are usually decisions on specific matters and on specific persons (e.g. the appointment and removal of government officials, temporary delegation of power, and the conferral of honors and awards). MBL, arts 50(4)–(5).

174 Organic Statute of Macau (n 171), art 41(1) (1990). Vitalino Canas, 'The General Regime of Fundamental Rights in the Basic Law and in the International Instruments' in Jorge Oliveira and Paulo Cardinal (eds), *One Country Two Systems, Three Legal Orders – Perspectives of Evolution* (Springer 2009) 673.

175 Basic Law of Judiciary Organization (澳門司法組織綱要法), art 17 (1991); Paulo Cardinal and Luís Pessanha, 'Macau' in David S. Law et. al., (eds), *Oxford Handbook of Constitutional Law in Asia* (OUP 2023), Part 7.

176 Simon N. M. Young, 'Fundamental Rights and the Basic Laws of the Hong Kong and Macau Special Administrative Regions' in Jorge Oliveira and Paulo Cardinal (eds), *One Country Two Systems, Three Legal Orders – Perspectives of Evolution: Essays on Macau's Autonomy After the Resumption of Sovereignty by China* (Springer 2009) 681.

177 On 1 October 1999, the NPCSC adopted all laws, decrees, and other normative documents, save for 33 which it found wholly or partly inconsistent with the MBL (3.86 percent of all laws reviewed). *The Yearbook of Macau 2020*, page 121, available at https://yearbook.gcs.gov.mo/uploads/yearbook_pdf/2020/myb2020c.pdf, accessed 11 October 2024.

has been criticized for delivering what some scholars have called a "deadly blow" to constitutional review immediately after the handover.[178]

In Case 1/2000 and Case 2/2000, the applicants filed applications to the High Court of Justice for the leave of constitutional appeal to the Constitutional Court of Portugal in Lisbon. Nonetheless, the High Court of Justice did not grant the leave for appeal before 20 December 1999. According to Article 70(2) of the Basic Law on Judicial Organization, the following pending proceedings must be terminated: appeals against a court's decision where (1) the court refuses to apply a rule on the ground that the rule is inconsistent with the Constitution of Portugal; or (2) the court has applied a rule that violates the Constitution of Portugal. Article 70(4) of the same law states that the courts of the MSAR cannot adjudicate cases filed on the ground of violating the Constitution of Portugal. Eventually, the two constitutional appeals were terminated. Against this background, the applicants appealed to the TUI and raised two issues: Whether the two pending constitutional appeals have been terminated? If yes, whether the applicants have the right to file a new petition of constitutional review?

First, the TUI affirmed that the Basic Law on Judicial Organization had brought the two pending constitutional appeals to an end. Second and more importantly, the TUI held that the legal system of Macau after the handover did not encompass any appeal procedure for addressing the issues of whether a law violates the MBL.[179]

Moving to a Weak-Form Constitutional Review

Changes occurred in 2006. In Case 9/2006, the TUI changed its opinion and affirmed that the courts of the SAR have the competence in interpreting the MBL and examining the compliance of a law with the MBL:

> When adjudicating cases, the courts can scrutinize whether or not a law violates the Basic Law. The courts should enforce Article 11 of the Basic Law and should not apply a law that contradicts the Basic Law and its principles thereof, without prejudice to Article 143 of the Basic Law. As there is no specialized appeal procedure for reviewing whether a law is in compliance with the Basic Law in the legal system of Macau, the courts can review the conformity of laws with the Basic Law when adjudicating specific cases.[180]

178 Paulo Cardinal, 'Fundamental Rights in Macau: From Territory Under Portuguese Administration to Special Administrative Region of the PRC' in Jorge A. F. Godinho (ed), *Study on Macau Civil, Commercial, Constitutional and Criminal Law* (LexisNexis 2011) 28–29.

179 Case 1/2000, page 3; Case 2/2000, page 2.

180 Case 9/2006, page 3.

In Case 28/2006, the TUI elaborated in detail upon the necessity and constitutional foundation of constitutional review carried out by the courts of Macau:

> The power (of constitutional review) is derived from an integrated interpretation of various provisions of the Basic Law.
>
> In fact, in accordance with Article 19 (2) of the Basic Law, Macau courts have the power to adjudicate all cases in Macau, without prejudice to the restriction on the judicial power imposed by the legal system and principles previously in force in Macau.
>
> Article 11 of the Basic Law also states that no statute, decree, administrative regulation or normative instrument shall contradict this Law.
>
> Nonetheless, the Basic Law does not establish any mechanisms, particularly political mechanisms, for settling the potential conflicts emerging in litigations between the Basic Law and other laws in force. Consequently, the courts must solve these conflicts in specific adjudications.
>
> ...
>
> If a court can interpret the Basic Law when adjudicating cases, the court for sure can reach a conclusion that certain legislation or administrative regulations contravene the Basic Law. Under this circumstance, the court must enforce the provision of Article 11 of the Basic Law: therefore, it must not apply the law that is in contradiction with the provisions or general principles of the Basic Law, without prejudice to Article 143 of the Basic Law.[181]

The TUI eventually reintroduced constitutional review to Macau, but it just established a weak-form constitutional review. This form of review contrasts sharply with the strong-form judicial review practiced by the TCC and the CFA. In the case of the TCC and CFA, once they declare legislation or a rule unconstitutional, the law or rule is rendered null and void. By contrast, the TUI has asserted that courts in Macau should not apply legislation or administrative rules that are incompatible with the MBL.[182] However, this disapplication is only applicable to the specific case under review and does not carry general binding force.[183] This means that even after a law or rule is found unconstitutional in a particular instance, it remains valid and can still be applied in future cases unless amended or repealed by the legislative or administrative authorities. In Case 8/2007, the TUI reiterated:

181 Case 28/2006, pages 28–31.
182 Case 28/2006, page 31.
183 Jorge Oliveira and Paulo Cardinal, 'Macau's Court of Final Appeal' in Simon N. M. Young and Yash Ghai (eds), *Hong Kong's Court of Final Appeal: The Development of the Law in China's Hong Kong* (CUP 2014) 609.

> The finding that a provision violates a rule with a higher hierarchy is nothing more than an integral part of the court's reasoning. It is one step within the logical process that leads to the final judgment but does not form a part of the determination. The court cannot use this as a basis to give a judgment that that provision is illegal with concrete and binding force. The finding is only valid in the case itself and does not yield any effect toward other cases or even other courts. The provision deemed illegal does not become invalid because of this particular determination.[184]

Two Tracks of Judicial Review of Administrative Rules

Besides reviewing the constitutionality and legality of administrative rules in concrete legal disputes, Articles 88 to 93 of the Code of Administrative Litigation of Macau (CAL) provide an alternative procedure for scrutinizing administrative rules – abstract review. Prosecutors, high commissioners of the Macau Commission Against Corruption, and any persons aggrieved by administrative regulations can petition the court to invalidate the administrative regulations.[185] Although only administrative regulations are subject to abstract review based on the literal meaning of the CAL, the TUI purposively interpreted the purview of the abstract review to embrace all kinds of administrative rules that have the characteristic of generality and abstraction, including administrative regulations, executive orders, dispatches, and policies, which can be repeatedly applied to a group of unspecific people.[186]

Abstract review of administrative rules is distinct from concrete review of administrative rules in two aspects. First, a concrete review takes place in the context of adversarial litigation which focuses on the legal effects of the impugned administrative rules on the parties to a case. An abstract review can be initiated without a challenge against a concrete administrative decision. Second and more importantly, whereas the legal effect of a concrete review is disapplying unconstitutional or illegal administrative rules to the case itself, once courts declare an administrative rule illegal in an abstract review, such a rule becomes null and void. The declaration has a general and legal binding force on all courts and citizens.[187] The TUI stated that the abstract review of administrative rules aimed to remove an illegal administrative rule from the legal system.[188]

184 Case 8/2007, page 9.
185 CAL (n 18), art 91(1).
186 Case 5/2005, page 9.
187 CAL (n 18), art 89(1). As a civil law jurisdiction, Macau courts do not follow the common law traditions, and the TUI's decisions are not considered a source of law as in the common law. Jorge Godinho and Paulo Cardinal, 'Macau's Court of Final Appeal' in Simon N. M. Young and Yash Ghai (eds), *Hong Kong's Court of Final Appeal: The Development of the Law in China's Hong Kong* (CUP 2014) 609.
188 Case 28/2006, page 33.

Nonetheless, procedural restrictions attached to the abstract review procedure significantly hinder its effectiveness in safeguarding individual rights. First, individuals cannot request an abstract review unless the courts have deemed an administrative rule provision unlawful on three separate occasions.[189] But there is an exception rule: if a provision has an immediate effect on people's rights and interests, people can file abstract reviews and are not bound by the "three illegal declarations" requirement.[190] Second, the courts can only review the compliance of administrative rules with higher laws rather than the MBL, national laws of China applied in Macau, and international treaties.[191] Essentially, abstract review focuses on whether the administrative rule aligns with prior domestic laws, not with the broader constitutional framework or international legal standards. The constitutionality of administrative rules, particularly their consistency with the MBL, can only be evaluated in concrete review proceedings.

Judicial Review of Concrete Executive Actions

Due to the influence of the Portuguese centralized model of judicial review of executive action, Macau established the Administrative Tribunal as a component of the Court of First Instance, which specializes in resolving disputes concerning administrative, tax, and customs duties matters. The Administrative Tribunal enjoys common and residual jurisdiction in first instance over cases against government decisions.[192] However, Macau does not establish a high administrative court nor a supreme administrative court, given its small size of territory and population.[193] The Court of Second Instance is empowered to adjudicate the appeals against the decisions of the Administrative Tribunal, and the TUI hears appeals from the Court of Second Instance.[194]

Besides hearing appeals from the Administrative Tribunal, the Court of Second Instance can decide administrative litigation cases at the first instance against (i) acts, crimes, and misdemeanors of high officials in relation to the discharge of their duties,[195] and (ii) acts of the Chief Executive and high officials relating to administration, tax, and customs.[196] The TUI has original

189 CAL (n 18), art 90(1).

190 *Ibid.*

191 *Ibid.*, art 88 (2).

192 Basic Law of Judicial Organisation (n 175), art 30 (2019).

193 João Nuno Calvão da Silva, 'The Administrative Litigation of the MASAR' in Manual Trigo (ed), *Report on Macau Law* (LexisNexis 2014) 125.

194 CAL (n 18), arts 8, 9.

195 Basic Law of Judicial Organisation (n 175), art 36(2) and (3) (2019). These high officials include the president and secretaries of the Legislative Assembly, the commissioners against corruption, the commissioners of audit, the commander-general of the Unitary Police Office, the director-general of the Customs Office, members of the Executive Board, and members of the Legislative Assembly, as well as judges and prosecutors.

196 *Ibid.*, art 36(8).

Table 2.1 Judicial Review Decisions of the Four Apex Courts in Greater China (1999–2019).

Types Courts	*Review Primary Legislation*	*Review Administrative Rules*	*Review Executive Acts*	*In Total*
SPC	0	10	92	92
TCC	161	138	0	299
CFA	33	8	37	78
TUI	13	2	302	317
In total	207	158	433	786

Source: Author.

jurisdiction over the cases against acts, crimes, and misdemeanors of the Chief Executive in connection to the discharge of his duties.[197] It also has exclusive jurisdiction over appeals in respect of restrictions on the right of assemblies and demonstrations[198] and disputes arising from the election of the Chief Executive and Macau Legislative Assembly members.[199]

Judicial Review Activity of the Four Apex Courts in Greater China

The statutory law and case law in each area of Greater China delimit the competences of judicial review for their courts. However, one must question the meaningfulness of the comparison of the judicial review schemes without comparing the actual exercise of judicial review power, as the jurisdiction delimited by law hardly reflects the operation of judicial review in practice. To what extent each apex court substantively and effectively supervises legislative and executive actions ultimately depends on the actual exercise of judicial review power on the ground. Straightforward indicators of the practice of judicial review include the number of cases the courts have decided and how often they exercise their judicial review power. This section compares the statistics on the four apex courts' judicial review decisions. Table 2.1 contains the numbers of judicial review cases decided by the four apex courts between 1999 and 2019.

Before detailing the statistics contained in Table 2.1, clarifications of the case selection are necessary. This book focuses on substantive decisions. Decisions dealing with purely procedural issues, such as a decision to grant/dismiss leave to appeal and a decision to stay proceeding, are excluded. As for

197 *Ibid.*, art 44(2).

198 Law on the Right of Assembly and Demonstration (第2/93/M號法律——集會權和示威權), art 12(1).

199 Law on the Chief Executive Election (行政長官選舉法), arts 96–101; Law on the Legislative Assembly Election of the Macau SAR (澳門特別行政區立法會選舉法), arts 22, 28A, 36, 47B and 136–138.

the SPC decisions, this book includes decisions published in the Gazette of the Supreme People's Court (SPC Gazette)[200] and the Guiding Cases System.[201] The SPC has delivered enormous administrative litigation judgments per year.[202] It is nearly impossible to study all of them and unnecessary to do so. The Gazette cases and Guiding cases are published by the SPC as sample cases. They have higher authority than ordinary judicial decisions.[203] The Gazette cases are meant to provide an adjudication paradigm for all Chinese courts.[204] As for Guiding cases, the SPC expressly requires courts at all levels to refer to and imitate them when adjudicating cases.[205] Lower courts in practice tend to follow the Gazette cases and Guiding cases to avoid their decisions being overturned on appeals.[206]

From Table 2.1, the number of judicial review cases in China against primary legislation is zero, as the courts are not entitled to constitutional review of any legislation. There are 92 Gazette cases and Guiding cases where the courts reviewed concrete executive action. Among these 92 cases, the citizens challenged and the court reviewed administrative rules in 10 cases. In Taiwan, the TCC reviewed the constitutionality of statutes in 161 interpretations and scrutinized administrative rules in 138 interpretations in the last 20 years.

Hong Kong Court Final Appeal Reports (HKCFAR) is the law reports endorsed by the CFA. According to the HKCFAR, the CFA delivered 730 judicial decisions from 1997 to the end of 2019, of which 33 decisions relate to the constitutionality of ordinances, eight decisions relate to the review of administrative rules, and 37 decisions relate to the review of administrative actions.[207] In Macau, the TUI delivered 1068 judgments which are publicly

200 The Gazette is the official journal of the SPC, a compilation of judicial interpretation, judicial statistics, and representative cases and judgments. The first issue of the Gazette was published in 1985. The cases and judgments included in the Gazette are not legally binding. However, they provide an adjudication paradigm for courts at all levels.

201 The SPC established the Guiding cases scheme by promulgating the Provisions of the Supreme People's Court Concerning Work on Case Guidance (最高人民法院关于指导案例工作的规定) in 2010.

202 Searching the SPC administrative litigation decisions on the PKULAW.COM (北大法宝) website on 20 February 2022, it was found that the SPC has made 57,987 administrative litigation decisions since the ALL came into force on 1 October 1990.

203 Ahl (n 31) 267.

204 Hao Dong (董浩), *Judicial Interpretation* (司法解释论) (Chinese University of Political Science and Law Press 1999) 356–364.

205 The Provisions of the Supreme People's Court Concerning Work on Case Guidance (n 201), art 7.

206 Yougen Li (李友根), 'Why Leading Cases Are Not Binding' (指导案例为何没有约束力) (2010) 4 *Law and Social Development* (法制与社会发展) 86. The author used leading cases to refer to the Gazette cases.

207 According to the case classification on the HKCFAR, there were 50 human rights cases, 30 constitutional law cases, 29 administrative law cases, 25 immigration cases, and 8 election cases from 1999 to 2019. This book recategorizes these cases according to the three kinds of government actions.

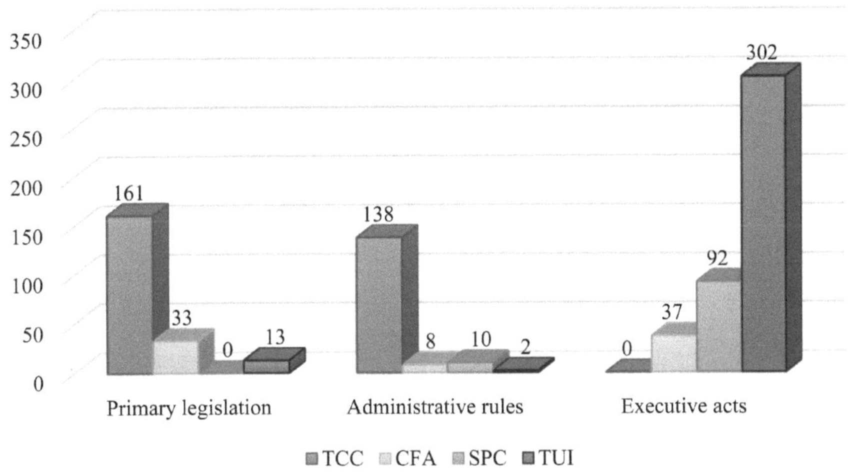

Figure 2.2 Judicial Review Decisions of the Four Apex Courts in Greater China (1999–2019).

Source: Author.

accessible on its database until the end of 2019.[208] The TUI reviewed laws and decrees in 13 decisions and scrutinized administrative rules and rules in 2 decisions. The vast majority of the TUI's judicial review decisions are reviewing concrete administrative actions (302 decisions).[209]

There are some interesting findings from Figure 2.2:

- The TCC and the CFA are much more active than the SPC and the TUI in reviewing primary legislation.
- When combining administrative rules, the TCC and the CFA are still more active than the SPC and the TUI in terms of judicial review of legal provisions. The SPC and the TUI are inactive in this regard.
- The SPC and the TUI are active in reviewing concrete executive actions.

Judicial review of primary legislation and administrative rules is often considered a symbolic aspect of judicial activeness and assertiveness. Primary

208 According to the statistics published by the TUI, it made more than 1068 decisions from 1999 to 2019, available at www.court.gov.mo/zh/subpage/statisticstui, accessed 17 April 2020. However, only 1068 are open to the public, available at www.court.gov.mo/zh/subpage/welcome.

209 The TUI decided 422 administrative litigation cases between 1999 and 2019. There are 45 decisions written in Portuguese without Chinese translation. There are around 90 cases that were dealing with procedural issues, for example suspending the enforcement of the executive actions. The TUI usually did not substantively review executive actions in those cases. Therefore, those decisions are excluded from this book.

legislation is the most important source of law, lying at the top of the hierarchy of domestic legal systems beneath the constitution.[210] Judicial review of primary legislation can profoundly influence the state's policy, people's rights and freedoms, as well as the landscape of a domestic legal system.[211] Administrative rules are an essential source of law in domestic legal systems. Some also have democratic foundations because they are promulgated with the delegation from legislatures or reviewed by legislatures.[212] The TCC's and the CFA's judicial review practice reveals their willingness and activeness to supervise and control legislative action of the legislative and executive branches. On the contrary, the SPC and the TUI are either unable to or unwilling to do so; instead, they tend to supervise the implementation of laws by reviewing concrete administrative decisions.

Conclusion

This chapter has compared the four judicial review schemes in Greater China and the actual exercise of judicial review power of the four apex courts in the last two decades. It finds that the CFA's and the TUI's jurisdictions of judicial review are broad, covering primary legislation, administrative rules, and concrete executive actions. The TCC's jurisdiction of judicial review covers primary legislation and administrative rules. The power of reviewing concrete administrative decisions is primarily vested in the administrative courts.[213] The SPC's jurisdiction of judicial review is the narrowest. It has no authority to interpret the Constitution of the PRC and lacks power to review the constitutionality of any legislative and executive action. It can only review the legality of administrative rules low rank. The central judicial review purview of the SPC is to review concrete administrative decisions.

The comparison of the statistics on the four apex courts' judicial review cases decided during the last two decades reveals that the TCC and the CFA are more active in the judicial review of primary legislation and administrative rules. On the contrary, the TUI and the SPC are more focused on reviewing concrete executive actions. Reviewing primary legislation and administrative

210 Roscoe Pound, 'Common Law and Legislation' (1908) 21 *Harvard Law Review* 383, 383–384.

211 *Ibid.* Roscoe Pound commented that the legislation is the outcome of "long and patient study by experts, careful consideration by conferences or congresses or associations, press discussion in which public opinion is focused upon all important details, and hearings before legislative committees".

212 Kevin M. Stack, 'Rulemaking Regimes in the Modern State' in Peter Cane and others (eds), *The Oxford Handbook of Comparative Administrative Law* (OUP 2021) 555.

213 It is necessary to point out that, in Taiwan, concrete administrative decisions are subject to judicial review by administrative courts. Therefore, judicial review in Taiwan covers three types of government action. However, this book focuses on the TCC's and the other three apex courts' judicial review activities. Judicial review carried out by Taiwan's administrative courts are not examined by this book.

rules symbolizes more intrusive judicial activities, but the SPC and the TUI lack power or confidence in doing so. It is a general presumption that the TCC's and the CFA's scrutiny over legislative action has a wider influence than the SPC's and the TUI's review of administrative decisions. The following three chapters will look closely into these cases, with the purpose of drawing a spectrum of judicial activism/deference, encapsulating the stance assumed by the four apex courts.

3 Judicial Review of Primary Legislation

Introduction

The preceding chapter provided an overview of the judicial review competence of the four apex courts across Greater China, along with an overall snapshot of their judicial review activities from 1999 to 2019. The forthcoming chapters, spanning Chapter 3 to Chapter 5, will delve into judicial review decisions delivered by the four apex courts. These illustrative case studies explore and compare each court's approaches to law interpretation, standards of judicial review they applied, and intensity of judicial review. By doing so it aims to map a spectrum of judicial activism and deference, which encapsulates the stance assumed by each court.

Judicial review of primary legislation often serves as a symbol of the judiciary's activeness and assertiveness, given that primary legislation is the most important source of law, occupying a higher echelon of a domestic legal system, usually positioned immediately beneath the constitution.[1] Judicial review of primary legislation holds the potential to exert a profound impact on individual rights and freedoms and the landscape of a domestic legal system. This chapter presents judicial scrutiny of primary legislation by the TCC, the CFA, and the TUI. The SPC is excluded because constitutional review of statutes is beyond its competence.

Whereas the TCC and the CFA were intrusive in probing primary legislation, the TUI displayed a marked reluctance and circumspection in this arena. Noteworthy is the divergence between the CFA of Hong Kong and the TUI of Macau, two apex courts in hybrid regimes. The CFA is as assertive as its counterpart in democratic Taiwan, while the TUI is much more deferential. The TCC and the CFA have exhibited an inclination towards applying intrusive standards of review, including proportionality and the principle of

1 Roscoe Pound commented that legislation is the outcome of "long and patient study by experts, careful consideration by conferences or congresses or associations, press discussion in which public opinion is focused upon all important details, and hearings before legislative committees". Roscoe Pound, 'Common Law and Legislation' (1908) 21 *Harvard Law Review* 383, 383–384.

DOI: 10.4324/9781003482536-3

equality, which emerged as prominent facets in approximately 80 percent of the TCC's interpretations and over 50 percent of the CFA's decisions against primary legislation between 1999 and 2019. The TCC and the CFA were confident and fearless in striking down legislation by the two standards of review. Both courts declared the impugned legislation unconstitutional in over half of the decisions. In contrast, the TUI's approach to reviewing primary legislation appears markedly reticent. Over the last two decades, the TUI has only reviewed primary legislation, including laws and decrees, in 13 cases. Moreover, the TUI expressly declined to use proportionality to scrutinize Macau's primary legislation, including laws and decrees. When applying the principle of equality, the TUI merely conducted a formal equality review and did not conduct a substantive review.

The application of proportionality and equality by the TCC and the CFA is coupled with varying degrees of review intensity. Owing to the influence of German and American constitutional laws and jurisprudence, the German intensity of review and the American multi-tiered scrutiny have shaped the TCC's jurisprudence. The Grand Justices have tried to reconcile the two systems of intensity of judicial review and reached a tentative consensus: "one proportionality, three levels of intensity of review". Over the past two decades, the TCC has adopted a low level of intensity of review in many cases. But, after 2007, there was an increase in the reliance on intermediate and high levels of intensity of review. This overall trend indicates that the TCC becomes more confident and less deferential in constitutionally reviewing statutes. Likewise, the CFA developed a spectrum of intensity for proportionality, including the reasonable necessity test (a stricter test) and the "manifestly without reasonable foundation" test (a more lenient test). The CFA did not hesitate to use the reasonable necessity test to review ordinances, particularly where fundamental rights are involved. In stark contrast, the TUI was deferential in reviewing primary legislation. It stressed that the courts should play a passive role instead of an active role in judicial review. The courts could only invalidate legislation that results in manifest and intolerable inequality without justification, objectivity, or rationality. It did not strike down legislative provisions even when they were unconstitutional but just declared them meaningless.

The remainder of this chapter encompasses five parts. Part 2 to Part 4 examine the constitutional review of primary legislation in Taiwan, Hong Kong, and Macau, respectively. Part 5 concludes this chapter by comparing the convergence and divergence of constitutional review in these three areas.

Taiwan

An Overview

From 1999 to 2019, the TCC reviewed primary legislation, commonly referred to as statutes in Taiwan in 161 interpretations, many of which pertained to

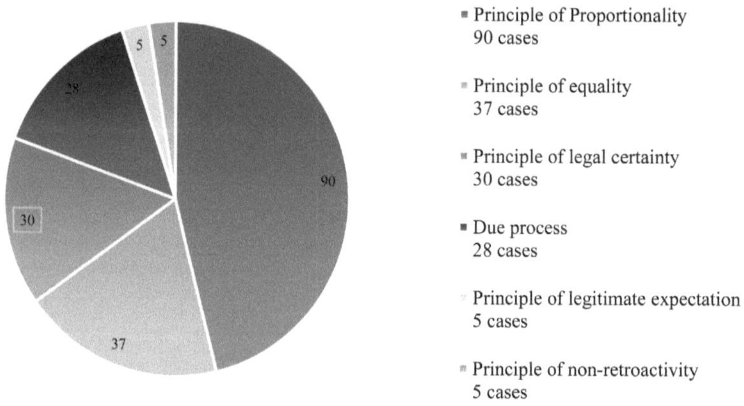

Figure 3.1 Standards of Review in J.Y. Interpretations against Statutes (1999–2019).
Source: Author.

fundamental rights and freedoms.[2] Figure 3.1 presents statistics on the standards of review applied in the interpretations against statutes.[3] These standards of review outline the court's analytical framework.[4]

It is evident that proportionality is the linchpin standard for reviewing statutes by the TCC.[5] This standard emerged in 90 cases, representing an estimated 55.9 percent of the total, which significantly outnumbers other standards of review. The principle of equality garners recurrent utilization, making an appearance in 37 cases, constituting roughly 23 percent. The principles of legal certainty and due process contribute to 30 cases (approximately 18.6 percent) and 28 cases (approximately 17.4 percent), respectively. In conjunction with these four cardinal standards, other standards also emerged occasionally in the TCC's review of statutes, such as the principle of legitimate

2 Jiunn-Rong Yeh and Wen-Chen Chang, 'An Evolving Court with Changing Functions: The Constitutional Court and Judicial Review in Taiwan' in Albert H.Y. Chen and Andrew Harding (eds), *Constitutional Courts in Asia: A Comparative Perspective* (CUP 2018) 112.

3 The numbers of cases in Figure 3.1 add up to more than 161 because more than one standard of review is applied in some cases.

4 Alec Stone Sweet and Jud Mathews, 'Proportionality Balancing and Global Constitutionalism' (2008) 47 *Columbia Journal Transnational Law* 72, 88–89.

5 Jau-Yuan Hwang (黃昭元), 'Development of Standards of Review by the Constitutional Court (1996–2011): Reception and Localization of the Proportionality Principle' (大法官解釋審查標準之發展 (1996–2011)：比例原則的繼受與在地化) (2013) 42 National Taiwan University Law Journal (台大法律論叢) 215, 234–241; Shu-Perng Hwang (黃舒芃), 'The Principle of Proportionality in the Trend of "Hierarchicalization": Critical Remarks on the Current Developments in Constitutional Review' (比例原則及其階層化操作：一個著眼於司法院釋憲實務發展趨勢的反思) (2016) 19 *Academia Sinica Law Journal* (中研院法學期刊) 1, 11–12.

expectation,[6] the principle of non-retroactivity,[7] protection against double jeopardy,[8] and the principle of the best interests of the child.[9]

Proportionality in the TCC's Review of Statutes

Adoption of Proportionality in Taiwan

The developmental trajectory of proportionality in Taiwan is akin to that in Germany. In Germany, this standard originated from nineteenth-century Prussian administrative law.[10] After WWII, the German Basic Law of 1949 embraced a catalog of human rights, and the German Federal Constitutional Court (GFCC) inherited proportionality and proclaimed it a constitutional principle for human-rights safeguarding.[11] In Taiwan, proportionality was first invoked in administrative litigation decisions in the 1980s and was then adopted by the TCC in the 1990s.[12] In 1994, the Taiwan Administrative Court declared that proportionality was a general principle with constitutional status.[13] Two years later, the TCC used the term "principle of proportionality" for the first time in its *holding* of Interpretation No. 409 (1996), stating that expropriation of privately owned land must be restricted by the principle of proportionality and any encroachment on property rights must be as minimal as possible.[14] Proportionality emerged in the TCC's *reasoning* for the first time in Interpretation No. 414 (1996), and thus, some scholars regarded this case as the first case where the TCC invoked proportionality.[15]

Interpretation No. 476 (1999) was a milestone decision where the TCC elaborated on the subtests of proportionality for the first time.[16] In this case, the TCC was confronted with a thorny issue of whether the life sentence and death penalty in the Narcotics Elimination Act and Drug Control Act were

6 J.Y. Interpretations Nos. 589, 751, 781, 782, 783.
7 J.Y. Interpretations Nos. 714, 751, 781, 782, 783.
8 J.Y. Interpretations Nos. 604, 775.
9 J.Y. Interpretations Nos. 587, 664.
10 Alec Stone Sweet and Jud Mathews, *Proportionality Balance and Constitutional Governance: A Comparative and Global Approach* (OUP 2019) 61.
11 *Ibid.*, 65.
12 Cheng-Yi Huang and David S. Law, 'Proportionality Review of Administrative Action in Japan, Korea, Taiwan, and China' in Francesca Bignami and David Zaring (eds), *Research Handbook in Comparative Law and Regulation* (Edward Elgar 2014) 317.
13 Judgment No. 2291 of 1994, available at https://legal.judicial.gov.tw/FINT/Default_AD.aspx, accessed 11 October 2024.
14 J.Y. Interpretation No. 409.
15 Chien-Chih Lin, 'Proportionality in Taiwan: American-German Fusion' in Po Jen Yap (ed), *Proportionality in Asia* (CUP 2020) 63; Hwang, 'Development of Standards of Review by the Constitutional Court from 1996 to 2011' (n 5) 218.
16 Between J.Y. Interpretation No. 414 and J.Y. Interpretation No. 476, there are several decisions where the principle of proportionality was invoked, such as J.Y. Interpretations Nos. 414, 428, 436, 445, 452, and 471.

constitutional. The TCC stated that a legislative measure was proportionate if they (a) pursue due purposes, (b) take necessary means, and (c) exert proper restrictions.[17] It is worth pondering this decision. First, in comparison with the standard model of proportionality that comprises four distinctive subtests,[18] the TCC did not include the suitability test in its formula of proportionality. It is unclear why the Grand Justices ignored the suitability test, especially because some of the Grand Justices on that bench have German doctoral degrees.[19] Second, the TCC used the term "proper restrictions". But it is the balance test in nature.[20]

The TCC eventually followed the standard model, adding the suitability test back to proportionality and using proportionality *stricto sensu* in place of "proper restrictions" in Interpretation No. 542 (2000). This case was about the relocation of some residents living near a reservoir catchment area. The TCC reiterated twice that the measures taken by the government must be capable of promoting legitimate purposes.[21]

Application of Proportionality in the TCC's Review of Statutes

Due to a large number of cases using proportionality, it is helpful to present an overview of the application of this standard before giving a detailed description. Table 3.1 includes interpretations against statutes where the TCC applied proportionality. According to the statistics in the row "Unconstitutional", the TCC ruled against the statutes in half of the cases where proportionality was applied.

Before 2003, the TCC's reasoning and conclusions were rendered in a simplistic manner,[22] and it did not always elucidate the subtest(s) of proportionality. After 2003, there was a shift in the TCC's reasoning, with a tendency to provide more informative justifications for its decisions and elucidate the subtest(s) of proportionality, particularly when striking down statutes. This

17 J.Y. Interpretation No. 476, [1].

18 Po Jen Yap (ed), *Proportionality in Asia* (CUP 2020) 9–13; Alec Stone Sweet, 'The Necessity of Balancing: Hong Kong's Flawed Approach to Proportionality, and Why It Matters' (2020) *Hong Kong Law Journal* 541. There are scholars, such as Robert Alexy, claiming that proportionality is composed of three subtests, instead of four subtests. Robert Alexy considers the legitimate aim test superfluous and threatening to the rationality of proportionality. Robert Alexy, 'Proportionality and Rationality' in Vicki C. Jackson and Mark Tushnet (eds), *Proportionality: New Frontiers, New Challenges* (CUP 2017) 18–20.

19 Lin, 'Proportionality in Taiwan' (n 15) 64; Hwang, 'Development of Standards of Review by the Constitutional Court from 1996 to 2011' (n 5) 220.

20 Alec Stone Sweet and Jud Mathews, 'Proportionality and Rights Protection in Asia: Hong Kong, Malaysia, South Korea, Taiwan – Whither Singapore?' (2017) 29 *Singapore Academy of Law Journal* 774, 786; Huang and Law (n 12) 320.

21 J.Y. Interpretation No. 542, [2]–[3].

22 Shu-Perng Hwang (n 5) 14; Hwang, 'Development of Standards of Review by the Constitutional Court from 1996 to 2011' (n 5) 226.

Table 3.1 The Application of Proportionality in J.Y. Interpretations against Statutes (1999–2019).

	J.Y. Interpretations	*Total Interpretations*[a]
Constitutional	476, 490, 509, 512, 515, 517, 528, 531, 544, 554, 564, 575, 577, 578, 580, 584, 585, 588, 596, 604, 617, 618, 623, 630, 633, 634, 636, 637, 642, 646, 656, 659, 664, 665, 672, 673, 675, 678, 688, 689, 690, 697, 699, 702, 709, 714, 716, 719, 739, 746, 751, 764, 767, 768, 775, 777, 778, 780, 781, 782, 783	61 (67.8%)
Unconstitutional	487, 507, 523, 535, 551, 558, 573, 580, 583, 585, 588, 603, 616, 633, 636, 641, 644, 649, 654, 664, 669, 670, 673, 677, 685, 702, 709, 710, 711, 712, 716, 718, 732, 733, 744, 746, 749, 756, 766, 775, 777, 781, 782, 783, 786	45 (50.0%)

Source: Author.

[a] The figures in the column "Total Interpretations" add up to 105 instead of 90 because, in the underlined cases, the TCC upheld the constitutionality of some impugned provisions and struck down other impugned provisions.

book includes interpretations of the TCC made after 1999, thus allowing for the identification of the subtests in many cases.

The TCC did not always apply all four subtests in each interpretation. When an impugned statute fails one subtest, it is enough for the TCC to strike it down. Although the TCC applied the legitimate aim test most frequently, the TCC seldom questioned the aim and goal of a statute. The suitability test and the balance test have not played a significant role in the TCC's review of statutes either. The necessity test is the most powerful subtest. Around half of the unconstitutional statutes failed the proportionality test at this stage. The following parts will closely examine the implementation of the subtests of proportionality.

THE LEGITIMATE AIM TEST

Overall, the legitimate aim test does not have much "bite" in the TCC's review of statutes, which is consistent with the conventional practice that courts usually do not question the legitimacy and appropriateness of the goals that the government sets up.[23] Nonetheless, it is misguided to say the legitimate aim

23 Lin, 'Proportionality in Taiwan' (n 15) 68.

test is just window-dressing in the TCC's decisions. First, the TCC required the legislature to explicitly specify the purpose of any restrictive measures.[24] Additionally, impugned statutes and restrictive measures must pursue legitimate aims.[25] Otherwise, the legitimate aim test fails.

One illustrative decision is Interpretation No. 766 (2018), which pertains to social welfare legislation. According to Article 18-1(2) of the National Pension Act, if the insured persons did not apply for their pension when eligibility criteria were met, their family members could apply for the pension after the insured individual's death, and the pension payment started from the month when eligibility criteria were met (Situation A). By contrast, for insured persons who passed away before 29 February 2016, their surviving family members could only receive the pension from the month when they submitted the pension applications (Situation B). In Situation B, family members lost their pension incurred between the fulfillment of the eligibility criteria and the submission of the pension application. The legislative rationale behind this discrepancy was attributed to the challenges associated with verifying cases preceding 29 February 2016.

The TCC stated that when reviewing social welfare policies, the courts usually respect the legislative discretion and give broad deference to the Legislative Yuan due to the limited fiscal resources, demographical structure, and population changes.[26] Nonetheless, it still stressed that the courts should examine restrictions on the right to pension with a relatively high level of intensity because this right significantly impacted people's livelihood.[27] It required that limitations on the right to pension must pursue an important public interest and must be substantially connected to the public interest pursued.[28] A legislative document indicates that Article 18-1(2) aimed to save administrative expenditure and for administrative convenience. Those ends, in the TCC's opinion, were not important enough to justify the reduction of pension.[29]

THE SUITABILITY TEST

This subtest often emerged in cases against statutes, but the TCC rarely found statutes unsuitable or incapable of achieving the aims.[30] The first example is Interpretation No. 766. Besides failing the legitimate aim test, the impugned measure did not pass the suitability test. It was claimed that the different pension arrangements aimed to save fiscal resources. The TCC, however, considered that these arrangements did not promote this end because the number of pension applications in Situation B was small and did not help much with

24 J.Y. Interpretation 603, [12].
25 E.g. J.Y. Interpretations Nos. 580, 603, 744, 748, 760, 766.
26 J.Y. Interpretation No. 766, [2].
27 *Ibid.*, [3].
28 *Ibid.*
29 *Ibid.*, [5].
30 E.g. J.Y. Interpretations Nos. 551, 603, 710, 766.

saving fiscal resources.[31] Another example is Interpretation No. 551 (2002). The TCC applied the suitability test and invalidated Article 16 of the Drug Control Act. This provision stipulated that any person who brings false accusations or fabricates evidence to bring fictitious actions should be sentenced to the criminal punishment imposed for the offense which they accused others of.[32] The TCC held that this measure was not relevant to the objectives of the Drug Control Act, which are combating narcotics and mitigating the adverse impacts of drugs.[33]

THE NECESSITY TEST

The TCC applied the necessity test in over 60 cases and declared impugned statutes unconstitutional on this ground in over 20 cases.[34] The necessity test is undoubtedly the most potent subtest in the TCC's constitutional review.

In Interpretation No. 718 (2014), the TCC reviewed Article 8(1) of the Assembly and Demonstration Act, which mandated that all assemblies and demonstrations must obtain prior permission from authorities.[35] Impromptu gatherings and those out of urgency were not exempted. The TCC emphasized that Article 14 of the Constitution of Taiwan protected people's right to assembly and demonstration and guaranteed that people express their opinions peacefully.[36] Any restrictions on this right must comply with the principle of proportionality.[37] The prior permission enabled the authority to gather the information necessary for law enforcement and to act properly. The TCC thought that if permission was required, it would be unlikely to hold those assemblies and demonstrations that arise from urgent circumstances, where the effectiveness of the protest relies on immediate action. Furthermore, since impromptu assemblies typically lack a designated organizer or responsible person to apply for permission, the TCC argued that the prior permission requirement essentially made urgent and spontaneous assemblies impossible, thereby infringing on the constitutional right to assemble and demonstrate.

THE BALANCE TEST

The TCC less frequently applied the balance test, which is reminiscent of the Canadian and Hong Kong approaches as opposed to the German approach.[38]

31 J.Y. Interpretation No. 766, [5].
32 J.Y. Interpretation No. 551.
33 *Ibid.*, [1].
34 E.g. J.Y. Interpretations Nos. 523, 573, 588, 603, 616, 636, 644, 654, 664, 670, 673, 677, 685, 702, 711, 716, 718, 732, 733, 744, 749, 756, 777.
35 J.Y. Interpretation No. 718, [2].
36 *Ibid.*, [1].
37 *Ibid.*
38 Huang and Law (n 12) 321; Dieter Grimm, 'Canadian and German Constitutional Jurisprudence' (2007) 57 *University of Toronto Law Journal* 383, 398; Johannes Chan, 'Proportion-

The TCC only struck down statutes based on imbalance in a limited number of cases.[39]

One notable example exception is Interpretation No. 712 (2013), where the TCC overturned Article 65 of the Act Governing the Relations Between People of Taiwan and Mainland China using the balance test. This provision prohibited Taiwanese people from adopting children from Mainland China if they already had children, including cases where Taiwanese individuals sought to adopt their spouses' children from Mainland China. The TCC recognized the Legislative Yuan's contention that lifting the prohibition could lead to an influx of children from Mainland China immigrating to Taiwan, potentially threatening Taiwan's societal stability and safety.[40] The TCC agreed that the prohibition could be seen as a suitable measure to protect the interests and well-being of the public of Taiwan. But the TCC still ruled against this prohibitive measure on the grounds that the harm caused by this measure to people's right to marriage and family exceeded the benefits it was intended to secure.[41] It also ignored the right to enjoy family union and happiness, as well as the physical and mental well-being of the adopted children.

Principle of Equality in the TCC's Review of Statutes

The principle of equality, which emerged in 37 cases, is the second most frequently applied standard of review. The TCC held that there was no violation of the principle of equality in 20 cases.[42] It overturned statutes based on this principle in 17 cases.[43]

The principle of equality is enshrined in the Constitution of Taiwan.[44] It can be perceived as a fundamental right or a basic principle of constitutional law. The TCC uses it in both senses.[45] In the TCC's opinion, the principle of equality has two meanings: formal equality and substantive equality. Formal

ality after Hysan: Fair Balance, Manifestly without Reasonable Foundation and Wednesbury Unreasonableness' (2019) 49 *Hong Kong Law Journal* 265, 268.

39 E.g. J.Y. Interpretations Nos. 487, 551, 603, 641, 649, 712.

40 J.Y. Interpretation No. 712, [4].

41 *Ibid.*, [5].

42 J.Y. Interpretations Nos. 485, 490, 560, 575, 578, 596, 618, 639, 647, 667, 675, 688, 697, 698, 719, 727, 728, 739, 764, 768.

43 J.Y. Interpretations Nos. 477, 573, 610, 624, 649, 666, 687, 694, 696, 701, 745, 748, 760, 779, 781, 782, 783.

44 Constitution of Taiwan (中華民國憲法), arts 5, 7; Amendment to the Constitutional of Taiwan, art 10 (1997).

45 Jau-Yuan Hwang (黃昭元), 'Evolution of Equality Theory and Difficulties Concerning the Constitutional Application of the Conception of Substantive Equality' (從平等理論的演進檢討實質平等觀在憲法適用上的難題) in Chien-Liang Lee (李建良) (ed), *Theory and Practice of Constitutional Interpretation* (憲法解釋之理論與實務) (San Min Book 2017) 271–272.

equality is a requirement that "like cases should be treated alike, unlike cases should not be treated alike".[46] Although the TCC does not define "substantive equality",[47] it reiterates in many interpretations that:

> The principle of equality prescribed by Article 7 of the Constitution does not mean absolute and mechanical formal equality, but rather the protection of people's substantive equality in legal status. The legislature, based on the value system of the Constitution and legislative intention, should consider the differences between the subject matters and make reasonable differences in treatment.[48]

Substantive equality encapsulates positive and beneficial measures responsive to those who are disadvantaged, in need, and ignored. When the TCC assesses whether a statute violates substantive equality, it takes an approach comprising two tests: (1) whether differences in treatment pursue a legitimate aim, and (2) whether there is a certain level of nexus between the differences in treatment and the aim pursued.[49] These two tests are nearly identical to the subtests of proportionality.[50] However, there is still a debate among the Grand Justices about whether proportionality should be applied to discrimination cases.[51]

The most striking example case of equal protection in recent years is Interpretation No. 748 (2017), which led to Taiwan being the first area in Asia that legalizes same-sex marriage. In that case, the TCC applied the two tests of substantive equality. The TCC considered that the freedom of marriage was a fundamental right vital to personality development and human dignity.[52] The Marriage Chapter of Taiwan's Civil Code prohibited two persons of the same sex from marrying. This unfavorable treatment against homosexuals in their freedom of marriage was made on the basis of sexual orientation. The TCC held that it should adopt a relatively intense standard of review to determine the constitutionality of this differential treatment based on sexual orientation.

46 *Ibid.*, 287.

47 *Ibid.*, 273.

48 J.Y. Interpretations Nos. 485, 526, 547, 565, 584, 596, 605, 614, 647, 648, 666, 675, 694, 696, 711, 727.

49 *Ibid.*

50 Jau-Yuan Hwang (黃昭元), 'Choosing the Standard of Scrutiny for the Equality Right Cases: Questioning the Applicability of the Proportionality Principle' (平等權審查標準的選擇問題：兼論比例原則在平等權審查上的適用可能) (2008) 12 *National Taiwan University Law Journal* (台大法律論) 253, 257.

51 Grand Justices Jen-Shou Yang and Tzu-Yi Lin hold an opinion that proportionality should be applied to equal protection cases. Grand Justice Tzong-Li Hsu thinks that proportionality could be applied to equal protection cases, but it has to be adjusted. Grand Justice Jau-Yuan Hwang holds a different opinion that proportionality is a not a suitable standard for equal protection cases. *Ibid.*, 260–266; Shu-Perng Hwang (n 5) 12.

52 J.Y. Interpretation No. 748, [13].

The differential treatment can only be justified when it pursues an important public interest and is substantially related to the aim.[53]

The TCC acknowledged that the legislature had taken manifold considerations into account when it constructed the institution of marriage. The main purpose of banning same-sex marriage was to maintain reproduction and safeguard fundamental ethical orders.[54] But the TCC held that these purposes were not important enough to justify the different treatment against homosexuals:

> The Marriage Chapter (of the Civil Code) does not set forth the capability of reproduction as a requirement for concluding an opposite-sex marriage. Nor does it regard being unable or unwilling to procreate as reasons for declaring a marriage void or voidable and for decreeing a divorce. Therefore, reproduction is not an essential element of marriage. The fact that two persons of the same sex are incapable of natural reproduction is the same as the result of two opposite-sex persons' inability or unwillingness to procreate. Prohibiting two persons of the same sex from marrying, for the consideration that they are unable to reproduce, obviously has no rational basis. Marriage is expected to safeguard the fundamental ethical orders. Minimum age of marriage, monogamy, prohibition of marriage between close relatives, the obligation of fidelity, and supporting each other are fairly legitimate aims. These ethical orders built upon opposite-sex marriage will remain unaffected if allowing two persons of the same sex to enter a legally recognized marriage, given that same-sex marriage is subject to the formal and substantive requirements of the Marriage Chapter, and both parties are subject to the rights and obligations during the marriage and after the marriage. Apparently, disallowing the marriage of two persons of the same sex for the sake of safeguarding basic ethical orders is irrational.[55]

Other Standards of Review in the TCC's Review of Statutes

Besides the principle of proportionality and the principle of equality, legal certainty, and due process also frequently emerged in the interpretations against statutes. This part will look at the application of these standards of review.

Principle of Legal Certainty

Legal certainty is an intrinsic element of the rule of law and the requirement of "prescribed by law" enshrined in Article 23 of the Constitution of Taiwan.

53 *Ibid.*, [15].
54 *Ibid.*
55 *Ibid.*, [16].

This principle requires laws to be clearly defined so that they are accessible and formulated with sufficient precision to enable citizens to foresee the consequences of their behavior.[56] Nonetheless, absolute certainty is unattainable. Grand Justice Chang-Fa Lo stressed that the necessary degree of certainty depends on the subject matters of the law, the content of law, and the socio-economic backgrounds.[57] Criminal punishment and encroachments on fundamental rights call for a high degree of legal certainty.[58] The laws concerning people's rights and obligations must be clearer than those regulating technical and trivial matters.[59] Due to the increasingly sophisticated socio-economic activities, social networks, and technology, laws are expected to be more definite than ever.[60]

In the TCC's opinion, clear and unambiguous legislation is understandable by citizens and courts based on their literal meaning and legislative purpose.[61] If the interpretation of legislation in accordance with its plain or ordinary meaning in its context and in light of legislative intent leads to multiple and divergent meanings, it does not comply with the principle of legal certainty.[62]

From Figure 3.1, the TCC applied the principle of legal certainty in 30 cases[63] and struck down some statutes on this ground.[64] For example, in Interpretation No. 636 (2008), the TCC reviewed Articles 2(3) and 2(5) of the Act for Eliminating Hoodlums which punished the acts of "oppressing the good", "bad behavior", and "vagrancy and villainy". The TCC considered those expressions to be overly vague and imprecise, offering little guidance to citizens. Ordinary people are not able to make informed choice about their action and cannot foresee whether their conduct amounts to the behavior punished by those provisions. The TCC held that these provisions were constitutionally invalid on account of unclear, imprecise, and ambiguous.[65]

Due Process

Due process is another standard of review that the TCC frequently employs to review statutes. The TCC applied this standard in 28 decisions.[66] In Interpretation No. 710 (2013), the TCC struck down Article 18(1) of the Act

56 J.Y. Interpretations No. 636.
57 J.Y. Interpretations No. 697 (concurring opinion of Grand Justice Chang-Fa Lo), at 2–4.
58 *Ibid.*, at 2.
59 *Ibid.*, at 3.
60 *Ibid.*, at 3.
61 J.Y. Interpretations Nos. 432, 491, 521, 594, 602, 617, 623.
62 J.Y. Interpretations No. 713 (concurring opinion of Grand Justice Chang-Fa Lo), at 5.
63 J.Y. Interpretations Nos. 491, 521, 522, 523, 524, 545, 564, 573, 585, 594, 602, 617, 623, 633, 636, 659, 664, 655, 669, 672, 689, 690, 697, 702,710, 734, 761, 767, 768, 777.
64 J.Y. Interpretations Nos. 523, 564, 573, 585, 636, 664, 710, 777.
65 J.Y. Interpretation No. 636, [5].
66 J.Y. Interpretations Nos. 491, 585, 588, 631, 633,636, 639, 653, 654, 663, 665, 667, 677, 689, 690, 708, 709, 710, 731, 736, 737, 752, 755, 761, 762, 763, 755, 785.

Governing Relations between People from Taiwan and Mainland China. This provision allowed security agencies to repatriate people from Mainland China immediately without opportunities for defense.[67] The TCC stated:

> When depriving or restricting people's liberty, irrespective of whether the person is facing criminal charges, the state must have a legal basis and follow mandatory judicial procedures and other due processes. The principle of due process under the Constitution requires legislators to promulgate adequate procedures after considering all factors, including the fundamental rights at stake, the intensity and scope of the restrictions, the public interests pursued, the proper functions of the decision-maker, and the availability of alternative procedures and possible costs of the possible procedures.[68]

The TCC also applied due process in Interpretation No. 762 (2018). According to Article 33(2) of the Criminal Procedure Code, an unrepresented defendant can request copies of records in dossiers upon paying fees. In contrast, the defendant with legal counsel cannot enjoy this right.[69] The TCC struck down the impugned provision on the grounds that Article 33(2) unconstitutionally limited the defendants' right to defend their case effectively. It held that all defendants should enjoy the right of access to dossiers, evidence, and other information.[70]

Intensity of the TCC's Review of Statutes

The TCC's jurisprudence of constitutional law is significantly influenced by both German and American constitutional jurisprudence,[71] which is attributed to the educational experience of the Grand Justices. Unlike other influential supreme courts and constitutional courts comprising experienced judges and lawyers, the TCC boasts a significant presence of legal scholars, and a large majority of Grand Justices have studied overseas, especially in Germany and the United States.[72] They have brought what they learned overseas back to Taiwan, both in classrooms and in courtrooms.[73] As a result, two systems of

67 J.Y. Interpretation No. 710, [3].
68 *Ibid.*, [1].
69 J.Y. Interpretation No. 762, [5].
70 *Ibid.*, [7].
71 Shu-Perng Hwang (n 5) 18–20.
72 Lin, 'Proportionality in Taiwan' (n 15) 66.
73 Wen-Chen Chang (張文貞), 'An Empirical Study on the Reference of Foreign Laws and Precedents by Constitutional Court Interpretations: The Study-Abroad Backgrounds as the Key (司法院大法官解釋引用外國法及判決之實證研究—大法官留學背景作為引用的關鍵因素)' in Yun-Chien Chang (張永健) (ed), *Empirical Studies of the Judicial System 2011* (2011司法制度實證研究) (The Institutum Iurisprudentiae Academia Sinica 2013) 44–49.

intensity of judicial review exist in the TCC's decisions: the German intensity of review and the American multi-tiered scrutiny. Each system has its dominant terrains. Whereas German intensity of review primarily applies to restrictions on occupational freedom, American multi-tiered scrutiny mainly emerges in disputes relating to freedom of speech and discrimination. Over time, the jurisprudential contention among the Grand Justices has fostered an integration of these two systems. Grand Justices have reached a tentative consensus: "one proportionality, three levels of intensity of review".[74]

Overall, the TCC mainly adopted a low level of intensity of review in the past two decades. However, since 2007, there has been an increase in the reliance on the intermediate and high levels of intensity of review, indicating that the TCC has become less deferential in constitutional review of statutes and more confident about exerting strict review against statutes.[75]

German-American Fused Intensity of Proportionality Test[76]

ADOPTION OF GERMAN INTENSITY OF REVIEW

The *Pharmacy case* decision is arguably one of the most significant decisions of the GFCC. In this decision, the GFCC established varying levels of intensity of constitutional review associated with proportionality after differentiating limitations on the freedom of occupation.[77] The provision under challenge was Article 3(1) of Bavaria's Apothecary Act, which required special authorization from the relevant authorities before the operation of a pharmacy. Such authorization could be granted if opening a new pharmacy was commercially viable and would not result in economic harm to nearby competitors. The issue before the GFCC was whether this provision was consistent with the freedom of occupation guaranteed by Article 12(1) of the German Basic Law. In the GFCC's opinion, the rigor of scrutiny varied, depending on the types of limitations on the freedom of occupation.

- To regulate the practice of an occupation, the legislature is freest to do so. It can impose limitations to prevent damage and danger to the public and achieve greater total performance in society. Only excessively onerous and

74 Hwang, 'Development of Standards of Review by the Constitutional Court from 1996 to 2011' (n 5) 237–241.

75 Readers may think this conclusion is simplistic because the level of intensity of review is influenced by many factors, including the nature of legislation being reviewed, and because the intensity of review is not entirely a subjective choice of judge. Indeed, the intensity of review in a particular decision is determined by many subjective and objective factors. Nonetheless, this book collected all constitutional review decisions of the TCC, which is a rather decent number of cases for studies. Moreover, these cases span twenty years. The scale of cases and their time span adequately demonstrate the judges' assertiveness or deference in judicial review.

76 I would like to thank former Grand Justice Te-Chung Tang for his sharing on this point.

77 7 Entscheidungen des Bundesverfassungsgerichts (BVerfGE) 377 (1958).

unreasonable encroachments are unconstitutional. (Low-level intensity of review)

- When the legislature imposes subjective conditions on the access to an occupation, such as possessing qualifications, obtaining education, and training, the conditions can be justified when it is absolutely necessary to protect some particularly important community interests. (Intermediate-level intensity of review)
- When the legislature sets up objective conditions on the access to an occupation, it is permissible on very narrowly defined terms. They are allowed when there is a need for preventing demonstrably and highly possible dangers to the public interests with overriding importance.[78] (High-level intensity of review)

These three levels of intensity of the proportionality test were introduced to Taiwan via Interpretation No. 584 in 2004,[79] and, since then, the TCC has consistently adopted this set of intensity of judicial review in cases relating to occupational freedom.[80] For example, it adopted the low-level intensity of review in Interpretation 711 (2013). Article 11 of the Pharmacists Act provided that a pharmacist could practice only at one medical institute. This limitation was related to the practice of an occupation, and the TCC employed the low-level intensity of review.[81] The TCC invalidated that provision on the basis that a complete prohibition on practicing pharmaceutical businesses in more than one institute without reasonable exceptions constituted an unnecessary encroachment on the freedom of occupation.[82]

Interpretation No. 702 (2012) is an example case in which the TCC carried out an intermediate level review.[83] Article 14(1)(6) of the Teachers' Act provided that teachers cannot be dismissed unless competent authorities carry out an investigation and confirm that their action is inconsistent with teachers' morals and dignity rules. The TCC reiterated: "The issue of whether a particular restriction on occupational freedom is constitutional is governed by various standards. The appropriate standard reviewing the constitutionality of a restriction depends on the content of the restriction".[84] The TCC determined

78 J.Y. Interpretation No. 711 (concurring opinion of Grand Justice Te-Chung Tang); Norman Dorsen and others, *Comparative Constitutionalism: Cases and Materials* (West 2003) 1340–1341.

79 J.Y. Interpretation No. 584, [1]–[2].

80 J.Y. Interpretation No. 778 (concurring opinion of Grand Justice Chih-Hsiung Hsu); e.g. J.Y. Interpretations Nos. 584, 634, 637, 649, 659, 688, 689, 702, 711, 714, 716, 719, 749, 768, 778, 780, 781, 782, 783.

81 J.Y. Interpretations No. 711, [5].

82 *Ibid.*, [7].

83 J.Y. Interpretation No. 702.

84 *Ibid.*, [1].

that this provision imposed subjective conditions on the freedom to choose an occupation and applied the intermediate level review.[85]

In another example, Interpretation No. 649 (2008), the TCC applied the high-level intensity of review. In this case, Article 37(1) of the Physically and Mentally Disabled Persons Protection Act excluded non-blind persons from providing massage therapy. The petitioner argued that this provision deprived people without vision impairment of the right to become a massage therapist. The TCC considered that the limitation imposed by Article 37(1) was physically objective and beyond control.[86] The TCC acknowledged that the impugned provision pursued a compelling public interest.[87] But it still ruled against this provision on the grounds that the adverse consequence caused to the non-vision-impaired person exceeded the benefits gained for the vision-impaired person. Consequently, it overturned the impugned provision.

In addition to occupational freedom, the German graduated scale of proportionality test has been occasionally applied to other rights, including personal liberty,[88] privacy,[89] and freedom of movement.[90]

TRANSPLANTATION OF AMERICAN MULTI-TIERED SCRUTINY TO TAIWAN

As its name indicates, multi-tiered scrutiny includes multiple standards of review with different levels of intensity of review. The first standard is rational basis review which requires legislative and executive measures to be rationally related to a legitimate governmental interest.[91] The second standard is intermediate scrutiny, which demands legislative and executive measures to be "substantially related" to "important governmental objectives".[92] The last standard is strict scrutiny. This standard requires legislative and executive measures to be "narrowly tailored" to further "compelling" public interest.[93]

The TCC first applied tiered scrutiny along with the two-track theory in association with freedom of speech in Interpretation No. 414 (1996).[94] The two-track theory classifies restrictions on freedom of speech into two categories – content-based restrictions and content-neutral restrictions. The courts usually scrutinize content-based restrictions more intensively than content-neutral restrictions. Regarding the content-based restrictions, the courts make

85 *Ibid.*, [3].
86 J.Y. Interpretation No. 649, [5].
87 *Ibid.*, [5].
88 E.g. J.Y. Interpretations Nos. 588, 664, 669, 690.
89 E.g. J.Y. Interpretation No. 603.
90 E.g. J.Y. Interpretation No. 689.
91 Thomas B Nachbar, 'The Rationality of Rational Basis Review' (2016) 102 *Virginia Law Review* 1627, 1629.
92 Craig v Boren, 429 U.S. 190, 197 (1976).
93 Miller v Johnson, 515 U.S. 900,920 (1995); Johnson v California, 543 U.S. 499, 505 (2005).
94 Hwang, 'Development of Standards of Review by the Constitutional Court from 1996 to 2011' (n 5) 229.

further distinctions. According to Justice Frank Murphy's dictum in *Chaplinsky v New Hampshire*, speech could be distinguished into high-value speech, such as political speech and religious speech, and low-value speech, including commercial speech.[95] The courts scrutinize restrictions on high-value speech more intensively than low-value speech. Correspondingly, the courts apply the strict scrutiny standard to assess restrictions on high-value speech and apply the standards of intermediate scrutiny and rational basis review to restrictions on low-value speech.[96]

In Interpretation No. 414, the issue at stake was whether the prior censorship of pharmaceutical advertisements unconstitutionally restricted the freedom of speech. The TCC determined to apply intermediate scrutiny.[97] It considered that commercials normally did not enjoy a high degree of protection as other types of speech because they are irrelevant to the formation of public opinion, fact-finding, and expression of beliefs. Moreover, drug advertisements were closely related to the health of nationals. Consequently, they must be strictly regulated by law in order to protect public interest.[98]

Since Interpretation No. 414, the TCC has consistently applied multi-tiered scrutiny in freedom of speech cases.[99] For example, it applied the intermediate scrutiny standard to statutes relating to cigarette package regulation (Interpretation No. 577) and used the strict scrutiny standard to review the restrictions on political speech and association advocating communism and secession from the State (Interpretation No. 644).[100]

In addition to freedom of speech, multi-tiered scrutiny has also been applied to address discrimination cases and has deep roots in the TCC's constitutional review. As discussed above, the TCC follows two steps when applying the

95 315 U.S. 568 (1942), 571–572. Justice Frank Murphy said, "There are certain well defined and narrowly limited classes of speech, the prevention and punishment of which have never been thought to raise any Constitutional problem. These include the lewd and obscene, the profane, the libellous and the insulting or "fighting" words – those which, by their very utterance, inflict injury or tend to incite an immediate breach of the peace. It has been well observed that such utterances are not essential part of any exposition of ideas and are of such slight social value as a step to truth that any benefit that may be derived from them is clearly outweighed by the social interest in order and morality".

96 Tzu-Yi Lin (林子儀), *Freedom of Speech and Freedom of Press* (言論自由與新聞自由) (Angle Publishing 1999) 157–160.

97 Hwang, 'Development of Standards of Review by the Constitutional Court from 1996 to 2011' (n 5) 228.

98 J.Y. Interpretation No. 414, [1].

99 E.g. J.Y. Interpretations Nos. 509, 577, 617, 623, 634, 644, 656, 678, 689, 733, 744, 756.

100 The State territory includes the Mainland, Taiwan, Hong Kong, and Macau according to the Constitution of Taiwan and the Act Governing Relations between the People of Taiwan and Mainland China. In this case, the petitioner applied to Taipei City Government to establish an association to promote Taiwan independence. This application was declined for violating Article 2 of the Civil Associations Act, which prohibited the establishment of an association advocating communism or secession from the State. This article was deleted from the Act in 2007.

principle of equality. The first step is to examine whether differential treatment pursues a legitimate aim. The second step is to determine whether there is a certain level of nexus between the differential treatment and the aim pursued. The TCC applies the two steps in association with multi-tiered scrutiny.[101]

In Interpretation No. 760 (2018), the Police Personnel Management Act stipulated the training requirements for police officers. However, this Act did not designate the institute responsible for police training. In practice, the Ministry of Internal Affairs always arranged for the Taiwan Police College to train candidates without degrees from the police education system.[102] Candidates who have degrees from the police education system were trained by the Central Police College. The former group of candidates, who were trained by the Taiwan Police College, were not qualified for certain positions of high rank, while the latter group was qualified. The TCC considered that the impugned Act and arrangement had led to differential treatment between the candidates having degrees from the police education system and those without such degrees in terms of their right to take public examinations and hold public offices. The Court decided to apply the intermediate scrutiny standard, explaining:

> The right to take public examinations and to hold public office is entailed in the right to political participation in a broad sense, which involves participating in the state's decision-making and performing public duties and closely relates to the shaping of civic life and order. Differential treatment of this right should be subject to a relatively strict review. Besides pursuing important public interests, the differential treatment must be substantially connected to the purpose. Only in this case, the differential treatment could comply with the constitutional right to equal treatment.[103]

After going through the materials of the case, the TCC held that none of the two tests of the principle of equality was passed. It found the training arrangement was designed for three reasons: maintaining the police education system, limited training capacity of the Central Police College, and a limited number of positions of high rank. In the TCC's opinion, those purposes were to save administrative costs, which was not an important public interest.[104] It also considered that the Police Personnel Management Act aimed to select police officers based on merit and uphold the principles of fair competition

101 E.g. J.Y. Interpretations Nos. 618, 639, 647, 649, 666, 675, 688, 694, 696, 701, 719, 727, 745, 748, 760, 764, 768, 779, 781, 782, 783.

102 J.Y. Interpretation No. 760.

103 *Ibid.*, [5].

104 *Ibid.*, [9].

and merit-based employment. The training arrangement did not contribute to the realization of this aim.[105]

FUSION OF AMERICAN MULTI-TIERED SCRUTINY AND GERMAN INTENSITY OF REVIEW

The co-existence of the German graduated scale of the proportionality test and the American tiered scrutiny resulted in debate among Grand Justices of the TCC.[106] Many Grand Justices have systematically discussed the intensity of review in their separate opinions, and they have apparent preferences for particular standards of review that tend to be correlated with their educational background.[107] Grand Justices who studied in Germany are familiar with the graduated scale of proportionality test. In contrast, Grand Justices who studied in the United States prefer multi-tiered scrutiny and try to extend the application of multi-tiered scrutiny to cases beyond freedom of speech and discrimination cases.[108]

Although most of the Grand Justices defend and develop the judicial review intensity systems that they are familiar with,[109] some Grand Justices support a unified judicial review intensity system. Grand Justice Pai-Hsiu Yeh pointed out in his separate opinion to Interpretation No. 712 that "The systems of review standards from the United States and Germany are not clearly distinguished by the Court. Instead, the Court perceived them to be parallel and exchangeable".[110] Grand Justice Yeong-Chin Su also emphasized that, "The methodological question of how to localize the standards of review [proportionality and American tiered standards of scrutiny] and integrate them is inevitable when the Court learns from different jurisdictions".[111]

Over time, although contention continues, the Grand Justices have reached partial consensus on a fusion of the German graduated scale and the American tiered scrutiny. Grand Justice Jau-Yuan Hwang called this fusion "one proportionality, three levels of intensity of review".[112] The four subtests of proportionality are necessary steps and constitute a basic framework of constitutional review of the TCC, and, at the same time, proportionality is applied with three levels of intensity of review:

105 *Ibid.*, [9].
106 Shu-Perng Hwang (n 5) 19–20.
107 Hwang, 'Development of Standards of Review by the Constitutional Court from 1996 to 2011' (n 5) 231–232.
108 *Ibid.*
109 Chang (n 73), 66–73.
110 J.Y. Interpretation No. 712.
111 J.Y. Interpretation No. 719.
112 Hwang, 'Development of Standards of Review by the Constitutional Court from 1996 to 2011' (n 5) 237–241.

- Low level of intensity of review: the aims pursued must be legitimate public interests and the means should be rationally connected with the ends pursued.
- Intermediate level of intensity of review: the aims pursued must be important and substantial public interests and the means chosen shall be substantially related to the aims.
- High level of intensity of review: the aims pursued must be compelling/extraordinarily important public interests and the means chosen shall be directly related to the aims pursued or narrowly tailored for the purposes.[113]

One might wonder whether the test of the connection between the aims and means is the suitability test or the necessity test or entails both. Grand Justice Te-Chung Tang thinks that this test entails the suitability test, the necessity test, and the balance test.[114] These three subtests are about the relationship between the means and the aims. In practice, the TCC does not always distinguish the suitability test and the necessity test in its interpretations.[115]

The integration process between multi-tiered scrutiny and proportionality is still ongoing. The integration is not easy because American constitutional jurisprudence and German constitutional jurisprudence are peculiar to each other. The current fusion is innovative and unique, which may become a new engine for the further globalization of proportionality and convergence of constitutional law, bridging civil law and common law constitutional jurisprudence.

Intensity of the TCC's Review of Statutes

The TCC articulated the intensity of review it adopted in very few decisions, but its increasingly detailed reasoning indicated the intensity of review.[116] The terms it often used, such as "compelling public interest", "important public interest", "the last resort and necessary means", and "fairly reasonable means", help us identify the intensity of review.

113 The Grand Justices used different terminologies to describe the three levels of intensity of review. 寬松的審查標準 or 低度的審查標準 or 合理審查標準 for the low level of intensity of review. 較嚴格的審查標準 or 中度審查標準for the intermediate level of intensity of review. 嚴格審查標準 or 從嚴審查標準 for the high level of intensity of review. Ibid., 257–258; Te-Chung Tang (湯德宗), 'A Primary Study on the Establishment of Intensity System of Constitutional Review – An Idea of Hierarchicalised Proportionality Principle' (違憲審查基準體系建構初探—"階層式比例原則"構想) in Fu-Te Liao (廖福特) (ed), *Theory and Practice of Constitutional Interpretation* (憲法解釋之理論與實務) (San Min Book 2009) 1, 39–45.

114 Tang, *ibid.*, 42.

115 *Ibid.*

116 Shu-Perng Hwang (n 5) 20.

Table 3.2 Intensity of Proportionality Test in J.Y. Interpretations against Statutes (1999–2019).

Intensity of Review	*Constitutional*	*Unconstitutional*	*Total Interpretation*
Low level	476, 512, 517, 528, 544, 554, 564, 578, 580,[a] 604, 617, 618, 642, 656, 672, 673, 675, 688, **689**,[b] 699, 709, 714, 716, 719, 746, 751, 764, 767, 768, 778, **781**, **782**, **783**	551, 580, 641, 673, 709, 711, 712, 716, 732, 733, 746, 756, 786	41 (45.6%)
Intermediate level	577, 584, 588, 623, 634, 637, 646, 659, 665, 678, **689**, 702, 780, **781**, **782**, **783**	588, 603, 669, 702, 749, 766	20 (22.2%)
High level	664, 690, 777	644, 649, 664, 744, 777	6 (6.7%)
Unclear	490, 509, 515, 531, 575, 585, 596, 630, 633, 636, 697, 739, 775	487, 507, 523, 535, 558, 573, 583, 585, 616, 633, 636, 654, 667, 670, 677, 685, 710, 718, 775	28 (31.1%)

Source: Author.

[a] In these 16 underlined J.Y. Interpretations, the TCC declared some statutory provisions constitutional and some statutory provisions unconstitutional.

[b] Four J.Y. Interpretations in bold are decisions where more than one statutory provision was questioned and the TCC applied different levels of intensity of review.

From Table 3.2, the TCC tends to apply proportionality leniently over the past two decades. It adopted the low level of intensity of review in 41 cases (approximately 45.6 percent). By contrast, it adopted the high level of intensity of review in only six cases and the intermediate-level intensity in 20 cases. According to Table 3.3, the TCC applied the principle of equality deferentially as well. It adopted the low level of intensity of review in 11 cases, while the intermediate and high levels of intensity of review were invoked in only 10 cases in total. When reading Table 3.2 and Table 3.3 together, the TCC adopted the low level of intensity of review in 52 cases, more than the total number of cases where the intermediate level and high level of intensity of review were adopted (36 interpretations in total).

After 2007, however, there was an increased reliance on the intermediate level and high level of intensity of review. The TCC has adopted them in 32 cases and adopted the low level of intensity of review in 38 cases from 2007 to 2019 (Figure 3.2). Particularly, the intermediate level of intensity of review is frequently suggested in the Grand Justices' separate opinions. Grand Justice Jau-Yuan Hwang commented that the intermediate level of intensity of

Table 3.3 Intensity of Review of the Principle of Equality in J.Y. Interpretations against Statutes (1999–2019).

Intensity of Review	*Constitutional*	*Unconstitutional*	*Total Interpretation*
Low level	618, 639, 647, 675, 688, 719, 727, 764, 768	745, 779	11 (29.7%)
Intermediate level		666, 694, 696, 701, 748, 760, 781, 782, 783	9 (24.3%)
High level		649	1 (2.7%)
Unclear	485, 490, 560, 575, 578, 596, 667, 697, 698, 728, 739,	477, 573, 610, 624, 687	16 (43.2%)

Source: Author.

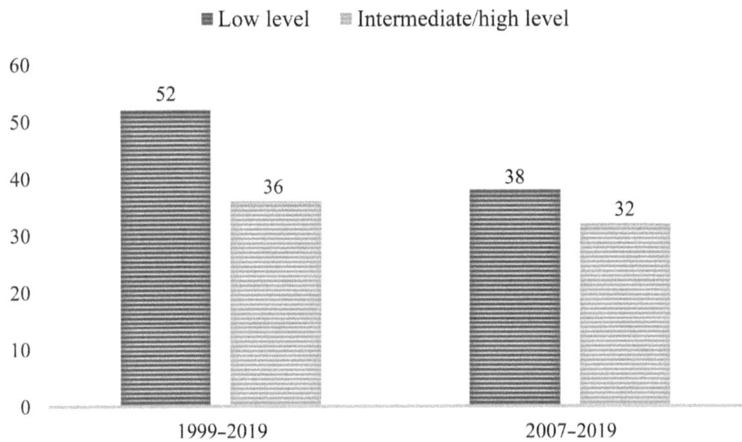

Figure 3.2 A Comparison Between Low Level and Intermediate/High Level of Intensity of Review in J.Y. Interpretations against Statutes (1999–2019).[a]

Source: Author.

[a] As the TCC often applies both proportionality and the principle of equality in the same interpretation (for example, Interpretations Nos. 618, 675, 688, 719), Figure 3.2 contains double counting. But it is proper to keep double counting because the numbers show the frequency of different levels of intensity of review adopted by the TCC.

review became the "new love" of the Grand Justices,[117] signifying the increasing intrusiveness and assertiveness of the TCC's constitutional review against statutes.

117 Hwang, 'Development of Standards of Review by the Constitutional Court from 1996 to 2011' (n 5) 244.

Hong Kong

An Overview: The CFA's Approach to Constitutional Review

This section examines the CFA's judicial review of ordinances enacted by the Legislative Council of Hong Kong. In assessing whether legislation breaches constitutional rights, thereby violating the Basic Law, the CFA has consistently employed a structured approach comprising a series of established questions:

(1) The first question asks whether constitutional rights are engaged in the dispute. If the answer is in the affirmative, the examination proceeds to the next question.
(2) The second question asks whether an impugned legislative provision amounts to a restriction on this right. If so, the analysis advances to the subsequent question.
(3) The third question asks whether the right is absolute. If the rights are absolute, restrictions are prohibited, and the impugned provision will be considered unconstitutional. If the right is qualified, the final question is posed.
(4) The last question asks whether the restriction can be justified. The proportionality test is typically employed as the standard of review.[118]

In terms of identifying constitutional rights and restrictions on them, it relates to the interpretation of the HKBL, the BORO, and the relevant laws imposing restrictions. The CFA has reiterated that the HKBL and the BORO are "living instruments intended to meet the changing needs and circumstances",[119] and that the interpretation of the constitution must "consider the purpose of the instrument and its relevant provisions as well as the language of its text in light of the context".[120] The CFA also emphasized that constitutional rights should be generously interpreted while the restrictions on rights should be narrowly interpreted.[121] Notwithstanding the generous approach to rights interpretation, there are still cases dismissed in the stage of the first and second questions.

118 *Catholic Diocese of Hong Kong v Secretary for Justice* (2011) 14 HKCFAR 754, [65]; *Kong Yunming v Director of Social Welfare* (2013) 16 HKCFAR 950, [39]; *Official Receiver v Zhi Charles* (2015) 18 HKCFAR 467, [22]–[23]; *Kwok Cheuk Kin v Secretary for Constitutional and Mainland Affairs* (2017) 20 HKCFAR 353, [29]–[30].

119 *Ng Ka Ling and Others v Director of Immigration* (1999) 2 HKCFAR 4, 28D–E; *W v Registrar of Marriages* (2013) 16 HKCFAR 112, [115].

120 *Ng Ka Ling, ibid.*, 28F–G; *Vallejos v Commissioner of Registration* (2013) 16 HKCFAR 45, [27]–[29].

121 *Ng Ka Ling, ibid.*, 34E–G; *HKSAR v Ng Kung Siu and Another* (1999) 2 HKCFAR 442, 455H–I; *Gurung Kesh Bahadur v Director of Immigration* (2002) 5 HKCFAR 480, [24]; *Official Receiver and Trustee in Bankruptcy of Chan Wing Hing and Another v Chan Wing Hing and Another and (Third Party)* (2006) 9 HKCFAR 545, [36]; *HKSAR v Lam Kwong Wai and Another* (2006) 9 HKCFAR 574, [36].

In *Catholic Diocese of Hong Kong v Secretary for Justice* (2011), the CFA confirmed the constitutionality of ss. 40BK(2) and (3)(a) and 40BU(2) and (3) of the Education Ordinance (Cap 279) because no constitutional right was infringed.[122] The impugned provisions changed the way of school management so that the applicant lost "absolute control" over Diocesan schools.[123] The applicant argued that those provisions were inconsistent with the right to freedom of religion under Article 141(3) of the HKBL and thus unconstitutional.[124] Article 141(3) entitles religious organizations in Hong Kong to continue to run schools and provide other social services according to their previous practice before the handover. The CFA held, however, that the applicant's asserted authority to appoint one hundred percent of a school's management committee, supervisors, and principals in accordance with the previous practice prior to the handover was not encompassed by the freedom of religion under the HKBL. The CFA gave the following explanation:

> The meaning given to the phrase 'according to their previous practice' relates to the core freedom addressed by Article 141. It is the religious dimension of their previous practice that receives protection as part of the core constitutional right to religious freedom as applicable to religious organizations ... However, policies which have no religious content, for instance, as to the teaching of second languages, providing more physical education or information technology classes, or providing student travel or textbook subsidies, would not engage the protections.[125]

Yeung Chung Ming v Commissioner of Police (2008) is a case in which the CFA dismissed the applicant's claim on the grounds that no violation of constitutional rights had been identified.[126] The applicant was a policeman and was charged with criminal offenses. During the pending trial, the Commissioner of Police withheld seven percent of his salary pursuant to s. 17(2)(a) of the Police Force Ordinance (Cap. 232).[127] The applicant contended that s. 17(2)(a) violated his right to be presumed innocent and was unconstitutional.[128] The CFA held that the statutory power vested in the Commissioner of Police by s. 17(2)(a) did not constitute an infringement of the applicant's right to be presumed innocent.[129] The CFA considered that decisions made by the Commissioner of Police to withhold a portion of an officer's pay did not imply any view that the officer was guilty, but merely implied a view that he might be found guilty

122 (2011) 14 HKCFAR 754, [66].
123 *Ibid.*, [20]–[21].
124 *Ibid.*, [3].
125 *Ibid.*, [79].
126 (2008) 11 HKCFAR 513.
127 *Ibid.*, [1]–[2].
128 *Ibid.*, [3].
129 *Ibid.*, [31].

after trial.[130] Due to no infringement of the right to be presumed innocent, the CFA dismissed the appeal without further inquiring about the proportionality of the statutory provision.

In terms of the third question of whether the rights involved are absolute rights, the CFA has not struck down any ordinance on this ground yet. But in *Ubamaka v Secretary for Security* (2012), the applicant raised questions about the constitutionality and effect of s. 11 of the BORO, which provides that, "As regards persons not having the right to enter and remain in Hong Kong, this Ordinance does not affect any immigration legislation governing entry into, stay in and departure from Hong Kong, or the application of any such legislation". The CFA held that s. 11 of the BORO was constitutional, but it was qualified by s. 5 and not applicable to these absolute rights protected by the BORO.[131] The CFA also stressed that the government could not justify any encroachment on the absolute BORO by proportionality.[132]

When the court confirms that an impugned ordinance restricts a qualified constitutional right, it will ask whether the restriction can be justified. The principle of proportionality is the most frequently utilized standard of review in this step. In the last two decades, the CFA addressed challenges to ordinances in 34 cases. It employed proportionality in 16 cases and declared ordinances unconstitutional in 11 cases (Table 3.4). Proportionality is undoubtedly a linchpin standard and has "bite". The following part particularly delves into the application of proportionality by the CFA to review ordinances.

Proportionality in the CFA's Review of Ordinances

Adoption of Proportionality in Hong Kong

Prior to the British handover of Hong Kong to China in 1997, the courts of colonial Hong Kong had already applied proportionality in judicial review. After the handover, Hong Kong courts continue to rely on proportionality to adjudicate judicial review cases.

As early as the colonial era, the then Court of Appeal of Hong Kong had applied proportionality.[133] In *R v Sin Yau Ming*, the issue presented before the Court of Appeal was whether a mandatory presumption contained in ss. 46

130 *Ibid.*, [30]–[31].
131 15 HKCFAR 743, [114]–[115].
132 *Ibid.*, [145].
133 Rehan Abeyratne, 'More Structure, More Deference? Proportionality in Hong Kong' in Po Jen Yap (ed), *Proportionality in Asia* (CUP 2020) 28; Stone Sweet and Mathews, 'Proportionality and Rights Protection in Asia' (n 20) 789; Danny Gittings, *Introduction to the Hong Kong Basic Law* (2nd edn, Hong Kong University Press 2016) 291.

Table 3.4 Proportionality in the CFA Decisions against Ordinances (1999–2019).

	CFA Decisions	*In Total*
Constitutional	HKSAR v Ng Kung Siu and Another (1999) Solicitor v Law Society of Hong Kong (2006) So Wai Lun v HKSAR (2006) Fu Kor Kuen Patrick v HKSAR (2012) Kwok Cheuk Kin v Secretary for Constitutional and Mainland Affairs (2017)	5 (31.3%)
Unconstitutional	Solicitor and Law Society of Hong Kong v Secretary for Justice (2003) Leung Kwok Hung and Others v HKSAR (2005) (Severance) Official Receiver and Trustee in Bankruptcy of Chan Wing Hing and Another v Chan Wing Hing and Another and (Third Party) (2006) HKSAR v Lam Kwong Wai and Another (2006) (Remedial Interpretation) HKSAR v Hung Chan Wa and Another (2006) (Remedial Interpretation) Secretary for Justice v Yau Yuk Lung (2007) HKSAR v Ng Po On (2008) (Remedial Interpretation) Koon Wing Yee v Insider Dealing Tribunal (2008) Mok Charles v Tam Wai Ho (2010) Lee To Nei v HKSAR (2012) (Remedial Interpretation) Official Receiver v Zhi Charles (2015)	11 (68.7%)

Source: Author.

and 47 of the Dangerous Drugs Ordinance (Cap. 134) contradicted the right of the presumption of innocence enshrined in the BORO.[134]

The Court of Appeal asserted that when interpreting the BORO, the Hong Kong courts would no longer employ the ordinary cannon of construction of law nor the dicta of the common law,[135] as the BORO aimed to make the ICCPR enforceable in Hong Kong.[136] The courts should look to the purposes of the ICCPR and ensure the legislation is consistent with the Covenant.[137] Citing *R v Oakes*,[138] a leading Canadian case applying proportionality, the Court of Appeal concluded that even though the BORO contained no "justification" provision, the justification test, namely the proportionality test, was

134 [1992] 1 HKCLR 127.
135 *Ibid.*, 140.
136 Hong Kong Bill of Rights Ordinance (Cap. 383), pt II.
137 *Sin Yau Ming* (n 134) 142.
138 [1986] 1 SCR 103.

implied in the Hong Kong context by the reference to a "free and democratic society",[139] which serves as a constitutional bedrock of the application of proportionality.

On 1 July 1997, China resumed sovereignty over Hong Kong, and the HKBL replaced the Letters Patent to be the mini-constitution of the HKSAR. The BORO survived the transfer of sovereignty and remained an important instrument for human rights in Hong Kong.[140] The CFA, the newly established apex court of this region, substituted for the Privy Council, becoming the court of final adjudication of Hong Kong.[141]

The CFA continues to apply proportionality in constitutional review decisions.[142] *HKSAR v Ng Kung Siu and Another* (1999) is the first landmark case in which the CFA applied proportionality.[143] The case concerned the constitutionality of s. 7 of the National Flag and National Emblem Ordinance (No. 116 of 1997) and s. 7 of the Regional Flag and Regional Emblem Ordinance (No. 117 of 1997).[144] These provisions created restrictions on the freedom of expression by criminalizing desecrating the national flag and the regional flag. The respondents were convicted because they cut and tore off Chinese and Hong Kong flags and wrote the Chinese character "shame" on both flags in a public demonstration. They argued that these provisions violated their freedom of speech enshrined in Article 27 of the HKBL and Article 16 of the BORO.

The CFA asserted that the provisions of the ICCPR had been incorporated into Hong Kong's legal system through the BORO. A restriction on the freedom of expression could not contradict the ICCPR.[145] The CFA recognized flag desecration as a form of non-verbal speech or expression.[146] At the same time, the CFA admitted that the freedom of expression was not absolute and subject to restrictions provided by law and necessary for respect of others' rights and freedom and protection of the national security, public order, or public health or morals.[147]

The CFA applied proportionality, an ideally suitable standard for the issue of whether the restriction on the freedom of expression was justified. Nonetheless, the application of proportionality in the *Ng Kung Siu* case was neither complete nor structured.[148] The CFA only applied the legitimate aim test and necessity test. It started by examining whether the impugned ordinances

139 *Sin Yau Ming* (n 134) 142.
140 Gittings (n 133) 264.
141 HKBL, arts 19, 81.
142 Abeyratne (n 133) 30.
143 (1999) 2 HKCFAR 442.
144 *Ibid.*, 447E–H.
145 *Ibid.*, 455E–G.
146 *Ibid.*, 455F–G.
147 *Ibid.*, 456I–457A.
148 Abeyratne (n 133) 32.

aimed to protect public order (*ordre public*). The CFA defined "public order" broadly, including "what was necessary for the protection of the general welfare or for the interests of the collectivity as a whole".[149] The CFA thought that this concept varied with the time, place, and circumstances changing.[150] It held that the legitimate interests in protecting the national and regional flags were interests within this concept against the background of the resumption of sovereignty over Hong Kong under the principle of OCTS.[151] The CFA then used the necessity test to examine whether the restriction on the freedom of speech was necessary for the protection of public order. The CFA concluded that the restriction was not wide but limited because only one mode of expression, desecrating the flags, was banned, while other modes of expression were not prohibited. The CFA emphasized at the end of its reasoning:

> The implementation of the principle of 'One Country, Two Systems' is a matter of fundamental importance, as is the reinforcement of national unity and territorial integrity. Protection of the national flag and the regional flag from desecration, having regard to their unique symbolism, will play an important part in the attainment of these goals.[152]

While the suitability test and balance test were not explicitly invoked in the *Ng Kung Siu* case, the CFA's reasoning connoted the suitability of the restrictive measures in question.

In 2005, the CFA added the suitability test to the formula of proportionality in *Leung Kwok Hung and others v HKSAR*,[153] where it articulated the formula that was used for the next decade: after examining the aims pursued, the court has to ensure: "(i) the restriction must be rationally connected with one or more of the legitimate purposes; (ii) the means used to impair the right ... must be no more than necessary to accomplish the legitimate purpose in question".[154] Proportionality in Hong Kong became more harmonious with the standard model.[155] An observable lacuna persists in the form of the absence of the balance test. But the CFA did take the balance test into consideration in *Leung Kwok Hung*, stating:

> By applying a proportionality test for considering any restriction on the right of peaceful assembly, a proper balance is struck between the

149 *Ng Kung Siu* (n 143) 459I–460A.
150 *Ibid.*
151 *Ibid.*, 460A–D.
152 *Ibid.*, 461D–E.
153 (2005) 8 HKCFAR 229.
154 *Ibid.*, [90].
155 Alec Stone Sweet, 'The Necessity of Balancing: Hong Kong's Flawed Approach to Proportionality, and Why It Matters' (2020) *Hong Kong Law Journal* 541, 542.

> interests of society on the one hand and the individual's right of peaceful assembly on the other.[156]

The demarcation of the balance test as an independent subtest within the framework of proportionality was a development realized in *Hysan Development Co Ltd v Town Planning Board* (2016).[157] This case concerned restrictions on property rights imposed by the Town Planning Board's Outline Zoning Plans. The Outline Zoning Plans imposed a series of building restrictions on the applicant-owned extensive properties on various sites in Causeway Bay and Wan Chai.[158] The applicant claimed that the building restrictions unconstitutionally encroached on its property right in contravention of Articles 6 and 105 of the HKBL.[159] The CFA went through the first two subtests of proportionality quickly because the purpose and suitability of the building restrictions were of little dispute. These building restrictions aimed at promoting "the health, safety, convenience and general welfare of the community" by "facilitating air ventilation and pedestrian flow and setting appropriate building heights".[160] Before applying the necessity test, the CFA added the balance test to the formula of proportionality. It referred to the decisions of the Supreme Court of the United Kingdom, the Supreme Court of Canada, and the ECtHR, and stated that the case for accepting in principle the applicability of a fourth step in proportionality analysis is logically compelling.[161] There was "a meaningful distinction to be drawn" between the balance test and the other three subtests as the balance test required "placing colliding values and interest side by side and balancing them according to their weight".[162] The four subtests of proportionality were conceptually interrelated and interdependent so that courts could apply them fluidly and flexibly.[163]

Implementation of Proportionality in the CFA's Review of Ordinances

Table 3.5 exhibits the statistics on the application of each subtest of proportionality in the CFA's review of ordinances. The numbers in the column "All Decisions" indicate that the CFA did not always apply a complete set of subtests in every decision. Instead, it tended to apply the legitimate aim test, suitability test, and necessity test. The balance test emerged only once, which is

156 *Ibid.*, [35].
157 (2016) 19 HKCFAR 372.
158 *Ibid.*, [4].
159 *Ibid.*, [9].
160 *Ibid.*, [55].
161 *Ibid.*, [73].
162 *Ibid.* [71]–[72], citing *Alberta v Hutterian Brethren of Wilson Colony* [2009] 2 SCR 567.
163 *Ibid.* [60], citing *Bank Mellat v Her Majesty's Treasury (No. 2)* [2014] AC 700.

Table 3.5 The Application of the Subtests of Proportionality in the CFA Decision against Ordinances (1999–2019).

	All Decisions	*Unconstitutional*	*Constitutional*
Proportionality	16	11	5
Legitimate aim test	14	1	13
Suitability test	11	0	11
Necessity test	15	9	6
Balance test	1	0	1

Source: Author.

not surprising as it was not officially added to the formula of proportionality until 2016.[164]

Comparison between the column "Unconstitutional" and the column "Constitutional" shows that while the legitimate aim test and suitability test frequently emerged in the CFA's analysis, they had no "bite". In particular, the CFA did not strike down any ordinances by the suitability test during this period. This stands in stark contrast to the necessity test, which is, according to this table, the most potent subtest. The CFA used it to strike down nine ordinances. The balance test has not yet shown significant influence. The CFA once commented that the application of the fourth step would usually not invalidate a restriction which has satisfied the requirements of the first three stages of the inquiry.[165]

THE LEGITIMATE AIM TEST

The CFA struck down ordinances at the first stage of the proportionality test in one case – *Secretary for Justice v Yau Yuk Lung* (2007).[166] In this case, two men were charged with having committed buggery with each other in private.[167] They argued that s. 118 F(1) of the Crimes Ordinance (Cap. 200) constituted discrimination based on sexual orientation and infringed their constitutional right to equal treatment because this provision criminalized only homosexual buggery; by contrast, heterosexuals were not subject to any criminal liability in relation to the same and comparable conduct.[168]

164 This table counted the cases where the balance test was applied after the 2016 *Hysan* case. Before *Hysan*, there were some cases where the CFA's reasoning displayed the spirit of balancing. However, the CFA did not explicitly demarcate the four subtests of proportionality until the *Hysan* case. Consequently, those cases involving implicit balancing test were not counted. *Leung Kwok* Hung case is accounted as unconstitutional. It passed proportionality test after the severance of public order from ordre public.

165 *Hysan* (n 157) [73].

166 (2007) 10 HKCFAR 335.

167 *Ibid.*, [4].

168 *Ibid.*, [24].

Apparently, this case concerns equal protection. The CFA applied the principle of proportionality to assess whether the differences in treatment were more than necessary to accomplish an aim pursued. The Secretary for Justice argued that s. 118 F(1) was codifying the common law offense of committing an act outraging public decency and obviated such difficulties as there may be in proving the common law offense. The Legislative Council must have taken into consideration that there was a genuine need for such offense as "part of the package to reform law relating to homosexual conduct".[169] However, in the CFA's opinion, no genuine need for this differential treatment was identified.[170] The mere act of legislative enactment was insufficient to establish such a need.[171] In other words, the Secretary for Justice failed to demonstrate that s. 118 F(1) was enacted in pursuit of a legitimate aim. As a result, the differential treatment could not be justified, and there was an encroachment on the right to equal treatment.[172] Due to the failure at the first stage of the proportionality test, the CFA did not proceed to assess the remaining three subtests.

THE SUITABILITY TEST

Even though the suitability test frequently emerged in the CFA's proportionality analysis (11 out of 16 cases), no ordinance failed this subtest. Normally, the CFA just skated over it.[173]

THE NECESSITY TEST

The necessity test was the most frequently applied subtest when the CFA constitutionally reviewed ordinances. The CFA applied this subtest in 15 out of 16 decisions. The only decision in which the proportionality test was invoked while the necessity test was not applied was *Yau Yuk Lung*, because the court had already struck down the impugned legislation by the first subtest.[174] Among these 15 cases, the CFA declared the impugned ordinances unconstitutional in nine cases.[175] The necessity test appeared to be the most "devastating" weapon in the CFA's arsenal against ordinances.

169 *Ibid.*, [26].
170 *Ibid.*, [27].
171 *Ibid.*
172 *Ibid.*, [30].
173 For example, *Fu Kor Kuen Patrick v HKSAR* (2012) 15 HKCFAR 524, [90]; *Zhi Charles* (n 118) [35]; *Kwok Cheuk Kin* (n 118) [54].
174 *Yau Yuk Lung* (n 166).
175 *Solicitor and Law Society of Hong Kong v Secretary for Justice* (2003) 6 HKCFAR 570; *Official Receiver and Trustee in Bankruptcy of Chan Wing Hing and Another v Chan Wing Hing and Another and (Third Party)* (2006) 9 HKCFAR 545; *HKSAR v Hung Chan Wa and Another* (2006) 9 HKCFAR 614; *HKSAR v Ng Po On* (2008) 11 HKCFAR 91; *Koon Wing Yee v Insider Dealing Tribunal* (2008) 11 HKCFAR 170; *Mok Charles v Tam Wai Ho* (2010)

Reviewing *Official Receiver v Zhi Charles* (2015) as an example,[176] this case concerned the restriction on the right to travel.[177] A bankruptcy order was made against the respondent in December 2006.[178] He failed to attend an examination pursuant to s. 29 of the Bankruptcy Ordinance (Cap.6), and then a prohibition order and a warrant for arrest were issued against him in May 2012.[179] The respondent applied for a declaration that he was automatically discharged from bankruptcy in December 2010 (four years after the issuance of the bankruptcy order). Additionally, he argued that s. 30A(10)(a) of the Bankruptcy Ordinance was unconstitutional for encroaching on his right to travel, a right protected by Article 31 of the HKBL and Article 8(2) of the BORO.[180] Section 30A(10)(a) provides that the bankruptcy period should, if a person has left Hong Kong before the commencement of the bankruptcy, start to run once he returns to Hong Kong and notifies trustees of this return.

The CFA adopted the well-established approach mentioned above to examine the constitutionality of s. 30A(10)(a) of the Bankruptcy Ordinance.[181] It started with identifying the scope of the right to travel. It took the customary interpretation approach and gave the right to travel a generous interpretation,[182] holding that the right to travel must include the freedom to enter and stay away from Hong Kong.[183] In its view, the impugned provision restricted the right to travel as it imposed a sanction, namely the non-commencement of the bankruptcy period, on a person who was declared bankrupt but was absent from Hong Kong.[184] Given that the right to travel is not an absolute right, the CFA moved to assess whether the restriction imposed by s. 30A(10)(a) was proportionate.[185] The first and second subtests of proportionality were satisfied. The restriction was rationally connected to a legitimate aim, which was to keep the bankrupt on the trustee's radar so as to facilitate the management of estates and protect the interests of creditors and public interests.[186] But the CFA held that the restriction on the freedom to travel did not satisfy the constitutional requirement of necessity for three reasons. First, s. 30A(10)(a) operated automatically without exception. When the bankrupt was willing to cooperate with the trustee but might not come back because of some reasons beyond his control, he could not be exempted from the sanction. Second,

---

13 HKCFAR 762; *Lee To Nei v HKSAR* (2012) 15 HKCFAR 162; *Lam Kwong Wai* (n 121); *Zhi Charles* (n 118).

176 *Zhi Charles, ibid.*

177 *Ibid.*, [24]–[27].

178 *Ibid.*, [5].

179 *Ibid.*, [7].

180 *Ibid.*, [10].

181 *Ibid.*, [22].

182 *Ibid.*, [24].

183 *Ibid.*, [31].

184 *Ibid.*, [32].

185 *Ibid.*, [35].

186 *Ibid.*, [35].

even if the bankrupt was willing to cooperate with the trustee by providing all relevant documents and information needed for effective management, the bankruptcy period still did not run. Third, s. 30A(10)(a) did not give any discretion to the courts to disapply the sanction.[187] The CFA concluded that the applicant failed to prove:

> Why a materially less rigid regime would not equally protect the rights of creditors and the public interest in the administration of the estates of bankrupts; why, for example, the same objective would not reasonably be met if there were provision to cater for innocent cases and cases of cooperation notwithstanding the absence from Hong Kong and which afforded the courts a discretion to mitigate the sanction.[188]

THE BALANCE TEST

In *Kwok Cheuk Kin v Secretary for Constitutional and Mainland Affairs* (2017),[189] the CFA applied a full set of proportionality subtests. The applicants were members of the Legislative Council, and they resigned in order to trigger a by-election.[190] They all took part in the by-election, and they were re-elected.[191] Later, the Government of HKSAR introduced and the Legislative Council passed the Legislative Council (Amendment) Bill of 2012.[192] According to s. 39(2A) of that Bill, members who had resigned within six months of the date of a by-election were disqualified from being nominated for the by-election unless an intervening general election was held. The applicants questioned the constitutionality of s. 39(2A), arguing that it infringed on their right to stand for election under Article 26 of the HKBL and Article 21 of the BORO.[193]

The CFA confirmed that the right to stand for election had been infringed by restrictions contained in s. 39(2A).[194] It went through the four subtests of proportionality in sequence. In the CFA's opinion, the impugned provison passed all subtests. At the stage of the balancing test, the CFA gave three reasons. First, if the impugned legislation passes the first three subtests, they are unlikely to fail the balance test.[195] Second, the restriction on the right to stand for election was minor because it only applied to by-elections and prohibited the resigned members merely for six months. Thirdly, the voters in relevant

187 *Ibid.*, [55].
188 *Ibid.*, [56].
189 *Kwok Cheuk Kin* (n 118).
190 *Ibid.*, [8].
191 *Ibid.*, [9].
192 *Ibid.*, [16].
193 *Ibid.*, [19].
194 *Ibid.*, [32].
195 *Ibid.*, [61].

constituencies could vote for candidates without restriction, except for the resigning members.[196]

The Principle of Equality

Unlike the TCC hesitating to include equal protection cases in the terrain of proportionality,[197] the CFA expressly stated that proportionality constituted the justification test for scrutinizing discrimination. In *So Wai Lun v HKSAR* (2006), the applicant was convicted according to s. 124 of the Crimes Ordinance (Cap. 200), which criminalized men's conduct of sexual intercourse with a girl under the age of 16.[198] The applicant argued that s. 124 criminalized the conduct of the male to the exclusion of the female, and this deprived the male of equality before the law.[199] The CFA referred to the case *R v Man Wai Keung (No 2)* that was decided before the handover:

> Clearly, there is no requirement of literal equality in the sense of unrelentingly identical treatment always. For such rigidity would subvert rather than promote true even-handedness. So that, in certain circumstances, a departure from literal equality would be a legitimate course and, indeed, the only legitimate course. But the starting point is identical treatment. And any departure therefrom must be justified.[200]

In the CFA's opinion, impugned legislation, which departs from identical treatment, can be justified by reference to genuine need, rationality, and proportionality.[201] The CFA examined the reasoning in similar cases determined by American and Canadian courts and revealed that the impugned different treatment pursued genuine needs, including the problem of teenage pregnancies, not criminalizing the female's conduct because that might deter them from reporting the matter, and the legislature's role in resolving issues engaging society's code of sexual morality.[202] Even though the CFA merely examined the genuine needs without exerting a detailed proportionality test, this case established the place of proportionality in equal protection cases.

In *Yau Yuk Lung*, the relationship between proportionality and equal protection was more clearly elucidated. The facts and reasoning of this case were presented in the previous section.[203] In the case, the CFA stated that the principle of equal protection generally required like cases to be treated alike, and

196 *Ibid.*
197 See supra note 51 and accompanying text.
198 (2006) 9 HKCFAR 530, [2].
199 *Ibid.*, [4].
200 *Ibid.*, [20].
201 *Ibid.*, [28].
202 *Ibid.*, [21]–[27].
203 See above, the implementation of the legitimate aim test.

unlike cases not to be treated alike, but this principle did not invariably require exact equality.[204] Differences in treatment may be justified by showing:

> (1) The difference in treatment must pursue a legitimate aim. For any aim to be legitimate, a genuine need for such difference must be established; (2) The difference in treatment must be rationally connected to the legitimate aim. (3) The difference in treatment must be no more than is necessary to accomplish the legitimate aim.[205]

These three inquiries are, in fact, the first three subtests of proportionality.

Intensity of the CFA's Review of Ordinances

Spectrum of Intensity of Proportionality Test in Hong Kong

REASONABLENESS NECESSITY

Like the TCC, the CFA also introduced variable intensity of review associated with the proportionality test. When the CFA applies proportionality, the intensity of review differentiates at the third stage, the necessity test. The CFA introduced the test of reasonable necessity (a stricter test) and the "manifestly without reasonable foundation" test (a more lenient test) for the necessity assessment.

According to conventional wisdom, at the core of the necessity test is the least-intrusive means test or a requirement of "minimum impairment".[206] Legislatures and executive authorities must adopt the least-restrictive means among all viable means that promote legitimate aims.[207] Nonetheless, the CFA does not take this rigid and strict reading of the necessity test. Instead, it holds an opinion that the words "no more than necessary" lay down a test of reasonable, not strict, necessity.[208] It cited the ECtHR decision *James and Others v United Kingdom*.[209] In that case, the applicants claimed that the Leasehold Reform Act 1967 deprived them of property rights when lessees were entitled to purchase their freehold reversion. The ECtHR dismissed the applicants' argument of the strict necessity and adopted a test of reasonable necessity, commenting:

204 *Yau Yuk Lung* (n 166) [19].
205 *Ibid.*, [20].
206 Aharon Barak, *Proportionality: Constitutional Rights and Their Limitations* (CUP 2012) 317.
207 Robert Alexy, 'Constitutional Rights and Proportionality' (2014) 22 *Journal for Constitutional Theory and Philosophy of Law* 51, 52.
208 *Hysan* (n 157) [83].
209 (1986) 8 EHRR 123, [50]–[51].

> The availability of alternative solutions does not in itself render the leasehold reform legislation unjustified; it constitutes one factor, along with others, relevant for determining whether the means chosen could be regarded as reasonable and suite to achieving the legitimate aim being pursued, having regard to the need to strike a "fair balance".[210]

The CFA adopts a similar deferential approach to the necessity test. In the CFA's opinion, the legislative or executive authority must show that the measure impairs the right as little as reasonably possible in order to achieve the legislative objective.[211] The courts should not invalidate legislation or quash an executive act only because of the existence of an alternative means which might be less intrusive to the protected rights, because "a judge would be unimaginative indeed if he could not come up with something a little less 'drastic' or a little less 'restrictive' in almost any situation, and thereby enable himself to vote to strike legislation down".[212] The courts will strike down legislation or quash an executive act if the authority fails to explain why a significantly less intrusive and equally effective measure is not chosen.[213]

MANIFESTLY WITHOUT REASONABLE FOUNDATION

Besides the reasonable necessity, the CFA introduced another standard for carrying out the necessity test – "manifestly without reasonable foundation" ("manifest" standard), which is a far more deferential standard than the test of "reasonable necessity".

The CFA first articulated "manifestly without reasonable foundation" in *Fok Chun Wa v Hospital Authority* in 2012.[214] In *Fok Chun Wa*, the applicant was representative of women from what the CFA called "A2 Group": Mainland women marry Hong Kong residents and hold a Two-Way Permit that is issued by the Mainland authorities and allows them to stay in Hong long up to 90 days. She gave birth to a child in a local public hospital and was asked to pay more fees for obstetric services than Hong Kong- resident women.[215] The applicant alleged that charging Mainland Chinese women married to Hong Kong residents higher obstetrics fees was discriminatory and violated Article 25 of the HKBL and Article 22 of the BORO.[216]

The CFA took a usual approach to address discriminatory issues: (1) to identify relevant comparators; (2) to examine whether the different treatments

210 *Ibid.*, [51].
211 *Hysan* (n 157) [121].
212 *Ibid.*, [87]–[88].
213 *Ibid.*, [121].
214 [2012] 15 HKCFAR 409.
215 *Ibid.*, [1]–[2].
216 *Ibid.*, [39].

can be justified by the proportionality test.[217] Before applying the justification test to *Fok Chun Wa*, the CFA explained that giving the government adequate leeway was appropriate in this case and introduced "manifestly without reasonable foundation".[218] The CFA stated its position that "in the socio-economic context ... considerations are best left to the executive, legislative and other authority ... unless the solution or alternative is manifestly beyond the spectrum of reasonableness (or manifestly without reasonable foundation) the court will not interfere".[219] Ma CJ articulated this "manifest" standard:

> Where a number of alternatives, but reasonable, solutions to a problem exist, the court will not put itself in a place of the executive or legislature or other authority to decide which is the best option. That is not its role. The court will only interfere where the option chosen is clearly beyond the spectrum of reasonable options; in other words, the option has clearly gone too far (or further than necessary) to deal with the problem. In this situation, the court will not have been satisfied under the third limb of the justification test.[220]

THE SPECTRUM OF INTENSITY OF REVIEW FOR ASSESSING PROPORTIONALITY

Hysan undoubtedly stands as a milestone case in the evolution of proportionality in Hong Kong, given that, in this case, the CFA not only reintroduced the balance test to the framework of proportionality,[221] but also elaborated upon the spectrum of intensity for the proportionality test.[222] Additionally, in this case, the CFA introduced some factors for the court to consider when determining the intensity of judicial review.[223]

As discussed above, the applicant argued that the Town Planning Board imposed a series of building restrictions on its properties and violated its right to property. The applicant advocated the reasonable necessity as the intensity of review for the necessity test, while the Town Planning Board argued for the "manifest" standard.[224] This contention provided the CFA with an excellent chance to compare the test of reasonable necessity and the "manifest" standard. The CFA emphasized that the test of reasonable necessity and the "manifest" standard were not independent concepts; instead, they distinguished from each other merely by the degree of intensity of review.[225] The CFA

217 *Ibid.*, [57].
218 *Ibid.*, [61].
219 *Ibid.*, [76].
220 *Ibid.*, [75] (3).
221 *Hysan* (n 157) [73].
222 *Ibid.*, [119].
223 *Ibid.*, [107].
224 *Ibid.*, [82].
225 *Ibid.*, [119].

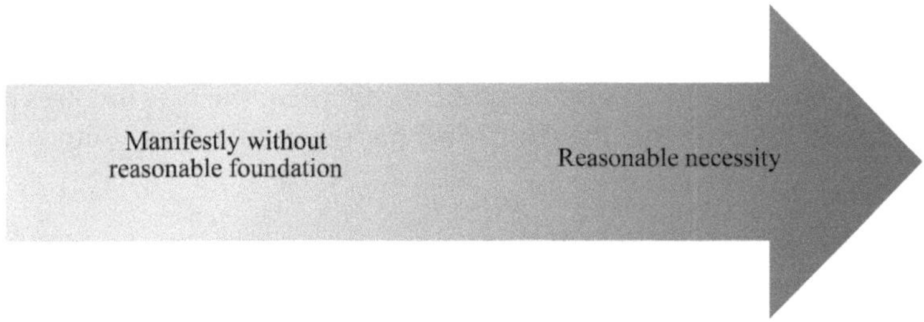

Figure 3.3 The Spectrum of Intensity of Review for Assessing Proportionality in the CFA Adjudication.

Source: Author.

considered that they were located at positions on one continuous spectrum of reasonableness, although they were differently named[226] (see Figure 3.3.).

When confronting distinct levels of intensity of review, the issue of which one should be adopted is critical. The intensity of review depends on many factors.[227] The CFA highlighted several factors for the courts to consider in determining which standard to apply, including (i) the significance of and extent of interference with the right at stake; (ii) the identity and constitutional role of decision-makers and the content and feature of the measures taken by governments;[228] (iii) the relevance of margin of appreciation.[229]

The more serious the interference with individual rights, the narrower the margin of appreciation the court will accord, and the more intense scrutiny the court will conduct. Where the impugned measures encroach on core social values or destroy the very essence of rights and where the court has expertise and constitutional duty to provide protection, the court should give narrow and even no margin of appreciation.[230] In these cases involving "fundamental rights" or "fundamental concepts", the courts will regard the restriction as disproportionate unless it fails the test of reasonable necessity.[231] These fundamental rights include freedom of expression, freedom of peaceful assembly, and rights bearing on criminal liability, such as the presumption of innocence.[232] In discrimination cases, where the discrimination is based on "suspect grounds" such as race, color, sex, or sexual orientation, the court will subject the impugned legislative and executive act to intense scrutiny.[233]

226 *Ibid.*, [122].
227 Harry Woolf and others, *De Smith's Judicial Review* (7th edn, Sweet and Maxwell 2013) 635.
228 *Hysan* (n 157) [107].
229 *Kwok Cheuk Kin* (n 118) [38].
230 *Hysan* (n 157) [113]; *Fok Chun Wa* (n 214) [81].
231 *Kong Yunming* (n 118) [40].
232 *Ibid.*
233 *Ibid.*

Where the restriction involves socio-economic policy regarding the allocation of limited public funds without restricting fundamental rights or involving discrimination not based on suspect grounds, or where the case involves political or policy considerations, the courts incline to the "manifest" standard.[234]

Intensity of the CFA's Review of Ordinance

The CFA did not hesitate to apply proportionality intensely in cases where fundamental rights were violated. According to Table 3.6, it adopted the test of reasonable necessity in eight cases (50 percent). All these cases related to fundamental rights, including the freedom of peaceful assembly,[235] the right of presumption of innocence,[236] the right to a fair trial,[237] the right to travel,[238] and discrimination on the grounds of sexual orientation.[239] There was merely one case – *Kwok Cheuk Kin* – where the CFA adopted the "manifest" standard and the case pertained to a by-election of the Legislative Council.[240] The CFA held that in the context where political judgment and prediction were concerned, due weight should be given to the legislature and the proper test was the "manifest" standard.[241]

In comparison with the TCC, the CFA adopted the high level of intensity of review more frequently. The TCC applied intermediate scrutiny and strict scrutiny in around 30.7 percent of decisions, which is lower than 50 percent. This comparison shows that when reviewing primary legislation, the CFA is not less strict than the TCC. When applying proportionality, the CFA was more likely to strike down primary legislation than the TCC (Figure 3.4).

Macau

Although the TUI affirmed the MSAR courts' competence of constitutionally reviewing laws and decrees in 2006, it demonstrated reluctance and caution in exercising this authority. It had undertaken constitutional review of laws and decrees in only 13 cases spanning from 1999 to 2019 (Table 3.7). This section examines the standards and intensity of judicial review in these cases. The analysis reveals that the TUI primarily relied on the principle of equality (five cases). Additionally, it also applied the principle of legitimate expectation (three cases) and the principle of justice (one case). The most striking finding

234 *Fok Chun Wa* (n 214) [71], [76]; *Kwok Cheuk Kin* (n 118) [42].
235 As in *Leung Kwok Hung* (n 153).
236 As in *Lam Kwong Wai* (n 121); *Hung Chan Wa* (n 175); *Ng Po On* (n 175); and *Lee To Nei* (n 175).
237 As in *Koon Wing Yee* (n 175).
238 As in *Zhi Charles* (n 118).
239 As in *Yau Yuk Lung* (n 166).
240 *Kwok Cheuk Kin* (n 118).
241 *Ibid.*, [55].

Table 3.6 Intensity of Proportionality Test in the CFA Decisions against Ordinances (1999–2019).

Intensity of Review	*Constitutional*	*Unconstitutional*	*In Total*
"Manifest" standard	Kwok Cheuk Kin v Secretary for Constitutional and Mainland Affairs (2017)		
	1		**1 (6.25%)**
Reasonable necessity		Leung Kwok Hung and Others v HKSAR (2005) HKSAR v Lam Kwong Wai and Another (2006) HKSAR v Hung Chan Wa and Another (2006) Official Receiver and Trustee in Bankruptcy of Chan Wing Hing and Another v Chan Wing Hing and Another and (Third Party) (2006) HKSAR v Ng Po On (2008) Koon Wing Yee v Insider Dealing Tribunal (2008) Lee To Nei v HKSAR (2012) Official Receiver v Zhi Charles (2015)	
	0	**8**	**8 (50%)**
Unclear	HKSAR v Ng Kung Siu and Another (1999) Solicitor v Law Society of Hong Kong (2006) So Wai Lun v HKSAR (2006) Fu Kor Kuen Patrick v HKSAR (2012)	Solicitor and Law Society of Hong Kong v Secretary for Justice ((2003) Secretary for Justice v Yau Yuk Lung (2007) Mok Charles v Tam Wai Ho (2010)	
	4	**3**	**7 (43.75%)**

Source: Author.

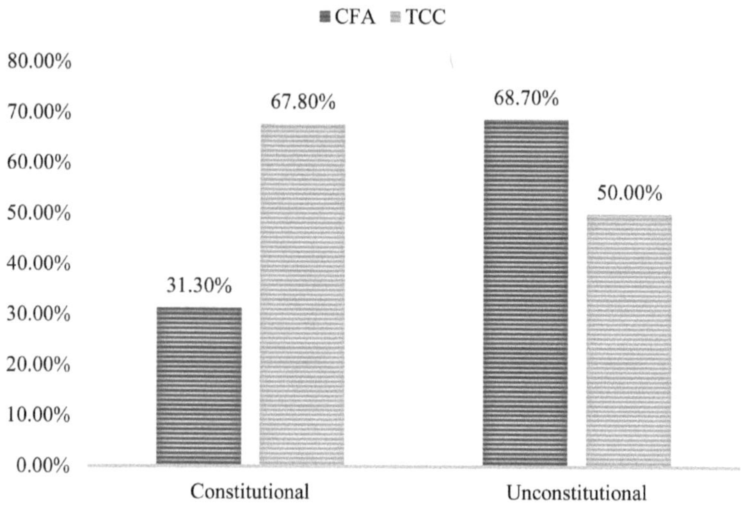

Figure 3.4 A Comparison of the Application of Proportionality in the CFA and the TCC Decisions against Primary Legislation (1999–2019).

Source: Author.

is the TCC's express refusal to apply proportionality to scrutinize laws and decrees.[242]

Principle of Equality in the TUI's Review of Laws and Decrees

In Case 5/2010, the Applicant, a secondary school teacher employed by the Education and Youth Development Bureau, contended that they faced unconstitutional discrimination regarding the calculation of service hours.[243] Decree No. 21/87/M, reading together with Decree No. 87/89/M, outlined two different methods for calculating service time: one for school teachers hired by the Education and Youth Development Bureau and another for teachers at public universities.[244] For the former group of teachers, medical leave that was less than 30 cumulative days annually was not factored into their length of service, while for the public university teachers, only the portions of medical leave exceeding 30 days were excluded from their service time. Invoking Article 25 of the MBL, the TUI stated that the principle of equality requires laws to treat like cases alike and treat unlike cases unlike.[245] In this context, the Government argued that the disparity in calculating service time was not

242 Case 112/2018, page 13.
243 Case 5/2010, page 20.
244 Case 5/2010, page 28.
245 *Ibid.*, page 31.

Table 3.7 The TUI Decisions against Primary Legislation and Standards of Review (1999–2019).

Case	*Law or Decree Reviewed*	*(Un)constitutional*	*Standards of Review*
2/2004	Article 1(3) of Decree No. 39/99/M – Civil Code	*Unconstitutional*	Unclear
5/2010	Article 5(2)(b) of Decree No. 21/87/M on Restructuring the Career Regime for Teacher of Education Bureau	*Unconstitutional*	Principle of equality
25/2011	Article 5(3) of Law No. 2/93/M on the Right to Assembly and Demonstration[a]	*Unconstitutional*	Unclear
33/2011	Article 26, 27 and 70 of Decree No. 110/99/M – Code of Administrative Litigation Procedure	Constitutional	Unclear
9/2012 19/2012 27/2012 33/2012	Article 40 of Law No. 18/2009 on Career Regime for Nurses	Constitutional	Principle of equality
23/2015	Article 123(3) of Decree No. 110/99/M – Code of Administrative Litigation Procedure	Constitutional	Principle of justice
88/2018 90/2018 102/2018	Article 48(1) of Law No. 10/2013 – Land Law	Constitutional	Principle of legitimate expectation
112/2018	Article 14, Law No. 10/2016 - Amendment to Law No. 17/2009 on Prohibition of the Illicit Production, Trafficking and Consumption of Narcotic Drugs and Psychotropic Substances	Constitutional	Unclear

Source: Author.

[a] Law 2/93/M was subsequently amended three times by Law No. 2/96/M, Law No. 16/2008, and Law No. 11/2018.

arbitrary; instead, it aimed to discourage short-term absences.[246] The TUI found this argument inadequate, as it failed to justify why short-term absences would only affect schools under the Education and Youth Development

246 *Ibid.*, page 37.

Bureau without impacting public universities.[247] Ultimately, the TUI held that Decree No. 21/87/M violated the principle of equality.[248] Thus, the decree was inapplicable to this case, and the executive decision based on it was quashed.[249]

In a group of cases where applicants challenged the constitutionality of Article 40 of Law No. 18/2009, the TUI also invoked the principle of equality.[250] In Macau, there are three ways of hiring nurses: civil servant nurses, government contract nurses, and nurses employed through an employment contract. The applicants were nurses hired through employment contracts. The Legislative Assembly passed Law No. 18/2009, which came into force on 18 August 2009 and aimed to increase nurses' salaries. According to Article 40 of this law, the salaries of civil servant nurses and government contract nurses were retroactively increased according to the new salary scales from 1 July 2007. In contrast, nurses hired via employment contracts only saw their salaries adjusted starting 18 August 2009. Therefore, nurses hired via employment contracts lost a sum of money equivalent to the difference between the two salary scales.[251] The TUI held that the differential treatment did not violate the principle of equality because the three groups of nurses were intrinsically different. After examining the relevant laws before and after the establishment of MSAR, the TUI held that the nurses hired via employment contracts had been treated differently from the civil servant nurses and government contract nurses since the colonial period. The former provides services and is paid according to the contract signed between the nurses and their employers. The latter groups are regulated according to the public service law applicable to Macau civil servants.[252] The TUI's reasoning appears contentious. The fact that nurses have been historically discriminated against is used as a justification for present unequal treatment.

Legitimate Expectation and Principle of Justice in the TUI's Review of Laws and Decrees

In March 2010, the Government of the MSAR started reviewing the implementation of land leases, and it had terminated over 70 land leases by 2020.[253]

247 *Ibid.*, page 36.

248 *Ibid.*, pages 39–40.

249 In 2010, Decree No. 21/87/M was revoked by Law No. 12/2010 on Career Regime for Teachers and Teaching Assistants in Government Non-higher Education Schools. This new law abandoned the differential treatment.

250 Cases 9/2012, 19/2012, 27/2012, 33/2012.

251 Case 9/2012, page 9.

252 *Ibid.*, page 34.

253 Commission Against Corruption of Macau, *Report on the Investigation of 74 Land Approval Files Declaring Provisional Land Leases Void* (關於74個被宣告臨時性租賃批給失效之土地審批卷宗之調查報告), available at www.ccac.org.mo/cn/news/rpt20201230_cn.pdf, accessed 12 August 2021.

A group of cases challenging these terminations were appealed to the TUI.[254] The decisions to terminate the leases were made according to the new Land Law, Law No. 10/2013, based on two grounds: first, the lessees failed to develop land in line with their leases and development plans, and second, the lease term had expired.

In Cases 88/2018, 90/2018, and 102/2018, the applicants argued inter alia that Article 48(1) of Land Law was inconsistent with Article 120 of the MBL.[255] Since the facts of these cases are similar, this book takes Case 88/2018 as an example. In this case, the Macau government granted a land lease to the applicant on 3 August 1994. Under this land lease, the applicant ought to construct a cable manufacturing factory on the land specified in the lease before 2 August 1996. But the applicant failed to implement the development plan on time. In 2016, the Chief Executive revoked the lease on the basis that provisional land leases cannot be renewed according to Article 48(1) of the Land Law (prohibition clause).[256]

The applicant claimed that revoking the leases violated the principle of legal expectation because Law No. 6/80/M (Land Law in force before the handover) did not contain any clause prohibiting the renewal of leases. Moreover, according to Article 120 of the MBL, "land leases granted or renewed before the establishment of the MSAR and extended beyond 1 December 1999, and all rights in relation to such leases must continue to be recognized and protected by the Region". The TUI held that no legitimate expectation derived from the old Land Law as the applicant claimed. On the contrary, Articles 49, 54, and 55 of the old Land Law, when read together, prevented provisional land leases from renewing in certain circumstances.[257] The TUI concluded that revoking the land concession contract did not undermine the applicant's legitimate expectation and that the new Land Law was consistent with Article 120 of the MBL.[258]

In Case 23/2015, the applicant argued that Article 123(3) of the Code of Administrative Litigation Procedure violated the principle of justice, since this provision excluded the testimony of a witness in the procedure to suspend the enforcement of administrative decisions.[259] The TUI dismissed this argument and held that no provision of the MBL prohibits the exclusion of testimonial evidence. It considered that the application for suspension of enforcement of administrative decisions should be dealt with expeditiously and the impugned

254 Including Cases 81/2016, 28/2017, 38/2017, 69/2017, 1/2018, 7/2018, 13/2018, 43/2018, 79/2018, 88/2018, 90/2018, 95/2018, 96/2018, 102/2018, 111/2018, 6/2019, 12/2019, 13/2019, 16/2019, 26/2019, 72/2019, 75/2019, and 118/2019.

255 Case 88/2018, page 8.

256 *Ibid.*, pages 3–7.

257 *Ibid.*, page 12.

258 *Ibid.*, page 13.

259 Case 23/2015, page 7.

provision was consistent with this purpose and did not seriously hamper the judicial justice.[260]

Intensity of the TUI's Review of Laws and Decrees

Overall, the TUI is more deferential than the TCC and the CFA in constitutionally scrutinizing primary legislation, evidenced by three aspects. First, in stark contrast to the TCC's and CFA's consistent application of proportionality when reviewing primary legislation, the TUI has never applied proportionality in constitutional review of laws and decrees. It even expressly declined to use proportionality to scrutinize legislative actions. In Case 112/2018, Article 14 of Law No. 10/2016 criminalized acts of unlawful cultivating, manufacturing, and possessing narcotic drugs and psychotropic substances for exclusive personal consumption if the quantity was over five times the daily reference intakes. People who violate this provision will be sentenced according to Articles 8 and 11, provisions that punish the acts of manufacturing and trafficking in narcotic drugs and psychotropic substances. Two applicants argued that Article 14 of Law No. 10/2016 was unconstitutional for encroaching on their right to be presumed innocent.[261] They claimed that this provision assumed people who possess drugs exceeding a certain amount to be drug manufacturers or drug traffickers, and the assumption could not be rebutted. The TUI dismissed their claims and gave the following reasons:

> The provision imposes harsher penalties for drug use when the quantity of drugs in possession is larger. This is a choice made by the legislature, which is not prohibited by the Basic Law and is not subject to courts' judgment. *The disproportionality of a discretionary action by executive authorities is a ground for annulment by the courts. But this (the disproportionality) does not apply to legislative actions.*[262]

This decision revealed itself as an unfortunate decision for constitutional review in Macau. Proportionality has been an impartial element of the "global model of constitutional rights"[263] and the rule of law.[264] It is widely employed by courts to review the legislation to safeguard individual rights. The TUI voluntarily diminished its essential role in safeguarding the constitutionality of legislation and protecting individual rights by rejecting a more rigorous standard of review that favors human rights protection.

260 *Ibid.*
261 Case 112/2018, page 13.
262 *Ibid.* (emphasis added).
263 Kai Möller, *The Global Model of Constitutional Rights* (OUP 2012).
264 David M. Beatty, *The Ultimate Rule of Law* (OUP 2003); Stone Sweet and Mathews, *Proportionality Balance and Constitutional Governance* (n 10) 1; Vicki C. Jackson, 'Constitutional Law in An Age of Proportionality' (2015) 124 *Yale Law Journal* 3094.

Second, the TUI has demonstrated a notably deferential approach to equal protection. Both the TCC and the CFA admit the principle of equality has two dimensions – formal equality and substantive equality – and they have consistently applied the substantive equality. However, the TUI predominantly relied on formal equality. In the school teachers case, the TUI considered school teachers employed by the Education and Youth Development Bureau the same as teachers at public universities; thus, their service hours ought to be calculated according to the same rules. In the nurse cases, the non-civil service nurses were regulated by different systems so that their salary adjustment rules could be different.

The TUI repeated its opinion that the scope of the principle of equality contains a prohibition of arbitrariness: no different treatment without justification.[265] When the legislation does not have adequate proper justifications for differential treatment, the principle of equality is violated from the perspective of prohibition of arbitrariness.[266] On the other hand, the TUI emphasized that the prohibition of arbitrariness determines the limits of judicial review.[267] Although the legislature is bound by the principle of equality, they still enjoy legislative freedom.[268] The courts only make a "negative judgment" in judicial review,[269] The TUI articulated the "negative judgment":

> The supervision of the validity of legislation is based on the provisions of the Basic Law. It is crucial to bear in mind that the relevant institutions [here is the judiciary] should not make "positive judgments" on the solution prescribed by law. In other words, when making judgments, the supervisory institutions [the judiciary] ought not to replace the legislature to second-guess the reasonableness of legal solutions on the grounds of "reasonable", "just", or "ideal". Constitutional review authority cannot go that far: they should conduct a "negative" judgment, which means removing a legal solution that, in all respects, cannot be considered reasonable[270]

Bearing this deferential attitude in mind, the TUI stated that when applying the principle of equality, the courts could only invalidate legislation that results in manifest and intolerable inequality without any justification, objectivity, or rationality.[271]

Lastly, the TUI's deferential attitude in judicial review of legislation is seen in Case 2/2004 and Case 25/2011, where the TUI found inconsistency

265 Case 5/2010, page 32; Case 9/2012, page 35.
266 Case 5/2010, page 32.
267 Case 5/2010, page 35; Case 9/2012, page 37.
268 Case 5/2010, page 32; Case 9/2012, page 35.
269 Case 5/2010, page 34; Case 9/2012, page 37.
270 Case 5/2010, page 34; Case 9/2012, page 37.
271 Case 5/2010, page 35; Case 9/2012, page 37.

between legislative provisions and the MBL but did not declare them unconstitutional. In Case 2/2004, Article 1(3) of the Civil Code provided that international conventions applicable to Macau prevail over domestic laws. The TUI held that no norm could confer another norm status superior to itself. Only the constitution could confer on international treaties status superior to legislation.[272] Instead of declaring Article 1(3) of the Civil Code unconstitutional, the TUI concluded that "Article 1(3) of the Civil Code is an expression of goodwill of ordinary legislators. For the purpose of adjudicating this case, this provision is meaningless".[273]

In Case 25/2011, the text of Article 5(4) of Law No. 2/93/M on the Right to Assembly and Demonstration stipulated that any notice of intention to hold an assembly must bear the signatures of three organizers. The applicant submitted a notice with only one signatory, leading to the rejection of the submission.[274] The applicant challenged that Article 5(4) of Law No. 2/93/M encroached on the right to assembly and demonstration and argued that one or two individuals could exercise this right alone.[275] The TUI admitted that the MBL did not contain a requirement of the minimum number of persons for mounting an assembly and demonstration. It held that if reading the text of Article 5(4) literally, this provision contradicts the MBL and is hence inapplicable. Instead of striking down the restriction, the TUI adopted a remedial interpretation to render the impugned provision consistent with the MBL, that the maximum number of signatories of a notice of intention to hold assemblies is three.[276]

Conclusion

This chapter has investigated the standards and intensity of judicial review in cases decided by three apex courts against primary legislation. It finds that the TCC and the CFA are far more active and intrusive in scrutinizing primary legislation than the TUI, which is timid and deferential in this regard.

Both the TCC and the CFA are intrusive in reviewing primary legislation by using proportionality and the principle of equality. They were confident and fearless in declaring legislation unconstitutional on the grounds of these two standards. In the TCC's decisions against statutes, the principles of proportionality and equality were the most frequently applied standards of review. By the two standards of review, the TCC conducted substantive reviews and struck down statutes in half of the cases. The CFA also often relied on proportionality to review ordinances (16 out of 34 cases) and declared the

272 Case 2/2004, page 6.
273 *Ibid.*, page 7.
274 Case 25/2011, page 2.
275 *Ibid.*, page 2.
276 *Ibid.*, page 6.

impugned ordinances unconstitutional in 11 cases by this standard of review. Additionally, both the TCC and the CFA developed varying levels of intensity of review for proportionality and equality. Since 2007, a trend of increase in the reliance on the intermediate and high levels of intensity of review has been seen in the TCC's decisions. The CFA developed a spectrum of intensity for the proportionality test, including the test of reasonable necessity and the "manifest" standard. In practice, the CFA was not timid in applying proportionality intensely, particularly where fundamental rights were engaged.

Standing in stark contrast to the TCC and the CFA, the TUI only reviewed primary legislation in 13 cases between 1999 and 2019. It has never applied proportionality to review laws and decrees. Moreover, it expressly refused to apply proportionality to scrutinize legislation. The TUI applied the principle of equality, but it is confined to a formal equality review. The TUI explicitly stated its deferential attitude towards judicial review that the courts should play a "passive" role and make negative judgment in judicial review. It would only invalidate legislation that results in manifest and intolerable inequality without any justification, objectivity, or rationality.

At this stage, this book could draw a spectrum of judicial activism/deference for the TCC, the CFA, and the TUI about their constitutional review of primary legislation. The TCC and the CFA have converged and assumed a position on the activism side, while the TUI takes a place on the deferential side. The subsequent chapters will continue to examine the judicial activism and deference among the four apex courts in their judicial review of government actions, including administrative rules and concrete administrative decisions.

4 Judicial Review of Administrative Rules

Introduction

The preceding chapter examined the standards and intensity of review against primary legislation. This chapter will continue comparing the courts' activism and deference by shifting the focus to judicial review of administrative rules. It will address the following questions: what standards of review have these courts applied to review administrative rules? How did they apply them? And how rigorously did they scrutinize administrative rules?

Recalling Chapter 2, all four apex courts of Greater China have jurisdiction over administrative rules. But in China and Macau, the SPC and the TUI are inactive in reviewing administrative rules. Besides the procedural obstacles, such as individuals cannot challenge administrative rules without petitions against concrete administrative decisions (China) and individuals cannot request an abstract review unless the courts have deemed an administrative rule provision unlawful on three separate occasions (Macau), the SPC's and the TUI's reluctance to review administrative rules also explains the small portion of cases against administrative rules despite the high volume of administrative litigation cases. Even when the SPC entertains appeals against administrative rules, it typically limits its review to the textual differences between the impugned rules and superior laws, rarely engaging with the substance of the rules. By contrast, the TCC and the CFA adopted a more assertive stance in reviewing administrative rules.

The main standards deployed by these four courts were divergent. Specifically, the SPC frequently employed the standard of contravening superior laws, which appeared in seven out of ten cases against administrative rules. The TCC made a large number of interpretations (138 interpretations) against administrative rules and deployed the principle of statutory reservation in approximately 72.5 percent of the cases, serving as a pillar standard for reviewing administrative rules. The CFA, on the other hand, invoked proportionality in seven out of eight cases and "prescribed by law" in four cases. The TUI reviewed administrative rules in merely two cases and declared the impugned rules illegal on the grounds of contravening superior laws and not being prescribed by law.

DOI: 10.4324/9781003482536-4

Notably, the four courts have distinct attitudes toward the application of proportionality in the judicial review of administrative rules. In China, the SPC once enabled the courts to review the proportionality of administrative normative documents in Minutes 2004. However, it excluded proportionality in the list of standards of review when promulgating the ALL Interpretation of 2018. Proportionality did not emerge in these Guiding cases and Gazette cases. Likewise, the TUI did not employ proportionality in cases against administrative rules. It is not imprudent to speculate that it will not deploy this standard in the future because it has explicitly refused proportionality for reviewing legislative actions 112/2018, which was discussed in Chapter 3. In the TCC's jurisprudence, proportionality is the pillar standard for reviewing primary legislation. However, this is not the case for the judicial review of administrative rules, where the principle of statutory reservation is the predominant standard of review. Among the four apex courts, only the CFA still relied mainly on proportionality in reviewing administrative rules.

In terms of the intensity of review, the TCC and the CFA were stricter in reviewing administrative rules than the SPC and the TUI. The TCC developed varying levels of intensity of review for the principle of statutory reservation and adopted the intermediate-level and the high-level intensity of review in over 70 percent of the cases, indicating the TCC's stringent attitude toward the government's rule-making power. Furthermore, the TCC extended its review to the content of administrative rules by applying standards such as proportionality and equal protection. The CFA placed particular emphasis on the proportionality of restrictions on rights. When applying proportionality, the CFA adopted the standard of reasonable necessity to scrutinize restrictions on freedom of expression and discrimination on the grounds of sexual orientation, and it employed the "manifest" standard to restrictions on socio-economic rights. This was consistent with its practice and jurisprudence on the judicial review of ordinances. The CFA's application of the "prescribed by law" principle differs from that of the TCC. The CFA paid little attention to whether the restrictions on rights and freedoms take the form of an ordinance or not. It placed its focus on the accessibility and precision of the restrictions on rights and freedoms.

This chapter is divided into six parts. Part 1 is an introduction. From Part 2 to Part 5, each part details one apex court's standards and intensity of judicial review of administrative rules. Part 6 is a summary of the main findings of this chapter.

China

Recalling Chapter 2, the SPC confirmed Chinese courts' competence to review rules (*guizhang*) and administrative normative documents (ANDs) in Minutes 2004, and the amendment to the ALL in 2014 further explicitly granted individuals the right to challenge ANDs in administrative litigation.[1] In practice, however, judicial review against administrative rules has been less frequently carried out than expected, which is evidenced by the relatively small number of cases in contrast to a huge number of cases against government decisions. According to the SPC's national statistics, from January 2016 to October 2018, over 650,000 administrative litigations were filed nationwide, of which approximately 3,880 cases, or about 0.6% of all cases, involved petitions against administrative rules.[2] Gazette cases and Guiding cases included in this book also reflect this inactive judicial practice. The SPC Gazette and Guiding cases included 92 administrative litigation cases, and only 10 involved scrutinizing administrative rules. In these cases, contravening superior laws was the most frequently applied standard (Table 4.1).

Regarding the intensity of review of administrative rules, the Chinese courts have been significantly deferential to their governments. Besides the courts' various strategies deployed to avoid reviewing administrative rules, it is evident in four aspects. First, the reasonableness and proportionality of administrative rules are beyond the courts' purview. In China, the SPC initially allowed courts to review the reasonableness and proportionality of ANDs through Minutes 2004. However, in the SPC ALL Interpretation of 2018, reasonableness and proportionality were notably excluded from the list of review standards. Second, when applying the standard contravening superior laws, the courts usually focused on the textual difference between the impugned rules and superior laws, with little attention paid to the substance of impugned provisions. Third, the standard of violating people's rights did not emerge in the decisions against administrative rules. Fourth, the standard violating rule-making procedures has never been employed as this standard is potent enough to render the whole administrative rule invalid.

Refusal to Review the Reasonableness and Proportionality of Administrative Rules

The ALL of 2014 entitled Chinese citizens to challenge the legality of ANDs.[3] But it does not specify the grounds of challenge and review. To fill this gap, the SPC issued the ALL Interpretation of 2018, where it listed several grounds for judicial review of ANDs, which are also applicable to the judicial review of rules. These grounds are as follows:

(1) Making ANDs in excess of statutory authority or the delegation granted by superior laws, including legislation, regulations, and rules;

1 See Chapter 2.
2 Haibo He (何海波), 'Court's Collateral Review of Normative Document' (论法院对规范性文件的附带审查) (2021) 3 *China Legal Science* (中国法学) 139, 140.
3 Administrative Litigation Law (ALL) (行政诉讼法), art 53.

Table 4.1 Judicial Review Cases against Rules and ANDs (1999–2019).

Case	*Year*	*Series Number / Gazette Issues*	*Rules and ANDs under Review*	*(Il)Legal*	*Standard of Review*
Tian Yong v The University of Science and Technology Beijing	1999	No. 38 1999(4)	Emergency Notice on Strict Administration of Examinations	Illegal	Contradicting superior laws
Fengxiang Company v The Salt Affairs Bureau of Shanghai Municipality	2002	2003(1)	Several Provisions of Salt Management of Shanghai Municipality	Illegal	Contradicting superior laws
Lu Tingzuo v The Housing and Land Management Bureau of Zhabei District, Shanghai Municipality	2006	2007(8)	Detailed Implementing Rules of Demolition and Management of Urban House of Shanghai Municipality	Legal	Contradicting superior laws
He Xiaoqiang v Huazhong University of Science and Technology	2009	No. 39	Detailed Implementation Rules of Bachelor's Degree Conferment on Undergraduates of Huazhong University of Science and Technology Wuchang Campus	Legal	Contradicting superior laws
Shanghai Dike Paper Packaging Co., Ltd v The Human Resources and Social Security Bureau of Shanghai Municipality	2009	2013(11)	Several Opinions of the Ministry of Labor on the Implementation of the Labor Law, art 1	Legal	Contradicting superior laws
Luwei (Fujian) Salt Industry Import and Export Co., Ltd. Suzhou Branch v The Salt Administration Bureau of Suzhou Municipality	2011	No. 5	Implementing Rules of Jiangsu Province on the Salt Industry Administration Regulation, art 42	Illegal	In excess of power

(*Continued*)

Table 4.1 (Continued)

Case	*Year*	*Series Number / Gazette Issues*	*Rules and ANDs under Review*	*(Il)Legal*	*Standard of Review*
Gan Lu v Jinan University	2011	2012(7)	Interim Provisions of Jinan University concerning Students affairs, art 53(5) Detailed Implementing Rules of Jinan University for Disciplinary Rules, art 25	Legal	Contradicting superior laws
Chen Aihua v The Housing and Urban-Rural Construction Bureau of Jiangning District, Nanjing Municipality	2013	2014(8)	Joint Notice of the Ministry of Justice and the Ministry of Construction on Enhancing Notarization in Housing Registration Management	Illegal	Illegally imposing obligation
Hongrun Supermarket v The Market Inspection and Management Bureau of Danyang Municipality	2015	2018(6)	Administrative Normative Document No. [2012] 29 of the People's Government of Danyang Municipality	Illegal	Contradicting superior laws
Cui Longshu v Feng County People's Government	2017	2017(11)	Notice on Circulation of Preferential Policy of Feng County on Business Invitation and Fundraising; Interpretations on Several Provisions of the Notice on Circulation of Preferential Policy of Feng County on Business Invitation and Fundraising	Legal Illegal	Principle of good faith

Source: Author.

(2) Contradicting superior laws;
(3) Imposing additional obligations on people or restricting people's rights and interests, without any basis in superior laws;
(4) Violating ANDs-making procedural rules;
(5) Other situations that violate laws, regulations, or rules.[4]

In the Minutes 2004, the SPC confirmed that the courts could review *the legality of rules* as well as *the legality, validity, reasonableness, and proportionality of ANDs.*[5] However, the ALL of 2014 and the ALL Interpretation of 2018 only refer to "illegal", omitting any mention of "unreasonable" or "disproportionate". In the Chinese legal context, "legality" means formal legality, a concept that contrasts with the substantive reasonableness and proportionality of governmental actions.[6] A literal and narrow interpretation of the ALL and the ALL Interpretation of 2018 will result in a constrained judicial review. Some scholars have suggested interpreting "illegal" generously so as to extend judicial review to the substantive reasonableness and proportionality of administrative rules.[7] However, in *He Xiaoqiang v Huazhong University of Science and Technology*, the SPC established a tone of deferential scrutiny toward administrative rules, emphasizing that legality review is a fundamental principle of judicial review of administrative rules.[8]

In this case, the respondent university refused to grant the appellant a bachelor's degree because he did not pass College English Test (Band Four).[9] The impugned AND, the Detailed Implementation Rules of Bachelor's Degree Conferment on Undergraduates of Huazhong University of Science and Technology Wuchang Campus, included College English Test (Band Four) as one of the prerequisites for granting undergraduate degrees. The appellant brought the case to the court and challenged the AND. The SPC stated:

> Each higher education institution determines its measuring standards for the requisite academic levels for undergraduate degrees…(which) is a specific manifestation of the principle of academic autonomy…Judicial

4 The Interpretation of the SPC on the Application of the Administrative Litigation Law (SPC ALL Interpretation of 2018) (最高人民法院关于适用《中华人民共和国行政诉讼法》的解释), art 148(2) (2018)
5 Minutes of the Symposiums of the Supreme People's Court concerning Application of Laws in Adjudicating Administrative Cases (Minutes 2004) (关于审理行政案件适用法律规范问题的座谈纪要) s 1 (2004).
6 Jianfu Chen, *Chinese Law: Context and Transformation* 248 (Brill 2008).
7 Qi Yu (余祺), 'Authority of Normative Document and Various Levels of Intensity of Judicial Review' (规范性文件的权威性与司法审查的不同层次) (2016) *Administrative Law Review* (行政法学研究) 51, 52.
8 SPC Guiding Case No. 39.
9 Decisions made by universities are considered executive actions and are subject to judicial review. Wei Cui, Jie Cheng, and Dominika Wiesner, 'Judicial Review of Government Actions in China' (2019) *China Perspectives* 35, 37.

review of the conferral of bachelor's degrees must not interfere with or influence the principle of higher education institutions' academic autonomy. Legality review should be the basic principle of judicial review of education institutions' act of conferring degrees.[10]

As the following case studies demonstrate, judicial review of administrative rules is predominantly confined to a formal legality review. Standards of substantive review, such as reasonableness and proportionality, did not appear in any SPC Guiding cases and Gazette cases against rules and ANDs.[11]

Standards in Judicial Review of Administrative Rules

According to Table 4.1, four standards of review were employed in the ten cases against rules and ANDs, namely, contravening superior laws (seven cases), making rules in excess of power (one case), acting in bad faith (one case), and imposing obligations on people (one case). This part details the application of these standards.

Contravening Superior Laws – Linchpin Standard of Review

Contravening superior laws is undoubtedly the linchpin standard of review in Gazette cases and Guiding cases against administrative rules. Research examining a larger number of cases supports this finding. Wang and Yi's research randomly selected 947 judicial decisions by all levels of courts and found that the courts deployed the standard of contravening superior laws to review ANDs in 99 percent of cases.[12]

When courts apply this standard, they usually adopt one approach: comparing the textual differences between the impugned provisions and the relevant superior laws and then concluding whether the impugned provision contradicts superior laws.[13] The comparison of textual differences is mechanical. This approach appears to be the courts' strategy to prevent their decisions from

10 *He Xiaoqiang* (n 8).

11 Some assertive judges applied proportionality and reasonableness in their adjudications, which is rare. Chao Lu (卢超), 'Judicial Predicament and Cohesive Function of Normative Documents Incidental Review' (规范性文件附带审的司法困境及其枢纽功能) (2020) 3 *Journal of Comparative Law* (比较法研究) 127, 137.

12 Guohua Wang (王国华) and Qingqing Yi (易清清), 'Empirical Study of Judicial Review Administrative Normative Instrument: A Study based on 947 Judgements' (行政规范性文件附带审查的实证分析 – 以947份裁判文书为样本) (2019) *Law and Modernisation* (法治现代化研究) 28, 35–39.

13 Cheng Li (李成), 'Judicial Construction of the Approach to Normative Documents Incidental Review' (行政规范性文件附带审查进路的司法构建) (2018) *The Jurist* (法学家) 61, 68; Ting Zhang (张婷), 'The Constitutional Propositions and Unfolding of Administrative Litigation Incidental Review' (行政诉讼附带审查的宪法命题及其展开) (2018) *Legal Forum* (法学论坛) 120, 123.

being overturned by superior courts and avoid criticism from the government, indicating the court's cautious attitude in reviewing administrative rules. After all, conspicuous violations of superior legal provisions or glaring inconsistency are the most moderate grounds to declare an administrative rule unlawful. Rarely do the courts delve deeply into the substantive content of the relevant laws. Empirical research indicates that, in most decisions against administrative rules, the courts do not give adequate justifications for their conclusions.[14] This adheres to a long-lasting political dogma among Chinese judges – "the less you say, the fewer mistakes you make".[15]

In the seven cases examined in this book, the courts declared the impugned provisions inconsistent with superior laws in three cases. All these impugned provisions patently contradict superior laws. Take *Tian Yong v The University of Science and Technology Beijing* as an example.[16] This case was published in the SPC Gazette in 1999 and later selected as a Guiding case in 2014. Tian Yong was an undergraduate student at the University of Science and Technology Beijing. An examination invigilator caught him carrying a note with electromagnetic formulas in an examination in February 1996 and stopped him from continuing the examination. According to No. 068 Emergency Notice on Strict Administration of Examinations, if students cheat on examinations, the university will terminate their university placement. The University decided to terminate Tian Yong's studies but failed to deliver the decision to him. Tian Yong continued his studies and passed all course examinations and satisfied the prerequisites for an undergraduate degree. However, the University refused to grant him an undergraduate degree because his studies had been terminated. Tian Yong brought a case before the court against the University. Regarding the validity of No. 068 Notice, the court held:

> Higher education institutions have the corresponding educational autonomy in accordance with the law. They have the right to issue rules and regulations to manage teaching and discipline for students. However, these school rules, regulations, and disciplinary actions must comply with the provisions of laws, regulations, and rules, and must respect and protect the legal rights and interests of the parties involved. In this case, the plaintiff carried notes during an examination, constituting a violation of examination discipline. The defendant is competent to handle this matter according to relevant laws, regulations, rules, and their provisions. However, the decision to expel the plaintiff based on the school's Notice

14 Xiaohui Xue (薛小惠), 'Solution to the Dilemma in the Implementation of Incidental Review of Administrative Normative Documents – An Observation on Typical Cases of the Supreme People's Court' (行政规范性文件附带审查制度实施困境的解决之道 – 基于最高人民法院典型案例的观察) (2020) Journal of Shandong University of Science and Technology (Social Science) (山东科技大学学报(社会科学版)) 61, 65.

15 Wang and Yi (n 12), 41.

16 SPC Guiding Case No. 38, SPC Gazette 1999(4).

> No. 068, which conflicts with the statutory rules for expulsion stipulated in Article 29 of the Regulations on the Administration of Students in Regular Higher Education Institutions, making the defendant's expulsion decision illegal.[17]

The superior law, Article 29 of the Regulations on the Administration of Students in Regular Higher Education Institutions, stipulates serious situations under which the universities can withdraw students from their studies. Cheating on an examination is not on the list. The court held that No. 068 Notice contradicted a superior rule by expanding the punishable actions.

Making Rules in Excess of Power

In *Luwei (Fujian) Salt Industry Import and Export Co., Ltd. Suzhou Branch v The Salt Administration Bureau of Suzhou Municipality*[18], the respondent made an administrative punishment decision against the plaintiff on the grounds that the plaintiff purchased and transported industrial salt but did not obtain a license from the government. This license was created by Articles 23, 32(2), and 42 of the Implementing Rules of Jiangsu Province on the Salt Industry Administration Regulation (Implementing Rules). The court found that the Salt Industry Administration Regulation, which is superior to the Implementing Rules, did not require a license for industrial salt transportation. The Implementing Rules could not introduce a new license or impose punishments for failing to obtain such a license because the Administrative Licensing Law and the Administrative Penalty Law prohibited local government from creating new licenses or imposing new penalties .[19] As a result, the court refused to apply the Implementing Rules and quashed the administrative punishment decision.

Acting in Bad Faith

In *Cui Longshu v Feng County People's Government*,[20] the High Court of Jiangsu Province rendered an AND invalid on the grounds of acting in bad faith. In this case, the respondent, the People's Government of Feng County, publicized a notice committing to reward individuals for introducing investments to the area. The plaintiff successfully facilitated an investment by a company from Chongqing in local sewage treatment facilities. However, the government refused to pay the promised reward. The plaintiff brought the case before the Intermediate Court of Xuzhou Municipality. During the trial, the respond-

17 *Ibid.*
18 Guiding Case No. 5.
19 Administrative Licensing Law, arts 15(1), 16(3); Administrative Penalty Law, art 13.
20 SPC Gazette 2017(11).

ent issued an Interpretation of the Notice, which restricted "investments" to those made by "foreign companies or local companies", thereby disqualifying the investment from Chongqing. The Intermediate Court dismissed the plaintiff's claims based on this Interpretation of the Notice. The plaintiff then appealed to the High Court Jiangsu Province. The High Court held that the Interpretation of the Notice had no binding force on the courts. It further determined that the government's narrow interpretation of "investment" was an attempt to evade its obligations and an abuse of administrative power, violating the principle of good faith. Consequently, the High Court ordered the government to pay the reward to the plaintiff as stipulated in the original notice.

It is noted that this principle is not listed in Article 148 of the ALL Interpretation of 2018. The introduction of the principle and the inclusion of this case in the SPC Gazette shows, to some extent, the SPC's support of judicial innovation and activism.

Creating New Obligations

In *Chen Aihua v The Housing and Urban-Rural Construction Bureau of Jiangning District, Nanjing Municipality*,[21] Cao Zhenlin bequeathed his house and assets to the plaintiff in a will. The respondent, the Housing and Urban-Rural Construction Bureau, refused to transfer the house into the plaintiff's name, citing the lack of a notarized will. The respondent submitted that it made the decision according to Article 2 of the Joint Notice of the Ministry of Justice and the Ministry of Construction on Strengthening Notarization in the Administration of Housing Property Registration, which required wills to be notarized for real estate transactions. The Court of Jiangning District, Nanjing Municipality, found that neither the Property Law, the Succession Law, nor the Housing Registration Measure mandated notarized wills for property transfers. The Court held that the Joint Notice was illegal and contradicted superior laws, as it imposed an additional obligation on individuals beyond the existing rules.

The Intensity of Judicial Review of Administrative Rules

Unlike the TCC and the CFA, which have developed spectra of intensity of review for some standards of judicial review, the Chinese courts have neither established levels of intensity of review nor offered explanations regarding the contexts and factors that influence the rigor of their review. The discussion about intensity of review is notably absent in their decisions. Despite that, their markedly deferential stance in reviewing administrative rules is evident.

21 SPC Gazette 2014(8).

First, Chinese courts are reluctant to scrutinize rules and ANDs, which accounts for the small caseload.[22] Although the decisions included in this book do not show the grounds for refusal to review administrative rules, some research revealed that the courts avoided judicial reviews on various grounds, including claiming there is no connection between impugned administrative rules and concrete executive decisions, asserting the court's lack of jurisdiction over the documents jointly promulgated by governments and the CCP organs, and citing the absence of relevant superior law.[23] The first and primary task of Chinese administrative litigations is to check the legality of concrete executive action and to solve disputes between individuals and the administrative authorities. Judicial review of administrative rules is deliberately designed to be subordinate and collateral, which may act as a disincentive for courts to engage in the judicial review of administrative rules.[24]

Second, the courts decline to review whether the impugned rules and ANDs are reasonable and proportionate. They instead rely mainly on the standard of contravening superior laws. Reasonableness and proportionality, as standards of review, are more invasive than complying with superior laws. The former group of standards of review involves a normative comparison between individual rights and public interest pursued by impugned measures.[25] In such a normative context, the courts attribute values to competing rights and interests and make value and morality judgments, which give the courts considerable discretion.[26] However, the concept of reasonableness and proportionality are excluded from the court's purview in their review of rules and ANDs.

Third, as demonstrated above, contracting the superior laws is the most frequently employed standard of review against administrative rules. The courts usually favor the impugned provisions unless there are evident violations of superior legal provisions or glaring inconsistencies. If they cannot identify a superior legal provision directly relevant to the impugned one, they either reject review requests or uphold the impugned provision.[27]

Fourth, the standard of violating people's rights has been conspicuously absent in decisions challenging administrative rules. One key reason is that the Constitution of the PRC is not justiciable, meaning its provisions, including those concerning human rights, cannot be directly invoked in court. This non-justiciability poses a significant obstacle for Chinese courts in assessing whether administrative rules infringe upon individuals' rights.

Lastly, the Chinese courts have largely refrained from applying the standards of violating rule-making procedures, despite its potency. This standard

22 Lu (n 11) 128–129.
23 *Ibid.*; Wang and Yi (n 12) 35–37.
24 Li (n 13) 65.
25 Niels Petersen, *Proportionality and Judicial Activism: Fundamental Rights Adjudication in Canada, Germany and South Africa* (CUP 2017) 38.
26 *Ibid.*, 39.
27 Wang and Yi (n 12) 44.

is powerful because a court's declaration that an administrative rule violates procedural requirements could invalidate the entire document.[28] Some scholars have even argued that the courts should not engage in reviewing the rule-making process,[29] contending that China's lack of a uniform administrative procedure law leaves courts without a clear procedural framework to assess the legitimacy of rule promulgation.[30] Additionally, the legality of administrative rules is already confirmed through the recording and review procedure conducted by the people's congress standing committees, which the courts should respect.[31] However, those arguments are untenable. Article 148 of the 2018 Interpretation of the Administrative Litigation Law (ALL) explicitly lists the violation of rule-making procedures as a standard for judicial review. Courts are indeed empowered to examine the rule-making process, and while there is no uniform procedural standard at the national level, procedural rules promulgated by provincial governments or people's congresses do exist.[32] These rules provide a framework within which courts can assess the legality of rule-making procedures.

Taiwan

In addition to constitutional review of statutes, reviewing the constitutionality of administrative rules is another essential part of the TCC's undertaking. Between 1999 and 2019, the TCC reviewed administrative rules in 138 interpretations, considerably more than the other three apex courts. This section examines the standards and intensity of review in these decisions.

The first and most striking finding is that unlike the predominance of proportionality in the review of statutes, the principle of statutory reservation is the pillar standard in the decisions against administrative rules. The TCC deployed the principle of statutory reservation in 100 out of 138 cases (approximately 72.5 percent) (Figure 4.1). When the TCC reviewed the constitutionality of administrative rules, it paid adequate attention to assess whether the restrictions on rights and freedoms are stipulated by statutes and whether the legislators explicitly grant executive authority power with clear and precise delegation to promulgate administrative rules. Once an administrative rule passed this statutory reservation test, its substance is still subject to scrutiny by principles of proportionality and equality, which emerged in only 21 and 23 cases, respectively.

28 Lu (n 11) 135.
29 Zhang (n 13) 125.
30 Lu (n 11) 135.
31 Zhang (n 13) 125.
32 E.g. Provisions on the Promulgation and Recording of Administrative Normative Documents in Yunnan Province (云南省行政规范性文件制定和备案办法) Provisions on the Administration of Administrative Normative Documents of Guangdong Province (广东省行政规范性文件管理规定); Provisions on the Administration of Administrative Normative Documents of Zhejiang Province (浙江省行政规范性文件管理规定); etc.

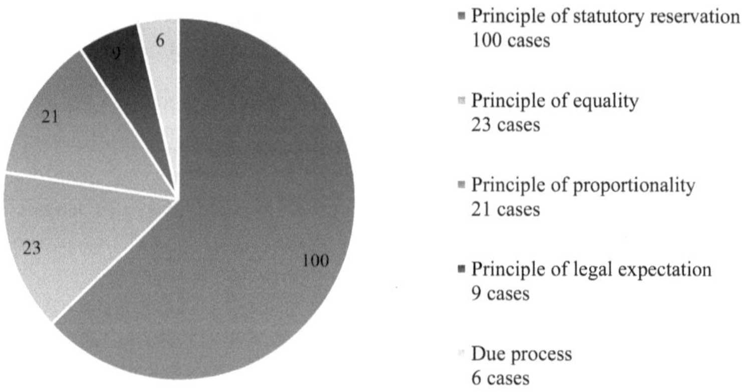

Figure 4.1 The Main Standards of Review in J.Y. Interpretations against Administrative Rules (1999–2019).

Source: Author.

The TCC developed varying intensity of review for the principle of statutory reservation, comprising of three levels, depending on the subject matters. In the last two decades, the TCC adopted the intermediate-level and high-level intensity of review in around 70 percent of the cases and struck down the impugned administrative rules in over 40 percent of the cases (Table 4.2). It shows that the TCC was stringent when assessing whether the executive

Table 4.2 Application of the Principle of Statutory Reservation in J.Y. Interpretations against Administrative Rules (1999–2019).[a]

	J.Y. Interpretations	*Total Interpretations*
Constitutional	480, 481, 493, 497, 500, 501, 506, 508, 510, 511, 519, 526, 530, 536, 537, 538, 539, 547, 548, 555, 561, 565, 571, 575, 593, 597, 598, 600, 606, 607, 608, 611, 612, 614, 615, 626, 628, 629, 635, 643, 648, 651, 660, 671, 676, 682, 685, 693, 697, 698, 700, 710, 715, 738, 745, 746, 750, 753, 779, 785	60 (60%)
Unconstitutional	478, 479, 492, 505, 514, 524, 532, 562, 566, 567, 568, 570, 581, 586, 598, 602, 609, 619, 620, 622, 638, 640, 650, 657, 658, 661, 674, 692, 703, 705, 706, 707, 710, 711, 723, 724, 730, 734, 739, 756, 765, 778	42 (42%)

Source: Author.

[a] The figures in the column "Total Interpretations" add up to 102 instead of 100 because, in these underlined cases, the TCC affirmed the invalidity of some provisions and the validity of other provisions.

agencies have authority to make administrative rules and whether they act in excess of their authority. By contrast, the TCC appeared deferential when applying the principles of proportionality and equality in judicial review of administrative rules. The TCC adopted intermediate scrutiny in only 4 out of 46 cases (8.7 percent) and did not use strict scrutiny. In more than half of the cases, the intensity of review was unclear.

Principle of Statutory Reservation in the TCC's Judicial Review of Administrative Rules

Article 23 of the Constitution of Taiwan provides that "All the freedoms and rights enumerated in the preceding articles should not be restricted by law except such as is necessary to prevent infringement upon the freedoms of other persons, to avert an imminent crisis, to maintain social order, or to advance public welfare". Besides proportionality, this provision contains another constitutional limitation of the restrictions on rights and freedoms: the principle of statutory reservation, a doctrine commonly used in Taiwan and other civil law jurisdictions.[33]

The core of the principle of statutory reservation is that only statutes enacted by legislatures can impose restrictions on constitutional rights.[34] In other words, the restrictions on constitutional rights should not arise simply from administrative actions.[35] In addition to restrictions on constitutional rights,[36] the Constitution of Taiwan reserves the exclusive legislative powers of the Legislative Yuan over taxation,[37] election and referendum,[38] and claiming compensation from the state.[39] But restrictions on rights and freedoms are a genetic and core area of the Legislative Yuan's exclusive legislative powers.[40]

The logic of the principle of statutory reservation is present when a constitution or a bill of rights guarantees a series of individual rights, in the first step, then empowers the legislature to restrict these rights by means of a clause such as "these rights can only be limited by law", in the second step.[41] Chapter II of

33 Grand Justice Tieh-Cheng Liu stated that, to comply with Article 23 of the Constitution of Taiwan, a valid restriction on people's rights must satisfy three conditions: (1) it is imposed for the purpose of protecting public interest; (2) it is stipulated by statutes; (3) it is necessary. J.Y. Interpretation No. 236 (dissenting opinion of Grand Justice Tieh-Cheng Liu).

34 Tzong-Li Hsu (許宗力), *Law and State Power* (法與國家權力) (Angle Publishing 1999) 118.

35 Vitalino Canas, 'The General Regime of Fundamental Rights in the Basic Law and in the International Instruments' in Jorge Oliveira and Paulo Cardinal (eds), *One Country Two Systems, Three Legal Orders – Perspectives of Evolution* (Springer 2009) 669.

36 Constitution of Taiwan (中華民國憲法), art 23.

37 *Ibid.*, art 19.

38 *Ibid.*, arts 129–136.

39 *Ibid.*, art 24.

40 Hsu (n 34) 120–126.

41 Alex Robert, 'The Construction of Constitutional Rights' (2010) 4 *Law and Ethics of Human Rights* 20, 23.

the Constitution of Taiwan has enshrined a series of individual rights (the first step).[42] The Constitution also mandates all restrictions on individual rights to be stipulated by statutes (the second step). Executive authorities should not restrict individual rights unless the legislature explicitly grants power to them.[43] Any restriction on rights and freedom imposed by administrative rules or administrative decisions without authority delegated by the legislature is unconstitutional and should be invalidated.[44]

The principle of statutory reservation has been defended on multiple normative grounds, such as democracy, the rule of law, and protection of rights and freedoms.[45] In a democracy, legislators are elected by the people, and the legislature has more substantial legitimacy to enact statutes that limit people's rights than any other branches of government. Statutes are the end production of a slow deliberate process in modern democracies.[46] Many voices could be heard and discussed in the deliberative procedure.[47] The rule of law account holds that all persons and authorities within a state are bound by law[48] – especially the executive power, which must be constrained by laws – and people's rights must be protected according to laws. The laws must be applied generally and be accessible, intelligible, clear, and predictable.[49] Grand Justice Chien-Hua Yang, Grand Justice Zu-Zan Yang, and Grand Justice Geng Wu elaborated upon the normative foundation of the principle of statutory reservation in their joint separate opinion, as follows:

> The rule of law is a fundamental principle of the Constitution of the Republic of China. Articles 23 and 172 of the Constitution expressly lay down the elements of the rule of law: the principles of statutory reservation and the supremacy of law. For the important matters relating to the rights and obligations of individuals, they must be stipulated by a statute. The content of a statute must conform to the established standards in Article 23 of the Constitution. A statute can grant power to executive authorities if necessary. But the enabling provision must contain sufficiently clear conditions and procedures, on which the executive authorities make administrative decisions. The executive authorities cannot make regulations to regulate matters concerning restrictions on people's rights without a statutory delegation of power.[50]

42 Constitution of Taiwan (n 36) ch 2.
43 Hsu (n 34) 118.
44 Aharon Barak, *Proportionality: Constitutional Rights and Their Limitations* (CUP 2012) 109.
45 J.Y. Interpretations No. 723 (concurring opinion of Grand Justice Sea-Yau Lin); Hsu (n 34) 131–138; Barak, *ibid.*, 107.
46 Ronan Cormacain, 'Legislation, Legislative Drafting and the Rule of Law' (2017) *The Theory and Practice of Legislation* 115, 127.
47 *Ibid.*, 128.
48 Tom Bingham, *The Rule of Law* (Penguin 2011) 8.
49 Barak (n 44) 108, 113–118; Cormacain (n 46) 116.
50 J.Y. Interpretation No. 276 (dissenting opinion of Grand Justice Chien-Hua Yang, Grand Justice Zu-Zan Yang, and Grand Justice Geng Wu).

When the TCC applies the principle of statutory reservation, it takes an approach that comprises three tests:

- The first test inquires whether the Legislative Yuan is allowed to grant legislative power to executive authority to promulgate administrative rules on a particular subject matter; If the answer is affirmative,
- The second test inquires whether the delegation of power is clear and precise; If the answer is again affirmative,
- The last test inquires whether the administrative rule exceeds the scope of delegation. If it falls within the scope of delegation, it is valid; If it falls outside the scope of delegation, it is invalid.[51]

In practice, it is relatively easy to pass the first test. Very few constitutional challenges arise when the Legislative Yuan delegates power to executive authorities for the purpose of enacting binding rules.[52] Many matters are subject to regulation by administrative rules provided that the delegation of power is granted by the Legislative Yuan. However, some matters cannot be entrusted to the executive and must be prescribed by statutes. These include crimes and penalties,[53] administrative punishments,[54] restrictions on personal liberty,[55] and taxation.[56] However, Grand Justice Tzung-Jen Tsai[57] and Professor Cheng-Yi Huang[58] observed that the TCC sometimes turned a blind eye to the Legislative Yuan's delegation of power to the executive to make rules concerning crimes and penalties, administrative punishments, and taxation.

Constitutional challenges against administrative rules relating to taxation are frequently appealed to the TCC.[59] Take Interpretation No. 597 (2005) as an example. The Minister of Finance announced a directive which stated to the effect that any interest of inheritance accrued after the death of a decedent

51 J.Y. Interpretation No. 612 (concurring opinion of Grand Justice Feng-Zhi Peng and Grand Justice Pi-Hu Hsu) at 6–14.
52 Barak (n 44) 112.
53 J.Y. Interpretations No. 601, 765.
54 J.Y. Interpretations No. 313, 324, 390, 394, 402.
55 J.Y. Interpretations No. 588, 710.
56 J.Y. Interpretations No. 635, 640, 660, 674, 685, 692, 693, 697, 700, 703, 746.
57 Tzung-Jen Tsai (蔡宗珍), 'Examining the Related Institutional Factors of the Thoughts and Development of the "Requirement of a Specially Enacted Statute"' (法律保留思想及其發展的制度關聯要素探微) (2010) 39 *National Taiwan University Law Journal* (台大法律論叢) 1, 47.
58 Cheng-Yi Huang, 'Judicial Deference to Legislative Delegation and Administrative Discretion in New Democracies: Recent Evidence from Poland, Taiwan, and South Africa' in Susan Rose-Ackerman and Peter L. Lindseth (eds), *Comparative Administrative Law* (Edward Elgar 2010) 467.
59 J.Y. Interpretations No. 478, 493, 500, 506, 508, 519, 536, 537, 565, 566, 593, 597, 606, 607, 608, 615, 620, 622, 635, 640, 650, 651, 657, 660, 661, 674, 685, 692, 693, 697, 698, 700, 703, 705, 706, 745, 746, 779.

should be included among the income of an inheritor and thus subject to taxation. At issue was the constitutionality of the directive. The TCC stated:

> Article 19 of the Constitution provides that people have the duty to pay taxes by the law. It should be construed to mean that the elements of taxation, such as taxpaying bodies, taxable objects, tax bases, and tax rates, must be provided by statutes...But it is impossible to specify all details in statutes. For technical and detailed matters, necessary clarifications in the form of administrative regulations are permissible. Thus, the executive authority could elaborate upon the legislative provisions based on its statutory powers ... There is no violation of 'taxation in accordance with law' to the extent that its clarifications are in line with the statute's legislative purposes, the economic purposes of taxation, and the principle of equality.[60]

This passage is a classic articulation of "taxation in accordance with law" that the TCC reiterated many times in its jurisprudence on statutory reservation.[61] According to this principle, except for these fundamental elements of taxation, the technical and detailed elements could be regulated by administrative regulations.

If the Legislative Yuan empowers the executive to make administrative rules, the empowerment must be clear and precise. This is the second test of the principle of statutory reservation. In practice, the TCC places reliance on this test.[62] The TCC reiterated that the purpose, content, and scope of the delegation of legislative power must be stated with precise and clear language.[63]

The TCC developed different levels of legal certainty when scrutinizing enabling provisions, depending on subject matters.[64] In criminal law, the required clarity and precision are the highest. When the Legislative Yuan entitles the executive authorities to make regulations related to crimes and penalties, the enabling statute must be so clear and so precise that individuals can foresee

60 J.Y. Interpretation No. 597, [1].

61 J.Y. Interpretations No. 765. Grand Justice Shin-Min Chen considered the principle of taxation by law as essentially the same as the principle statutory reservation. See J.Y. Interpretation No. 700 (dissenting opinion of Grand Justice Shin-Min Chen) at 4. Grand Justice Yeong-Chin Su holds a different opinion. He considers that when the principle of statutory reservation is perceived broadly, taxation by law can be considered a sub-principle of statutory reservation. However, taxation laws and regulations specify basic obligations that are not restrictions on rights. Hence, the principle of statutory reservation contained in Article 23 of the Constitution of Taiwan is not applicable in taxation cases. J.Y. Interpretation No. 700 (dissenting opinion of Grand Justice Yeong-Chin Su) at 2.

62 Tsai (n 57) 47.

63 J.Y. Interpretations 390, 514, 522, 570, 602, 643, 680, 734, 739.

64 J. Y. Interpretation No. 612 (concurring opinion of Grand Justice Feng-Zhi Peng and Grand Justice Pi-Hu Hsu) at 1–3.

the consequences their action may entail.[65] In other fields of law, the degree of required clarity and certainty is lower. Empowerment is considered clear and unambiguous if the meaning of enabling clauses is ascertained within the context or if the legislature's intention of delegating the power is ascertained after reading the enabling statute as a whole.[66] As for technical and detailed matters in relation to the enforcement of laws, the executive authorities have the greatest freedom to promulgate administrative regulations.[67]

In Interpretation No. 765 (2018), the TCC struck down the Enforcement Rules of the Land Expropriation Act on the grounds that the statutory delegation of power was not clear. Article 52(1) of the Enforcement Rules stated that land users must pay for water pipeline installation. The TCC considered that this provision impacted land users' property rights, the benefits of land development, the land users' financial plan, and the financial affordability of the executive authorities. Installing pipelines was not a technical and trivial matter that had a minor impact on people's rights. It must be prescribed by a statute or by administrative rules with a clear statutory delegation of power.[68] The Ministry of the Interior promulgated the impugned Enforcement Rules per Article 62 of the Land Expropriation Act, which states: "the enforcement rules of this Act should be stipulated by a central authority".[69] This enabling clause, in the TCC's opinion, was not clear enough in terms of whether the executive authority could decide the pipeline installation expenses sharing. Therefore, the impugned provision could not require the land users to bear the pipeline installation cost.

If the executive is empowered to make administrative rules and the enabling provisions are clear and precise, the TCC must assess whether the administrative rule exceeds the scope of the delegated power, which is the third test of the principle of statutory reservation. In Interpretation No. 756 (2017), Article 82 of the Enforcement Rules of the Prison Act failed this test. Article 66 of the Prison Act entitled prison officers to delete parts of the inmates' correspondence that posed a risk to prison discipline. Article 93-1 of the Prison Act authorized the Ministry of Justice to promulgate the rules for the implementation of Article 66.Article 82 of the Enforcement Rules of the Prison Act allowed prison officers to delete "correspondence that is false, deceptive, insulting or intimidating and that put others at risk of being deceived, causing psychological distress or anxiety". The TCC held that correspondence posed a risk to prison discipline only if the addressee was an inmate. If the addressee was not an inmate, the correspondence could not impact the prison

65 J.Y. Interpretations No. 522, [1].
66 J.Y. Interpretations No. 538, 612, 643, 676, 710, 765.
67 J.Y. Interpretation No. 562 [2].
68 J.Y. Interpretation No. 765, [5].
69 *Ibid.*, [6].

Table 4.3 The Application of Proportionality in J.Y. Interpretations against Administrative Rules (1999–2019).

	J.Y. Interpretations	*In Total*
Constitutional	480, 510, 542, 575, 593, 600, 612, 628, 643, 682, 717, 738, 750, 753, 754	15 (65.2%)
Unconstitutional	620, 713, 715, 732, 755, 756	6 (34.8%)

Source: Author

discipline.[70] The restrictions on the freedom of expression contained in Article 82 of the Enforcement Rules of the Prison Act were broader than that of the Prison Act.

Proportionality in the TCC's Judicial Review of Administrative Rules

Proportionality emerged in 21 cases (Table 4.3), which contrasts sharply with the interpretations against primary legislation, where proportionality emerged in 90 cases. One of the reasons for the less frequent application of proportionality in judicial review of administrative rules is that prior to a proportionality test, the TCC typically applies the principle of statutory reservation,[71] which serves as a gatekeeper to human rights restriction analysis.[72] Once the court finds a provision violates the principle of statutory reservation, the TCC can declare it unconstitutional and hence there is no need to conduct a proportionality test.[73]

The necessity test is still the most potent subtest in the TCC's review of administrative rules.[74] By contrast, other subtests nearly had no "bite" in judicial review against administrative rules. The TCC in Interpretation No. 715 (2013) struck down the Recruitment and Admission Guidelines relying on the necessity test. The Ministry of Defense was entitled by the Conscription

70 J.Y. Interpretation No. 756, [10].

71 There are very few cases in which the TCC skipped the principle statutory reservation but directly applied the principle of proportionality. For example, J.Y. Interpretations No. 542, 713, 717, 732, 754, 755.

72 Simon N. M. Young, 'Does it Matter if Restrictions on the Right to Social Welfare in Hong Kong are Prescribed by Law or Policy?' (2014) *Hong Kong Law Journal* 25, 26.

73 J.Y. Interpretation No. 638 (concurring opinion of Grand Justice Feng-Zhi Peng) 1. For example, J.Y. Interpretations No. 480, 510, 575, 593, 600, 612, 628, 643, 682, 738, 750, and 753. But there are some exceptional cases where the TCC still invoked proportionality even when the impugned administrative rules contradicted the principle of statutory reservation. For example, the TCC overturned Article 81(3) of the Enforcement Rules of the Prison Act on both grounds in J.Y. Interpretation No. 756.

74 E.g. J.Y. Interpretations No. 713, 715, 732, 755, 756.

Table 4.4 The Application of the Principle of Equality in J.Y. Interpretations against Administrative Rules (1999–2019).

	J.Y. Interpretations	*In Total*
Constitutional	481, 526, 542, 547, 555, 565, 571, 575, 593, 605, 607, 614, 626, 648, 682, 693, 698, 750,	18 (65.2%)
Unconstitutional	485, 620, 624, 722, 779	5 (34.8%)

Source: Author

Act and the Selection and Training Enforcement Regulations to stipulate rules on military officer recruitment and training.[75] The impugned Guidelines prohibited people with a conviction record from registering for the military officer examination. The TCC first confirmed that the impugned Guidelines conformed to the principle of statutory reservation because it fell within the legislative delegation.[76] The TCC then applied proportionality to review the substantive content of the Guidelines. The TCC accepted that the qualifications for military officer candidates were necessary for ensuring national and military security instead.[77] However, it considered that convictions resulting from intentional crimes should have been distinguished from those resulting from crimes of negligence.[78] It held that a prohibition of citizens who committed crimes of negligence from registering for the military officer examination was more than necessary and disproportionate.[79]

Principle of Equality in the TCC's Judicial Review of Administrative Rules

The principle of equality emerged in 23 cases where administrative rules were challenged (Table 4.4). Likewise, the equality test usually arises after the TCC confirms that the principle of statutory reservation is not violated.[80] But there are several cases where the TCC did not invoke the principle of statutory reservation but only applied the principle of equality.[81] In Interpretation No. 779 (2019), the TCC overturned a letter issued by the Ministry of Finance on the ground of violating the principle of equality. The impugned letter exempted urban land preserved for public infrastructure from land value-added tax. But

75 J.Y. Interpretation No. 715, [3].
76 *Ibid.*
77 *Ibid.*, [4]–[5].
78 *Ibid.*, [6].
79 *Ibid.*
80 E.g. J.Y. Interpretations No. 481, 547, 555, 565, 571, 575, 593, 607, 614, 626, 648, 682, 693, 698, 750.
81 J.Y. Interpretations No. 485, 526, 542, 605, 624, 779.

the land preserved for public infrastructure in non-urban areas is excluded from tax exemption. The TCC held that even though the tax exemption pursued a legitimate aim, there were no reasonable grounds to justify the differential treatment between urban and non-urban land preserved for public infrastructure.[82]

When the TCC applies the principle of equality to scrutinize the administrative rules, it takes the classic approach composed of two tests: (1) whether the differences in treatment pursue a legitimate aim; and (2) whether there is a certain level of nexus between the differences in treatment and the aim pursued.[83] In Interpretation No. 750 (2017), the petitioner argued that the Enforcement Rules of the Physicians Act and the Dentist Examination Rules were unconstitutional and violated the right to equal treatment. According to the Enforcement Rules, an overseas graduate is eligible for a dentist examination (second phase) only after completing an internship in Taiwan. It is the same requirement that applies to local graduates. But for students from domestic universities, the universities always arrange internships for them in accredited institutes, and they usually receive their internship certificates before graduation. By contrast, overseas graduates do not have equal opportunities to finish the internship as domestic students. The TCC held that the impugned rules did not constitute unlawful discrimination. The TCC considered that as medical care was intimately related to the health of citizens, physicians should be equipped with adequate clinical skills besides professional knowledge. The Enforcement Rules pursued a legitimate aim of ensuring overseas graduates familiarize themselves with Taiwan's medical environment, including local common diseases.[84] Overseas graduates could equip themselves with clinical skills through internships, and this internship requirement was reasonable as regards the aim pursued.[85]

The Intensity of the TCC's Judicial Review of Administrative Rules

The Intensity of Review of Statutory Reservation

In Interpretation No. 443 (1997), the TCC articulated the prototype of variable levels of intensity of review for statutory reservation.[86] In that case, the issue was whether the Regulation for Exit of Draftees unlawfully restricted the freedom of movement as it prohibited draftees from international travel. The TCC held that the Regulation was unconstitutional. It reiterated that any restriction on people's rights must be regulated by statutes enacted by the legislature or regulations promulgated with authority delegated by the

82 J.Y. Interpretation No. 779, [8].
83 J.Y. Interpretations No. 542, 565, 571, 575, 593, 605, 626, 648, 682, 722, 750, 779.
84 J.Y. Interpretation No. 750, [14].
85 *Ibid.*, [15].
86 Huang (n 58) 471.

legislature. It affirmed that the Conscription Act and the Enforcement Act of Conscription Act did not impose restrictions on freedom of movement on draftees, nor did these Acts explicitly empower the executive authority to impose such restrictions. The TCC elaborated upon the intensity of statutory reservation:

> The Constitution contains an extensive range of freedoms and rights. Any freedoms and rights not in contravention of social order and public interest are protected by the Constitution. However, not every freedom and right is protected in the same way... *The subject matters that must be stipulated by statutes or can be regulated by regulations relate to the so-called "intensity of regulation". The intensity of regulation varies depending on the subject matters, content, legal interest (involved), and the extent of restriction.*[87] [emphasis added]

The TCC frequently referred to this passage above in its subsequent decisions when applying the principle of statutory reservation. The intensity of regulation became fledged gradually.[88] Grand Justice Yu-Hsiu Hsu articulated the intensity of regulation for assessing the principle of statutory reservation in her separate opinion in Interpretation No. 612 (2006). She pointed out the TCC had set up three levels of intensity of review for statutory reservation, including:

- When depriving people of their lives or imposing limitations on their right to liberty, the legislature must enact statutes in full accordance with the principle of no penalty without a law. This represents a high level of intensity of review.
- When imposing restrictions on people's rights and freedoms, other than the rights to life and liberty, the restrictions should, in principle, be prescribed by statutes. If the legislature delegates power to the executive authorities to promulgate supplementary rules, this delegation of power must be articulated in clear and precise terms. This represents an intermediate level of intensity of review.
- The executive authorities can stipulate administrative rules without statutory delegation of power if the rules pertain to the technical and detailed matters related to law enforcement and do not impose restrictions on people's rights. This represents a low level of intensity of review.[89]

87 J.Y. Interpretation No. 443, [1].
88 J.Y. Interpretation No. 710 (opinion concurring in part and dissenting in part of Grand Justice Pai-Hsiu Yeh); Tsai (n 57) 43.
89 J.Y. Interpretation 612 (dissenting opinion of Grand Justice Yu-Hsiu Hsu) at 2–3

Table 4.5 Intensity of Review of the Principle of Statutory Reservation in J.Y. Interpretations against Administrative Rules (1999–2019).

Intensity of Review	*Constitutional*	*Unconstitutional*	*In Total*
Low level	480, 493, 508, 519, 526, 536, 537, 539, 548, 561, 571, 575, 597, 607, 608, 611, 615, 626, 628, 629, 635, 660, 697, 698, 700, 738, 745, 746, **750**,[a] 779		30 (30%)
Intermediate level	481, 497, 501, 506, 510, 511, 530, 538, 547, 500, 555, 565, 593, 598, 600, 606, 612, 614, 643, 648, 651, 671, 676, 682, 710, 715, **750**, 753, 785	479, 492, 505, 514, 524, 532, 562, 568, 570, 581, 586, 598, 602, 609, 619, 638, 640, 650, 657, 658, 661, 707, 710, 711, 724, 730, 734, 739, 756, 765, 778	60 (60%)
High level	685, 693	478, 566, 567, 620, 622, 674, 692, 703, 705, 706, 723	13 (13%)

Source: Author

[a] In this case, the TCC applied two levels of intensity of review to scrutinize the impugned administrative rule provisions.

In the last two decades, the TCC adopted the high and intermediate levels of intensity of review in around 70 percent of the cases. The low level of intensity of review was adopted in around 30 percent of the cases (Table 4.5). This shows the TCC was strict when reviewing the restrictions on people's rights and freedoms. When the TCC reviewed the impugned administrative rules with the low intensity of review, the TCC upheld them all. By contrast, when the TCC adopted the high level of intensity of review, 11 out of 13 were declared unconstitutional. When using the intermediate level of intensity of review, the TCC announced around half constitutional (29 cases) and half unconstitutional (31 cases). The correlation between the intensity of review and the result of review is substantial.

The Intensity of the Proportionality and Equality Tests

The intensity of proportionality and equality tests in cases against administrative rules was ascertained in 22 cases (Table 4.6 and Table 4.7). It is conspicuous from the two tables below that the TCC did not apply them with the high level of intensity of review. The intermediate level of intensity of review merely emerged in four out of 44 cases (9.1 percent). The TCC appeared deferential when applying proportionality and equality to review administrative rules.

Table 4.6 Intensity of Proportionality Test in J.Y. Interpretations against Administrative Rules (1999–2019).

Intensity of Review	*Constitutional*	*Unconstitutional*	*Total Interpretation*
Low level	480, 542, 612, 643, 682, 738, 750		7 (33.3%)
Intermediate level	575	715, 756	3 (14.3%)
High level			0
Unclear	510, 593, 600, 628, 717, 753, 754	620, 713, 732, 755	11 (52.4%)

Source: Author

Table 4.7 Intensity of Review of the Principle of Equality in J.Y. Interpretations against Administrative Rules (1999–2019).

Intensity of Review	*Constitutional*	*Unconstitutional*	*Total Interpretation*
Low level	542, 565, 571, 575, 593, 605, 648, 682, 750, 779	722	11 (47.8%)
Intermediate level	626		1 (4.3%)
High level			0
Unclear	481, 526, 547, 555, 607, 614, 620, 624, 693, 698	485	11 (47.8%)

Source: Author

In over half of the cases the intensity of review was unclear for several reasons. First, the TCC just mentioned the terms "the principle of proportionality"[90] or "the principle of equality",[91] but it did not actually apply them. Second, even though the subtests of proportionality appeared in some cases, the TCC just stated that "the punishment is more than necessary"[92] or "the measure is reasonable and necessary" in its conclusions.[93] In some cases, the TCC did not conduct substantive equality review.[94] Third, even though the TCC applied the subtests of proportionality, the intensity of review was confusing and unclear.

90 For example, J.Y. Interpretations No. 510, 568, 600, 620, 638, 754.
91 For example, J.Y. Interpretations No. 481, 485, 620, 698.
92 J.Y. Interpretation No. 713, [2]; J.Y. Interpretation No. 755, [12].
93 J.Y. Interpretation No. 628, [4].
94 For example, J.Y. Interpretations No. 526, 547, 555, 607, 614, 624,

For example, whereas the TCC considered the aims important (intermediate level), it required the impugned measures to be reasonably connected to the aims (low level).[95] In Interpretation No. 732 (2015), the TCC asks the executive authority to use the least intrusive means (high level) to pursue a legitimate aim (low scrutiny).

Hong Kong

Between 1999 and 2019, the CFA reviewed administrative rules, including subsidiary legislation and policies, in eight decisions (Table 4.8). This section examines the standards and intensity of review the CFA adopted in these decisions.

Proportionality remained a dominant standard of review in the CFA's judicial review of administrative rules, the same as its review of ordinances. The CFA invoked proportionality in seven out of eight decisions. This stands in contrast with the SPC and the TCC. The SPC excluded proportionality and the TCC relied mainly on the principle of statutory reservation to review administrative rules. Additionally, the CFA applied the standard of "prescribed by law" in four cases. However, unlike the TCC, the CFA placed its focus on the accessibility and precision of the restrictions on rights and freedoms and paid less attention to the question of whether the restrictions on rights and freedoms take the form of statutory instruments or not.[96]

Proportionality in the CFA's Judicial Review of Administrative Rules

The CFA applied proportionality in seven decisions against administrative rules, out of which it struck down the impugned administrative rules in three cases[97] and upheld the constitutionality of the impugned rules in four cases[98].

Kong Yunming v Director of Social Welfare (2013) is a milestone case in the CFA's judicial review; as Cora Chan commented, "The CFA in *Kong Yunming* is the first to have made clear that proportionality is the standard of review for assessing restrictions on all constitutional rights and applied such standard to scrutinize restrictions on the right to social welfare".[99] Kong Yunming is a Mainland Chinese woman and married a Hong Kong

95 J.Y. Interpretations No. 579, 717, 753.

96 Young (n 72) 26.

97 *Kong Yunming v Director of Social Welfare* (2013) 16 HKCFAR 950; *QT v Director of Immigration* (2018) 21 HKCFAR 324; *Leung Chun Kwong v Secretary for Civil Service* (2019) 22 HKCFAR 127.

98 *Chow Shun Yung v Wei Pih and Another* (2003) 6 HKCFAR 299; *Medical Council of Hong Kong v Helen Chan* (2010) 13 HKCFAR 248; *Fok Chun Wa v Hospital Authority* (2012) 15 HKCFAR 409; *HKSAR v Fong Kwok Shan Christine* (2017) 20 HKCFAR 425.

99 Cora Chan, 'Focus: Kong Yunming v Director of Social Welfare: Introduction' (2014) *HKLJ* 1, 2.

Table 4.8 The CFA Decisions against Administrative Rules (1999–2019).

Case Name	*Administrative Rules Reviewed*	*Rights Involved*	*(Un)Constitutional*	*Standard of Review*
Chow Shun Yung v Wei Pih and Another (2003) 6 HKCFAR 299	Hong Kong Court of Final Appeal Rules (Cap. 484, Sub Leg): Rule 7	Right to a hearing	Constitutional	Proportionality and prescribed by law
Lam Siu Po v Commissioner of Police (2009) 12 HKCFAR 237	Police (Discipline) Regulation (Cap. 232A, Sub. Leg.): Regulations 9(11) and 9(12)	Right to legal representation	Unconstitutional	Procedural fairness
Medical Council of Hong Kong v Helen Chan (2010) 13 HKCFAR 248	Medical Practitioners (Registration and Disciplinary Procedure) Regulation: Regulation 32(4); Medical Registration (Miscellaneous Provisions) Regulation: Regulation 6(1); Professional Code and Conduct: Part III	Right to fair hearing and freedom of expression	Constitutional	Proportionality and prescribed by law
Fok Chun Wa v Hospital Authority (2012) 15 HKCFAR 409	Policies concerning the obstetric service	Right to social welfare and Right to equal treatment	Constitutional	Proportionality
Kong Yunming v Director of Social Welfare (2013) 16 HKCFAR 950	Comprehensive Social Security Assistance System	Right to social welfare	Unconstitutional	Proportionality and prescribed by law
HKSAR v Fong Kwok Shan Christine (2017) 20 HKCFAR 425	Administrative Instructions for Regulating Admittance and Conduct of Persons (Cap. 382A, Sub. Leg.): ss. 11 and 12(1)	Freedom of expression	Constitutional	Proportionality and prescribed by law
QT v Director of Immigration (2018) 21 HKCFAR 324	Immigration policy on spousal dependant visa that excluded same-sex civil partnerships	Right to equal treatment	Unconstitutional	Proportionality
Leung Chun Kwong v Secretary for Civil Service (2019) 22 HKCFAR 127	Policy on civil servant medical and dental benefits and joint assessment of salaries for tax that excluded same-sex partner	Right to equal treatment	Unconstitutional	Proportionality

Source: Author

permanent resident. She came to Hong Kong on a one-way permit to join her husband on 21 December 2005. Unfortunately, her husband died the next day. In 2006, Kong Yunming's application for Comprehensive Social Security Assistance (CSSA) was rejected on the grounds that she did not meet the seven-year residence requirement. She was granted leave for judicial review and raised the question of whether the residence requirement for the CSSA was inconsistent with Articles 25, 36, and 145 of the HKBL and Article 22 of the BORO. In terms of the CSSA system, a ten-year residence requirement was first introduced in the 1940s as a condition of eligibility for public welfare assistance. It was reduced to five years in 1959 and further reduced to one year in 1970. Kong Yunming challenged a new requirement of seven years that was adopted in 2004.[100] In the CFA's opinion, the right to social welfare enshrined in Article 36 of the HKBL was subject to modification pursuant to policies promulgated by the Government of the Hong Kong SAR, according to the empowerment entitled by Article 145, on the one hand. The CFA emphasized that any restriction placed on the right to social welfare was amenable to judicial review on the basis of proportionality, on the other hand.[101] The Government claimed that the residence requirement was in favor of the sustainability of the social security system. Three factors contributed to the need for the impugned measure to safeguard the system's sustainability: (i) the policy of accepting immigrants from the Mainland under the one-way permit scheme; (ii) Hong Kong's aging population; (iii) the rise in expenditure on CSSA.[102] After examining whether those factors provide a rational justification for the seven-year restriction, the CFA held that none of those factors justified the need for the seven-year residence requirement.[103] First, the residence requirement conflicted with the family reunion policy of the one-way permit scheme. Most arrivals under this scheme were children. When mainland parents came to take care of their children without adequate income to meet their basic needs, they expected the social security system to provide CSSA benefits. Second, given Hong Kong's low fertility rate, the one-way permit scheme is the most important immigration policy, serving as a rational response to the aging-population issue. Third, the savings from the residence requirement constituted only a very small fraction of the overall expenditure on CSSA. In conclusion, the impugned legislation failed the suitability test as there was no rational connection between the seven-year residence requirement and the CSSA system's sustainability.

QT v Director of Immigration (2018) and *Leung Chun Kwong v Secretary for Civil Service* (2019) are two landmark cases relating to the rights of same-sex partners. In both cases, the CFA decided in favor of the rights of same-sex

100 *Kong Yunming* (n 97) [11]–[16].
101 *Ibid.*, [36].
102 *Ibid.*, [53].
103 *Ibid.*, [55]–[97].

partners. QT entered a civil partnership in the United Kingdom with her partner, SS. When SS secured employment in Hong Kong, QT applied for a dependent visa to join her as her spouse. However, her application was refused on the ground that "spouse" means a party to an opposite-sex marriage. QT challenged the decision on the ground of *Wednesbury* unreasonableness and claimed the refusal encroached upon her constitutional right to equal treatment.[104] The CFA considered that her challenge was made to an administrative policy and not to primary legislation and that there was no need to exert the judicial power of constitutional review.[105] Additionally, the CFA stated that the principle of equality was an important aspect of administrative rationality, and a violation of this principle sustained "an application for judicial review on the ground of *Wednesbury* unreasonableness".[106] Thus, the CFA framed the applicant's claim as one for judicial review on the ground of irrationality or unreasonableness in the *Wednesbury* sense.[107] It asserted that "the proportionality concepts developed in constitutional law, including *Hysan* fourth step, are equally applicable to deciding whether the differential treatment entailed by the policy is justified or whether it may be impugned as *Wednesbury* unreasonable".[108] The Director of Immigration said that impugned policy had two aims: (i) encourage persons with needed skills and talent to join Hong Kong's workforce, accompanied by their dependants; and (ii) maintain strict immigration control.[109] However, the CFA held that the refusal of granting dependent visas to same-sex spouses was not rationally connected to the legitimate aims pursued, in particular the first aim.[110] Thus, the CFA struck down the decision against QT.

In *Leung Chun Kwong*, the applicant, Mr Leung, is an Immigration Officer and married his partner in New Zealand, where same-sex marriage is legal.[111] Mr Leung sought to update his marital status with the Civil Service Bureau so that various medical and dental benefits would be available to his partner. The Secretary for Civil Service rejected his request on the ground that same-sex marriage was not a marriage within the meaning of Hong Kong law. Mr Leung was also unable to include his partner for joint tax assessment when filing his income tax return online. The Commissioner of Inland Revenue informed Mr Leung that in the context of the Inland Revenue Ordinance, marriage was a heterosexual marriage between a man and a woman. Mr Leung challenged the decisions of the Secretary for Civil Service and the Commissioner of Inland Revenue, claiming that their decisions constituted unlawful discrimination on

104 *QT* (n 97) [9].
105 *Ibid.*, [24].
106 *Ibid.*, [22]–[23].
107 *Ibid.*, [24].
108 *Ibid.*, [87].
109 *Ibid.*, [88].
110 *Ibid.*, [91]–[93].
111 *Leung Chun Kwong* (n 97) [2].

the grounds of his sexual orientation. The CFA applied proportionality that was articulated and applied in *QT*.[112] The CFA held that "the protection of the institution of marriage as defined by the laws of Hong Kong was a legitimate aim", but denying Mr Leung employment and tax benefits did not rationally contribute to the protection of the institution of marriage in Hong Kong.[113]

In the rest of the four cases where proportionality was deployed, the CFA upheld the constitutionality of the impugned administrative rules. *Fok Chun Wa v Hospital Authority* (2012) is one of them. The issue of the case was whether the differential treatment between Hong Kong resident women and women from Mainland China in terms of obstetrics fees is no more than necessary. The CFA concluded that the Hospital Authority justified the differential treatment after it confirmed: first, the Hospital Authority had given due regard to the long-term sustainability of Hong Kong's social service; second, the Hospital Authority had noticed that the finite resource might have been affordable but no longer be the case in modern society; third, the Hospital Authority had considered the problems of the healthcare system; fourth, the Hospital Authority had noticed there was a problem of dangerous behavior of Mainland pregnant women who try to seek admission at the public hospitals just after midnight and then discharge themselves against medical advice within 24 hours in order to save money; and lastly, the Hospital Authority had recognized the adverse effect on Hong Kong mothers brought about by providing the obstetric service to Mainland women.[114]

Prescribed by Law in the CFA's Judicial Review of Administrative Rules

In contrast to the TCC, which focused in the first instance on whether the restrictions on people's rights and freedoms are prescribed by primary legislation and whether the executive authority has been conferred power to promulgate administrative rules and impose restrictions, the CFA appears to pay little attention to whether the restrictions on rights and freedoms take the form of an ordinance. It placed its focus on the accessibility and precision of the restrictions on rights and freedoms.

"Prescribed by law" or "in accordance with law" is a recognized constitutional stipulation of any restriction on people's rights in Hong Kong. It is written in Article 39 of the HKBL and Article 11(1) of the BORO. The question of "prescribed by law" first came to the CFA in *Shum Kwok Sher v HKSAR* (2002).[115] The issue in this case was whether the offense of public misconduct was so uncertain as to be unconstitutional. To address this issue, the CFA referred to the jurisprudence of the ECtHR. In the ECtHR's opinion, to com-

112 *Ibid.*, [15]–[22].
113 *Ibid.*, [62]–[76].
114 *Fok Chun Wa* (n 98) [89]–[90].
115 (2002) 5 HKCFAR 381.

ply with the constitutional stipulation "prescribed by law", the relevant law must be certain and adequately accessible.[116] In *Winnie Lo v HKSAR* (2012), the CFA further stated that "People must be able to access an adequate indication of the legal rules applicable to any given situation. And those rules must be stated with sufficient precision to enable people, with appropriate advice if need be, to foresee to a reasonable degree in the circumstances whether their conduct would be lawful or unlawful".[117]

In *Kong Yunming*, the council for the appellant raised an argument that the seven-year residence restriction on the right to CSSA benefits was unconstitutional because this restriction was imposed by administrative rules rather than legislation.[118] The CFA rejected this argument, holding that the social welfare system in Article 145 of the HKBL could be regulated by a non-statutory system of administrative rules and policies as long as the system comprises rules that are accessible and systematically applied and the system is subject to administrative appeal.[119] However, the CFA's reasoning is far from adequate to answer the question of whether the seven-year residency requirement satisfied the constitutional stipulation "prescribed by law" in the sense of restriction taking the statutory form.[120]

In *Medical Council of Hong Kong v Helen Chan* (2010), the Medical Council found that Dr Chan was guilty of professional misconduct as she promoted health products, which were sold by a company with which she had a financial relationship. The presence of the legal adviser in the Medical Council's disciplinary inquiry is permitted in accordance with the Medical Registration Ordinance and by Regulation 6(1) of the Medical Registration (Miscellaneous Provisions) Regulation. The legal adviser will retire with the Medical Council and be present at the deliberation and give legal advice if necessary. The adviser will prepare the first draft of the decision of the Medical Council in their presence. The first challenge Dr Chan raised was against the presence of the legal adviser at the deliberation of the Medical Council and their role during the drafting of the judgment.[121] The CFA held that the relevant procedural limits could be set by law, including primary or subsidiary legislation, common law, and the constitution. The Court also held that "within limits, a body like the Medical Council is master of its own procedure".[122] It found that no express or implied statutory provision that prohibits the presence of the adviser at the Medical Council's deliberation or permits or prohibits the adviser from

116 *Ibid.*, [62]–[65].
117 *Winnie Lo v HKSAR* (2012) 12 HKCFAR 16, [19].
118 *Kong Yunming* (n 97) [24].
119 *Ibid.*, [25].
120 Young (n 72) 26.
121 *Helen Chan* (n 98) [28]. The relevant provisions are provided by reg 32(4) of the Medical Practitioners (Registration and Disciplinary Procedure) Regulation and reg 6(1) of the Medical Registration (Miscellaneous Provisions) Regulation.
122 *Ibid.*, [32].

drafting the Council's decision.[123] The CFA contended that the presence of legal advisers in the Medical Council's deliberation did not compromise the competence, independence, and impartiality of the tribunal.[124] As for drafting the judgment, the CFA held that this practice was accepted as long as the draft embodied the tribunal's findings and reasoning.[125]

Dr Chan raised another argument related to the standard of "prescribed by law". She argued the rule that doctors were barred from public promotion of commercial medical or health-related products constituted a restriction on freedom of speech not prescribed by law.[126] The CFA considered that the Medical Registration Ordinance established the Medical Council that was entitled to functions including professional discipline. The Medical Council published "Professional Code and Conduct" that included broadly defined professional misconduct. The CFA endorsed the Medical Council's argument that there had been a consensus among doctors concerning the impugned rule. The CFA considered that there were no difficulties for professional practitioners to recognize the widely accepted ethical rules.[127]

In *HKSAR v Fong Kwok Shan Christine* (2017), Ms Fong argued that s. 11 of the Administrative Instructions for Regulating Admittance and Conduct of Persons was invalid because a restriction on the freedom of expression was legally uncertain.[128] The CFA contended that, to ascertain whether a provision is legally uncertain, it was necessary for it to be interpreted and the interpretation must consider the context and purpose in the first instance.[129] In the CFA's opinion, "behave in an orderly manner" should not be taken in isolation; instead, the meaning of this rule was clear after considering other sections and the purpose of the administrative instruction.[130] It held that in light of the context and purpose of other provisions in the Administrative Instructions, s.11 was not uncertain and it was a conclusion any layman would have no difficulty reaching with common sense.[131]

Intensity of the CFA's Judicial Review of Administrative Rules

Intensity of Review of Proportionality

The spectrum of the intensity of proportionality test in the CFA's jurisprudence includes two levels: the standard of reasonable necessity and the "manifest" standard.[132] The choices of the intensity of review in cases against

123 *Ibid.*, [33].
124 *Ibid.*, [58]–[61].
125 *Ibid.*, [62].
126 *Ibid.*, [67].
127 *Ibid.*, [70].
128 *Fong Kwok Shan Christine* (n 98) [19].
129 *Ibid.*, [78].
130 *Ibid.*, [79]–[91].
131 *Ibid.*, [91].
132 The spectrum of proportionality review is discussed in Chapter 3 of this book.

administrative rules were consistent with the CFA's practice and jurisprudence on judicial deference in cases against ordinances. It conducts more intense scrutiny in cases involving restrictions on fundamental rights, such as discrimination on the grounds of sexual orientation, and uses a deferential standard when the restrictions on socio-economic rights are concerned. The CFA adopted the standard of reasonable necessity in *QT* and *Leung Chun Kwong*. The CFA stated that where a person faces discrimination on the grounds of sexual orientation, the court would subject the impugned measure to "particularly severe scrutiny".[133] Additionally, it is noteworthy that in *QT*, the CFA applied proportionality to the terrain of traditional *Wednesbury* unreasonableness. Proportionality is a standard of review more assertive than *Wednesbury* unreasonableness. The CFA's application of proportionality in place of *Wednesbury* unreasonableness could enable its deeper scrutiny into the government's discretion.

Fok Chun Wa and *Kong Yunming* are related to the qualification for social welfare.[134] The CFA considered that economic and social policies regarding allocating finite resources should be left to the government.[135] It emphasized in the two cases that "it would not usually be within the province of the courts to adjudicate on the merits or demerits of government socio-economic policies".[136] It held that it had the duty to intervene only where the impugned measure was "manifestly without reasonable foundation".[137]

Intensity of Review of Prescribed by Law

Like the TCC, the CFA also adopted varying levels of legal certainty,[138] holding that a law must be accessible and sufficiently precise and that legal certainty is not rigid but depends on particular circumstances. In *Shum Kwok Sher*, the CFA referred to *Sunday Times v United Kingdom* and stated:

> A norm cannot be regarded as a 'law' unless it is formulated with sufficient precision to enable the citizen to regulate his conduct: he must be able – if need be with appropriate advice – to foresee, to a degree that is reasonable in the circumstances, the consequences which a given action may entail. Those consequences need not to be foreseeable with absolute certainty: experience shows this to be unattainable. Again, whilst certainty is highly desirable, it may bring in its train excessive rigidity and the law must be able to keep pace with changing circumstances.[139]

133 *QT* (n 97) [108]; *Leung Chun Kwong* (n 97) [79].
134 *Fok Chun Wa* (n 98) [72]; *Kong Yunming* (n 97) [17]–[19].
135 *Fok Chun Wa* (n 98) [72]; *Kong Yunming* (n 97) [41].
136 *Fok Chun Wa* (n 98) [66]; *Kong Yunming* (n 97) [41].
137 *Kong Yunming*, *ibid.*, [41].
138 *Shum Kwok Sher* (n 115) 402G–403B; *Helen Chan* (n 98) [77]–[82].
139 *Shum Kwok Sher*, *ibid.*, 402G–403B.

Among others, the importance of rights and freedoms involved is one factor determining the degree of legal certainty. In *Helen Chan*, Dr Chan argued that a rule that prohibited doctors from promoting health products was an unlawful restraint of free speech and inconsistent with "prescribed by law". The CFA distinguished commercial speech, which the case concerned, and political speech. Although it thought restrictions on both categories of speech must be sufficiently precise, it upheld the Court of Appeal's opinion that the speech involved was commercial speech rather than political speech, and restrictions on drug promotions were necessary for the protection of public interest.[140] In the opinion of the CFA, political speech deserves a higher level of protection and legal certainty than commercial speech.

Nonetheless, as Simon Young observed, "There are a plethora of authorities recognizing the legal certainty dimension of 'prescribed by law' in Art 39 of the Basic Law … Less attention, however, has been paid to the public law-making dimension of 'prescribed by law'".[141] The CFA, distinct from the TCC, gives more leeway to the government in the sense of ignoring whether the restrictions on rights are created by ordinances. The TCC has paid sufficient attention to assess the nature and quality of the laws that create restrictions on rights and freedoms. It establishes a set of rules asking what restrictions must be created by statutes, what restrictions can be promulgated in regulations with a delegation from the legislature, and what restrictions can be promulgated by the executive without delegation. These rules aim to prevent the executive from ultra vires their regulative power, making rules that restrict people's rights. However, they did not emerge in the CFA's decisions.

Macau

Macau's legal system provides two channels for courts to check administrative rules: concrete and abstract review proceedings.[142] Despite two channels being available, the TUI reviewed administrative rules in only two cases from 1999 to 2019 (Table 4.9). In these cases, the TUI applied the standards of contravening superior laws and "prescribed by law". Although the TUI at no point discussed the intensity of review, its deferential attitude to the review of administrative rules is perceived.

Contravening Superior Laws in the TUI's Judicial Review of Administrative Rules

In Case 7/2007, the applicant challenged Resolution No. 154/CA of the Board of Administrative Directors of the Monetary Authority of Macau. The

140 *Helen Chan* (n 98) [81].
141 Young (n 72) 29–30, 35.
142 See 'Two-tracks of Judicial Review of Administrative Rules' in Chapter 2 of this book.

Table 4.9 The TUI Decisions against Administrative Rules (1999–2019).

Case	*Administrative Rules under Review*	*(In)Valid*	*Standards of Review*
7/2007	Resolution No. 154/CA of the Board of Administrative Directors of the Monetary Authority of Macau	Invalid	Contravening superior laws
2/2017	Internal Regulation of the Judicial Police: art. 17	Invalid	Prescribed by law

Source: Author

applicant, who had served as a deputy director of the Monetary Authority between 1996 and 2003, contested the cessation of certain benefits, including electricity, water, and telephone charges, car parking space, and an individual office room, upon leaving the deputy director position.[143]

Prior to this case, in Case 5/2005, the TUI had determined that Resolution No. 154/CA should be considered an administrative regulation with general effect and was therefore subject to the court's scrutiny through the abstract review proceeding.[144] In Case 7/2007, the TUI overturned this Resolution, citing its contravention of a superior law – the Monetary Authority Specialized Regulation of Personnel. Article 51 of this Regulation stipulates that remuneration includes basic remuneration, annual bonus, supplementary remuneration, and any other monthly payments on a permanent basis. The Monetary Authority argued that the discontinued fringe benefits were not part of the remuneration as defined in Article 51, but rather special bonuses provided to directors and deputy directors. The TUI made a distinction between remuneration and special bonuses. In its opinion, remuneration is periodic and related to the continuous enforcement of employment contracts, while special bonuses are rewards for good performance. However, the TUI also clarified that certain special bonuses should be regarded as part of remuneration when their quantity and regularity of payment are considered. Benefits such as electricity, water, and telephone charges fall into this category because they are directly connected with the officers' willingness to provide service. It is not a means to reward the employees for their performance of special work.[145] The TUI concluded that these discontinued benefits were parts of the remuneration package defined by the Monetary Authority Special Regulation of Personnel and were independent of the applicant's performance as a deputy director. Therefore, the court ruled that Resolution No. 154/CA was illegal for eliminating these benefits.

143 Case 7/2007, pages 17–18.
144 Case 5/2005, page 9.
145 Case 7/2007, pages 28–29.

Prescribed by Law in the TUI's Judicial Review of Administrative Rules

The TUI applied the standard "prescribed by law" in Case 2/2017. The case involved a judicial police officer who was punished by the Director of the Judicial Police under Article 17 of the Internal Regulation of the Judicial Police. This provision required judicial police officers to ensure their work phones were operational 24 hours 7 days a week. The applicant had changed his mobile phone number without notifying the police department, which caused communication issues. As a consequence, the department imposed a disciplinary punishment on the applicant, fining him an amount equivalent to 30 days' salary.[146] While the TUI acknowledged that the Director had the authority to issue internal regulations related to the administration of judicial police, it emphasized that such regulations could not impose new restrictions or punishments that were not already presented in existing laws and administrative regulations.[147] Therefore, the TUI declared Article 17 of the Internal Regulation of the Judicial Police illegal and overturned the punishment decision.

The Intensity of the TUI's Judicial Review of Administrative Rules

Although the TUI never explicitly discussed the intensity of its judicial review of administrative rules, it is evident that the TUI afforded significant leeway to the government in this area.

First, the TUI's reluctance to scrutinize administrative rules is evidenced in the very small number of cases it accepted for review. In nine cases where the applicants contested the legality of administrative rules, the TUI declined to hear their appeals.[148] The TUI reasoned that for applicants to challenge administrative rules through concrete review proceedings, the administrative rules must directly underpin the administrative decisions being contested. If no direct link existed, the court refused to examine the administrative rules. This approach closely aligns with the stance taken by the SPC.

Second, the TUI's decisions against administrative rules conspicuously lack the application of substantive standards of review, such as proportionality and equality, which would enable the court to evaluate the merits of governmental actions. While the TUI has not outright rejected the use of proportionality in reviewing administrative rules, its explicit refusal to apply this standard in the review of laws and decrees makes it highly unlikely that it would apply proportionality in this context.

146 Case 2/2017, page 15.

147 *Ibid.*, page 18.

148 Cases 8/2007, 9/2007, 10/2007, 13/2007, 14/2007, 16/2007, 17/2007, 18/2007, 19/2007.

Conclusion

This chapter has examined and compared the standards and intensity of judicial review adopted in decisions delivered by the four apex courts against administrative rules. It is not easy to compare the intensity of judicial review of the four courts against administrative rules, since the caseloads and standards of review vary between them. Nonetheless, their decisions and jurisprudence on the intensity of review still show their deferential or assertive judicial attitude toward reviewing administrative rules. The SPC and the TUI were reluctant to review administrative rules. Both courts declined to respond to challenges against administrative rules on various grounds. For example, both used the same ground that impugned administrative rules were not directly related to administrative decisions subject to review. Even when they entertained appeals against administrative rules, they did not substantively review their content and merits. The SPC emphasized that the judicial review of administrative rules was a legality review and that a court should avoid judging their reasonableness and proportionality. When using the standard of contravening superior laws, the Chinese courts simply contrasted the textual differences between the impugned rules and superior laws without substantively reviewing their content. Although the TUI did not expressly refuse proportionality, it did not apply proportionality in practice. Since it expressly declined to apply proportionality to primary legislation, it is not imprudent to speculate the same attitude to the judicial review of administrative rules.

Reviewing the constitutionality and legality of administrative rules was an essential part of the TCC's work. It also developed varying intensity of review for the principle of statutory reservation and applied the intermediate-level and the high-level intensity of review in over 70 percent of the cases. This indicates the TCC's strict interpretation of "prescribed by law". Any restrictions on individual rights and freedoms should generally be provided for by statutes passed by the democratic legislature and administrative authorities could only do so with clear and precise delegation of power from the legislature. Even when an administrative rule passed the statutory reservation test, the TCC continued reviewing its substantive content. At this stage, proportionality and equality were deployed. As for the CFA, proportionality is still the predominant standard of review for administrative rules. It adopted the standard of reasonable necessity to review discriminations on the grounds of sexual orientation and the "manifest" standard to restrictions on socio-economic rights, which is consistent with the cases against ordinances. The CFA also applied "prescribed by law", but it afforded leeway to the form of law that the government could adopt to impose restrictions on rights and freedoms, including enacting administrative rules without legislative delegation. The CFA is less concerned with whether the restrictions on rights take the form of statutory instruments. But it required the administrative rules to be accessible and sufficiently precise.

5 Judicial Review of Concrete Executive Acts

Introduction

Following the previous examination of the judicial review concerning primary legislation and administrative rules, this chapter shifts focus to the judicial review against concrete executive actions. It delves into the decisions of three apex courts: the SPC, the CFA, and the TUI, noting that concrete executive actions fall outside the jurisdiction of the TCC. This chapter seeks to address several questions: what standards have these courts employed to review concrete executive actions? How did they apply them? And how rigorously did they scrutinize executive actions? An investigation into over 400 decisions reveals that, while the SPC and the TUI took a markedly deferential approach to reviewing concrete executive actions, the CFA took a relative assertive stance toward concrete administrative decisions.

The SPC demonstrated a clear preference for reviewing the formal legality of concrete executive acts, steering off examining the substance of those acts. Its focus was primarily on whether the decision-makers act within the four corners of the power conferred on them, whether the decision-makers violate legally prescribed procedures, and whether the decision is reached based on sufficient evidence and correct facts. The SPC infrequently employed substantive standards such as proportionality or abuse of power because of a high threshold for substantive review. It emphasized and reiterated that the courts could only interfere with government actions that are significantly and manifestly unreasonable and could strike down those actions only if they are grossly disproportionate. Additionally, in the SPC's jurisprudence, public interest takes precedence over individual rights. The courts do not even revoke an illegal executive action if the revocation causes significant harm to national security and public interest.

Like the SPC, the TUI primarily relied on standards that focus on the formal legality of administrative decisions, such as violation of administrative procedure, failure to give reasons, and failure to perform duty. While the TUI applied proportionality when examining administrative actions, its application was more rhetorical than substantive, having no "teeth". The TUI echoed the SPC's stance, holding that the courts would not strike down administrative

DOI: 10.4324/9781003482536-5

decisions unless they are manifestly disproportionate. Additionally, the TUI often adopted a rigid and strict approach to the interpretation of the laws relating to individual rights, often limiting the scope of people's rights and freedoms.

Unlike the SPC and the TUI, the CFA did not circumvent substantive review. It often employed proportionality, unreasonableness, legal certainty, and legitimate expectation to review administrative decisions. Nonetheless, it was less assertive in certain areas, such as disciplinary proceedings and immigration. In those cases, it mainly adopted a low level of intensity of review.

This chapter comprises of five parts. Part 2 to Part 4 detail the standards and intensity of judicial review in the decisions of the SPC, the CFA, and the TUI against concrete executive acts, respectively. Part 5 is a summary of the main findings of this chapter.

China

An Overview

Scrutinizing concrete executive actions is the primary and most crucial domain of judicial review of Chinese courts. This is the only area where the courts could flex their muscles over the government, as they are excluded from reviewing primary legislation and administrative rules of superior rank. The ALL and the ALL Interpretation of 2018 provide 11 grounds for reviewing administrative decisions, on which the courts can declare impugned administrative decisions invalid or revoke them. These grounds for review are:

(1) Inadequacy of essential evidence.
(2) Misapplying laws and regulations.
(3) Violating procedures prescribed by law.
(4) Acting in excess of its power.
(5) Abuse of power.
(6) Decision that is manifestly improper.
(7) Failing to perform statutory duties.
(8) The decision-maker does not qualify as an executive authority.
(9) Restricting people's rights or imposing obligations without legal basis.
(10) It is objectively impossible to enforce administrative decisions.
(11) Other serious and obvious violations of laws.[1]

These standards of review can be divided into two groups. The first group is concerned with the formal legality of executive actions, including standards

1 Administrative Litigation Law (ALL) (行政诉讼法), arts 70, 72, 75; The Interpretation of the SPC on the Application of the Administrative Litigation Law (SPC ALL Interpretation of 2018) (最高人民法院关于适用《中华人民共和国行政诉讼法》的解释), art 99 (2018).

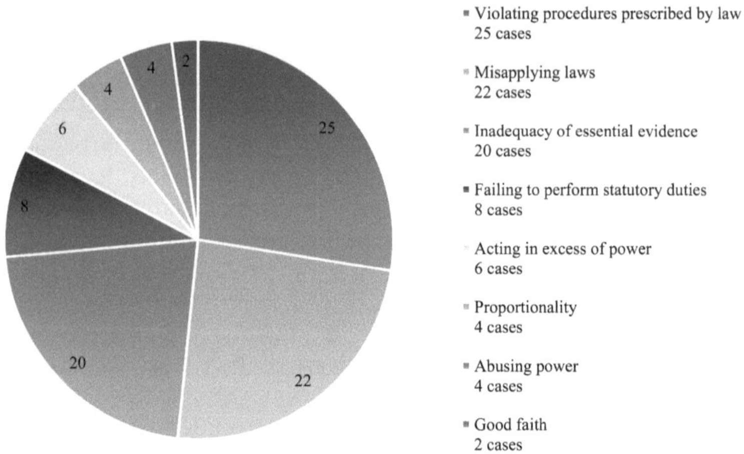

Figure 5.1 The Main Standards of Review in the SPC Decisions against Executive Actions (1999–2019).

Source: Author.

(1) to (4), and (7) to (8).[2] The second group focuses on the exercise of discretionary power and the substance of administrative decisions, including standards (5) to (6), and (9) to (10).[3]

After examining 92 Guiding cases and Gazette cases against administrative decisions, it was clear that Chinese courts prefer using the first group of standards of review (which emerged over 80 times) and tend to circumvent the second group of standards of review. Violating procedures prescribed by law (25 cases), misapplying the law (22 cases) and inadequacy of essential evidence (20 cases) were the most frequently applied standards of review. The second group of standards has been less frequently employed. Abuse of power emerged in four cases. Despite being absent from the list, the courts introduced and applied proportionality (four cases) and acting in good faith (two cases) (Figure 5.1).[4]

2 Xuexian Huang (黄学贤) and Lingyu Li (李凌云), 'Theoretical Research and Practical Development of the Principle of Legality Review in Administrative Litigation' (行政诉讼合法性审查原则的理论研究与实践发展) (2020) 5 *Study and Exploration* (学习与探索) 61, 65.

3 Lingyun Yu (余凌云), 'Reasonableness Review in Administrative Proceedings' (论行政诉讼上的合理性审查) (2022) 1 *Journal of Comparative Law* (比较法研究) 145, 149–151.

4 In addition to these standards of review, standards such as protection of legitimate expectations, protection of public moralities, and fair compensation in expropriation were also applied but on only one or two occasions.

Main Standards of Review in the SPC's Judicial Review of Concrete Executive Acts

Violating Statutory Procedure

In the SPC Guiding cases and Gazette cases, violating statutory procedure is the most frequently applied standard of review, emerging in 25 out of 92 cases (approximately 27.2 percent). Chinese administration has long been criticized for ignoring procedural fairness,[5] which explains why people often challenge decision-making procedures before the courts. Additionally, this standard requires the executive to act in line with the procedure prescribed law. Violation of this requirement means a breach of clearly stated rules. Therefore, the courts have less pressure to quash the impugned decisions on this ground.

Administrative decisions were often struck down for denying people's right to a hearing (8 out of 25 cases).[6] For example, in *Huang Zefu, He Boqiong, and He Yi v The Jintang Administration for Industry and Commerce of Chengdu Municipality, Sichuan Province*, the court struck down a confiscation decision and gave the reasons as follows:

> Following the general procedures of administrative penalties, the Jintang Administration for Industry and Commerce only informed the three persons ... of their rights to make a statement and their rights to defense but failed to inform them of their rights to request a hearing. [The administrative penalty decision] violated statutory procedures, and [it] should be revoked according to law.[7]

Besides denying the right to a hearing, Chinese courts have overturned executive decisions for violating other procedural rules. Examples include instances where administrative decisions were not delivered to those affected,[8] where

5 Jiansheng Zhang (章剑生), 'Judicial Review on the Grounds of Violating Statutory Procedure: Based on the Typical Cases Issued by the People's Supreme Court (1985–2008)' (对违反法定程序的司法审查——以最高人民法院公布的典型案例(1985 2008)为例) (2009) 2 *Chinese Journal of Law* (法学研究) 150, 162.

6 *Huang Zefu, He Boqiong, and He Yi v The Jintang Administration for Industry and Commerce of Chengdu Municipality, Sichuan Province*, Guiding Case No. 6; *Tian Yong v The University of Science and Technology Beijing*, Guiding Case No. 38; *Zhang Chengyin v The People's Government of Xuzhou Municipality*, SPC Gazette 2005(3); *Kunming Wei Heng Li Trade Co., Ltd. v The Planning Bureau of Kunming Municipality*, SPC Gazette 2009(10); *Ding'an Chengdong Building Decoration Engineering Company v The People's Government of Ding'an County*, SPC Gazette 2015(2); *Shanxi Anye Group Co., Ltd v Taiyuan Municipality People's Government*, SPC Gazette 2017(1); *Sheyang County Red Flag Cultural Troupe v The Culture, Radio, Television, Press and Publication Bureau of Sheyang County*, SPC Gazette 2018(8); *Shouguang PetroChina Kunlun Gas Co., Ltd v The People's Government of Shouguang Municipality and the People's Government of Shouguang Municipality*, SPC Gazette 2018(9).

7 Guiding Case No. 6.

8 *Tian Yong v The University of Science and Technology Beijing*, Guiding Case No. 38; *Lanzhou Changde Materials Office v The People's Government of Lanzhou Municipality*, SPC Gazette 2000(4).

the executive authority unduly delayed responding to the information disclosure requests,[9] where decisions were made by officials who did not hear the case,[10] and where construction permits were granted before the environmental impact assessment report was approved.[11]

The "procedure prescribed by law" encapsulates those procedural requirements explicitly written into the laws.[12] However, not all decision-making procedural requirements are captured in written laws, and it is impossible to do so. In situations where laws, regulations, and rules do not explicitly spell out procedural requirements, Chinese courts have introduced the principle of "administrative procedural justice" (*xingzheng chengxu zhengdangxing*)[13] or "due process" (*zhengdang chengxu*).[14] This represents one of the few instances of judicial activism by Chinese courts.[15]

The principle of "due process" first appeared in *Zhang Chengyin v The People's Government of Xuzhou Municipality*.[16] Zhang lived with her mother-in-law for many years until her mother-in-law passed away. During this period, their house was repaired and rebuilt and registered under Zhang's name. Zhang's sister-in-law filed an administrative reconsideration request to revoke the property ownership registration. The respondent decided in favor of Zhang's sister-in-law and invalidated the property ownership registration. However, the respondent did not inform Zhang of the administrative reconsideration proceeding.[17] Zhang lost her property without being given an opportunity to state her case. Under the Administrative Reconsideration Law, the government is not obliged to inform Zhang, who was regarded as a third party to the reconsideration proceeding. However, the court held:

9 *Li Jianxiong v Department of Transport of Guangdong Province*, Guiding Case No. 26.

10 *Xixia Longcheng Special Materials Co., Ltd v The Intellectual Property Administration of Yulin Municipality*, SPC Gazette 2018(5).

11 *Shen Xixian and others v The Planning Commission of Beijing Municipality*, SPC Gazette 2004(3).

12 Bixin Jiang (江必新), *Understanding and Applying the Articles the Administrative Litigation Law of the People's Republic of China and its Judicial Interpretation* (中华人民共和国行政诉讼法及其司法解释条文理解与适用) (People's Court Press 2015) 469–470.

13 Bixin Jiang (江必新), 'Judicial Review of the Justifiability of Administrative Procedure' (行政程序正当性的司法审查) (2012) 7 *Social Sciences in China* (中国社会科学) 123.

14 Youyong Zhou (周佑勇), 'Strengthening the Development of the Principle of Due Process through Judicial Decisions' (司法判决对正当程序原则的发展) (2019) 3 *China Legal Science* (中国法学) 26; Haibo He (何海波), 'The Principle of Due Process in Judicial Decisions' (司法判决中的正当程序原则) (2009) 1 *Chinese Journal of Law* (法学研究) 124.

15 Zhou, *ibid.*, 27.

16 *Zhang Chengyin* (n 6); He, 'The Principle of Due Process in Judicial Decisions' (n 14)137–138.

17 Administrative reconsideration is a control mechanism that allows internal self-correction by administrative authorities. Xin He, 'Administrative Reconsideration's Erosion of Administrative Litigation in China' (2014) *Chinese Journal of Comparative Law* 252, 255.

> In accordance with due process, the executive authorities, before making decisions, should hear arguments from interested parties whose rights and interests are adversely affected, albeit with no statutory obligation to inform third parties.[18]

Although the court did not give a clear definition to the principle of "due process", the judgment indicated that this principle had the constituent very similar to common law rules of natural justice, that "the parties should be given a proper opportunity to be heard and this end be given due notice of the hearing".[19] This is significant progress in judicial review of administrative decisions in the sense of enhancing judicial supervision of administrative decision-making and judicial protection of people's right to hearing, and consequently substantive rights.[20] Haibo He commented that Chinese judges had wanted the principle of "due process" for a long time and finally included it in their judgments, which was a big step forward for Chinese judicial review.[21]

Misapplying Laws

The standard of misapplication of law emerged in 22 Guiding cases and Gazette cases against administrative decisions. In ***He Wenliang v The Labor Bureau of Wuhou District***, the court dismissed the respondent's argument that injuries that happened in a lavatory were not work-related and that going to the bathroom was not a part of work.[22] In ***Wang Mingde v The Human Resources and Social Security Bureau of Leshan Municipality***,[23] the appellant's son died in a car accident on his way to work, and the police issued a Road Traffic Accident Certificate. However, the respondent suspended the work-related injuries determination proceeding on the grounds that the police had not issued a Written Determination of the Traffic Accident. According to Article 20(3) of the ***Regulation on Work Injury***, the determination of work-related injuries must proceed based on an official conclusion by the relevant authorities. In the respondent's opinion, a Written Determination of the Traffic Accident was the only valid form of conclusion, and the Certificate was not acceptable. The SPC considered the Certificate issued by the police to be a valid conclusion under

18 *Zhang Chengyin* (n 6).

19 Harry Woolf and others, *De Smith's Judicial Review* (7th edn, Sweet & Maxwell 2013) 348.

20 Although the NPCSC worried that the principle of due process was too theoretical and gave the courts discretion to decide its contents, it still acquiesced to the usage of this principle. Chunying Xin (信春鹰), *Interpretation of the Administrative Litigation Law of the People's Republic of China* (《中华人民共和国行政诉讼法》释义) (Law Press 2014) 188.

21 He, 'The Principle of Due Process in Judicial Decisions' (n 14) 139.

22 SPC Gazette 2004(9). The courts rejected similar narrow interpretation of the work injury in *Yang Qingfeng v The Labor and Social Security Bureau of Wuxi Municipality*, SPC Gazette 2008(1); *Deng Jinlong v The Social Security Funding Management Bureau of Shenzhen Municipality*, SPC Gazette 2019(11).

23 Guiding Case No. 69.

Article 20(3) and held that the respondent's narrow interpretation of Article 20(3) was erroneous, declaring the suspension of the injuries determination proceeding illegal.

When the executive authority did not specify the legal provisions on which their decisions were based, the court would strike down the decision on the grounds of misapplication of law.[24] The executive authority should provide reasons for their decisions and clearly state the legal provisions underpinning their decisions. In *Xuan Yicheng et al. v Bureau of Land and Resources of Quzhou Municipality*, the courts stated:

> When the respondent issued the Notice, [it] just stated that it made [the Notice] based on the Land Administration Law and relevant regulations of Zhejiang Province but failed to cite specific legal provisions. The administrative act did not have a clear legal basis, and [contained] an erroneous application of law.[25]

Inadequacy of Essential Evidence

Assessing the factual basis of administrative decisions is not the courts' expertise. Nonetheless, the ALL has included making decisions based on insufficient evidence and an error of facts as grounds for judicial review since 1989. This standard is one of the major grounds for reviewing executive decisions in China. It was invoked in 20 Guiding cases and Gazette cases, out of which only 3 stood this test.[26] In *Su Haiyan v Haikou Re-Education through Labor Management Commission*,[27] the respondent made an administrative punishment decision of re-education through labor of three years' incarceration for the appellant, accused of assault. The court acknowledged that, in making the decision, the respondent had considered the facts that the appellant had

24 *Lu Shiwei v The People's Government* of *Lanzhou Municipality*, SPC Gazette 2002(3); *Luo Lunfu v The Third Traffic Police Brigade of the Public Security Bureau of Luzhou Municipality*, SPC Gazette 2002(5); *Xuan Yicheng et al. v Bureau of Land and Resources of Quzhou Municipality*, Guiding Case No. 41. It is noticed that in *Lanzhou Changde Materials Office* Case, the respondent did not cite the legal provisions it relied on when making decisions, and the court considered it as a violation of statutory procedure, rather than misapplication of law.

25 *Xuan Yicheng et al., ibid.*

26 *Liao Zongrong v The Second Branch of Transportation Management Bureau, Public Security Bureau of Chongqing Municipality*, SPC Gazette 2007(1); *Wuxi Meitong Food Science and Technology Co., Ltd. v The High and New Technology Industrial Development Zone Branch, Wuxi Quality and Technology Supervision Bureau*, SPC Gazette 2013(7); *Shanghai Dike Paper Packaging Co., Ltd v The Human Resources and Social Security Bureau of Shanghai Municipality*, SPC Gazette 2013(11).

27 SPC Gazette 2000(3). Re-education through labor (*laodong jiaotang or laojiao*) is a type of administrative punishment imposed by the police according to laws, regulations, or even policies, under which the police can subject a person guilty of "minor offenses" to a maximum of three years' incarceration. Hualing Fu, 'Re-education through Labor in Historical Perspective' (2005) *China Quarterly* 811, 811.

emotional entanglements and pecuniary disputes with the victims and that the appellant appeared at the scene of the fight. However, the court still revoked this decision on the ground that the evidence was insufficient to prove the appellant was involved in the alleged assault. The fact was still unclear because the decision was based mainly on the victim's statement without any other supporting evidence.

Failing to Perform Statutory Duties and Acting in Excess of Power

When mandatory duties are conferred on the executive authority to perform public functions, failing to fulfill these duties constitutes administrative omission. Article 72 of the ALL entitles the Chinese courts to order the executive authorities to perform their duties within a fixed time if they fail to do so. This standard was invoked in 8 out of 92 Guiding cases and Gazette cases. Examples include instances where the Post and Telecommunication Office rejected setting up the "120" emergency number for a local hospital,[28] where the police did not take any action after receiving a theft report,[29] and where an environmental protection bureau illegally refused to disclose the environmental impact assessment report.[30]

When the laws confer power on the executive authorities, they must act within the confines of that power. If their actions exceed the scope of conferred power, those actions should be quashed. The courts invoked the standard of acting in excess of power in six cases and overturned the decisions in five cases.[31] In *Lu Shiwei v The People's Government of Jingyuan County*,[32] a garment and embroidery factory went bankrupt and entered insolvency proceedings. The trustees made a property disposal plan, and the court ruled in favor of it. According to the asset disposal plan, the appellant would acquire factory buildings and land tenure for 360,000 renminbi. The trustees submitted the plan to the respondent for approval. The respondent replied and approved the plan. However, the respondent revoked its approval after the appellant paid. The High Court of Gansu Province struck down the respondent's revoca-

28 *Chinese Medicine Hospital of Xupu County v The Post and Telecommunication Office of Xupu County*, SPC Gazette 2000(1).

29 *Yin Chenhui v The Public Security Bureau of Lushi County*, SPC Gazette 2003(2).

30 *All-China Environment Federation v The Environmental Protection Bureau of Xiuwen County*, SPC Gazette 2013(1).

31 *Lanzhou Changde Materials Office v The People's Government of Lanzhou Municipality*, SPC Gazette 2000(4); *Division 1 of Luobiancao Village v The People's Government of Chongqing Municipal*, SPC Gazette 2000(6); *Lu Shiwei v The People's Government of Jingyuan County*, SPC Gazette 2002(3); *Ji Deren v The People's Government of Yancheng Municipality*, SPC Gazette 2003(4); *Zhang Chengyin v The People's Government of Xuzhou Municipality*, SPC Gazette 2005(3). The only case in which the court made a decision in favor of the government is *Yi'erku Company v The Administration for Industry and Commerce of Wuxi Municipality*, SPC Gazette 2006(3).

32 *Lu Shiwei, ibid.*

tion decision on the grounds that local governments had no power to make decisions either in favor of or against property disposal plans in insolvency proceedings. According to the Bankruptcy Law, the trustees should enforce the property disposal plan after the court's approval. The respondent had no power to assess or approve the disposal plan.

The standards of review above focused on the formal legality of administrative action. The following parts will look at three standards of review that emerged in the SPC Guiding cases and Gazette cases by which the courts examined the substance of executive acts.

Proportionality

THE ADOPTION OF PROPORTIONALITY IN CHINA

The landmark case that first applied the principle of proportionality was *Planning Bureau of Harbin Municipality, Heilongjiang Province v Huifeng Industrial Development Co Ltd*, in which the SPC applied proportionality to reverse an administrative penalty decision.[33] The respondent, Huifeng Company, undertook a reconstruction of two buildings located on Central Avenue, which is in a historic area of Harbin. Huifeng Company added four stories to each building without obtaining the required construction approval from the Planning Bureau. The newly added stories obstructed the street-level view of Xinhua Bookstore, a landmark of Central Avenue. The Planning Bureau ordered the appellant to tear down four stories of one building and two stories of the other building, and to pay a fine of nearly 400,000 renminbi.

The High Court of Heilongjiang Province held that Huifeng Company violated the law but the penalty was manifestly unfair and decided to reduce the demolition part and decrease the fine. On appeal, the Planning Bureau argued that it made the penalty decision in accordance with the Central Avenue Plan, which aimed to preserve the authenticity and integrity of the historic areas of Harbin. The SPC accepted the respondent's argument that the buildings should not destroy the view of the historic area. But the SPC held that the administrative penalty was manifestly unfair since the amount of demolition ordered by the applicant was more than necessary to implement the Central Avenue Plan and preserve the integrity of the historic area. The SPC's reasoning relied on the necessity test and the balance test from proportionality. It stated:

> When the Planning Bureau ordered Huifeng Company to take relevant corrective acts [to restore the buildings], its decision should reflect the degree of damage [to the view of Central Avenue]. [The Planning

33 Wang Jing (王静), 'Application of the Principle of Proportionality in Chinese Administrative Litigation' (比例原则在中国行政判决中的适用) (2017) 4 *Shanghai Jiaotong University Law Review* (交大法学) 22, 23.

> Bureau] ought to fulfil the purpose of the administrative management, and at the same time, respect the appellant's rights and interests. [The corrective acts] should be limited to the accomplishment of the administrative purposes and goals and should cause the least harm to the people's rights and interests.[34]

Proportionality in this statement did not contain the legitimate aim test or the suitability test. But the SPC's decision implied these two subtests. It upheld the lower court's decision to reduce the demolition part and decrease the fine, indicating that removing several stories was sufficient to protect the view of Central Avenue, which was the purpose of making the administrative decision.

It was not until 2010 that the SPC elaborated the subtests of proportionality in its comments on *Wang Liping v The Transportation Bureau of Zhongmou County* and *Chen Ning v The Public Security Bureau of Zhuanghe Municipality*.[35] In *Wang Liping*, the SPC confirmed the subtests of proportionality included the suitability test, the necessity test, and the balance test.[36] In *Chen Ning*, the SPC articulated the meaning of each subtest, which was not different from the subtests of the standard model of proportionality.[37] However, the SPC did not include the legitimate aim test in the formula of proportionality, although it intentionally or unintentionally examined the purposes and goals the executive tried to achieve in its adjudication. The reason for this omission is unclear, especially when some Chinese scholars have been arguing for four subtests of proportionality for decades prior to this decision.[38]

THE APPLICATION OF PROPORTIONALITY

In the last two decades, proportionality and its subtests were invoked in four Guiding cases and Gazette cases.[39] The term "proportionality" emerged in one case – *Chen Chao v The Urban Public Transportation Management and Service Centre of Ji'nan Municipality*. In the other three cases, the term "proportionality" did not appear in the court's decisions, but the courts employed

34 *The Planning Bureau of Harbin Municipality, Heilongjiang Province v Huifeng Industrial Development Co Ltd*, SPC, 19 January 2000.

35 The two cases were published in the SPC Gazette 2003 and later selected as typical cases by the Administrative Tribunal of the SPC in 2010.

36 The Administrative Tribunal of the SPC (ed), *Chinese Administrative Adjudication Cases (Volume I)* (中国行政审判案例(第1卷)) (China Legal Publishing House 2010) 92.

37 *Ibid.*, 96.

38 Quan Liu (刘权), 'The Legitimacy of Aims and Reconstructing the Principle of Proportionality' (目的正当性与比例原则的重构) (2014) 4 *China Legal Science* (中国法学) 133, 144.

39 *Wang Liping v The Transportation Bureau of Zhongmou County*, SPC Gazette 2003(3); *Chen Ning v The Public Security Bureau of Zhuanghe Municipality*, SPC Gazette 2003(3); *Suzhou Dingsheng Food Company v The Industry and Commerce Bureau of Suzhou Municipality*, SPC Gazette 2013(10); *Chen Chao v The Urban Public Transportation Management and Service Centre of Ji'nan Municipality*, SPC Gazette 2018(2).

the subtests of proportionality. Among the four subtests, the necessity test and the balance test that emerged in all four cases are the most frequently applied subtests. This practice is different from the TCC and the CFA, which rarely rely on the balance test.

In *Suzhou Dingsheng Food Company v The Industry and Commerce Bureau of Suzhou Municipality*, the Industry and Commerce Bureau of Suzhou Municipality imposed an administrative punishment on the appellant for unlawfully using trademarks similar to those registered by other companies. The appellant thought the punishment was too severe to be fair. The High Court of Jiangsu Province stated the respondent should exercise its discretionary power according to the principle "punishment commensurate with unlawfulness" when making the administrative punishment decision:

> [w]hen [the executive authorities] guarantee the accomplishment of administrative management aims, (they) should give due consideration to the people's rights and interests. Administrative punishment should be commensurable with the extent to which administrative actions' objectives and purposes are accomplished and should try to cause the least harm to people's rights and interests.[40]

In *Chen Chao*, the appellant was an online ride-hailing driver. The respondent found that the appellant had not obtained a taxi license and made an administrative punishment decision against him, including a fine of 20,000 renminbi and confiscation of profit. On appeal, the Intermediate Court of Ji'nan Municipality considered that, although providing taxi service without a license was unlawful, the administrative punishment was more than necessary. The court expressly stated that:

> Proportionality is an essential principle of administrative law ... When the executive authority makes punishment [decisions] according to existing laws and regulations, they should try their best to confine adverse impact on people to a minimum range and strike a balance between the accomplishment of administrative management aims and the protection of new inventions.[41]

Wang Liping is another vivid example. The appellant borrowed tractors and delivered pigs for sale. The respondent stopped her on her way and found the tractor owners did not pay road maintenance tax. The respondent decided to seize the tractors. The appellant requested to transport the pigs to the destination before seizing the tractors because the pigs might die from being exposed to high temperatures. The respondent refused this request and removed the

40 *Suzhou Dingsheng Food Company*, *ibid.*
41 *Chen Chao* (n 39).

tractors' engines. The trailers tilted and the pigs squashed each other and died from high temperatures. The SPC stated that the respondent disregarded the appellant's reasonable request and made a manifestly unreasonable decision. The respondent did not act in accordance with the principle of causing minimum adverse impact on people, and its actions resulted in a serious imbalance between the public interest the respondent tried to achieve and the appellant's rights and interests.[42]

As for the subtests of legitimate aims and suitability, they were only deployed in *Chen Ning*. In this case, the appellant and her husband had a serious car accident. Her husband was stuck in the driver's seat and lost consciousness. The police officers tried many means to open the driver's side door but failed. Eventually, they successfully rescued her husband by cutting the door with gas welding, which resulted in a fire and serious damage to the car. The appellant sued the police for causing damage to the car. According to the court's reasoning, the four subtests of proportionality were applied. First, the measure was taken for a legitimate aim, rescuing her husband's life; second, the measure is suitable. The police officers successfully removed her husband from the deformed car; third, the measure is necessary because it is the last resort; fourth, the measure struck a balance between the property interests and her husband's life. In its comment on the case, the SPC stated:

> The principle of proportionality applied in the case is a widely recognized standard for scrutinizing the exercise of discretionary power. It requires when carrying out administrative actions, an executive authority should balance the achievement of administrative objectives with the protection of individuals' rights and interests. If the accomplishment of administrative aims could result in adverse impacts on people's rights and interests, the adverse impact should be minimized and kept within an appropriate proportion.[43]

Abuse of Power and Good Faith

Acting in excess of power and abusing power are two independent grounds of judicial review in Chinese administrative law. The distinction on the surface between the two standards is whether executive authorities act within the confines of the power conferred by laws.[44] Acting in excess of power indicates that the executive authorities act outside the confines of their power. When

42 The Administrative Tribunal of the SPC (n 36) 92.

43 *Ibid.*, 96.

44 Haibo He (何海波), 'Obvious Improperness of Administrative Actions' (论行政行为"明显不当") (2016) 3 *Chinese Journal of Law* (法学研究) 70, 77–78; Jianjun Yao (姚建军), 'Judicial Review Against Administrative Abuses of Power' (对行政滥用职权的司法审查) (2011) 7 *People's Judicature* (人民司法) 86, 86.

the executive authorities abuse power, they still act within the four corners of their power, but in an inappropriate or irrational manner.[45]

The standard "abuse of power" was employed in four Guiding cases and Gazette cases.[46] In *Liu Yunwu v The First Traffic Police Brigade of the Public Security Bureau of Taiyuan Municipality, Shanxi Province*,[47] the respondent suspected that the appellant failed to complete an annual vehicle examination and therefore seized his van. After the appellant provided proof of the annual examination, the respondent refused to return the van, citing suspicions that the appellant had used a fake vehicle mark and replaced the original engine generator. Despite the appellant's submission of relevant evidence, the respondent continued to retain the van, claiming it was of unknown origin. The court considered that the seizure of a vehicle was intended as a provisional measure. The respondent should have returned the vehicle, or investigated the origin of the vehicle, or requested a guarantee of some sort and then released the vehicle. By repeatedly asking the appellant to submit evidence that was objectively unavailable, the respondent's actions constituted an abuse of power.

The principle of good faith was applied in two cases, and the courts struck down the executive decisions on this ground.[48] In *Pingxiang Yapeng Real Estate Development Co., Ltd. v The Bureau of Land and Resources of Pingxiang Municipality*,[49] the respondent publicized a land sale notice in a local newspaper, indicating that the land was designated for commercial and residential use. Following this, the appellant and the respondent signed a contract, and the respondent issued two land use certificates: one labeled "industrial land" and the other "commercial and residential land". The appellant asked the respondent to correct the "industrial land" certificate to reflect "commercial and residential land" as originally intended. The respondent agreed to make a change, but it demanded that the appellant pay additional land transfer fees. The Court stated that once an administrative contract was signed, all parties were bound to adhere to its items. The executive authority, in this case, must not unilaterally change or rescind the contract without proper reasons. The Court ultimately revoked the respondent's decision, holding that the request

45 Yu (n 3) 146.

46 *Wang Liping* (n 39); *Ding'an Chengdong Construction and Decoration Company v The People's Government of Sihong County*, SPC Gazette 2015(2); *Liu Yunwu v The First Traffic Police Brigade of the Public Security Bureau of Taiyuan Municipality, Shanxi Province*, SPC Gazette 2017(2); *Cui Longshu v The People's Government of Feng County*, SPC Gazette 2017(11).

47 *Liu Yunwu, ibid.*

48 *Pingxiang Yapeng Real Estate Development Co., Ltd. v The Bureau of Land and Resources of Pingxiang Municipality*, Guiding Case No. 76; *Cui Longshu v The People's Government of Feng County*, SPC Gazette 2017(11). The principle of good faith emerged in *Lu Hongxia v The Commission of Development and Reform of Nantong Municipality*, but the court held that the appellant acted in bad faith as she abused rights to information.

49 *Yapeng, ibid.*

for additional land transfer fees lacked factual or legal justification and violated the principle of good faith.

The Intensity of the SPC's Judicial Review of Concrete Executive Acts

The Chinese courts have not systematically discussed the intensity of review of executive actions in their decisions. But the Guiding cases and Gazette cases still indicate the court's deferential judicial approach in judicial review of executive actions, which is evident in three aspects. First, it is a cardinal principle of Chinese administrative law that the courts should primarily review the formal legality of executive actions and avoid reviewing their substance. This principle explains the courts' preference in applying these standards that focus on the formal legality of administrative decisions. Second, the threshold for conducting a substantive review is very high. The courts can only interfere with executive actions if they are significantly or manifestly unreasonable and can only strike them down when they are grossly disproportionate. Third, public interest is given more weight than individual rights and interests, resulting in the individuals being at a distinct disadvantage in judicial review. The courts cannot even revoke an illegal executive action if the revocation significantly harms national security and public interest.

"Legality" and "Reasonableness" in Chinese Administrative Law

To understand the deferential approach of Chinese courts in reviewing executive action, it is essential to understand the dichotomy between "legality" and "reasonableness" in Chinese administrative law. Legality means that the courts scrutinize the formal legality of executive actions: whether decision-makers act within the four corners of the power conferred on them, whether they correctly understand and apply the laws, whether the decision-making violates statutory procedures, and whether the decision is based on sufficient evidence and correct facts.[50] By reasonableness, the courts are concerned with the discretionary decision-making and substance of administrative decisions.

Since the incipient ALL was enacted in 1989, it has been an underlying principle of Chinese administrative law that courts are supposed to be concerned primarily with the formal legality of executive actions and not to substantively review the merits of executive acts.[51] Article 5 of the ALL of 1989 provided that "when the people's courts adjudicate administrative cases, they scrutinize the 'legality' of concrete executive actions".[52] This provision conveyed the legislature's attitude, albeit implicitly, that the courts are supposed not to substantively review the reasonableness of executive acts.

50 Huang and Li (n 2) 65.
51 The Administrative Tribunal of the SPC (n 36) 92, 98.
52 ALL (n 1), art. 6.

Legality and reasonableness in Chinese administrative law perform the function of demarcating the role of the judiciary and executive authorities.[53] In the early stage of judicial review of administrative decisions (1989–2014), the Chinese courts were nearly completely precluded from examining the reasonableness of executive actions. They were only charged with the responsibility of adjudicating upon the formal legality of executive actions. The executive discretion was not amenable to judicial review and the substance of administrative decisions was not subject to judicial scrutiny.[54] The NPCSC stated in its explanation of the ALL draft in 1989:

> To correctly deal with the relationship between judicial power and administrative power, the people's courts should hear administrative cases in accordance with the law and should not interfere with the executive actions that are within the confines established by statutes and regulations, and should not replace the executive authority in the exercise of administrative power, so as to ensure that the executive authorities effectively carry out administrative management according to the law.[55]

The constraint on judicial review was enhanced by the Interpretation of the SPC on Several Issues concerning the Implementation of the ALL of 2000, which expressly required the courts to dismiss people's claims in the cases where the impugned concrete executive decisions were unreasonable but formally legal.[56]

On the one hand, the legislature intended to confine judicial review to the formal legality of administrative actions; on the other hand, the ALL of 1989 provided two grounds of judicial review that enabled the courts to review the substance of executive actions: abuse of power and obviously unfair administrative penalties.[57] The ALL seemed to open a gate for judicial activism. As Haibo He observed, however, the courts tended to decline to use these two grounds of review.[58] They stopped themselves from intervening in executive decision-making. One reason for the rare usage of the two substantive grounds of review was that the two grounds were vague in law. The ALL of 1989 and

53 Weijie Tan (谭炜杰), 'Categorizing the Intensity of Administrative Reasonableness Review' (行政合理性原则审查强度之类型化) (2014) 12 *Journal of Law Application* (法律适用) 49, 49; He, 'Obvious Improperness of Administrative Actions' (n 44) 72.

54 The Administrative Tribunal of the SPC (n 36) 92.

55 Explanation of the Administrative Litigation Law of the People's Republic of China (Draft) (关于《中华人民共和国行政诉讼法》(草案)的说明》), SPC Gazette 1989(2).

56 Interpretation of the SPC on Several Issues concerning the Implementation of the ALL (最高人民法院关于执行《中华人民共和国行政诉讼法》若干问题的解释) art. 56 (2000).

57 ALL of 1989, art. 54.

58 He, 'Obvious Improperness of Administrative Actions' (n 44) 72.

the relevant judicial interpretations did not elucidate these grounds.[59] Another reason was that the courts strategically chose not to use these grounds to protect themselves from the criticisms and even punishments from the government and to prevent their decisions from being overturned by higher courts.

While it is generally accepted that constitutions delegate matters of political, social, and economic policy to the legislature and the executive, rather than the judiciary, this division of responsibilities does not entirely absolve the courts from examining the substantive merits of legislative and executive actions.[60] Courts are traditionally seen as ill-suited to address issues that are inherently matters of policy preference, are polycentric in nature, or fall outside their areas of expertise.[61] However, the courts' constitutional role and their responsibility to uphold the rule of law suggest that they should not be entirely passive in scrutinizing the actions of the other branches of government. The need for judicial oversight is particularly pressing when it comes to ensuring that executive discretion is exercised within reasonable bounds and does not infringe upon fundamental rights. Chinese scholars have long advocated for judicial review of the substance of executive acts and for strengthening judicial control over the exercise of administrative power.[62]

In 2014, the NPCSC amended the ALL and added a new ground of judicial review – manifest impropriety.[63] Chinese scholars believed this ground of review would enhance the court's judicial review over the substance and reasonableness of executive acts. But in practice, the judicial review of administrative actions is still dominated by formal legality review. The courts continue the self-constraint strategy and remain timid in judicial review. They predominantly relied upon those standards that do not touch upon the substance of executive decision, which the foregoing investigation into the judicial review decisions proves.

A High Threshold for Reasonableness Review

Manifest impropriety, disproportionality, and abuse of power are standards concerned with the substance and merits of executive decisions. But these standards have appeared in only a limited number of Guiding cases and Gazette cases, which echoes the national trend. A search on "China Judgments Online", a judicial decision database run by the SPC, found that,

59 Hu Cheng (程琥), 'A New Approach to the Principle of Legality in Administrative Litigation' (行政诉讼合法性审查原则新探) (2019) 9 *Journal of Law Application* (法律适用) 75, 86.

60 Harry Woolf and others (n 19) 19.

61 Eric C. Ip and Po Jen Yap, 'Substantive Review of Administrative Discretion in Hong Kong: Divergence between Judicial Rhetoric and Practice' (2019) 7(1) *Chinese Journal of Comparative Law* 190, 210.

62 He, 'Obvious Improperness of Administrative Actions' (n 44) 72, 75.

63 ALL (n 1), art. 70. At the same time, the obviously unfair administrative penalty was removed from the ALL.

among 786,669 administrative litigation judgments delivered between 1999 and 2022, proportionality was invoked in 883 judgments (0.11 percent) and abuse of power in 5,246 judgments (0.67 percent).[64] In contrast to the standards of review focusing on formal legality, the number of proportionality and abuse of power cases is also embarrassingly small. Via keyword searches in the same database and under the same conditions, it finds that inadequacy of evidence emerged in the reasoning of 68,401 cases (8.7 percent), erroneous application of laws and regulations in 45,848 cases (5.82 percent), violation of legally prescribed procedure in 28,378 cases (3.6 percent), and ultra vires in 9,929 cases (1.26 percent).[65] These statistics do not include judgments that use these standards but do not contain the exact terms. The infrequent application of these substantive review standards can be largely attributed to the high threshold for substantive review set by the courts. In the comment on *Chen Ning*, the SPC stressed:

> If courts strictly apply the principle of reasonableness to examine discretionary executive acts, administrative efficiency will suffer from excessive constraints. The judiciary may be suspected of displacing the executive when they intervene in-depth in the fields of administration. Thus, the scrutiny of executive discretion by applying the principle of reasonableness must be limited to a specially tailored level according to our domestic situations: discretionary executive decisions should be deemed lawful unless they are manifestly unreasonable.[66]

The SPC reiterated the high threshold for substantive review when commenting on *Wang Liping*:

> In administrative litigation, [the court] can apply the principle of proportionality to correct the executive action…only when a concrete executive action grossly violates the principle of proportionality and causes severe damage to people's legitimate rights and interests. The courts can interfere with it only if an executive action is manifestly unreasonable, constituting a fundamental breach of law[67]

These statements reveal an extraordinarily high threshold associated with substantive review and proportionality test in Chinese judicial review of administrative decisions. Proportionality applies only if a decision is grossly disproportionate. In the SPC's opinion, a grossly disproportionate decision

64 Shiling Xiao, 'State-centric Proportionality Analysis in Chinese Administrative Litigation' (2023) 21 *International Journal of Constitutional Law* 461, 472–473.

65 *Ibid.*

66 The Administrative Tribunal of the SPC (n 36) 97–98.

67 *Ibid.*, 92.

must be manifestly unreasonable and constitute a fundamental breach of law. This high threshold aimed to and did prevent the courts from using proportionality to interfere excessively with the administration of the executive authorities.

Public Interest Precedes Individual Rights

The deferential attitude of the Chinese courts in judicial review is reflected by their understanding of human rights and public interests as well. In the comment on *Yu Zhujun v The Traffic Police Brigade of the Public Security Bureau of Wujing District, Changzhou Municipality*, the SPC stated:

> When public interest conflicts with individual interests, how to strike a balance between them is a hard question for the courts… We think the courts should find an optimum balancing point between maintaining public interest and protecting individual rights in concrete cases. While following the principle of public interest taking priority [over private interests], [the courts] protect the private interests to the greatest extent so as to strike a reasonable and basic balance between them.[68]

In this passage, the SPC admitted that there should be a balance between public interest and individual rights, but it inserted a premise that, in balancing analysis, public interest should be given more weight than individual rights (taking priority). This stance reflects the Chinese understanding of individual rights within the context of judicial review.

Different from the Western concepts of individual liberty, rights, and dignity, China's understanding of individual rights has a peculiar feature that individual rights are associated with collectivism, nationalism, and patriotism.[69] The "individual is not an entity unto itself, but is inescapably collective in terms of the relatedness of family and society".[70] "Individualism" has strong negative connotations in China.[71] When public interest and individual rights emerge together, the former remains superior to the latter. In the Chinese legal system, "public interest takes priority" (*gongyi youxian*) has been enshrined in many laws as a general principle.[72] Due to this dogma, the Chinese courts treat public interest and individual rights differently when facing conflicts between

68 *Ibid.*, 31–32.

69 Xiangchen Sun (孙向晨), 'Individual Rights in Modern Time and "Individual" in Confucian Tradition' (现代个体权利与儒家传统中的"个体") (2017) 3 *Journal of Chinese Humanities* (文史哲) 90, 98.

70 Ronald Boer, *Socialism with Chinese Characteristics: A Guide for Foreigners* (Springer 2021).

71 Sun (n 69) 98.

72 After searching "Gongyi Youxian" (公益优先) in PKLAW.CN on 30 March 2021, the data retrieval tool found five regulations promulgated by the Departments of State Council and 93 regulations by local governments that embrace it as a general principle.

them. The former is given more weight than the latter. Chinese administrative litigation puts the individuals whose rights are encroached at a distinct disadvantage.

According to Article 74(1)(1) of the ALL of 2017, the courts should not strike down an illegal administrative decision if overturning the decision would significantly damage national security and public interest. This rule concretizes the perception that public interest precedes individual rights. In five SPC Guiding cases and Gazette cases, the courts referred to this provision and maintained illegal administrative actions that should have been overturned.[73] And these cases demonstrate that public interest has been unduly broadly interpreted.

In *Yimin Company v The People's Government of Zhoukou Municipality*,[74] the appellant obtained a gas and pipeline franchise from the respondent in 2000. However, the respondent decided to grant a franchise to Yixing Company three years later, despite the fact that the appellant's franchise remained in force. The SPC ruled that the decision to grant the gas franchise to Yixing Company was illegal because it violated statutory procedures and infringed upon the appellant's legitimate expectations. However, the SPC chose not to reverse this decision; instead, it stressed that annulling the decision would harm the public interest in two significant ways: first, it would delay the East-West Gas Pipeline Project and postpone the gas supply to the citizens of Zhoukou Municipality; second, the respondent government would be obliged to pay compensation to Yixing Company, resulting in public finance losses. Clearly, in this monetary conflict between the local government and the appellant company, the government's fiscal concerns prevailed over the appellant's rights and interests. The court ordered the respondent to compensate the appellant's legitimate investment, excluding expected profits.

Hong Kong

An Overview

From 1999 to 2019, the HKCFAR publicized 37 judicial review cases against governmental decisions, constituting around half of the CFA's judicial review decisions in this period. In Hong Kong, the main sources for the grounds of judicial review against concrete executive acts are (i) the HKBL; (ii) the

73 *Zhang Daowen, Tao Ren and others v The People's Government of Jianyang Municipality, Sichuan Province*, Guiding Case No. 88; *Yimin Company v The People's Government of Zhoukou Municipality*, SPC Gazette 2005(8); *Ding'an Chengdong Construction and Decoration Company v The People's Government of Sihong County*, SPC Gazette 2015(2); *Shanxi Anye Group Co., Ltd v Taiyuan Municipality People's Government*, SPC Gazette 2017(1); *Shouguang PetroChina Kunlun Gas Co., Ltd v The People's Government of Shouguang Municipality and the People's Government of Shouguang Municipality*, SPC Gazette 2018(9).

74 *Yimin*, *ibid*.

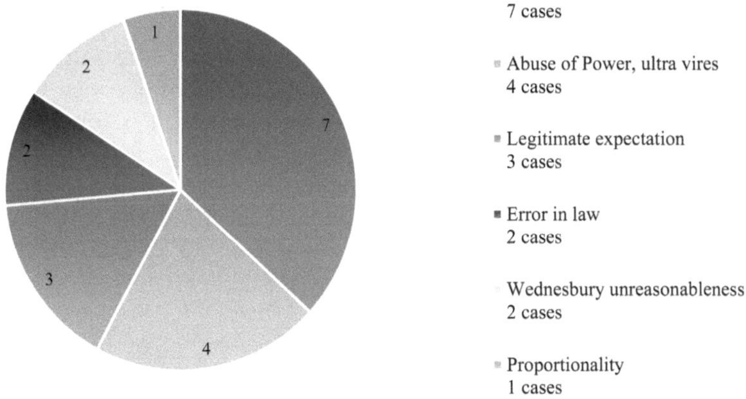

Figure 5.2 The Main Standards of Review in the CFA Decisions against Executive Actions (1999–2019).

Source: Author.

legislation, particularly the BORO; and (iii) the common law.[75] The HKBL and the BORO have become the primary vehicles for protecting individual rights from encroachment by the government.[76] The traditional common law grounds of judicial review include illegality, unreasonableness, and procedural impropriety.[77] Figure 5.2 presents the main standards of review deployed by the CFA in these cases against administrative actions. One might notice that the total numbers in Figure 5.2 are less than 37. Three reasons may explain that. First, the CFA did not apply any particular standard to review the administrative decision in some cases but merely interpreted and applied relevant laws.[78] In *Tam Nga Yin and Others v Director of Immigration* (2001), the issue is whether Chinese nationals born in Mainland China who are adopted by Hong Kong permanent residents have the right to abode in Hong Kong under Article 24(2)(3) of the HKBL.[79] The CFA adopted the common law approach to interpreting Article 24(2)(3) of the HKBL and held that the phrase "born…of" referred only to natural children and could not sustain an interpretation that adopted children were included. It also added that the time

75 Stephen Thomson, *Administrative Law in Hong Kong* (CUP 2018) 121.

76 Kate Olley, 'Introduction of Judicial Review in Hong Kong' (2003) 8 *Judicial Review* 108, 111.

77 *Council of Civil Service Union v Minister for the Civil Service* [1985] AC 374.

78 *Tam Nga Yin and Others v Director of Immigration* (2001) 4 HKCFAR 251; *Lai Tak Shing v Secretary for Home Affairs* (2007) 10 HKCFAR 655; *Ubamaka v Secretary for Security* (2012) 15 HKCFAR 743; *Gutierrez v Commissioner of Registration* (2014) 17 HKCFAR 518.

79 Article 24(2)(3) of the HKBL provides that "The permanent residents of the Hong Kong Special Administrative Region shall be: … (3) Persons of Chinese nationality born outside Hong Kong of those residents listed in categories (1) and (2)".

of birth requirement suggested that "the relationship is a natural relationship and does not include the relationship arising from adoption".[80]

Second, under the usual approach to scrutinizing the constitutionality of governmental acts,[81] there is no need to apply any standard of review to determine whether the restrictions on rights are justifiable if it is found that no rights are involved or violated in the case.[82] In *Comilang Milagros Tecson v Director of Immigration* (2019), two Filipino mothers, whose children are Hong Kong residents or permanent residents, challenged the government's refusal to extend permission to remain in Hong Kong to look after their children. The appellants argued that they and their children enjoyed the right to family under (i) Article 37 of the HKBL; (ii) Articles 14, 19(1) and 20(1) of the BORO; (iii) Article 10 of the ICESCR; and (iv) Article 3 of the Convention on the Rights of Child (CRC). The CFA ruled against all these grounds. The CFA held that the immigration reservation to the ICCPR contained in section 11 of the BORO excluded the mothers and their children from reliance on the rights under the BORO.[83] The appellants could not rely on the right to raise a family enshrined in Article 37 of the HKBL to support their extension application as section 11 of the BORO implies the limitation of the application of cognate rights in the Basic Law.[84] As for the appellant's arguments relying upon Article 10 of the ICESCR and Article 3 of the CRC, the CFA considered these conventions did not confer any rights on individuals because both the ICESCR and the CRC have not been incorporated into Hong Kong domestic legislation.[85] Lastly, there are some cases where the standards of review are just unclear.[86]

The numbers in Figure 5.2 show that, like the SPC, the CFA tended to check the decision-making procedure. On the other hand, unlike the SPC, the CFA did not hesitate to deploy proportionality, unreasonableness, abuse of power, legal certainty, and legitimate expectation, which are standards that enable it to review the substance of administrative decisions. The following section will examine the major standards of review relied upon by the CFA in the cases against executive acts.

80 *Tam Nga Yin* (n 78) 263F–G.
81 See the CFA's approach to scrutinizing the constitutionality of governmental actions in Chapter 3 of this book.
82 *GA v Director of Immigration* (2014) 17 HKCFAR 60; *Comilang Milagros Tecson v Director of Immigration* (2019) 22 HKCFAR 59.
83 *Comilang Milagros Tecson*, *ibid.*, [24]–[35].
84 *Ibid.*, [59]–[65].
85 *Ibid.*, [74]–[78].
86 *Secretary for Justice and Others v Chan Wah and Others* (2000) 3 HKCFAR 459; *Registrar of Births and Deaths v Syed Haider Yahya Hussain and Another* (2001) 4 HKCFAR 429; *Ho Man Kong v Superintendent of Lai Chi Kok Reception Centre* (2014) 17 HKCFAR 179; *Designing Hong Kong Ltd v Town Planning Board* (2018) 21 HKCFAR 237.

Main Standards of Review in the CFA's Judicial Review of Executive Acts

Procedural Fairness

Hong Kong inherits the common law of the UK after the handover, including the common law grounds of judicial review. Procedural fairness or procedural impropriety is one of the three grounds in Lord Diplock's trilogy of standards of review – illegality, irrationality, and procedural impropriety.[87] At the foundation of procedural fairness is natural justice. In administrative law, procedural fairness is a well-defined concept that comprises two fundamental rules: rules against bias and the right to a fair hearing.[88] Since governmental power grows more drastic, procedural fairness plays an essential role. As they control the substance of what the executive authorities do by means of the standards of unreasonableness and proportionality, the courts can control the decision-making process by controlling the procedure through which they do it.[89] The CFA applied the standard of procedural fairness in seven cases,[90] making it one of the most frequently employed standards of review.

Secretary for Security v Sakthevel Prabakar (2004) is an important case in the CFA's jurisprudence relating to procedural fairness and immigration management.[91] Prabakar fled from Sri Lanka as a refugee to escape threats to his life. He arrived in Hong Kong using a forged Canadian passport and later was arrested. The Secretary for Security made a deportation decision against him because he had been guilty of an offense punishable with imprisonment of shorter than two years. While serving his sentence, Prabakar applied for refugee status claiming that he would be subjected to torture if he was sent back to Sri Lanka. The United Nations High Commission for Refugees (UNHCR) administers the recognition of refugees in Hong Kong. After interviewing Prabakar, the UNHCR rejected his application. In light of the UNHCR's decision, the Director of Immigration recommended the Secretary for Security to deport Prabakar from Hong Kong to Sri Lanka with no option of return. Subsequently, Prabakar submitted more evidence and underwent two more interview rounds. Eventually, the UNHCR recognized his refugee status. However, the Secretary for Security refused to revoke the deportation order. The Secretary for Security argued that it had not made its own assessment of Prabakar's situation by applying the criteria for torture risk; instead, it had

87 *Council of Civil Service Union* (n 77) 410C–E.

88 Willian Wade and Christopher Forsyth, *Administrative Law* (9th edn, OUP 2004) 440, 443.

89 *Ibid.*, 439.

90 *HKSAR v Lee Ming Tee and Another* (2001) 4 HKCFAR 133; *Secretary for Security v Sakthevel Prabakar* (2004) 7 HKCFAR 187; *Stock Exchange of Hong Kong Ltd v New World Development Co Ltd and Others* (2006) 9 HKCFAR 234; *Solicitor v Law Society of Hong Kong* (2008) 11 HKCFAR 117; *C v Director of Immigration* (2013) 16 HKCFAR 280; *HLB Hodgson Impey Cheng v Hong Kong Institute of Certified Public Accountants* (2013) 16 HKCFAR 460; *Asia Television Ltd v Communications Authority* (2013) 16 HKCFAR 773.

91 *Prabakar, ibid.*

relied upon the UNHCR's opinion that was not amenable to judicial review and did not give any reason.

The CFA pointed out that the question of the case concerned procedural fairness and emphasized that the appropriate standard of fairness depended on "an examination of all aspects relating to the decision in question, including its context and its nature and subject".[92] The CFA held:

> To him, life and limb are in jeopardy and his fundamental rights not to be subjected to torture is involved. Accordingly, high standards of fairness must be demanded in the making of such determination ... Having regard to the gravity of what is at stake, the courts will on judicial review subject the Secretary for Security's determination on rigorous examination and anxious scrutiny to ensure that the required high standards of fairness have been met.[93]

The CFA articulated the high standards of fairness that should be adopted in that case:

- "The potential deportee, who has the burden of establishing his torture claim ... should be given reasonable opportunities to establish his claim".
- "The claim must be properly assessed by the Secretary" and the following relevant matters should be considered: (i) "is there evidence of a consistent pattern of gross, flagrant or mass violations of human rights in that country? Has the situation changed"; (ii) "has the potential deportee been tortured in the past and how recently?"; (iii) "is there medical or other independent evidence to support the claim of past torture?"; (iv) "has the potential deportee engaged in political or other activity within or outside that country concerned which would make him vulnerable to the risk of being subjected to torture on return?"; (v) "is the claim credible?"
- "Where the claim is rejected, the Secretary should give reasons. The reasons ... must be sufficient to enable the potential deportee to consider the possibilities of administrative review and judicial review".[94]

The CFA held that the Secretary for Security did not meet these standards as it merely followed the UNHCR's unexplained rejection decision. Without undertaking any independent assessment, the Secretary fell below the high standard of procedural fairness.[95]

Two developments from the case which introduced the high standard "procedural fairness" are noteworthy. First, the CFA created a sliding scale of

92 *Ibid.*, [43].
93 *Ibid.*, [44]–[45].
94 *Ibid.*, [51]–[52].
95 *Ibid.*, [48].

procedural fairness review by asserting that the more important the rights and interests at stake, the more anxiously the court will scrutinize the fairness of executive decisions. Swati Jhaveri contends that the higher standards of fairness open up a new aspect of review under the heading of "fairness".[96] Second, together with subsequent cases, such as *C v Director of Immigration* (2013),[97] *Prabakar* led the government to transform the torture screening mechanism and pass legislation in 2012 to put the scheme on a statutory basis.[98]

Stock Exchange of Hong Kong Ltd v New World Development Co Ltd and Others (2006) is a case concerning the right to legal representation.[99] In that case, the applicants challenged the punishment against them before the Disciplinary Committee. The Disciplinary Committee made procedural directions for the hearing, providing that while legal advisers could accompany the applicants to the hearing, they would not be allowed to make oral submissions. The applicants argued that the procedural directions breached Article 35 of the HKBL and the common law principles of procedural fairness. The CFA concluded that "court" under Article 35 of the HKBL did not include the Disciplinary Committee.[100] Hence, the right to legal representation under this provision could not assist the applicant. But the CFA considered that the common law rules on procedural fairness still applied. The Court stressed that:

> The common law principles of fairness operate flexibly, requiring the tribunal to respond reasonably to the requirements of fairness arising in each case, balancing any competing interests and considering what, if any limits may proportionately be imposed on legal representation in consequence.[101]

96 Swati Jhaveri, 'Transforming "Fairness" as a Ground of Judicial Review in Hong Kong' (2013) 11 *International Journal of Constitutional Law* 358, 365.

97 *C* (n 90) [86]. In this case, the Director of Immigration ordered to remove C from Hong Kong on the ground that the UNHCR rejected his refugee status. The CFA stated that, "In the light of the nature of the Director's decision and its drastic consequences for the appellants, it follows from *Prabakar* in particular and other cases mentioned that the Court is bound to: ... subject the [Director's] determination to rigorous examination and anxious scrutiny to ensure that the required high standards of fairness have been met ... If the courts decide that they have not been met, the determination will be held to have been made unlawfully".

98 Simon N. M. Young, 'Human Rights' in Simon N. M. Young and Yash Ghai (eds), *Hong Kong's Court of Final Appeal: The Development of the Law in China's Hong Kong* (CUP 2014) 402.

99 *Stock Exchange of Hong Kong Ltd* (n 90).

100 *Ibid.*, [52].

101 *Ibid.*, [101]. The CFA also lists some factors that it thinks should be considered: The factors include: (1) the seriousness of the charge and potential penalty; (2) whether any points of law are likely to arise; (3) the capacity of the individual to present his own case; (4) procedural difficulties; (5) the need for reasonable speed in making the adjudication; (6) and the need for fairness among the individuals concerned.

The other three cases concerned the standard of proof in disciplinary proceedings,[102] disclosure of the materials and evidence,[103] as well as the independence and impartiality of decision-makers.[104] In all three cases, while the CFA adopted the traditional common law rules of procedural fairness, it gave them flexible contents that vary according to the context and issues. In *Solicitor v Law Society of Hong Kong* (2008), the Court held:

> The standard of proof for disciplinary proceedings in Hong Kong is a preponderance of probability under the *Re H* approach. The more serious the act or omission alleged, the more inherently improbable must it be regarded. And the more inherently improbable it is regarded, the more compelling will be the evidence needed to prove it on a preponderance of probability.[105]

Likewise, the CFA in *HLB Hodgson Impey Cheng v Hong Kong Institute of Certified Public Accountants* (2013) stated:

> The concept of independence and impartiality does not vary in its meaning as between different kinds of administrative bodies, but its practical content varies according to circumstances which include the functions assigned to the body, and its place in a wider statutory scheme. Conduct that may compromise the appearance of independence and impartiality of one person or body required to form an opinion for the purposes of one statutory scheme may not have that effect in the case of another.[106]

Abuse of Power and Ultra Vires

The CFA applied the standards of abuse of power and ultra vires in four cases.[107] Before detailing the application of these standards of review, it is worth mentioning a relevant case, *PCCW-HKT Telephone Ltd v Telecommunications Authority* (2005).[108] In this case, the CFA stated a test for determining whether an authority has discretionary power when the law neither expressly prohibits nor permits the power. It held that the correct test for deciding whether an inferior court or tribunal had such implied ancillary powers was whether they

102 *Solicitor (2008)* (n 90).
103 *Asia Television Ltd* (n 90).
104 *HLB Hodgson Impey Cheng* (n 90).
105 *Solicitor (2008)* (n 90) [116].
106 *HLB Hodgson Impey Cheng* (n 90) [68].
107 *Noise Control Authority and Another v Step In Ltd* (2005) 8 HKCFAR 113; *PCCW-HKT Telephone Ltd v Telecommunications Authority* (2005) 8 HKCFAR 337; *Lo Siu Lan v Hong Kong Housing Authority* (2005) 8 HKCFAR 363; *Shiu Wing Steel Ltd v Director of Environmental Protection and Airport Authority* (2006) 9 HKCFAR 478.
108 *PCCW-HKT Telephone Ltd, ibid.*

were derivable by statutory implication and required for the effective exercise of the jurisdiction conferred on it.[109] This loose test may lead to interpretations in favor of government.

Lo Siu Lan v Hong Kong Housing Authority (2005) is an influential case relating to public housing management in Hong Kong.[110] In the case, the applicant was a tenant of public rental housing. The Housing Authority was established as a corporation under the Housing Ordinance. The core function of the Housing Authority is to provide subsidized public rental housing to low-income families. The applicant instituted judicial review proceedings against the Housing Authority's decision to divest the retail and carpark facilities and sell these facilities to a unit trust (Link REIT). The CFA thought the key question was whether the sale of these facilities to Link REIT was consistent with the object of "securing the provision of" the facilities. If it is inconsistent, then the sale would be beyond the capacity of the Authority, that is, ultra vires the corporation.[111] The CFA held that the sale of the retail and carpark facilities was within the capacity of the Authority. It reasoned that it was vital to distinguish "to provide" and "to secure the provision of". The statutory object under the Housing Ordinance did not use the phrase "to provide", but rather "to secure the provision of". To secure the provision of facilities does not mean that the Authority must itself be the direct provider.[112]

In *Noise Control Authority and Another v Step In Ltd* (2005), the applicant argued that the Noise Control Ordinance and the Technical Memorandum did not confer power on the Noise Control Authority to impose the "not audible" requirement. The CFA held that the Authority did not act ultra vires. It reasoned that, although the Technical Memorandum prescribed limits in terms of decibels, the circumstances would warrant the prescribing of a different limit, and the Authority could impose a requirement that was not expressed in decibels.[113]

Legitimate Expectations

The CFA is the first apex court in the common law world to affirm the principle of substantive legitimate expectations.[114] This principle can be understood in the context of procedural fairness and in the context of unreasonableness.[115] Correspondingly, it has two main focuses as a ground of review: (i) procedurally, a person who has a legitimate expectation will expect the executive

109 *Ibid.*, [36].
110 *Lo Siu Lan* (n 107).
111 *Ibid.*, [35].
112 *Ibid.*, [37]–[39].
113 *Noise Control Authority* (n 107) [25].
114 *Ng Siu Tung and Others v Director of Immigration* (2002) 5 HKCFAR 1; Ip and Yap (n 61) 194.
115 Wade and Forsyth (n 88) 500.

authority to reach a decision by following a particular procedure; and (ii) substantively, they will expect the authority to make a particular decision.[116] In general words, a legitimate expectation requires the government to honor promises, representations, practices, or policies they made, adopted, or announced. The CFA relied on this standard to scrutinize the administrative decision in three cases.[117]

Take *Ng Siu Tung and Others v Director of Immigration* (2002) as an example, a leading case concerning the principle of legitimate expectations in Hong Kong. After the British handover of Hong Kong to China, numerous Mainland-born children of Hong Kong permanent residents claimed permanent resident status and raised challenges against the Immigration Ordinance. There were over 5,000 claimants who applied for legal aid to take out proceedings. In order to reduce the number of cases and costs, some cases were selected as test cases brought before the court. The Legal Aid Department said to the rest of the claimants that it was unnecessary to initiate separate proceedings for each legally aided person.[118] The Secretary for Security also made a representation that "after the whole litigation process is completed, the Immigration Department will follow the final judgment of the courts in dealing with the applicants for the Certificate of Entitlement".[119]

In the two test cases, namely, *Chan Kam Nga* and *Ng Ka Ling*, the CFA overturned part of the Immigration (Amendment) (No. 2) Ordinance and part of the Immigration (Amendment) (No. 3) Ordinance, respectively. The CFA's decisions were later reversed by the NPCSC's interpretation. Nonetheless, the NPCSC's interpretation did not apply retroactively, stating that it did not affect the right of abode of the litigating party under the decisions. *Ng Siu Tung* and other applicants, over 5,000 in total, claimed that they were in the same position as the parties in the test cases on the ground that they had legitimate expectations that they would receive the same treatment as the parties in *Ng Ka Ling* and *Chan Kam Nga*.

The CFA accepts that the principle of legitimate expectations has formed a part of the administrative law of Hong Kong and was an important element in the exercise of the court's supervisory function.[120] The CFA articulated the contents of this standard that:

- A legitimate expectation arises from a promise or representation the authority makes;

116 Christopher Forsyth and Rebecca Williams, 'Closing Chapter in the Immigration Children Saga: Substantive Legitimate Expectation and Administrative Justice in Hong Kong' (2002) *Asia Pacific Law Review* 29, 35.

117 *Ng Siu Tung* (n 114); *Director of Immigration v Lau Fong* (2004) 7 HKCFAR 56; *Ho Choi Wan v Hong Kong Housing Authority* (2005) 8 HKCFAR 628.

118 *Ng Siu Tung, ibid.*, [64].

119 *Ibid.*, [66].

120 *Ibid.*, [91].

- The authority should give effect to the legitimate expectation unless there are reasons recognized by law for not giving effect to the expectation;
- Even if the decision involves the making of a political choice by reference to policy considerations, the authority must make the choice in light of the legitimate expectations of the parties. Failing to do so, the decision will be vitiated by reason of failure to take account of relevant considerations and thereby constituting an abuse of power;
- Only in an exceptional case, the court would be satisfied that the failure to take account of a relevant consideration has not affected the decision.[121]

The CFA emphasized that the representation and policy statement made by the authority must be clear and unambiguous. The interpretation of the representation or policy should be subject to the *Wednesbury* unreasonableness test.[122] At the same time, the expectation could not result in the authority acting contrary to law or undermining the entire legislative scheme.[123] The CFA in *Ng Siu Tung* considered that, if the court enforced the expectations of the applicants who had merely relied on the representations made by the government to the general public, this would allow more than 600,000 to enter and reside in Hong Kong, which would undermine the statutory immigration scheme.[124] As for the applicants who received specific written communication from the Legal Aid Department and the Secretary for Security, the CFA recognized their legitimate expectations. The exercise in their favor of the relevant discretionary power would not undermine the immigration scheme as a whole.[125]

An Error in Law

The standard of error in law emerged in two cases.[126] In *Town Planning Board v Society for Protection of the Harbour Ltd* (2004), the Town Planning Board decided to submit a plan which proposed reclaiming 26 hectares from Victoria Harbour to the Chief Executive. The respondent brought a judicial review proceeding against the decision on the ground that the Town Planning Board misinterpreted the Protection of the Harbour Ordinance, in particular Section 3.

Section 3 requires that the Town Planning Board must have regard to the principle of "protection and preservation of the harbour" when exercising its power. The Town Planning Board argued that it had taken a correct approach

121 *Ibid.*, [94]–[98].
122 *Ibid.*, [104].
123 *Ibid.*, [134].
124 *Ibid.*
125 *Ibid.*, [137].
126 *Lau Kong Yung and Others v Director of Immigration* (1999) 2 HKCFAR 300; *Town Planning Board v Society for Protection of the Harbour Ltd* (2004) 7 HKCFAR 1.

to interpreting the Ordinance: the decision-maker must take the presumption against reclamation into account as a compulsory material consideration and undertake a weighing exercise to decide whether the public interests of the proposed reclamation would outweigh the need to preserve the harbor.

The CFA adopted the purposive approach to interpret the Protection of the Harbour Ordinance, a usual approach to statutory interpretation.[127] It considered that in the present case, there was no difficulty in identifying the legislative purpose, which has been stated in the preamble that "protect and preserve the harbour by establishing a presumption against reclamation in the harbour".[128] The legislature recognized the great public need to protect and preserve the harbor because Victoria Harbour was a unique public asset and a central element of the natural heritage of Hong Kong's people. The CFA held that it was "wrong to interpret the presumption against reclamation merely as a compulsory material consideration to which the decision-maker must pay due regard" when making reclamation decisions.[129] It was also wrong to demote the strong public need to prevent permanent destruction and irreversible loss of the harbor to the same level as any town planning need.[130] In the CFA's opinion, the presumption against reclamation ought to be interpreted in such a way that "it can only be rebutted by establishing an overriding public need for reclamation".[131] A need is overriding if it is a compelling and present need.[132]

Unreasonableness

Associated Provincial Picture Houses Ltd v Wednesbury Corp[133] was considered the progenitor of the standard of unreasonableness in modern law.[134] In *Wednesbury*, Lord Greene identified two aspects of the standard: (1) a decision that takes into account irrelevant considerations or did not take into account relevant considerations; and (2) where a discretionary decision is "so unreasonable that no reasonable authority could ever have come to it" requiring "something overwhelming".[135]

127 *Town Planning Board, ibid.*, [29].
128 *Ibid.*, [30].
129 *Ibid.*, [43].
130 *Ibid.*
131 *Ibid.*, [44].
132 *Ibid.*, [46].
133 [1948] 1 KB 223.
134 Margit Cohn, "Legal Transplant Chronicles: The Evolution of Unreasonableness and Proportionality Review of the Administration in the United Kingdom" (2010) 58 *American Journal of Comparative Law* 583, 603.
135 Lord Greene articulated the classic formulation of unreasonableness: "It is true the discretion must be exercised reasonably. Now what does that mean? Lawyers familiar with the phraseology commonly used in relation to exercise of statutory discretions often use the word 'unreasonable' in a rather comprehensive sense. It has frequently been used and is

In *Council of Civil Service Union v Minister for Civil Service*, Lord Diplock lifted *Wednesbury* unreasonableness to a high point by expressing the standard in terms of "irrationality", which is the second in his trilogy of grounds of judicial review.[136] Lord Diplock articulated the definition of "irrationality" as follows:

> By 'irrationality' I mean what can by now be succinctly referred to as '*Wednesbury* unreasonableness'. It applies to a decision which is so outrageous in its defiance of logic or of accepted moral standards that no sensible person who had applied his mind to the question to be decided could have arrived at it.[137]

According to the articulation of Lord Greene and Lord Diplock, the threshold of *Wednesbury* unreasonableness is very high,[138] and a broad discretionary power is conferred on the decision-maker. Paul Craig has commented that, "If this is the generally applicable standard of substantive review, there can be no presence of any meaningful substantive oversight and it is difficult to think of a single real case in which the facts meet this standard".[139]

With the growing realization that the traditional *Wednesbury* unreasonableness is not protective of human rights sufficiently, intense scrutiny was called for when fundamental rights and important interests are involved.[140] In *R v Secretary of State for the Home Department, Ex p Bugdaycay* (1987),[141] where the claimants challenged a refusal to grant asylum, Lord Bridge, for the first time, introduced "anxious scrutiny". A clearer formulation of anxious scrutiny is to be found in *R v Ministry of Defence, Ex p Smith* (1996). In this case, the claimant challenged the exclusion of homosexual people from the military. The Court of Appeal held that "the more substantial the interference with human rights, the more the Court will require by way of justification before it is satisfied that the decision is reasonable".[142]

---

frequently used as a general description of the things that must not be done. For instance, a person entrusted with a discretion must, so to speak, direct himself properly in law. He must call his own attention to the matters which he is bound to consider. He must exclude from his consideration matters which are irrelevant to what he has to consider. If he does not obey those rules, he may truly be said, and often is said, to be acting 'unreasonably.' Similarly, there may be something so absurd that no sensible person could ever dream that it lay within the powers of the authority". *Wednesbury* (n 133) 229.

136 *Council of Civil Service Union* (n 77) 410C–E.

137 *Ibid.*, 410F–G.

138 Carnwath, "From Rationality to Proportionality in the Modern Law" (2014) 44 *Hong Kong Law Journal* 447, 449.

139 Paul Craig, "The Nature of Reasonableness Review" (2013) 66 *Current Legal Problems* 131, 161.

140 Harry Woolf and others (n 19) 638.

141 [1987] AC 514.

142 [1996] QB 517, 554.

The CFA relied on the standard unreasonableness in two cases. Take *Ghulam Rbani v Secretary for Justice* (2014) as an example.[143] In this case, the appellant, a Pakistani national, was under administrative detention by the Director of Immigration pending deportation after serving a prison term imposed by a criminal court. He sued the Director for damages resulted from false imprisonment, claiming that he was unlawfully detained after this release from prison. The CFA held that the initial detention between 23 August and 15 September was lawful as the Director had acted diligently and expeditiously to enable his return.[144] However, the detention between 16 September and 7 October was unlawful as the detention was inconsistent with common law *Hardial Singh* principles. Woolf J laid down the *Hardial Singh* principles in relation to a statutory detention power in *R v Governor of Durham Prison, ex p Hardial Singh* (1984).[145] The principles require:

> (i) The Secretary of State must intend to deport the person and can only use the power to detain for that purpose; (ii) The deportee may only be detained for a period which is reasonable in all the circumstances; (iii) If, before the expiry of the reasonable period, it becomes apparent that the Secretary of State will not be able to effect deportation within that reasonable period, he should not seek to exercise the power of detention; (iv) The Secretary of State should act with the reasonable diligence and expedition to effect removal.[146]

The CFA held that the second period of detention was inconsistent with the 2nd, 3rd, and 4th principles.[147]

Proportionality

Proportionality plays an essential role in the CFA's constitutional review of ordinances and administrative rules. This principle was also deployed in judicial review of government decisions. *Hysan* is an example case, and this is a milestone decision because the CFA added the balance test to the proportionality test and elaborated on the spectrum of intensity of this test.[148]

143 (2014) 17 HKCFAR 138; Another case is *Secretary for Transport v Delight World Ltd* (2006) 9 HKCFAR 720.
144 *Ghulam Rbani, ibid.*, [50]–[51].
145 [1984] 1 WLR 704.
146 *Ghulam Rbani* (n 143) [23].
147 *Ibid.*, [55]–[57].
148 *Hysan Development Co Ltd v Town Planning Board* (2016) 19 HKCFAR 372; See Chapter 3.

The Intensity of the CFA's Judicial Review of Executive Acts

Sliding Down to Low Intensity of Review

To examine the intensity of the CFA's review of executive acts, it is better to start with three standards of review for which the CFA applies on a sliding scale, namely procedural fairness, unreasonableness, and proportionality. The CFA applied them with low intensity in a vast majority of the cases. Eric Ip and Po Jen Yap have recently underlined the trend toward deference in Hong Kong courts' judicial review of administrative action.[149] This study echoes their observation. The CFA has acknowledged a higher standard of procedural fairness, anxious scrutiny, and reasonable necessity test. However, it has under-enforced these high standards of review in practice.

As discussed above, one of the developments the CFA introduced to procedural fairness is a sliding scale. The contents of procedural fairness vary depending on the context, nature, and subject matter of the decision in question. In particular, when the executive act puts people's right to life at risk, procedural fairness calls for anxious scrutiny.[150] The CFA applied a higher standard of procedural fairness in two out of seven cases, namely *Prabakar* and *C*. Both cases are concerned with immigration control and returning the refugees. In the remaining cases, the CFA did not adopt a higher standard of procedural fairness. The CFA has considered that the lack of full legal representation in disciplinary proceedings was not inconsistent with procedural fairness,[151] and applying civil standard of proof in disciplinary proceedings was not unreasonable.[152] It upheld the refusal to provide relevant information to the affected people on the grounds of confidentiality.[153]

The CFA applied the principle of unreasonableness in two cases. In both cases, the decisions indicate that the CFA conducted the *Wednesbury* unreasonableness test, not anxious scrutiny. In *Secretary for Transport v Delight World Ltd* (2006), the CFA followed the traditional *Wednesbury* unreasonableness formula and considered that the need for *Melhado* use permission should not be taken into consideration when compensation for the resumption of the land is assessed.[154] In *Ghulam Rbani*, the CFA applied the *Hardial Singh* principles, which are no more than a detailed unreasonableness principle in the context of detention for deportation. In *Hysan*, the CFA applied the standard "manifestly without reasonable foundation".[155]

149 Ip and Yap (n 61) 210.
150 Notes 92–93 above and text accompanying.
151 *Stock Exchange of Hong Kong Ltd* (n 90).
152 *Solicitor* (2008) (n 90).
153 *Asia Television Ltd* (n 90).
154 *Delight World Ltd* (n 143) [33]. The New Territories Land held under a lease that contained a restriction against buildings could be used for non-agriculture purposes, for example, container storage sites. This is *Melhado* use.
155 *Hysan* (n 148) [126].

Flexible Procedure in Disciplinary Proceedings

In four cases concerning procedural protections in disciplinary proceedings, the CFA endorsed the flexible procedures adopted by disciplinary committees. In *Stock Exchange*, the CFA considered that a restriction to the party's lawyer from addressing the Disciplinary Committee of the Stock Exchange did not violate Article 35 of the HKBL, which guarantees the "choice of lawyers for timely protection of their lawful rights and interests or for representation in the courts".[156] In *Solicitor (2008)*, the CFA reiterated that the appropriate standard of proof in disciplinary proceedings was the civil standard of review, although it stated that the more serious the act or omission alleged, the more compelling evidence would be needed.[157] In *Lam Siu Po*, a case concerning police disciplinary proceedings, the CFA referred to the case *Stock Exchange* and held that while a blanket restriction on professional legal representation in police disciplinary proceedings was systematically incompatible with the right to a fair hearing, the tribunal has a discretion to permit representation where procedural fairness is required.[158]

Leeway to Strict Immigration Control

As an international metropolis, Hong Kong attracts abundant immigrants and refugees from Mainland China and surrounding Asian countries. It is not surprising that the CFA heard many cases on rights in migration.[159] Many judicial review cases against concrete executive acts are concerned with immigration control and the right to abode. Because of the crisis as a result of the NPCSC's interpretation after *Ng Ka Ling*, the CFA became deferential and cautious. Also, due to Hong Kong's considerable economic attraction to many people, the CFA saw that there was a need to control immigration.[160] It displayed great respect for the strict immigration control policies.

These 13 cases can be generally divided into two groups: cases where the CFA substantively examined whether the applicants have the right to enter to enjoy their right of abode in Hong Kong and cases where the CFA examined the decision-making procedure but did not review the substance of executive decisions. In most cases from the former group, the CFA gave a less generous interpretation of the textual meaning. In *Tam Nga Yin*, the CFA interpreted "Persons of Chinese nationality born outside Hong Kong of those residents listed in categories (1) and (2)" to exclude the adopted children.[161] In the important case of *Ng Siu Tung*, the CFA decided only a small group of claim-

156 *Stock Exchange* (n 90) [37]–[38].
157 *Solicitor* (2008) (n 90) [116].
158 *Lam Siu Po v Commissioner of Police* (2009) 12 HKCFAR 237, [135]–[142].
159 Young (n 98), 395.
160 *GA* (n 82) [30].
161 *Tam Nga Yin* (n 78) 263F–G.

ants who had legitimate expectations based on specific representations could be treated favorably as those in *Ng Ka Ling*.[162] In *Comilang Milagros Tecson*, the Filipino mothers were forced to leave Hong Kong and could not stay to look after their juvenile children, who were Hong Kong residents.[163] This case reflects one of many problems foreign domestic helpers face in Hong Kong. They are not entitled to the right to abode because of working in Hong Kong for a fixed number of years, and they are forced to leave Hong Kong within two weeks after the termination of their employment.[164] In *Gutierrez*, the CFA thought the applicant, a son of a foreign domestic helper from the Philippines, had not established the eligibility for becoming a permanent resident provided in Article 24(2)(4) of the HKBL. The CFA considered that the applicant was ten years old and lacked independent capacity to take Hong Kong as his place of permanent residence; at the same time, his mother was not qualified for ordinary residence because she was a foreign domestic helper.[165]

In the second group of cases, including *Prabakar* and *C*, although the CFA struck down the decisions on the ground of violating fair procedure, the authority could make the same decision to deport the applicants (Prabakar had left Hong Kong and resettled in Canada before the case brought before the CFA) through proper procedures. The protection provided by the CFA was not adequate.

Having said that, the CFA has shown more deference when reviewing concrete administrative actions compared to its scrutiny of ordinance and subordinary legislation, it has not avoided reviewing the substance of these decisions. This is reflected by the frequent deployment of standards such as proportionality, unreasonableness, and substantive expectation. This practice differentiates the CFA from the SPC and the TUI, which tend to avoid substantive review. The following section delves into the judicial review of administrative decisions by the TUI.

Macau

An Overview

Previous chapters have revealed that, from 1999 to 2019, the TUI only reviewed primary legislation in 13 cases and administrative rules in 2 cases. The vast majority of judicial review decisions were against concrete administrative decisions (302 cases, around 95.3 percent of all judicial review cases). Articles 3 to 14 of the Code of Administrative Procedure (CAP) enshrines

162 *Ng Siu Tung* (n 114) [137].

163 *Comilang Milagros Tecson* (n 82).

164 Karen Kong, 'Applying the Right to Family in the Immigration Context of Hong Kong', available at https://blog-iacl-aidc.org/membership-and-exclusion/2019/6/18/applying-the-right-to-family-in-the-immigration-context-of-hong-kong, accessed 12 June 2021.

165 *Gutierrez* (n 78) [51]–[52].

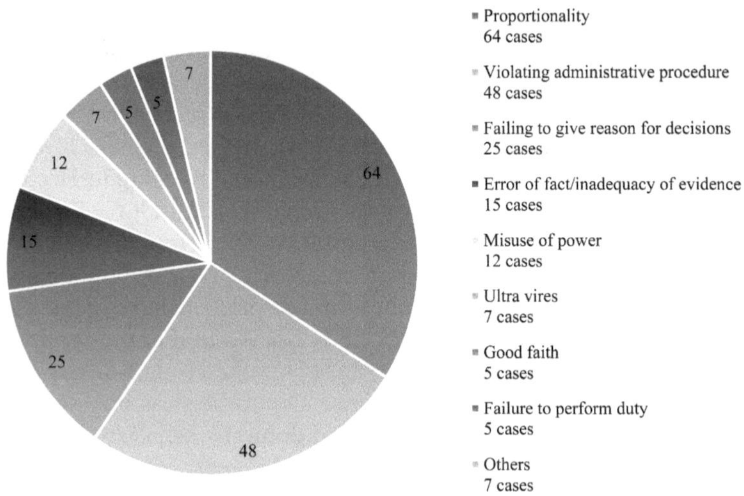

Figure 5.3 The Main Standards of Review in the TUI Decisions against Executive Actions (1999–2019).

Source: Author.

generic principles and requirements of administrative law, including legality, pursuing public interests and respecting people's rights and interests, equality, proportionality, using official language, fairness and impartiality, good faith, cooperation, participation, the obligation to act, non-bureaucracy and efficiency, and access to administrative justice.[166] Additionally, Article 122(2) of the CAP outlines nine situations under which the executive actions should be nullified: (1) exceeding decision-making authority; (2) actions beyond the responsibilities of the organization to which the official belongs; (3) pursuit of impossible, unclear, or criminal objectives; (4) infringement on fundamental rights; (5) decisions made under coercion; (6) lack of required legal form; (7) disorderly decision-making by collective bodies or decisions lacking the necessary quorum or majority; (8) violation of final judicial decisions; and (9) actions stemming from previously annulled or revoked administrative acts.[167]

Figure 5.3 presents some descriptive statistics on the standards applied in judicial review cases against executive decisions by the TUI from 1999 to 2019. The numbers in the chart, when added up, are less than 302 because the TUI did not apply any particular standards of review in over one-third of the decisions. Those cases were concerned mainly with the TUI's interpretation and application of the laws. As discussed later below, the TUI's approach to the interpretation of the laws is not human rights protective.

166 Code of Administrative Procedure (CAP) (行政程序法典), arts 3–14.
167 *Ibid.*, art 122(2).

It is striking that proportionality was employed in 64 cases, which is in sharp contrast to the judicial review of legislation where the TUI expressly declined to adopt proportionality. "Misuse of power" (*desvio de poder*) in the TUI's jurisprudence has a particular meaning, similar to the legitimate aim test of proportionality. It emerged in 12 cases. However, proportionality and misuse of power had no "teeth". The TUI holds an opinion identical to that of the SPC, that the courts do not strike down the administrative decisions unless they are manifestly disproportionate and utterly unreasonable. Consequently, very few impugned administrative decisions failed the proportionality test.

Besides proportionality, the standards focusing on the formal legality of an administrative decision – such as violation of administrative procedure, failure to give reasons for the administrative decision, decisions based on an error of facts or without adequate evidence, ultra vires, and failure to perform duty – remain the primary standards of review in the TUI's judicial review. The same tendency is seen in China's Guiding cases and Gazette cases. The following part examines the implementation of these standards of review in the TUI's decisions.[168]

Main Standards of Review in TUI's Judicial Review of Concrete Executive Acts

Proportionality and Misuse of Power

THE ADOPTION OF PROPORTIONALITY AND MISUSE OF POWER

Proportionality was introduced to Macau before the transfer of sovereignty from Portugal to China. Portugal adopted proportionality in 1982,[169] and it became a fundamental principle of Portuguese constitutional law.[170] Proportionality was further enshrined as a general principle in the Portuguese Code of Administrative Procedure in 1992.[171] The CAP of Macau passed in 1999, modeled on the Portuguese Code of Administrative Procedure, expressly stipulates proportionality as a general principle of Macau's administrative law.[172]

168 There are also some standards of review that were applied in a few cases, including legitimate expectation, the principle of equal treatment, and principle against double jeopardy.

169 Aharon Barak, *Proportionality: Constitutional Rights and Their Limitations* (CUP 2012) 182, 186–199; Alec Stone Sweet and Jud Mathews, *Proportionality Balancing and Constitutional Governance: A Comparative and Global Approach* (OUP 2019) 69–80.

170 Francisco Pereira Coutinho and Nuno Piçarra, 'Portugal: The Impact of European Integration and the Economic Crisis on the Identity of the Constitution' in Anneli Albi and Samo Bardutzky (eds) *National Constitutions in European and Global Governance: Democracy, Rights, the Rule of Law* (Routledge 2019) 591.

171 Lin Zhu (朱琳), 'Commenting on Portuguese Code of Administrative Procedure' (葡萄牙行政程序法典评介) (1996) 3 *Administrative Law Review* (行政法学研究) 88, 88.

172 CAP (n 166), art 5.

The TUI used the term "principle of proportionality" in Case 1/2000, the first case after the establishment of the SAR. In this case, the TUI dismissed a constitutional appeal, holding that there was no appeal procedure in MSAR's legal system for addressing the issue of whether a law violates the Basic Law. Since the constitutional appeal was terminated, the TUI held that the litigation cost should be exempted according to the principle of proportionality.[173] In this case, the TUI did not elaborate on the principle of proportionality.

Not until Case 6/2000 did the TUI elaborate upon proportionality and its subtests. The case relates to border control. The applicant was from Hong Kong and barred from entering Macau for three years on the grounds that he threatened public order and security as he was suspected of being a member of a crime organization conducting "bate-fichas"[174] in Macau and had been sanctioned twice for possessing drugs in Hong Kong. In the TUI's opinion, to assess whether the applicant would threaten Macau's public order and security was within the executive authority's discretion and normally not subject to judicial review.[175] However, it took a step back and emphasized that the executive discretion was not completely free from judicial supervision. When a decision manifestly violates the general principles of law, the courts could strike it down.[176] Proportionality is one of the general principles by which the executive is bound. The TUI elaborated on proportionality:

> The normative core of the principle of proportionality is prohibition of excess, which implies that there should be an appropriate relationship between means and purpose. This core meaning gives rise to the three elements of the principle of proportionality: suitability, necessity and balance. To achieve an aim, the measure to be taken should be suitable in relation to that aim. Amid all the suitable measures, the one that is least harmful to legitimate interests should be chosen. The conflicting interests should be balanced on a proportionate scale in light of the public interest at stake.[177]

173 Case 1/2000, page 4.

174 "Bate-fichas" is a Portuguese term made up by Portuguese police and the original expression in Cantonese is "Dap-ma". "Bate-ficha" simply means the rolling or exchanging of chips between the customers (gamblers) and the "bate-ficha" guys (*dap-ma-chai*) or chip rollers. The chip rollers carry "dead" chips and walk around the gambling rooms to seek customers. They exchange the "dead" chips for cash chips or cash with their customers. In return, the chip rollers get a commission for this kind of exchange. This business was not regulated by law until 2009. Angela Veng Mei Leong, 'The "Bate-Ficha" Business and Triads in Macau Casinos' (2002) *Queensland University of Technology Law and Justice Journal* 83.

175 Case 6/2000, page 11.

176 *Ibid.*, page 12.

177 *Ibid.*, page 13.

This formula of proportionality, which comprises three subtests, has been applied in the next two decades. The basic content of these three subtests is not different from the standard model of proportionality. But the legitimate aim test is missed.

Nonetheless, "misuse of power" (*desvio de poder*) in the TUI's jurisprudence has a particular meaning, similar to the legitimate aim test of proportionality. The TUI stated that "misuse of power is a typical defect in the exercise of discretionary power … [T]here is a misuse of power where the purpose of the impugned action is not the purpose the law intends when conferring that power".[178] In other words, the purpose the executive decisions pursue deviates from the legislative purpose. The TUI gives two specific situations of misuse of power: first, the decision-maker exercises administrative power to accomplish a public interest, which is not the one prescribed by law; second, the decision-maker does not pursue a public interest, but rather their self-interest.[179]

THE IMPLEMENTATION OF PROPORTIONALITY AND MISUSE OF POWER

Proportionality emerged in 64 out of 302 judicial review cases (approximately 19.3 percent),[180] and misuse of power emerged in 12 cases between 1999 and 2019.[181] The application of the two standards has three conspicuous features.

First, there was an apparent tendency of the TUI to apply proportionality and misuse of power to cases concerning border control and immigration (36 cases), disciplinary sanctions and administration of civil service (23 cases), and restrictions on assemblies and demonstrations (9 cases).[182] The typical issues before the TUI are whether the decisions to refuse a person entry to Macau or deny their residential permits are proportionate, whether the disciplinary sanctions are more than necessary to punish misconduct, and whether the prohibition and restriction of the right to assembly are more than necessary.

Second, even though proportionality has been invoked in many cases, the TUI rarely struck down administrative decisions on the grounds of

178 Case 9/2000, page 20.

179 Case 22/2018, pages 35–36.

180 Cases 6/2000, 9/2000, 26/2003, 27/2003, 1/2004, 21/2004, 22/2004, 14/2005, 15/2005, 1/2006, 8/2006, 31/2006, 36/2006, 21/2007, 34/2007, 32/2008, 28/2010, 50/2010, 53/2010, 56/2010, 63/2010, 12/2011, 13/2011, 45/2011, 8/2012, 13/2012, 25/2012, 38/2012, 41/2012, 65/2012, 68/2012, 69/2012, 76/2012, 83/2012, 30/2013, 32/2013, 59/2013, 13/2014, 26/2014, 28/2014, 29/2014, 33/2014, 103/2014, 104/2014, 112/2014, 123/2014, 5/2015, 62/2015, 71/2015, 15/2016, 69/2016, 74/2016, 83/2016, 17/2017, 18/2017, 22/2017, 22/2018, 65/2018, 8/2019, 11/2019, 35/2019, 66/2019, 94/2019, 101/2019.

181 Cases 9/2000, 26/2003, 29/2003, 21/2007, 50/2010, 12/2011, 8/2012, 68/2012, 19/2014, 25/2014, 29/2014, 22/2018.

182 The remaining cases applying proportionality are concerned with piers leases (two cases), obtaining and assessing tenders for public works project (two cases).

disproportionality (five cases)[183] and no administrative decision was quashed due to misuse of power. In Case 6/2000, mentioned above, the TUI held the decisions to prohibit the applicants from entering Macau were manifestly disproportionate because the applicants committed minor offenses.[184] In Case 45/2011, the applicant tendered for the Macau sewage treatment plant construction contract. The government rejected the applicant's tender because it thought the application documents did not comply with tender requirements. The TUI confirmed that the applicant's documents had included all the information required, although they did not comply with some formatting requirements.[185] It held that the refusal of tender submission because of the formatting irregularity was disproportionate. In the TUI's opinion, these formal defects can be remedied. Additionally, the more tenderers, the more opportunities for the best proposal, which is good for public interests. The TUI emphasized that individual rights could only be limited when they conflict with administrative management and the limitation must be proportionate and suitable.[186] In this case, there was no such conflict, and there was no ground for rejecting the applicant's tender.

The last feature of the application of proportionality by the TUI is the lack of a structured and progressive approach. Typically, when a court deploys proportionality, an administrative decision should pass all the subtests and failure in any subtest can lead to the decision being struck down. However, the TUI usually concluded whether an impugned executive act was proportionate or disproportionate without rigorously applying the subtests step-by-step. As observed by Albert Chen and P. Y. Lo, the TUI applied a methodology that looks into the matter more intuitively.[187] For instance, in cases related to restrictions on assemblies and demonstrations, the TUI concluded that the noise resulting from gatherings was manifestly disproportionate to other people's right to peace, quiet, and rest.[188] In cases concerning disciplinary punishment, the TUI deemed the penalties excessive and thus disproportionate.[189] The reasons behind these conclusions were not presented in the judgments.

183 Cases 6/2000, 9/2000, 45/2011, 8/2019, 11/2019.

184 Case 6/2000, page 14.

185 Case 45/2011, pages 18–19.

186 *Ibid.*, pages 20–21.

187 Albert H. Y. Chen and P. Y. Lo, 'The Constitutional Orders of 'One Country, Two Systems': A Comparative Study of the Visible and Invisible Bases of Constitutional Review and Proportionality Analysis in the Chinese Special Administrative Regions of Hong Kong and Macau' in Rosalind Dixon and Adrienne Stone (eds) *The Invisible Constitution in Comparative Perspective* (CUP 2018) 257.

188 Cases 2/2011, 44/2013.

189 Case 8/2019.

Violation of Administrative Procedure

The government's decision-making procedure was challenged in 48 cases. Among these cases, 20 cases concerned the termination of land leases,[190] 12 were related to disciplinary proceedings,[191] and 10 dealt with border control and immigration.[192] The remaining cases involved various issues, including public infrastructure project tender (two cases),[193] taxation (one case),[194] application for telegram fee exemption (one case),[195] application for construction permission (one case),[196] and building inspection (one case).[197]

In the vast majority of cases (41 out of 48 cases), the applicants argued that administrative decisions were illegal because the executive denied their right to a hearing before final decisions were made. According to Articles 93 to 98 of the CAP, decision-makers are required to hear the arguments from the person concerned after concluding investigations and before making final decisions. This requirement allows individuals to defend themselves and provide the decision-makers with more information to ensure the best possible decision.[198] The TUI stressed that:

> The right to a hearing not only guarantees the [realization] of substantive law but also aims to build consensus, increase the proximity of decision to the facts and increase the acceptance of decisions. It is a consequent product of modern administrative management that seeks communication, consensus and realization of justice.[199]

In practice, however, the TUI only quashed five administrative decisions on the grounds of denying the right to a hearing. Case 106/2019 is one of the five cases. In this case, the TUI overturned the Secretary for Economy and Finance's decision to refuse the extension of the applicant's residential permit on the grounds that the applicant had ceased to be an ordinarily resident of Macau in the past two years preceding the application for extension.[200]

190 Cases 11/2012, 48/2012, 39/2017, 81/2017, 1/2018, 7/2018, 13/2018, 30/2018, 42/2018, 43/2018, 89/2018, 90/2018, 91/2018, 96/2018, 98/2018, 6/2019, 16/2019, 78/2019, 118/2019.

191 Cases 5/2000, 8/2001, 6/2003, 7/2005, 22/2016, 52/2006, 30/2008, 32/2008, 8/2012, 41/2012, 62/2018, 104/2018.

192 Cases 13/2003, 39/2004, 1/2006, 48/2010, 13/2011, 11/2017, 28/2013, 29/2014, 17/2017, 106/2019.

193 Cases 31/2012, 35/2012.

194 Case 28/2012.

195 Case 2/2016.

196 Case 34/2017.

197 Case 54/2017.

198 José Eduardo de Figueiredo Dias, *Administrative Law of Macau* (Miguel Ângelo Loureiro Manero de Lemos tr, LexisNexis 2012) 181–182.

199 Case 28/2013, page 19.

200 Case 106/2019, pages 3–4.

The applicant was employed by a Macau company as a chief operating officer and often traveled abroad on official duty. According to Law No. 8/1999 on Permanent Resident and Right of Abode, when determining whether a person has ceased to be ordinarily resident in Macau, the Secretary for Economy and Finance should consider the following factors: (i) the reason, duration, and frequency of any absence from Macau; (ii) whether the person has a habitual residence in Macau; (ii) whether the person is employed by a Macau-based company; and (iv) the whereabouts of the principal members of the person's family (spouse and minor children). The TUI stressed that the Secretary for Economy and Finance should give the applicant a chance to explain her frequent absences from Macau. However, the Secretary for Economy and Finance did not provide the applicant with an opportunity to defend herself.[201]

An Error of Facts and Insufficient Evidence

The applicants argued that executive decisions were based on erroneous facts and insufficient evidence in 15 cases.[202] The TUI struck down the impugned administrative decisions in eight of these cases. Case 20/2019 serves as an example. The applicant, a Hong Kong permanent resident, worked for a Hong Kong company that operated a retail store in Macau. He was sent to Macau to provide technical support for the retail store and spent a total of 61 days in Macau between 2014 and 2015. The Secretary for Security barred the applicant from entering Macau for three years, accusing him of illegal work in Macau, including helping receive clients in the Macau retail store.

The applicant contended that the executive had misunderstood the facts. According to Article 4(1) of the Regulation on the Prohibition of Illegal Work, providing technical support and training employees should not be considered illegal work. The TUI upheld the applicant's argument.[203] Regarding the allegation of receiving clients, the TUI held that this activity was incidental and temporary, occurring in the context of training employees, and should not be classified as illegal work.[204]

Failure to Give Reasons for Administrative Decisions

The executive must give reasons for their administrative decisions, a straightforward requirement arising out of common sense. According to the CAP, the reasoning for an executive action must be congruent, clear, and sufficient to ensure that ordinary people can understand and reconstruct the cognitive and

201 *Ibid.*, page 10.
202 Cases 7/2010, 10/2010, 62/2010, 7/2012, 77/2013, 57/2016, 14/2017, 35/2017, 81/2017, 13/2018, 24/2018, 40/2018, 95/2018, 104/2018, 20/2019.
203 Case 20/2019, pages 11–12.
204 *Ibid.*, page 13.

evaluative process of the decision-maker. Obscure, contradictory, and insufficient reasoning is equivalent to no reason.[205] In essence, providing reasons for administrative decisions is a basic requirement of administration.[206] The Macau executive agencies have been accused before the TUI of not giving reasons for their administrative decisions in 25 cases. The TUI only struck down four administrative decisions on this ground[207] and dismissed the challenges in most cases.

In Case 70/2018, the TUI quashed the Secretary for Security's decision to annul the applicant's residential permit and prohibit him from entering Macau for five years. The applicant appealed to the TUI, arguing that the Secretary for Security did not provide reasons for his decisions. The decision to annul the applicant's residential permission was based on an order issued by the Interim Director of the Immigration Department, which merely mentioned that the applicant was prosecuted for abuse of trust on 6 May 2015, without details of the offenses. The decision to prohibit the applicant from entering Macau for five years was based on a statement of the Director of Public Security Police Force stating that the applicant broke his promise and did not hand over a large amount of money to two victims. Besides the order and the statement, the Secretary for Security's decision did not include adequate facts and gave no reason for the impugned decision.[208]

Ultra Vires and Failure to Perform Duty

The TUI applied ultra vires in seven cases and failure to perform statutory duty in five cases. It declared impugned administrative decisions illegal on the basis of these two standards in several cases.[209]

Case 12/2000, concerning denial of residential permit, was the first case in which the TUI declared an administrative decision invalid on the ground of ultra vires. The applicant applied for a special residential permit. The Secretary for Security and Administration of Portuguese Macau believed that the applicant did not meet the conditions for a special residential permit and decided not to submit the application to the Governor of Macau for consideration, ultimately rejecting the application. The TUI held that the Secretary for Security and Administration's decision was beyond his authority. According to Article 40(3) of Decree 55/95M, the power to grant a special residential permit belonged to the Governor of Macau and could not be delegated to other authorities. The Secretary had no power to assess and reject the special

205 CAP (n 166), art 115(2); Case 55/2017, page 19.
206 Figueiredo Dias (n 198) 225.
207 Cases 14/2002, 45/2016, 42/2017, 70/2018.
208 Case 70/2018, page 13.
209 E.g. Cases 12/2000, 14/2003, 16/2005, 16/2010, 55/2010.

residential permit application. He should have submitted the application to the Governor for a decision.[210]

In Case 55/2010, the applicant was granted a temporary residential permit after investing over one million patacas in real estate in Macau. In March 2006, the applicant sold one property, causing his investment to fall below the one million patacas threshold required for capital investment entrants. The applicant reported the sale to the Macau Trade and Investment Promotion Institute in June 2007 and bought another property in July to resume the investment status needed for a temporary residential permit. When the applicant applied for an extension of his residential permit in August, the Secretary for Economy and Finance rejected the application on the grounds that he did not maintain the investment status between March 2006 and July 2007. The TUI overturned the Secretary for Economy and Finance's decision on the ground of failing to perform the duty of notification. According to Article 7(3) of Decree 14/95M, the executive should have given the applicant at least 30 days to resume its investment status after receiving his report. However, the Secretary did not make any notification in June when the applicant reported the sale of the property.[211]

Acting in Good Faith

Good faith is a fundamental principle of administrative law enshrined in Article 8 of the CAP. According to this provision, the executive should consider the fundamental values of law, people's expectations, and the purpose of the executive action. The TUI applied this principle in five cases. In many cases, the applicant argued that the administrative decisions contradicted good faith, but the TUI refused to apply this principle, holding that this principle, along with fairness, legal expectation and proportionality, was not applicable to assess the defects of nondiscretionary administrative decisions.[212]

Only in one case, Case 1/2012, did the TUI overturn the decision on the ground of acting in bad faith. The applicant tendered for a local sewage treatment plant upgrade and maintenance project. His tender documents were rejected because the Chief Executive was not sure whether his certificate of sewage treatment operation experience was an official certificate, which was necessary according to the tender. The TUI held that the Chief Executive acted with bad faith in two aspects. First, he did not give the applicant the necessary time to prove that the certificate was an official document issued by a foreign government.[213] According to the judgment, the Chief Executive gave

210 Case 12/2000, page 6.

211 Case 55/2010, page 8.

212 E.g. Case 54/2011, page 24; Case 9/2016, page 29; Case 20/2016, page 20; Case 103/2018, page 89; Case 118/2019, page 11.

213 Case 1/2012, pages 12–13.

the applicant merely three days, which was far from enough. Second, the Chief Executive should have investigated the authenticity of the certificate if there was doubt, which was his duty. Moreover, this investigation was a relatively easy task for the government.[214] The failure to perform this basic investigative step indicated bad faith, as the government did not fulfill its obligation to verify important details before making a decision.

Intensity of the TUI's Judicial Review of Concrete Executive Acts

Overall, the TUI has taken a deferential approach to reviewing concrete executive actions. The intensity of review was at a low level, which is reflected by three aspects. First, the TUI's approach to the interpretation of the law was not protective of human rights. Second, while the TUI employed proportionality and misuse of power in many cases, the application of the two standards was more rhetorical than substantive. They hardly played any role in protecting individual rights from executive restrictions. Third, take the freedom of assembly as a case study: in those decisions concerning restrictions on the freedom of assembly, the TUI only struck down the administrative decisions which were manifestly erroneous or totally unreasonable. For sensitive political public meetings, the TUI rejected the petitions with unconvincing and far-fetched reasoning.

Interpretation of Law: Not Protecting Human Rights

Between 1999 and 2019, around one-third of the TUI's judicial review cases involved issues related to the interpretation and application of laws. In these cases, the TUI took a restrictive approach to the interpretation of individual rights and interests, dismissing the vast majority of people's claims. Unlike the CFA, which emphasizes the generous and purposive interpretation of individual rights and the narrow construction of restrictions to these rights, the TUI does not adopt a clear and protective stance on individual rights interpretation. Instead, its decisions have shown a rigid and narrow approach to interpreting individual rights.

As discussed above, many judicial review cases brought before the TUI challenged the denial of the right to a hearing. In most cases, the TCC dismissed the applicants' claims. The TUI's narrow interpretation of procedural fairness explained the low success rate of these challenges. The TUI distinguishes between essential procedures and non-essential procedures. Only procedures prescribed by law are considered as essential, and their violation could lead to the invalidation of administrative decisions. Conversely, the TUI does not strike down administrative decisions that violate non-essential procedures,

214 *Ibid.*, page 14.

those not explicitly prescribed by law.[215] In other words, the TUI would only strike down decisions that blatantly violate the right to a hearing explicitly required by law. Additionally, the TUI holds that a hearing is unnecessary if the decision-maker has no discretion but must make the only decision according to the law.[216] However, this interpretation is inconsistent with Articles 96 and 97 of the CAP, which list several circumstances under which a hearing is exempted. This situation is not one of these circumstances. The TUI has expanded the scope of the exemption, resulting in a high tolerance for violations of people's right to a hearing.

In Case 34/2021, the TUI interpreted the right to appeal in criminal cases narrowly. Article 389(1)(g) of the Code of Criminal Procedure clearly states that criminal sentences exceeding ten years can be appealed to the TUI. The Applicant was found guilty of two counts of drug trafficking by the Court of First Instance and received two sentences: nine years of imprisonment and six years and three months of imprisonment.[217] The Court of First Instance imposed an overall sentence of 11 years of imprisonment.[218] The applicant believed the sentence was disproportionate and appealed to the Court of Second Instance, which dismissed his claim.[219] Subsequently, the applicant sought a review of the penalty from the TUI. The Court ruled that an appeal was permissible only if each sentence exceeds ten years.[220] Consequently, the appeal was dismissed despite the overall sentence being 11 years, because it was derived from combining two sentences below the 10 years imprisonment threshold. Furthermore, the TUI ruled in Case 138/2021 that the courts would only entertain appeals if the actual sentence exceeded ten years, and not merely when the offense authorized a sentence above ten years.[221]

Additionally, the interpretation of law by the TUI appears to be surprisingly rigid. In Case 49/2007, the applicant, a Portuguese language teacher at the University of Macau, applied for special leave from 1 July to 30 July 2005, which was approved by the Director of the Education and Youth Affairs Bureau. He took a seven-day trip to Shanghai and returned to Macau, then departed to Portugal three days later to meet with his students. Upon his return, the University informed him that his absence from work between 7 to 30 July was unjustified because the special leave must be taken outside Macau for 30 consecutive days.[222] The TUI upheld the University's decision. It interpreted Article 3(3) of Decree 62/98M to mean that once the person concerned returns to Macau before the expiration of the special leave, the spe-

215 Case 11/2012, pages 7–8; Case 48/2012, pages 6–7.
216 Case 11/2012, page 15; Case 48/2012, page 15.
217 Case 34/2021, pages 1–2.
218 *Ibid.*, page 2.
219 *Ibid.*, page 3.
220 *Ibid.*, page 13.
221 Case 138/2021, pages 13–17.
222 Case 49/2007, pages 5–6.

cial leave terminates immediately, and they must return to service. The TUI emphasized that special leave should be taken continuously, not interruptedly.[223] The purpose of special leave is to give the teachers and civil servants a relatively long break from work.[224] Although the TUI acknowledged this legislative purpose, it considered that spending several days resting in Macau could not achieve this purpose, which is incomprehensible.

In Case 47/2008, the applicant, a lawyer, was appointed as a notary in Macau. His appointment was terminated because he had suspended his practice for over two years since September 2001. He applied for reappointment in May 2007, but his application was refused because he did not satisfy the appointment requirements stipulated in Articles 1 and 24 of Decree 66/99M, which included attending and passing the course provided by the Justice Affairs Bureau. The applicant appealed to the TUI, contending that he attended and passed the course before his first appointment and that re-attending the course was an unreasonable requirement for reappointment.[225] The TUI dismissed his claim based on a literal interpretation of Articles 1 and 24 of Decree 66/99M. It considered that the notaries who did not engage in notarial practice for over two years might no longer have the essential knowledge and competence, thus necessitating retaking the course for reappointment.[226] However, the TUI could not address the applicant's argument that some lawyers had not been appointed as notaries until five years after passing the course, suggesting that the applicant had more professional experience as a notary compared to them and that retaking the course was more than necessary.[227] The TUI simply stated they were different cases without further explanation.

Divergence Between Rhetoric and Practice in Proportionality and Misuse of Power Cases

Despite the frequent reiterations by the TUI that proportionality is a general principle of Macau administrative law, a clear gap exists between judicial rhetoric and actual effects. The TUI's application of proportionality and misuse of power has been notably restrained, with almost no judicial intrusion into administrative decision making. The TUI's approach is identical to that of the SPC in setting a high threshold for quashing administrative law based on these principles.

The TUI has consistently maintained that judicial intervention is warranted only if an administrative decision violates the principle of proportionality in

223 *Ibid.*, page 11.
224 *Ibid.*
225 Case 47/2008, page 13.
226 *Ibid.*, page 16.
227 *Ibid.*

an "intolerable manner".[228] It stated that "the court's duty is to determine whether the executive authorities' exercise of discretionary power is manifestly wrong or utterly unreasonable".[229] In the context of border control and immigration, the TUI held an opinion that an impugned decision should not be struck down unless it manifestly violates proportionality.[230] In the context of disciplinary sanctions and administration of civil service, the TUI reiterated that administrative decisions "are generally not subject to judicial review, except in cases where there are obvious errors, manifest injustice and violation of general principles of administrative law, including proportionality".[231]

In Case 69/2016, the applicant, a Hong Kong permanent resident, applied for a residential permit for a family reunion with his wife, a permanent resident of Macau. The Secretary of Security rejected his application because he was suspected of threatening the local public order and security. The facts on which the decision was made related to a minor offense occurred a decade ago and a fine of 1000 Hong Kong dollars, and the record was expunged.[232] The applicant argued that the decision was disproportionate and violated his right to family life guaranteed by Article 38 of the MBL. The TUI stated that it would intervene only when an administrative decision violates proportionality in an intolerable manner.[233] It held that having regard to the overall interest of safeguarding Macau's public order and security, the refusal of residential permits was not unacceptable or intolerable.

When the TUI assesses whether the executive misuses its power, the TUI grants leeway to the executive by imposing the burden of proof on citizens. People who challenge the intention of administrative actions must prove the executive pursues an illegal purpose. The TUI referred to Mário Aroso de Almeida's opinion and reiterated that the burden of proving administrative authorities pursuing illegal purposes rested on the appellants who challenge administrative actions.[234] However, proving personal intention, which is invisible and elusive, is a difficult task. It becomes even more difficult when an officer makes a decision for public interest and at the same time for personal interest.

Due to the high threshold for judicial intervention by proportionality and the imposition of the burden of proof on the applicants, the applicants have successfully challenged the proportionality of administrative actions in few

228 Cases 50/2010, 8/2012, 38/2012, 69/2012, 76/2012, 83/2012, 32/2013, 26/2014, 62/2015, 83/2016, 65/2018.

229 Cases 27/2003, 14/2005, 1/2006, 8/2006, 31/2006, 12/2011, 13/2011, 13/2012, 25/2012, 26/2014, 22/2017.

230 Case 36/2006, page 15.

231 Case 27/2003, 26/2014, 104/2014, 101/2019.

232 Case 69/2016, page 9.

233 *Ibid.*, page 17.

234 Case 29/2003, page 9; Case 68/2012, page 231.

cases and no administrative action has been quashed on the grounds of misuse of power.

The Right to Assembly and Right to Demonstration

Article 27 of the MBL guarantees Macau residents freedom of speech, assembly, and demonstration. Law No. 2/93/M on Right to Assembly and Demonstration enforces the right to assembly and demonstration by providing the timing, procedure, and legal remedies. Article 1 of this law stipulates that all Macau residents have the right to assemble in the public sphere or private sphere open to the public and that the right can be restricted only under the conditions prescribed by law. The exercise of freedom of assembly does not require government permissions, but organizers have an obligation to inform the Public Security Police Force.[235] If the Public Security Police Force prohibits or imposes conditions on assemblies, the organizers can appeal to the TUI, which has the original jurisdiction over these cases. The Public Security Police Force must submit their response within 48 hours and the TUI must address the case within 5 days upon their response.[236] If the TUI finds the decisions illegal, it can quash them and re-make a decision in place of the illegal one. This aims to ensure individuals can effectively and timely exercise their rights.[237]

Between 1999 and 2019, the TUI received 22 appeals against the administrative decisions prohibiting or restricting assemblies and demonstrations. The TUI awarded significant leeway to the executive when adjudicating these cases. In Case 75/2010, the applicant who was aggrieved by a decision of the government appealed to the TUI. The TUI stated that, "[i]n principle, courts should not judge whether the exercise of the discretionary power is appropriate in administrative litigation. It may only declare the illegality of an administrative decision and annul it in the circumstance where the exercise of discretionary power by the executive authorities is manifestly erroneous or totally unreasonable".[238]

Due to this restrained attitude, the TUI upheld most prohibitions and restrictions imposed by the government and only struck down nine decisions between 1999 and 2019.[239] The TUI supported the Public Security Police Force's bans on public assemblies on the grounds that the proposed meeting places were crowded with intensive traffic and close to historic buildings, which are popular tourism spots of Macau.[240] But Macau is known for its small

235 Law 2/93/M (Right to Assembly and Demonstration), art 5.
236 Law 2/93/M (Right to Assembly and Demonstration), art 12.
237 Case 16/2010, page 5.
238 Case 75/2010, page 6.
239 Cases 16/2010, 21/2010, 2/2011, 25/2011, 44/2013, 33/2014, 34/2014, 57/2017, 37/2018.
240 Case 31/2011, page 11.

territory and historic buildings dispersing over the congested roads and town. The TUI even upheld a prohibition decision even if only three persons would join the planned assembly.[241]

Additionally, the TUI tended to reject politically sensitive public gatherings. In Case 95/2014 and Case 100/2014, the TUI supported the prohibition of public meetings on the theme of "Promoting Civic Referendum on the Election of Chief Executive of 2014". The TUI stated that "an assembly (for the purposes of the freedom of assembly) means any gathering convened at some places for a common purpose of exchanging ideas, debating and forming opinions collectively".[242] In the TUI's opinion, the proposed public meetings were not an assembly, but a "opinion poll", aiming to survey Macau residents about their opinion regarding the election of Chief Executive by universal suffrage.[243] The TUI's reasoning and decision were, overtly, not logically persuasive. Public meetings that promoted universal suffrage were platforms for people to exchange ideas, express their preferences, and form collective opinions about the Chief Executive election, which fell within its definition of assembly. These two decisions were unfortunate decisions for Macau citizens' freedom of speech and civil society.

Case 94/2019 was more controversial. The TUI rejected a series of public meetings supporting the anti-extradition bill amendment protests in Hong Kong. The organizers intended to hold public meetings, of which the purpose was to urge the Hong Kong police to observe the Convention against Torture and not to use force unlawfully.[244] The TUI prohibited the meetings on two grounds. First, there was no evidence certified by any authorities showing that the Hong Kong police used force unlawfully or tortured any protestors. There was evidence showing that protests in Hong Kong involved crimes and the police had to maintain the social order. The public meetings were unsubstantiated attacks against the Hong Kong police and misleading.[245] Second, the TUI stated that under "One Country, Two Systems", Hong Kong and Macau were independent regions and should not interfere with each other's domestic affairs. The Macau government should not allow an assembly that might affect Hong Kong's local affairs.[246] These reasons were far from convincing. First, to urge the Hong Kong police to act according to international conventions is an expression of opinions and attitudes, which is the purpose of guaranteeing the right of assembly. Second, public meetings organized by civil society are not an act of government. The TUI regarded assemblies as interfering with

241 Case 34/2011, page 3.
242 Case 95/2014, page 6; Case 100/2014, page 5.
243 Case 95/2014, pages 7–8; Case 100/2014, page 5.
244 Case 94/2019, page 2.
245 *Ibid.*, pages 14–16.
246 *Ibid.*, pages 16–18.

domestic affairs of other regions, which is not persuasive according to any international law or domestic law.

In Case 6/2011, the TUI supported a decision prohibiting a demonstration outside the Liaison Office of the Central People's Government in Macau.[247] It stated that it was necessary to ensure that the facilities of the Liaison Office are not damaged and their operation is not disturbed, and to ensure the staff's safety, who enjoy protection and immunity provided to diplomatic institutions and personnel.[248] According to Article 8 of Law 2/93/M, assemblies held 30 meters away from government agencies and the Liaison Office should be allowed. Nonetheless, the TUI still rejected the proposed assembly and stated that the pavement outside the Liaison Office is narrow and the road next to it is a main road with a large traffic flow.[249] The TUI appeared sensitive and tended to reject assemblies and demonstrations nearby the Liaison Office and the government offices.[250]

Because the TUI is at the apex of Macau's judicial system, its decisions are first-instance decisions and final. Once it supports the impugned decisions restricting people's right to assembly, the applicants are unable to appeal to a higher court. The TUI's deferential attitude toward the government's restrictive measures has undermined its role in safeguarding people's freedom of assembly.

Conclusion

This chapter explored the standards and intensity of judicial review of concrete executive acts in China, Hong Kong, and Macau, revealing that the SPC and the TUI are significantly deferential in reviewing concrete executive actions. In contrast, the CFA is relatively invasive in the judicial review of concrete administrative decisions.

The SPC and the TUI primarily focus on the formal legality of executive acts, typically verifying whether decision-makers operate within their legal boundaries, apply the law correctly, adhere to required procedures, and base decisions on adequate evidence and accurate facts. The standards allowing an in-depth examination of the merits of administrative decisions are infrequently deployed by the SPC. Even when invoked, they are often ineffective in protecting individual rights. The SPC has emphasized and reiterated that the courts could only interfere with those decisions that are significantly and manifestly unreasonable and could strike down executive actions only if they are grossly disproportionate, setting a high bar for intervention. While the TUI employed proportionality in some cases, it has done so more rhetorically

247 Case 6/2011, pages 6–7.
248 *Ibid.*, page 6.
249 *Ibid.*, page 6.
250 Additional examples include Case 31/2011 and Case 34/2011.

than substantively, sharing the SPC's view that the courts do not strike down administrative decisions unless they are manifestly disproportionate. This stance minimizes proportionality's potential to protect human rights.

Moreover, in the SPC's jurisprudence, public interests generally supersede individual rights, with courts barred from revoking illegal executive actions if doing so would significantly harm national security or public interest. Likewise, the TUI's approach to human rights interpretation is rigid and not protective, favoring strict legal interpretations that narrow down individual rights and freedoms.

Conversely, the CFA engages more readily in substantive review. It frequently employs proportionality, unreasonableness, legal certainty, and legitimate expectation to assess administrative decisions. However, in cases involving disciplinary proceedings and immigration, it has adopted a lower intensity of review when evaluating procedural fairness, proportionality, and unreasonableness in these contexts.

6 Convergence, Divergence, and Reasons Behind

Convergence and Divergence in Judicial Review in Greater China

Judicial review has experienced expansion globally, and the four jurisdictions of Greater China have embraced judicial review as well. Chapter 2 to Chapter 5 examined the competence and activities of judicial review of the four apex courts in Greater China in the last two decades, revealing that the TCC and the CFA have converged on judicial activism and intrusive, while the SPC and the TUI have converged on strong judicial deference to the other branches of government. Judicial review in the four areas of Greater China has moved in two opposite directions.

Chapter 2 begins by examining the jurisdiction of the judicial review of the four apex courts in Greater China. The CFA and TUI enjoy broader jurisdiction than the TCC and the SPC to the extent of judicial review competence set up by law. The CFA and the TUI are vested with the power to review primary legislation, administrative rules, and concrete executive decisions. By contrast, the TCC enjoys the power to check primary legislation and administrative rules but lacks jurisdiction over concrete executive actions, which is assigned to the administrative courts of Taiwan. The SPC's jurisdiction for judicial review is the narrowest among the four courts. Chinese courts, including the SPC, have long been excluded from constitutionally reviewing any government actions. In the *Qi Yuling* case, judicial activism peaked when the SPC invoked the PRC Constitution and provided protection for the right to education.[1] However, this case did not usher in an era of judicial constitutional review as the SPC withdrew the *Qi Yuling* decision under political pressure. Judicial review, introduced to China in the late 1980s and known as administrative litigation, was initially limited to concrete administrative decisions. It was not until 2014 that Chinese courts were officially vested with the power to review administrative rules, but this power is still confined to rules of low rank.

1 Hualing Fu & Xiaobo Zhai, 'What makes the Chinese Constitution socialist?' (2018) 16(2) *International Journal of Constitutional Law* 655, 657.

DOI: 10.4324/9781003482536-6

In practice, the TCC and the CFA were much more active than the SPC and the TUI in reviewing primary legislation and administrative rules. The SPC and the TUI were either unable or unwilling to review primary legislation and administrative rules. The TCC and the CFA were confident and fearless in scrutinizing legislation and administrative rules. Via judicial review, the TCC and the CFA have shown an active and positive role in influencing government policy, protecting people's rights, safeguarding the rule of law, and refining local legal landscapes. By contrast, reviewing concrete executive actions is the main terrain of the SPC's and the TUI's judicial review. Consequently, their influence on law-making and policy formation is rather limited.

There is another essential difference between the TCC/CFA and the SPC/TUI in relation to the binding effect of their judicial review decisions against primary legislation and administrative rules. When the TCC and the CFA declare primary legislation or an administrative regulation unconstitutional or illegal, it becomes null and void. In China and Macau, however, a declaration of a law to be unconstitutional or illegal only leads to the disapplication of that law in the specific case where the claimant successfully challenges government decisions. The law remains in effect and is applicable in other cases. Although the TUI could render an administrative rule null and void via abstract review, this procedure was merely mounted one time in the past two decades.[2]

Chapter 3 focuses on the judicial review of primary legislation in Greater China and finds that the TCC and the CFA were more invasive than the TUI in reviewing primary legislation. The TCC and the CFA were liberal and had ruled in favor of various fundamental rights, such as same-sex marriage and transgender marriage,[3] same-sex partner benefits,[4] freedom of speech,[5] and the right to social welfare.[6] Both courts took a generous approach to interpreting human rights and were active in using proportionality and equal protection, which were invoked in around 80 percent of the TCC's interpretations and in over 50 percent of the decisions of the CFA against primary legislation. They declared impugned legislation unconstitutional in over half of the decisions when applying proportionality and equal protection.

In contrast, the TUI has shown broad and inappropriate leeway to Macau's legislature. It has never applied proportionality in cases against primary legislation. In Case 112/2018, it expressly rejected to apply proportionality to constitutionally scrutinize legislative actions.[7] It emphasized the passive and negative role of courts in judicial review, which means that the judiciary ought

2 Case 7/2007, page 31.

3 J. Y. Interpretation No. 748; *W v Registrar of Marriages* (2013) 16 HKCFAR 112.

4 *QT v Director of Immigration* (2018) 21 HKCFAR 324; *Leung Chun Kwong v Secretary for Civil Service* (2019) 22 HKCFAR 127

5 J.Y. Interpretation No. 718; *Leung Kwok Hung and others v HKSAR* (2005) 8 HKCFAR 229.

6 J.Y. Interpretation No. 766; *Kong Yunming v Director of Social Welfare* (2013) 16 HKCFAR 950.

7 Case 112/2018, page 13.

not to assess the rationality of legislation on the grounds of "reasonable", "just", or "ideal".[8] When applying the principle of equal protection, the TUI emphasized that, although the legislature is bound by the principle of equality, they still enjoy legislative freedom.[9] The courts only make a "negative judgment" in judicial review,[10] which means that the court could only invalidate legislation that results in manifest and intolerable inequality without any justification, objectivity, or rationality.[11] Additionally, the TUI has shown reluctance to strike down a law even when it found the law unconstitutional. In Case 2/2004, instead of declaring Article 1(3) of the Civil Code unconstitutional, it just declared the law meaningless.[12]

Chapter 4 continues by examining judicial review of administrative rules by the four apex courts in Greater China. It reveals that the TCC and the CFA were more assertive than the SPC and the TUI in reviewing administrative rules. The CFA was as active and intrusive as the TCC in reviewing administrative rules, although they relied on distinct standards and approaches. The TCC tended to examine whether the executive has the authority to promulgate administrative rules by applying the standard of statutory reservation. It has developed varying levels of intensity of review in association with this standard and has adopted the intermediate-level and high-level intensity of review in over 70 percent of the cases. When an impugned rule satisfies the statutory reservation test, the TCC still subjects it to substantive assessment by proportionality, equality, and other principles. Distinct from the TCC, proportionality remained the pillar standard in the CFA's scrutiny of administrative rules. The CFA paid less attention to whether the restrictions on individual rights take the form of ordinance – the primary legislation in Hong Kong. But it requires the law to be formulated with sufficient precision to enable the citizen to regulate his conduct.

The SPC and TUI have been notably restrained in reviewing administrative rules, with the TUI addressing only two cases over two decades. Besides the procedural obstacles, such as individuals not being able to challenge administrative rules without petitions against concrete administrative decisions (China) [13] and individuals not allowed to request an abstract review unless the courts have deemed an administrative rule provision unlawful on three separate occasions (Macau),[14] the SPC's and the TUI's reluctance to review administrative rules also explains the small portion of cases against administrative rules.

8 Case 5/2010, page 34; Case 9/2012, page 37.
9 Case 5/2010, page 32; Case 9/2012, page 35.
10 Case 5/2010, page 34; Case 9/2012, page 37.
11 Case 5/2010, page 34; Case 9/2012, page 37.
12 Case 2/2004, page 7.
13 Administrative Litigation Law (行政诉讼法), art 53(1).
14 Code of Administrative Litigation (行政訴訟法典), art 90(1). If a provision has an immediate effect on people's rights and interests, people can file abstract reviews and are not bound by the "three illegal declarations" requirement.

Even when entertaining appeals, the SPC usually concluded in favor of the impugned provisions unless there were evident violations of superior laws or glaring inconsistencies.

The predominant terrain of the SPC's and the TUI's judicial review lies on concrete executive actions. Chapter 5 demonstrates that they have granted significant leeway to their governments. The SPC has shown an apparent tendency to review the formal legality of concrete executive actions and avoid reviewing the substance of government decisions. It relied mainly on the standards of violating statutory procedures, insufficient evidence, an error of facts, failing to perform mandatory duties, and ultra vires. Although the SPC and the TUI employed proportionality in some cases, the application was no more than rhetoric. They stressed that the courts should not strike down administrative decisions unless they are manifestly disproportionate and cause severe harm to individual rights and interests.[15] *A fortiori*, in the SPC's jurisprudence, individual rights are outweighed by public interest.[16] The TUI's interpretation in relation to human rights is not protective either. It adopted a rigid and strict approach to interpreting the laws, resulting in the exclusion of people's rights and freedoms. The CFA appeared deferential in some cases relating to disciplinary proceedings and immigration. Nevertheless, it is still more assertive than the SPC and the TUI. Additionally, it often employed proportionality, unreasonableness, legal certainty, and legitimate expectation to review the substance of the administrative decisions.

The previous chapters demonstrated the convergence and divergence of judicial review in Greater China. The remainder of this chapter shows how the influence of foreign law associated with judges' educational background has shaped judicial review practices in each area.

Factors Directing Convergence and Divergence

Political, Institutional, and Historical Factors

The phenomenon of global expansion of judicial power along with growing public confidence in judicial review is explained through expanding literature providing various accounts. The classic comparative judicial review studies emphasized the relationship between modern democracies and judicial review and asserted that more established and vibrant democracies can host more activist courts and stronger judicial review.[17] Whether it is Alec Stone Sweet's

15 The Administrative Tribunal of the SPC (ed), *Chinese Administrative Adjudication Cases (Volume I)* (中国行政审判案例 (第1卷)) (China Legal Publishing House 2010) 92, 97–98; Case 36/2006, page 15.

16 The Administrative Tribunal of the SPC, *ibid.*, 31–32.

17 Democracy, by definition, is typically associated with fragmentation of power and implies political competitiveness. Besides political competition, modern democracy connotates respecting human rights and the rule of law. Bills of rights and independent judicial bodies to

incomplete contracting theory, Ginsburg's insurance model of judicial review, or Hirschl's hegemonic preservation theory, they are all built on democracy and fragmentation of power. Stone Sweet stated that a constitution could be conceived as a contract between political elites who jointly negotiate the constitutional framework of a state. In establishing a democracy, the contracting parties know that they will compete with each other for office through elections. They want to restrict the opponents who could be in power through elections. This is realized, in part, by constitutional rights and constitutional review.[18] Ginsburg suggested that judicial review was a form of political insurance that mitigates the risk of electoral loss. As democracy increases electoral uncertainty, no party can predict with confidence that it will maintain power indefinitely. It makes sense that parties that believe they could lose power in elections agree to adopt judicial review as a forum to challenge government action. It is more likely to adopt judicial review where each party's power is pretty even.[19] Hirschl offered another political account called "hegemonic preservation". When the ruling party foresees themselves losing power, they may initiate a constitutional entrenchment of rights and judicial review to transfer power to the courts. They assume that empowering courts is a way of ensuring their policy preferences are preserved.[20]

If the democratic theories are adequate to explain the judicial review activity in Greater China, one would expect a closer alignment between the judicial activism/deference spectrum and the political spectrum. In other words, the TCC, operating in Taiwan's liberal democracy, would indeed be expected to be the most assertive. The CFA and the TUI would likely exhibit a comparably deferential stance in judicial review, showing similar deference or slightly more assertiveness than the SPC. But this book has demonstrated that the TCC and the CFA stand on the side of judicial activism, while the SPC and the TUI lean towards judicial deference.

Some brilliant scholars have identified institutional, political, and historical factors that shape the different trajectories among the four apex courts. Po Jen Yap and Chien-Chih Lin stated that a fragmentation of power and an independent judiciary are two institutional explanations for the TCC's and CFA's

which any individual can bring a constitutional complaint are basic characteristics of modern constitutionalism. Tom Ginsburg, 'The Global Spread of Constitutional Review' in Keith E. Whittington, R. Daniel Kelemen, and Gregory A. Caldeira (eds) *The Oxford Handbook of Law and Politics* (OUP 2008) 88.

18 Alec Stone Sweet, *Governing with Judges: Constitutional Politics in Europe* (OUP 2000); Alec Stone Sweet and Jud Matthew, *Proportionality Balancing and Constitutional Governance: A Comparative and Global Approach* (OUP 2019).

19 Tom Ginsburg, *Judicial Review in New Democracies: Constitutional Courts in Asian Cases* (CUP 2003).

20 Ran Hirschl, *Towards Juristocracy: The Origins and Consequences of the New Constitutionalism* (Harvard University Press 2004).

convergence on structured proportionality and constitutional remedies.[21] Eric Ip suggested political transaction costs may account for the difference in the evolutionary path of CFA's and the TUI's constitutional review.[22] Political transaction costs refer to the expenses involved in running a political system, including decision-making, issuing orders, and enforcing rules. In judiciary–regime relations, these costs become significant when courts make decisions that conflict with regime preferences, often prompting regimes to limit judicial power. But fragmented regimes with high transaction costs may struggle to agree on or execute responses to judicial decisions. Consequently, when transaction costs are high, courts are more likely to adopt assertive constitutional reviews and aggressive judicial doctrines.[23] The factional infighting inside Hong Kong's ruling elites and formidable popular resistance to its initiatives disable the government from credibly threatening the CFA, reinforcing the demand for judicial review of unpopular policies. In contrast, Macau has a higher level of executive-legislative harmony, minimal civil unrest, and very weak pressure to democratization. The Macau government could preempt and discourage the TUI from engaging in any active judicial review. Albert Chen and P. Y. Lo suggested the legal traditions that already existed in Hong Kong and Macau at the time of their respective handovers explain the divergence between the CFA and the TUI.[24] Constitutional review enabling the courts to declare legislation invalid and void and null already existed in Hong Kong before the handover and was further reinforced subsequent to the enactment of the BORO. The Hong Kong judiciaries carried on constitutional review after the handover. By contrast, there was no well-developed constitutional review systems in colonial Macau.[25]

Judges' Education Background and Influence of Foreign Laws

Apart from these factors, this book suggests that the judges' education background and the foreign legal knowledge and jurisprudence they brought to the courts impact judicial review activities, shaping the convergence and divergence of judicial review in Greater China. Many judges on the TCC and the CFA obtained their legal education in Western countries, particularly in Germany, the US (for TCC judges), and the UK (for CFA judges). This

21 Po Jen Yap and Chien-Chih Lin, *Constitutional Convergence in East Asia* (CUP 2022).

22 Eric C. Ip, *Hybrid Constitutionalism: The Politics of Constitutional Review in the Chinese Special Administrative Regions* (CUP 2019).

23 *Ibid.*, 23–24.

24 Albert H. Y. Chen and P. Y. Lo, 'The Constitutional Orders of 'One Country, Two Systems': A Comparative Study of the Visible and Invisible Bases of Constitutional Review and Proportionality Analysis in the Chinese Special Administrative Regions of Hong Kong and Macau' in Rosalind Dixon and Adrienne Stone (eds) *The Invisible Constitution in Comparative Perspective* (CUP 2018) 261–262.

25 *Ibid.*

educational experience and legal knowledge they obtained have significantly influenced their decisions and reasoning, reflecting on the pervasive references to and citations of foreign laws and precedents, leading them to align more closely with the jurisprudence of Western democracies. At the same time, the TCC and the CFA have largely preserved their judicial review from Chinese laws' influence. By contrast, in Macau, three out of four TUI judges sitting on the bench between 1999 and 2019 were born in Mainland China, two judges obtained their first law degree in China, and two in Portugal. Chinese and Portuguese influence is overt and profound in the TUI's decisions and has led the court to a deferential and cautious stance in judicial review. It is plausible that the TUI cherry-picked Portuguese laws and scholarship to justify its deferential stance. In politically sensitive cases of constitutional importance, the TUI judges are very ready to Chinese laws, which played a decisive role in the TUI's rulings. In China, nearly all senior judges of the SPC are trained domestically, and they are cautious about referring to foreign authorities. But this does not mean that China completely isolates itself from foreign legal systems. Chinese judges are well-informed and sometimes embrace foreign laws. Nevertheless, these foreign doctrines are adjusted to fit China's unique political and legal context. For example, doctrines like proportionality, which are robust in other jurisdictions, have been weakened when applied within China.

Education Background of Judges

The TCC was established in 1948 and initially comprised 17 Grand Justices appointed by the President and approved by the Supervisory Yuan, with a term of office of nine years.[26] In 1997, the Constitution of Taiwan underwent its fourth amendment, which drastically changed the composition, appointment, and tenure of the TCC Grand Justices. Under the Fourth Amendment, since 2003, the TCC has comprised 15 Grand Justices appointed by the President and approved by the Legislative Yuan of Taiwan.[27] The Grand Justices are appointed for a term of eight years and cannot be consecutively reappointed,[28] except for eight Grand Justices appointed in 2003 with a term of four years.[29] Due to the different terms of office of the first batch of Grand Justices under the new rules and early resignations of some judges, 58 Grand Justices served on the bench of the TCC from 1999 to 2019.[30] More than half of the Grand

26 Constitution of Taiwan (中華民國憲法), art 79(2). Judicial Yuan Organization Act (司法院組織法), art 3 (1947). In 1992, the Constitution was amended to require the appointment of the Grand Justices to be approved by the National Assembly. The Second Amendment to the Constitution of Taiwan, art 13.

27 Amendment to the Constitutional of Taiwan, art 5(1) (1997).

28 *Ibid.*, art 5(2).

29 *Ibid.*, art 5(3).

30 The introduction of the judges of the TCC is available at https://cons.judicial.gov.tw/docdata.aspx?fid=9, accessed 30 November 2024.

Justices obtained degrees from top universities in Germany or America, many holding doctoral degrees.[31] They brought their acquired knowledge back to the courtrooms.[32]

The HKBL stipulates that judges of the HKSAR, including the CFA judges, "shall be appointed by the Chief Executive on the recommendation of an independent commission composed of local judges, persons from the legal profession and eminent persons from other sectors".[33] The CFA is composed of the Chief Justice and three permanent judges.[34] The Chief Justice must be a Chinese citizen who is a permanent resident of Hong Kong with no right of abode in any foreign country.[35] Additionally, there are two panels of non-permanent judges, one consisting of former Hong Kong judges and the other consisting of eminent judges from other common law jurisdictions.[36] Substantive appeals are heard on the CFA in panels of five.[37] Non-permanent judges are scheduled to hear substantive appeals with the permanent bench. In 2019, the retirement age of the CFA Chief Justice and permanent judges rose to the age of 70 from 65.[38] Their term of office can be extended by the Chief Executive but by no more than two periods of three years.[39] Since the establishment of the SAR in 1997 until 2019, the CFA had seen two Chief Justices and eight permanent judges.[40] Most permanent judges who have served on the HKCFA between 1997 and 2019 completed their primary legal education in England, and only two out of ten justices graduated with a first law degree at the University of Hong Kong.[41]

In Macau, the TUI comprises of three judges appointed by the Chief Executive based on the recommendation of an independent commission.[42]

31 Grand Justices who obtained degrees from American universities include: Vincent Sze, Yu-Tien Tseng, Tieh-Cheng Liu, Hsiang-Fei Tung, Pi-Hu Hsu, Tzu-Yi Lin, Syue-Ming Yu, Feng-Zhi Peng, In-Jaw Lai, Tsay-Chuan Hsieh, Shin-Min Chen (master's degree), Chang-Fa Lo, Dennis Te-Chung Tang, Chen-Huan Wu, and Jau-Yuan Hwang. Grand Justices who obtained degrees from German universities include: Tze-Chien Wang, Tong-Schung Tai, Jyun-Hsiung Su, Tzong-Li Hsu, Yih-Nan Liaw, Yu-Hsiu Hsu, Yueh-Sheng Weng, Chen-Shan Li, Mao-Zong Huang, Pai-Hsiu Yeh, Ming Chen, Chun-Sheng Chen, Shin-Min Chen (doctoral degree), Yeong-Chin Su, Ming-Cheng Tsai, Sheng-Lin Jan, Ming-Yan Shieh, and Tzung-Jen Tsai.

32 Chien-Chih Lin, 'Global Constitutionalism in Taiwan' (2021) 10 *Global Constitutionalism* 275, 285.

33 HKBL, art 88.

34 Court of Final Appeal Ordinance (Cap. 484), sec 5(1).

35 HKBL, art 90(1).

36 Court of Final Appeal Ordinance (n 34), sec 5(2) & (3).

37 *Ibid.*, sec 16(1).

38 *Ibid.*, sec 13A.

39 *Ibid.*, sec 14(2).

40 Since handover, the CFA has had three Chief Justices. Chief Justice Andrew Cheung Kui-nun was appointed as the third Chief Justice of the CFA on 11 January 2021.

41 They are Justice Patrick Chan and Chief Justice Andrew Cheung.

42 MBL, art 87(1).

Except for the Chief Justice, who must be a Chinese citizen and a permanent resident of Macau, there is no nationality requirement for other judges of the TUI and judges of lower courts.[43] In other words, foreign judges with professional qualifications can be appointed to the courts of Macau at all levels.[44] Substantive appeals to the TUI are typically adjudicated by this bench of three.[45] From 1999 to 2019, only four judges sat on the TUI.[46] In 1999, three judges – Sam Hou Fai, Chu Kin, and Viriato Manuel Pinheiro de Lima (foreign judge) – were appointed to the TUI.[47] At the end of 2011, the Chief Executive appointed Song Man Lei to the TUI after Judge Chu Kin died in a car accident.[48] The low turnover of TUI judges is due to the relative youth of the judges when they were appointed. Chief Justice Sam was 37 years old, Justice Chu 32, and Justice Song 46 when they were appointed. Among the four judges serving the bench from 1999 to 2019, Chief Justice Sam, Justice Chu, and Justice Song were born in Mainland China. Chief Justice Sam and Justice Song obtained their primary law degree from China, and Justice Chu and Justice Lima acquired their first law degrees in Portugal.[49]

In China, judges must hold Chinese nationality as required by the Law of Judges.[50] The SPC judges, including the Chief Justice, are appointed by the NPC. The presidents and judges of lower courts are appointed by the people's congress at the corresponding level. Information about the Chinese judges is usually opaque. Nonetheless, based on publicly available information, none of the Chief Justices of the SPC and very few high-ranking judges have obtained law degrees from overseas universities. Between 1999 and 2019, the SPC had three Chief Justices: Yang Xiao, Shengjun Wang, and Qiang Zhou. Chief

43 MABL, arts 87 & 88(2).

44 Different terms of appointment are applicable between local judges and foreign judges. Local judges appointed to the TUI are permanent judges and retire at the age of 65. Foreign judges are appointed to the TUI on a renewable contract for periods of two years. Statute of Magistrates, art 14 (4). Executive Order No. 4/1999, art 1; Executive Order No. 115/2011; Executive Order No. 177/2019.

45 A uniformization of jurisprudence is made by five judges, including three judges of the TUI, the president, and the most senior judge from the Court of Second Instance. Basic Law of Judiciary Organization of Macau (澳門司法組織綱要法), art 46(2).

46 At the time of writing, five judges have been appointed as TUI judges. In December 2019, the Chief Executive appointed José Maria Dias Azedo to the TUI in place of Justice Lima, who retired at the age of 65. Executive Order No. 177/2019.

47 Executive Order No. 4/1999, art 1(1).

48 Executive Order No. 115/2011.

49 Chief Justice Sam obtained an LLB degree from Peking University and later finished courses in Portuguese language, culture, and law at the University of Coimbra and obtained a graduate diploma in Macau law from the University of Macau. Judge Song obtained LLB and master's degrees from Peking University and later finished the Portuguese language course provided by the University of Coimbra. She also finished an Introduction to Macau Law Program and obtained a graduate diploma in Macau law. She served as a prosecutor of Macau since 1996 and later became an assistant prosecutor general in 2000.

50 Law on Judges (法官法), art 12.

Justice Xiao and Chief Justice Zhou earned their law degrees from Renmin University of China and Southwest University of Political Science and Law, respectively. Chief Justice Wang graduated with a bachelor's degree in history, not law. Among them, only Chief Justice Xiao had experience as the Deputy Attorney General of the SPP before his appointment to the SPC. Chief Justice Wang and Chief Justice Zhou worked in the government organs and CCP bureaus and lacked experience as judges, prosecutors, or lawyers before their appointments.[51]

Influence of Foreign Laws

The learning and training experience of judges deeply impact their courts' judicial review approach. They bring legal knowledge and jurisprudence they have learned to the courts.

The TCC Grand Justices frequently referred to German and American judicial decisions and courts' jurisprudence in their separate opinions. According to Professor Wen-Chen Chang's research, between 2003 and July 2010, the Grand Justices referred to foreign judgments and foreign laws 873 times in their separate opinions. Germany and the United States are the most frequently referred jurisdictions, with 508 and 155 references respectively.[52] Professor Chang's statistics provided evidence of a strong association between judges' overseas study experience and the foreign authorities they cited. In other words, Grand Justices who studied in Germany tended to refer to German authorities, while Grand Justices who obtained degrees from the United States were inclined to cite American authorities.[53] The German and American fusion of proportionality as demonstrated in Chapter 3 is an example. The insights of the Grand Justices into German and American constitutional jurisprudence demonstrated in their separate opinions substantiate the impact of German and American constitutional norms and jurisprudence on Taiwan, contributing to a convergence in outcome, standards of review, and intensity of review between the TCC and international high-level judicial review.[54]

51 Chief Justice Wang had worked in the CCP Central Political and Legal Affairs Commission for 15 years before his appointment as the President the SPC. Chief Justice Zhou worked in the Ministry of Justice and had been the Provincial Governor and Secretary of the CCP Committee of Hunan Province before his appointment.

52 Wen-Chen Chang (張文貞), 'An Empirical Study on the Reference of Foreign Laws and Precedents by Constitutional Court Interpretations: The Study-abroad Backgrounds as the Key (司法院大法官解釋引用外國法及判決之實證研究—大法官留學背景作為引用的關鍵因素)' in Yun-Chien Chang (張永健) (ed) *Empirical Studies of the Judicial System 2011* (2011司法制度實證研究) (The Institutum Iurisprudentiae Academia Sinica 2013) 44–49.

53 *Ibid.*, at 66–73.

54 Grand Justice Tzu-Yi Lin (J.Y. Interpretations No. 571, 584, 603, 617, 623, 644, 665, 682, 689)
Grand Justice Syue-Ming Yu (J.Y. Interpretations No. 577, 603)
Grand Justice Tzong-Li Hsu (J.Y. Interpretations No. 604, 623, 654, 665, 669, 767)

In Hong Kong, judges of the CFA obtained systematic common law education and training in British and local universities. Additionally, the Basic Law, the mini-constitution of this region, guarantees the laws previously in force in Hong Kong, including the common law, will continue to operate in Hong Kong after the handover and permits courts of Hong Kong to refer to precedents of other common law jurisdictions.[55] These provisions constitute a constitutional approval of citing foreign authorities.[56] The CFA emphasized that:

> The continuance of the common law was recognised as a major contributor to the maintenance of business and commercial confidence as well as confidence in the independence of the judiciary and the rule of law ... common law in Hong Kong should continue to apply and develop assisted by foreign, as well as local, precedent.[57]

Since the handover, the CFA has made extensive use of comparative law, especially authorities from the UK, Canada, Australia, and the ECtHR.[58] The application of proportionality in Hong Kong is an example of international influence. The High Court of colonial Hong Kong referred to the SCC's decision *R v Oakes* when introducing proportionality to Hong Kong.[59] When the CFA added balance – the fourth subtest of proportionality – to the justification test, it cited the Canadian case of *RJR-MacDonald Inc v A-G of Canada* and the British cases of *Huang v Secretary of State for the Home Department*

Grand Justice Yu-Hsiu Hsu (J.Y. Interpretations No. 604, 617, 630, 644, 646, 654, 678, 682, 689)
Grand Justice Feng-Zhi Peng (J.Y. Interpretation No. 638)
Grand Justice Chun-Sheng Chen (J.Y. Interpretations No. 659, 678, 682, 690, 697, 698, 738)
Grand Justice Chen-Shan Li (J.Y. Interpretations No. 682, 699, 718, 732)
Grand Justice Shin-Min Chen (J.Y. Interpretations No. 682, 688, 700, 702, 710, 711, 712, 715, 718, 719, 732, 733)
Grand Justice Yeong-Chin Su (J.Y. Interpretations No. 688, 700, 702, 709, 711, 712, 738)
Grand Justice Te-Chung Tang (J.Y. Interpretations No. 696, 699, 709, 711, 715, 718, 744 749, 756 760, 766)
Grand Justice Chang-Fa Lo (J.Y. Interpretations No. 715, 716, 733, 744)
Grand Justice Jau-Yuan Hwang (J.Y. Interpretations No. 745, 756, 767, 778)

55 HKBL, arts 8 and 84.
56 *Democratic Republic of the Congo v FG Hemisphere Associates LLC No.1* (2011] 14 HKCFAR 95, [441].
57 *Ibid.*, [440]–[441].
58 Sir Anthony Mason, 'The Common Law' in Simon N. M. Young and Yash Ghai (eds), *Hong Kong's Court of Final Appeal: The Development of the Law in China's Hong Kong* (CUP 2014) 347–348.
59 *R v Sin Yau Ming* (1992) 1 HKCLR 127, 142.

and *Bank Mellat v Her Majesty's Treasury (No 2)*.[60] When the CFA differentiated two levels of intensity of proportionality test, it relied on the ECtHR's innovation of "margin of appreciation",[61] and cited the British case of *R v Director of Public Prosecutions, ex p Kebilene* to justify the domestic application of this concept.[62] The CFA also widely cited British and ECtHR cases when articulating the factors that should be taken into account when courts choose the intensity of judicial review.[63] In another example, the CFA intensively cited the British and ECtHR authorities on same-sex marriage in *W v Registrar of Marriage* and *Leung Chun Kwong v Secretary for the Civil Service and Another*.[64]

The international influence over the CFA's judicial activities is further reinforced by overseas non-permanent judges sitting on this court.[65] Article 82 of the HKBL permits the CFA to invite judges from other common law jurisdictions to sit on the apex court of this region.[66] According to the Court of Final Appeal Ordinance, to be eligible to be appointed as an overseas non-permanent judge, a person should be (a) a judge or retired judge of a court of unlimited jurisdiction in either civil or criminal matters in another common law jurisdiction; (b) a person who is ordinarily resident outside Hong Kong; and (c) a person who has never been a judge of the High Court, a District Judge or a permanent magistrate, in Hong Kong.[67] The qualification requirements (b) and (c) mean that overseas non-permanent judges must be foreign, which guarantees they bring non-indigenous jurisprudence and wisdom to Hong Kong. Non-permanent judges, whether local or overseas, have no retirement age.[68] They are appointed for a term of three years and that term can be extended for one or more periods of three years by the Chief Executive on the recommendation of the Chief Justice.[69] From 1997 to 2019, there were 27 eminent judges from the UK, Australia, New Zealand, and Canada appointed as non-permanent judges of the CFA, including Baroness Hale of Richmond, the former President of the UKSC, Justice Beverley McLachlin, the former Chief Justice of the SCC, Sir Anthony Mason and Sir Gerard Brennan, former

60 *Hysan Development Co Ltd v Town Planning Board* (2016) 19 HKCFAR 372, [65]–[67].
61 *Fok Chun Wa v Hospital Authority* (2012] 15 HKCFAR 409, [61]–[62].
62 *Ibid.*, [62].
63 *Hysan* (n 60) [105]–[118].
64 Martin Kwan, 'Is the Hong Kong Courts' Ability to Refer to Foreign Authorities Unrestrained?' (2022) 4 *Amicus Curiae* 71, 74–75.
65 Joseph Fok, 'Judges from Other Common Law Jurisdictions on the Hong Kong Court of Final Appeal' in Anna Dziedzic and Simon N. M. Young (eds) *The Cambridge Handbook of Foreign Judges on Domestic Courts* (CUP 2023).
66 HKBL, art 82.
67 Court of Final Appeal Ordinance (n 34), sec 12(4).
68 *Ibid.*, sec 14(3).
69 *Ibid.*, sec 14(4).

Chief Justices of the High Court of Australia.[70] All overseas non-permanent judges are pre-eminent and well-respected judges who "had significant influence in shaping the jurisprudence of their own jurisdictions".[71] Overseas non-permanent judges have sat on more than 95 percent of all appeals heard by the CFA since 1997.[72] The positive influence of overseas non-permanent judges sitting on the CFA has been widely recognized by local and overseas judges, lawyers, and scholars.[73] Lord Cook of Thorndon explicitly once pointed out that:

> [A] function of a judge from other common law jurisdictions is to give particular consideration to whether a proposed decision of this Court (the CFA) is in accord with generally accepted principles of the common law.[74]

The appearance of overseas judges in the apex court of Hong Kong contributes to the convergence in judicial review jurisprudence between the CFA and the Western courts. The CFA has earned itself international reputations in protecting human rights and upholding the rule of law. Inviting overseas judges to sit on the CFA does not mean to dictate Hong Kong law by a single jurisdiction.[75] On the contrary, the system of foreign judges and pervasive uses of comparative law guarantee Hong Kong reaches the international high level, especially in the aspects of human rights protection and judicial independence.

In Macau, according to the Basic Law, the previously enforced laws, decrees, administrative regulations, and other regulatory documents are retained after the handover unless they conflict with the MBL or have been modified.[76] Before the handover, the Legislative Assembly of colonial Macau had enacted five statutes: the Penal Code, the Criminal Procedure Code, the Civil Code,

70 Until July 2024, the time of writing, there have been 30 overseas non-permanent judges appointed to the CFA, available at www.hkcfa.hk/en/about/who/judges/introduction/index.html, accessed on 12 July 2024.

71 Fok (n 65) 45.

72 Simon N. M. Young, 'Domestic Criticisms of Foreign Judges: The Case of Hong Kong' in Anna Dziedzic and Simon N. M. Young (eds) *The Cambridge Handbook of Foreign Judges on Domestic Courts* (CUP 2023) 284.

73 'The Chief Justice's Address at the Opening of the Legal Year', 11 January 1999, available at www.hkcfa.hk/en/documents/publications/speeches_articles/index.html, accessed 15 July 2024; Sir Anthony Mason, 'The Place of Comparative Law in Developing the Jurisprudence on the Rule of Law and Human Rights in Hong Kong' (2007) 37 *Hong Kong Law Journal* 299; Fok (n 65); Michael Thomas, 'A Practitioner's Perspective' in Simon N. M. Young and Yash Ghai (eds), *Hong Kong's Court of Final Appeal: The Development of the Law in China's Hong Kong* (CUP 2014) 201; Lo Pui Yin, *The Judicial Construction of Hong Kong's Basic Law: Courts, Politics and Society after 1997* (Hong Kong University Press, 2014) 84–85, 289

74 *Chen Li Hung v Ting Lei Miao* (2000) 3 HKCFAR 9, 23.

75 Young (n 72) 291.

76 MBL, art 8.

the Commercial Code, and the Civil Procedure Code. These statutes continue to operate after the handover and are known as the five foundational laws of the MSAR.[77] They were modeled on corresponding Portuguese statutes and inherited Portuguese legal traditions.

On the other hand, after the handover, Chinese law and jurisprudence have been permeating into Macau's legal system and courts' adjudication, despite the separation of legal systems under "One Country, Two Systems".[78] The coexistence of Portuguese and Chinese legal traditions is continuously nourished by the judges of Macau, especially the TUI judges. As noted above, between 1999 and 2019, two out of four judges sitting on the TUI acquired their first law degrees from Portugal and two from Mainland China. Additionally, 80 percent of Macau's judges had attended training sessions hosted by the SPC, where they learned about the Chinese judicial system.[79] The TUI judges have frequently referred to Chinese and Portuguese laws, opinions of Portuguese and Chinese courts, and academic views of Chinese and Portuguese scholars. The influence of Chinese and Portuguese law has led the TUI to a deferential and conservative stance in judicial review.

Portuguese scholars' opinions advocating for limited judicial review and restrained courts have informed the TUI in several leading cases. In Case 5/2010 and Case 9/2012, which concerned equal protection, the TUI cited the view of Jorge Miranda and Rui Medeiros, emphasizing that courts would play a passive and negative role in judicial review and that the courts should not assess a law on the grounds of "reasonable", "just", or "ideal".[80] The TUI also adopted Maria Lucia Amaral's opinion, asserting that the courts would declare a law violating the principle of equality only if it causes manifest and intolerable inequality without any justification, objectivity, or rationality.[81] Additionally, the TUI cited Portuguese scholars' opinions to underpin the deferential approach to proportionality, that judicial intervention is warranted only if an administrative decision violates this principle in an "intolerable manner".[82] It cited Mário Aroso de Almeida's opinion and required citizens to bear the whole burden of proving administrative authorities pursuing illegal purposes.[83]

77 Genliang Xie (謝耿亮), 'The Predicament of Macau Law and the Way Out: Inclination to Portugal and Local' (澳門法困局與出路：葡萄牙化或本地化) (2009) 2 *Journal of "One Country Two Systems" Studies* ('一國兩制'研究) 43, 51.

78 Dan Wei, 'Macao's Legal System Under Globalisation and Regional Integration: Between Tradition and Evolution' (2014) 9(2) *Frontiers of Law in China* 233, 238.

79 Chief Justice's speech at Ceremonial Opening of the Legal Year 2019–2020 (在2019至2020年澳門特別行政區司法年度開幕典禮上的講話) (18 October 2019).

80 Case 5/2010, page 34; Case 9/2012, page 37.

81 Case 5/2010, page 35; Case 9/2012, page 37.

82 Case 26/2003, page 11; Case 50/2010, page 27.

83 Case 29/2003, page 9.

The influence of Chinese law on the TUI is prominent in those politically sensitive cases of constitutional importance. The TUI has openly relied on Mainland laws, the decisions of the Central Government in Beijing, and the opinions of Chinese courts and Chinese scholars to underpin its decisions. For example, in Case 28/2006, the TUI addressed two critical issues: whether the courts of Macau are vested with the power of constitutional review and whether the Chief Executive is competent to promulgate administrative regulations even without delegation of power from the Legislative Assembly. On the first issue, the TUI referred to the opinion of Professor Zhenmin Wang, the then member appointed by Beijing to the Committee for the Basic Law of the MSAR, that the NPCSC and the courts of the SARs are the competent institutions for constitutional review.[84] The TUI's reliance on his opinion suggests that it only affirms the local courts' power of constitutional review after receiving approval from Mainland Chinese officials. When addressing the second issue, the TUI cited the PRC Constitution and the PRC Law on Legislation. It asserted that it must consider the Chinese constitutional provisions, theories, and practices in understanding administrative regulations in Macau because the MBL was passed by the NPC, drafted by the MBL Drafting Committee which comprised eminent persons from the Chinese legal sector, and influenced by the PRC Constitution and relevant theories.[85] Additionally, administrative regulation is derived from Chinese laws and did not exist in Macau before the handover.[86] The TUI concluded that Macau and China have parallel systems in terms of the relationship between administrative regulations and legislation.[87]

In another example, in Case 81/2021, the TUI upheld a ban on a candlelight vigil in memory of the Tiananmen Square military crackdown, citing the Resolution of the NPCSC on Stopping Riots and Quelling Anti-Revolution Unrest, which labeled events on 4 June as disturbances aimed at overthrowing the leadership of the CCP, overthrowing the Central Government, and subverting the PRC.[88] The TUI even asserted that the proposed gathering was a well-planned and deliberate attack on the reputation, dignity, and authority of

84 Case 28/2006, page 29. The Committee for the Basic Law of the MASR is a working committee under the NPCSC and was established in 1999 according to the Decision of the NPC Approving the Proposal by the Drafting Committee for the Basic Law of the Macao SAR on the Establishment of the Committee for the Basic Law of the Macao SAR under the NPCSC. The Committee's function is to advise the NPCSC on various matters concerning the MABL: see arts 17(3), 18(3), 143(4) and 144(3) of the MBL.

85 Case 28/2006, pages 103–104.

86 *Ibid.*, page 105.

87 *Ibid.*, pages 104–105.

88 Case 81/2021, page 50. Resolution of the NPCSC on Stopping Riots and Quelling Anti-Revolution Unrest (全国人民代表大会常务委员会关于制止动乱和平息反革命暴乱的决议) (Approved at the Eighth Session of the Standing Committee of the Seventh National People's Congress on 6 July 1989).

the Central Government.[89] The last example is Case 113/2021. In the latest Legislative Assembly election, all candidates from the pro-democracy camp were disqualified from running for direct elections. The TUI upheld the disqualification decisions and accepted the accusation that all pro-democracy candidates failed to uphold the MBL and the MSAR. The accusation was based on the fact that these candidates had organized and participated in assemblies to commemorate the Tiananmen Square military crackdown, Chinese dissident Liu Xiaobo, and the pro-democracy manifesto Charter 08.[90] The TUI cited Article 1 of the PRC Constitution, which stipulates that "the leadership of the CCP is the defining feature of Chinese socialism".[91] It interpreted these gatherings as challenges to the CCP's leadership. Additionally, referring to Liu Xiaobo's conviction handed down by the High Court of Beijing, the TUI regarded assemblies commemorating Xiaobo Liu and displaying Charter 08 as challenges against the constitutional orders of the PRC.[92]

By contrast, despite the same constitutional arrangement and more enormous pressure imposed on Hong Kong by Beijing, Chinese legal authorities hold little leverage on the CFA's judicial review.[93] The CFA has been guarding the expertise and authority of Hong Kong's courts in interpreting and applying laws following the common law approach.

In 2001, the CFA decided *Director of Immigration v Chong Fung Yuen*, another thorny case concerning the right to abode after *Ng Ka Ling*. Chong Fung Yuen is a Chinese citizen born in Hong Kong when his parents, who are Chinese citizens, came to Hong Kong as temporary visitors to visit Chong Fung Yuen's grandfather. Chong Fung Yuen claimed that he enjoyed the right to abode according to Article 24(2)(1), which provides that "Chinese citizens born in Hong Kong before or after the establishment of the HKSAR". The Director of Immigration rejected this claim. The counsel for the Director of Immigration requested the CFA to refer the provision in question to the NPCSC for interpretation in accordance with Article 158 of the HKBL.[94] The

89 Case 81/2021, page 57.

90 Liu Xiaobo was a leading figure among China's dissidents and a renowned human rights advocate. In December 2008, he was arrested and imprisoned for subverting state power. The charges against him stemmed from his public criticism of the Chinese government and his role as a principal author of Charter 08, a manifesto demanding democracy, respect for human rights, and the rule of law in China. Jean-Philippe Beja, Fu Hualing, and Eva Pils (eds), *Liu Xiaobo, Charter 08 and the Challenges of Political Reform in China* (Hong Kong University Press, 2012).

91 Case 113/2021, pages 208–209.

92 *Ibid.*, pages 209–210.

93 Because of the cross-strait situation, Taiwan is *de facto* an area beyond the control of Beijing, and Taiwan's legal system is completely independent from China's. Additionally, Taiwan holds high the banner of democracy, freedom, and constitutionalism in order to differentiate itself from authoritarian China. The TCC has played a role in safeguarding these values and isolated its public law jurisprudence from China's.

94 *Director of Immigration v Chong Fung Yuen* (2001) 4 HKCFAR 211, 225I–226D.

counsel also submitted that if the court chose not to make a judicial reference, it should take into account the statement in the NPCSC Interpretation of 26 June 1999 subsequent to *Ng Ka Ling*.[95] The CFA rejected both submissions. It held that the interpretation handed down by the NPCSC on 26 June 1999 did not express a clear view that Article 24(2)(1) was an excluded provision that should refer to the NPCSC for interpretation.[96] Article 24(2)(1), "a provision defining one category of permanent residents who are entitled to the right of abode", in the CFA's opinion, did not concern the affairs which are the responsibility of the Central People's Government or the relationship between the Central Authorities and the Region.[97] Having addressed the issue of judicial reference, the CFA proceeded to the interpretation of HKBL provisions, emphasizing the common law approach to interpretation:

> The courts of Hong Kong exercise independent judicial power under the Basic Law … This principle, which follows from the doctrine of the separation of power, is a basic principle of the common law and is preserved and maintained in Hong Kong by the Basic Law.
>
> The courts' role under the common law in interpreting the Basic Law is to construe the language used in the text of the instrument in order to ascertain the legislative intent as expressed in the language. Their task is not to ascertain the intent of the lawmaker on its own. Their duty is to ascertain what was meant by the language used and to give effect to the legislative intent as expressed in the language.[98]

On this common law approach, the CFA concluded that the meaning of Article 24(2)(1) was clear, and there was no ambiguity. It means that Chinese citizens born in Hong Kong before or after 1 July 1997 are permanent residents of Hong Kong.[99]

When the NPCSC passed the NSL and imposed it on Hong Kong on 30 June 2020, the CFA ruled that the common law approach should be applied in the interpretation of this law in *HKSAR v Lui Sai Yu*,[100] even though the NSL is a law of pervasive Chinese law elements as a consequence of a hasty legislative process.[101] The NPCSC underwent three readings of the NSL bill in approximately one month without publishing the bill for public inquiry nor engaging in meaningful consultation with the members of the HKBL

95 *Ibid.*, 231C–D.
96 *Ibid.*, 228I–J.
97 *Ibid.*, 229G–H.
98 *Ibid.*, 223G–H.
99 *Ibid.*, 233G.
100 *Hong Kong SAR v Lui Sai Yu* (2023) HKCFA 26 [45].
101 Albert H. Y. Chen, 'The National Security Law: A Contextual and Legal Study' in Hualing Fu and Michael Hor (eds) *The National Security Law of Hong Kong: Restoration and Transformation* (University of Hong Kong Press 2022).

Committee before promulgation.[102] The CFA emphasized that the NSL and Chinese law converged merely on the national law on safeguarding national security and not on any unrelated Chinese law which employs concepts using similar language.[103] It held that, under the umbrella of the policy of "One Country, Two Systems", Hong Kong's legal system is separated from the Mainland legal system and that the courts may not "search for and consider as possible aids to construction, similarity-worded Mainland laws".[104]

In China, judges have rarely cited foreign laws, precedents, or scholarship.[105] One significant reason for this is the general lack of knowledge of foreign law, as the vast majority of judges are trained domestically and do not possess overseas law degrees.[106] The limited reference to foreign law is further reinforced by the SPC's 2009 issuance of the *Rules on Citing Laws, Regulations, and Other Normative Legal Documents in Judicial Decisions.* Article 5 of these Rules provided that "Administrative litigation judgments should cite laws, (NPCSC's) legal interpretations, administrative regulations, or judicial interpretations. Local regulations, autonomous regulations and separate regulations, as well as interpretations of administrative regulations or *Guizhangs* issued by the State Council or departments authorized by the State Council, may be directly cited if applicable".[107] According to this provision, citing precedents or academic opinions, whether domestic or foreign, lacks legality and contradicts the SPC directives. Since 2011, the SPC has been publishing Guiding cases to be referred to by all judges when they adjudicate similar cases. Still, Chinese judges seldom explicitly cited decided cases even when they followed rulings of guiding cases.[108] It is therefore conceivable that judges are more reluctant and hesitant to openly cite foreign precedents. Despite the paucity of references to foreign authorities, international influence is inevitable given the global exchange of legal knowledge and Chinese judicial review is informed by foreign laws. As a matter of fact, the establishment, development, and refinement of Chinese administrative law since the Reform and Opening were informed by foreign laws and scholarship, including the

102 Jie Cheng, 'Hong Kong's Constitutional Order after the National Security Law' in Hualing Fu and Michael Hor (eds) *The National Security Law of Hong Kong: Restoration and Transformation* (University of Hong Kong Press 2022).

103 Lui Sai Yu (n 100), [47].

104 *Ibid.*

105 Zhihang Zheng (郑智航), 'Domestic Application of Foreign Laws and Precedents (外国法与案例在本国司法中的运用)' (2014) 2 *Global Law Review* (环球法律评论) 105, 118–122.

106 *Ibid.*, 121.

107 Rules of the SPC on Citing Laws, Regulations, and Other Normative Legal Documents in Judicial Decisions (最高人民法院关于裁判文书引用法律、法规等规范性法律文件的规定)

108 Benjamin M. Chen et al., 'Detecting the Influence of the Chinese Guiding Cases: A Text Reuse Approach' (2024) 32 *Artificial Intelligence and Law* 463–486.

Soviet Union, Germany, and the UK.[109] However, the introduction of foreign doctrines and principles has often been selective, with imported doctrines and principles being "tamed" to fit China's unique political and legal systems, where judicial review of government actions is seriously constrained.

Proportionality is one of the foreign doctrines imported to China. In 1988, Japanese scholar Koichi Aoyagi gave a lecture on proportionality at the Chinese University of Political Science and Law, and later his speech was translated into Chinese and published in a Chinese law journal, which was one of the first articles in Chinese that systematically introduced the principle of proportionality.[110] In his informative lecture, Koichi Aoyagi discussed the subtests of proportionality, the intensity of proportionality test, the factors influencing the intensity of review, and judicial deference. Since 1999, when the SPC first applied proportionality in judicial review, proportionality has been invoked in a negligible number of judicial review cases. Additionally, when proportionality was deployed, the courts had insufficient emphasis on the safeguarding of individual rights but had a bias towards public interest. According to Ma and Yu's statistics, people lost their claims in about 70 percent of all cases when the courts employed the balancing analysis, the last subtest of proportionality.[111]

Proportionality in China has been altered to accommodate the limited role of judicial review within the party-state government structure and China's long-held belief that state/collective interest takes precedence over individual rights. It becomes less intrusive in Chinese judicial review. By contrast, the TCC and the CFA intentionally keep in line with Western standards, despite their endeavor to reconcile foreign legal principles with local experience. In China, international influence is overshadowed by the unique domestic political and legal environment, which significantly shapes the application and interpretation of imported legal principles.

Conclusion

Judicial review trends over the past two decades show a clear divergence within Greater China: while the TCC and CFA exhibit assertive judicial review, the SPC and TUI demonstrate a more deferential approach. Apart from the

109 Xinli Zhu (朱新力) & Meiying Luo (骆梅英) 'Advancing Without Roadblocks: The Development of Comparative Administrative Law and Contemporary Administrative Law in China' (前行没有路障——比较行政法学与中国当代行政法学的发展) in Songnian Ying (应松年) (ed), *A Review and Outlook of Chinese Administrative Law* (中国行政法之回顾与展望) (Chinese University of Political Science and Law Press, 2006) 334–343.

110 Koichi Aoyagi, 'Infringements on Basic Rights and the Principle of Proportionality' (基本权利的侵犯和比例原则) (1988) *Journal of Comparative Law* (比较法研究) 34, 36.

111 Chao Ma (马超) & Xiaohong Yu (于晓虹), 'Application of Principle of Proportionality in Administrative Litigation – An Empirical Study Based in Published Judicial Decisions' (行政审判中比例原则的适用—基于公开裁判文书的实证研究) (2022) 4 *Journal of Shandong University* (山东大学学报 (哲学社会科学版)) 58, 62.

political, institutional, and historical reasons, this book suggests the influence of foreign legal systems, stemming from the educational backgrounds of judges is another factor that is shaping this divide.

Many judges on the TCC and the CFA obtained their legal education in Western countries, particularly in Germany, the US (for TCC judges), and the UK (for CFA judges). This educational experience and the legal knowledge they obtained have significantly informed their decisions and reasoning, as reflected in the pervasive references to and citation of foreign laws and precedents. The TCC judges frequently referred to and discussed German and American public law decisions and jurisprudence in their separate opinions, and the CFA has extensively used comparative law, especially authorities from the UK, Canada, Australia, and the ECtHR, leading them to align more closely with the judicial review in liberal democracies. Additionally, on the CFA, overseas non-permanent judges have played an additional and essential role in maintaining Hong Kong's judicial review in line with common law jurisprudence.

By contrast, in Macau, three out of four TUI judges sitting on the bench between 1999 and 2019 were born in Mainland China, two judges obtained their first law degree in China, and two in Portugal. Chinese and Portuguese influence is overt and profound in the TUI's decisions and has led the court to a deferential and cautious stance in judicial review. In politically sensitive cases of constitutional importance, the TUI readily invokes Chinese law, Chinese courts' decisions, and Chinese scholars' opinions. It is worthy highlighting that despite the same constitutional arrangement and even more enormous pressure imposed on Hong Kong by Beijing, Chinese laws hold little leverage on the CFA's judicial review. The CFA has been steadfastly guarding the expertise and authorities of Hong Kong's courts in interpreting and applying laws following the common law approach. In China, nearly all senior judges of the SPC are trained domestically, and they have rarely cited foreign laws, precedents, or scholarship. But this does not mean that China completely isolates itself from foreign legal systems. Chinese judges are well-informed and sometimes embrace foreign laws. Nevertheless, these foreign doctrines are adjusted to accommodate China's political and legal environment, where judicial review power is seriously restrained.

7 Conclusion

The global proliferation of judicial review attracted research into it, a subject which has been popular now for a few decades. This book adds judicial review in Greater China to this chorus by comparing the judicial review mechanisms in the four areas and comprehensively examining judicial review activities of the apex court in each area from 1999 to 2019. It reveals that the apex courts in Taiwan and Hong Kong (TCC and CFA) have embraced judicial activism and intrusion, while the SPC and the TUI, apex courts in Mainland China and Macau, have shown strong deference to the other branches of government. Judicial review in the four areas of Greater China has evolved in two opposite directions.

These findings partly support the current theory that, whereas democratic regimes provide fertile soil for developing judicial review and would host active and assertive judicial review – Taiwan being a case in point in this book – authoritarian regimes lack such a political and legal environment for strong and effective judicial review and authoritarian rulers could not tolerate powerful courts – China being the case here. On the other hand, statistics and judicial review decisions of the CFA and the TUI tell two entirely different stories, suggesting that the dichotomy between democratic and non-democratic in explaining the global expansion of judicial review oversimplifies the intricate political and legal systems in hybrid regimes. Hong Kong and Macau possess nearly identical constitutional frameworks, culture, language, and ethnicity. But the CFA and the TUI presented strikingly different judicial review practices in the last two decades. The CFA was active and assertive in judicial review, as was the TCC, a constitutional court of a democratic regime; on the contrary, the TUI was timid and deferential in judicial review, more or less the same as the SPC, the supreme court of the world's largest authoritarian regime.

Hybrid regimes are neither fully democratic nor outright authoritarian. They embrace the features of democracies and authoritarian regimes. The co-existence of judicial review supportive conditions and restrictive factors render the evolution of judicial review in hybrid regimes more complicated and indeterminate than those in democracies and authoritarian regimes. This book suggested that the educational background of judges and the influence

DOI: 10.4324/9781003482536-7

of foreign laws have influenced the development of judicial review in the four areas of Greater China. This attempt does not aim to simplify the complex and diverse forces influencing judicial review in Greater China or in hybrid regimes. Instead, it hopes to provoke broader research and discussions on judicial review evolution in Greater China and in hybrid regimes, which are worthy of further examination.

In Greater China, many factors that potentially influence the development of judicial review are emerging and changing. In Taiwan, the TCC started to hear constitutional complaints in 2022, which is believed to bring significant changes to the TCC constitutional review.[1] The National Security Law enacted by the NPCSC for Hong Kong changed this city's political and legal landscape.[2] In 2018, China amended its Constitution and removed the limits on the term of office of president. Xi Jinping wields extraordinary power and has become the most powerful leader since Mao Zedong,[3] resulting in China's hard-line policies towards Taiwan and Hong Kong. Judicial review in Greater China is undoubtedly a noteworthy and dynamic phenomenon in a changing political environment. The statistics and findings of this book could provide fundamental baseline data for evaluating the future development of judicial review in Greater China.

1 Huaxiang Fang (方华香), 'A Study on the Introduction and the Future Implementation of Constitutional Complaints' (裁判宪法审查制度之引进与未来施行相关疑义研析), available at www.ly.gov.tw/Pages/Detail.aspx?nodeid=6590&pid=179873, accessed 16 November 2021.

2 Simon N. M. Young, 'Hong Kong's Highest Court Reviews the National Security Law – Carefully' *Lawfare,* available at www.lawfaremedia.org/article/hong-kongs-highest-court-reviews-national-security-law-carefully, accessed 30 July 2024.

3 Po Jen Yap, 'Authoritarian Regimes' in Peter Cane, Herwig C. H. Hofmann, Eric C. Ip, and Peter L. Lindseth (eds), *Oxford Handbook of Comparative Administrative Law* (OUP 2020) 350.

Appendix

Appendix A: List of the SPC Judicial Review Decisions (1999–2019)

Types	*Cases*	*Case Number / Gazette Issue*	*In Total*
Review of normative documents	Luwei (Fujian) Salt Industry Import and Export Co., Ltd. Suzhou Branch v The Salt Administration Bureau of Suzhou Municipality	No. 5	10
	Tian Yong v The University of Science and Technology Beijing	No. 38	
	He Xiaoqiang v Huazhong University of Science and Technology	No. 39	
	Fengxiang Company v The Salt Affairs Bureau of Shanghai Municipality	2003(1)	
	Lu Tingzuo v The Housing and Land Management Bureau of Zhabei District, Shanghai Municipality	2007 (8)	
	Gan Lu v Jinan University	2012 (7)	
	Shanghai Dike Paper Packaging Co., Ltd v The Human Resources and Social Security Bureau of Shanghai Municipality	2013 (11)	
	Chen Aihua v The Housing and Urban-Rural Construction Bureau of Jiangning District, Nanjing Municipality	2014 (8)	
	Cui Longshu v The People's Government of Feng County	2017 (11)	
	Hongrun Supermarket v The Market Inspection and Management Bureau of Danyang Municipality	2018 (6)	
Review of executive acts	Huang Zefu, He Boqiong, and He Yi v The Jintang Administration for Industry and Commerce of Chengdu Municipality, Sichuan Province	No. 6	82

Appendix A: (Continued)

Types	*Cases*	*Case Number / Gazette Issue*	*In Total*
	Inner Mongolia Qiushi Real Estate Development Limited Liability Company v The Civil Air Defense Office of Hohhot Municipality	No. 21	
	Wei Yonggao and Chen Shouzhi v The People's Government of Lai'an County	No. 22	
	Li Jianxiong v Department of Transport of Guangdong Province	No. 26	
	Sun Lixing v The Labour and Personnel Bureau of Tianjin New Technology Industrial Park	No. 40	
	Xuan Yicheng and others v Bureau of Land and Resources of Quzhou Municipality	No. 41	
	Dai Shihua v The Public Security Fire Protection Brigade of Jinan Municipality	No. 59	
	The Dongtai Branch of Aokang Food Co., Ltd. of Yancheng Municipality v The Dongtai Administration for Industry and Commerce of Yancheng Municipality	No. 60	
	Wang Mingde v The Human Resources and Social Security Bureau of Leshan Municipality	No. 69	
	Pingxiang Yapeng Real Estate Development Co., Ltd. v Bureau of Land and Resources of Pingxiang Municipality	No. 76	
	Luo Rongrong v The Price Bureau of Ji'an Municipality	No. 77	
	Zhang Daowen, TAO Ren, et al. v The People's Government of Jianyang Municipality, Sichuan Province	No. 88	
	Beiyan Yunyi v Yanshan Police Station, Lixia District Branch, the Public Security Bureau of Jinan Municipality	No. 89	
	Bei Huifeng v The Traffic Police Brigade of the Public Security Bureau of Haining Municipality	No. 90	
	Chongqing Fuling Zhida Property Management Co., Ltd v The Human Resources and Social Security Bureau of Fuling District, Chongqing Municipality	No. 94	
	Luo Yuanchang v The Local Maritime Office of Pengshui Miao and Tujia Ethnic Minority Autonomous County, Chongqing Municipality	No. 101	

Appendix A: (Continued)

Types	*Cases*	*Case Number / Gazette Issue*	*In Total*
	Chinese Medicine Hospital of Xupu County v The Post and Telecommunication Office of Xupu County	2000 (1)	
	Su Haiyan v Haikou Labour Education and Rehabilitation Management Commission	2000 (3)	
	Lanzhou Changde Materials Office v The People's Government of Lanzhou Municipality	2000 (4)	
	Division 1 of Luobiancao Village v The People's Government of Chongqing Municipal	2000 (6)	
	Yichang Maternal & Child Care Center v The Administration for Commerce and Industry of Yichang Municipality	2001 (4)	
	Li Zhifang v The Traffic Police Brigade of the Public Security Bureau of Longyan Municipality	2001 (5)	
	Diantou Longsheng Stone Material Factory v The People's Government of Fuding County	2001 (6)	
	Lu Shiwei v The People's Government of Jingyuan County	2002 (3)	
	Luo Lunfu v The Third Traffic Police Brigade of the Public Security Bureau of Luzhou Municipality	2002 (5)	
	Guangzhou Municipality Hai Long Wang Investment and Development Co. Ltd v The Foreign Trade and Economic Committee of Guangzhou City, Guangdong Province	2002 (6)	
	Yin Chenhui v The Public Security Bureau of Lushi County	2003 (2)	
	Wang Liping v The Transportation Bureau of Zhongmou County	2003 (3)	
	Chen Ning v The Public Security Bureau of Zhuanghe Municipality	2003 (3)	
	Ji Deren v The People's Government of Yancheng Municipality	2003 (4)	
	Peng Xuechun v The Administration for Industry and Commerce of Shanghai Municipality	2003 (5)	
	Chen Li v The Urban Management Bureau of Quanshan District, Xuzhou Municipality	2003 (6)	

Appendix A: (Continued)

Types	*Cases*	*Case Number / Gazette Issue*	*In Total*
	Shen Xixian and others v The Planning Commission of Beijing Municipality	2004 (3)	
	Zhonghaiyayuan Management Committee v The Housing Management Bureau of Haidian District, Beijing Municipality	2004 (5)	
	Feng Haojiang and others v The Urban Planning Bureau of Dongguang Municipality	2004 (7)	
	Song Lili v The Construction Bureau Suqian Municipality	2004 (8)	
	He Wenliangv The Labour Bureau of Wuhou District, Chengdu Municipality	2004 (9)	
	China Everbright Bank v The People's Government of Wuhan Municipality	2004 (10)	
	35 Villagers from Building 28 of Niansisancun v The Planning Bureau of Yangzhou Municipality	2004 (11)	
	Zaishengyuan Company v The Health Bureau of Shanghai Municipality	2005 (1)	
	Meishan Sprayer Factory v The People's Government of Meishan Municipality and the National Land and Resources Bureau of Meishan Municipality	2005 (2)	
	Zhang Chengyin . The People's Government of Xuzhou Municipality	2005 (3)	
	Huang Jincheng and others v The Property Management Bureau of Wuhou District, Chengdu Municipality	2005 (6)	
	Yang Baoxi v Tianjin Clothes Technical School	2005 (7)	
	Songye Stone Materials Factory v The Labour Protection Bureau of Xingyang Municipality	2005 (8)	
	Yimin Company v The People's Government of Zhoukou Municipality	2005 (8)	
	Jianming Food Company v The People's Government of Sihong County	2006 (1)	
	Yierku Company v The Administration for Industry and Commerce of Wuxi Municipality	2006 (3)	
	Shanghai Jingang Economic and Trade Corporation v The Administration for Industry and Commerce of Xinjiang Uygur Autonomous Region	2006 (4)	
	Zhaoqing Foreign Trade Company v The Customs of Zhaoqing Municipality	2006 (5)	

Appendix A: (Continued)

Types	*Cases*	*Case Number / Gazette Issue*	*In Total*
	Botan Company v The Customs of Xiamen Municipality	2006 (6)	
	Shao Zhongguo v The Safety Inspection Bureau of Huangpu District, Shanghai Municipality	2006 (8)	
	Xia Shanrong v The Construction Bureau of Xuzhou Municipality	2006 (9)	
	Jiao Zhigang v Heping District Branch, the Public Security Bureau of Tianjin Municipality	2006 (10)	
	Liao Zongrong v The Second Branch of Transportation Management Bureau, the Public Security Bureau of Chongqing Municipality	2007 (1)	
	Lingwang Company v The Labour Bureau of Wuxi Municipality	2007 (1)	
	Bai Guanghua v Tianjin Labour Education and Rehabilitation Management Commission	2007 (3)	
	Yang Yimin v The People's Government of Sihong County	2007 (10)	
	Yang Qingfeng v The Labour and Social Security Bureau of Wuxi Municipality	2008 (1)	
	Beijing National Jade Hotel v The Labour and Social Security Bureau of Chaoyang District, Beijing Municipality	2008 (9)	
	Kunming Wei Heng Li Trade Co., Ltd. v The Planning Bureau of Kunming Municipality	2009 (10)	
	Shanghai ROYALSHE Cosmetics Co., Ltd. v Jinshan Branch of the Administration for Industry and Commerce of Shanghai Municipality	2009 (11)	
	Wang Changhuai v The Labour and Social Security Bureau of Xuyi County	2011 (9)	
	Beijing CU Lighting Equipment Co., Ltd .v The Commerce Committee Shanghai Municipality	2011(7)	
	Huang Lujun and Others v The Administration for Industrial and Commercial of Jinhua Municipality	2012 (5)	
	All-China Environment Federation v The Environmental Protection Bureau of Xiuwen County, Guiyang Municipality, Guizhou Province	2013 (1)	

Appendix A: (Continued)

Types	*Cases*	*Case Number / Gazette Issue*	*In Total*
	Wuxi Meitong Food Science and Technology Co., Ltd. v High and New Technology Industrial Development Zone Branch, Wuxi Quality and Technology Supervision Bureau	2013 (7)	
	Chen Shanju v The Human Resources and Social Security Bureau of Songjiang District	2013 (9)	
	Yu Xichu v The Housing and Urban-Rural Construction Bureau of Guiyang Municipality	2013 (10)	
	Suzhou Dingsheng Food Company v The Industry and Commerce Bureau of Suzhou Municipality	2013 (10)	
	Ding'an Chengdong Construction and Decoration Company v The People's Government of Sihong County	2015 (2)	
	Lu Hongxia v The Commission of Development and Reform of Nantong Municipality	2015 (11)	
	Sun Changrong v The People's Government of Jilin Province	2016 (12)	
	Shanxi Anye Group Co., Ltd v The People's Government of Jilin Province	2017 (1)	
	Liu Yunwu v The First Traffic Police Brigade of the Public Security Bureau of Taiyuan Municipality, Shanxi Province	2017 (2)	
	Shanghai Wenhe Foot Care Service Department v The Human Resources and Social Security Bureau of Putuo District, Shanghai Municipality	2017 (4)	
	Chen Chao v The Urban Public Transportation Management and Service Centre of Jinan City	2018 (2)	
	Xixia Longcheng Special Materials Co., Ltd v The Intellectual Property Administration of Yulin Municipality	2018 (5)	
	Sheyang County Red Flag Cultural Troupe v The Culture, Radio, Television, Press and Publication Bureau of Sheyang County	2018 (8)	
	Shouguang PetroChina Kunlun Gas Co., Ltd v The People's Government of Shouguang Municipality and the People's Government of Weifang Municipality	2018 (9)	
	Deng Jinlong v The Social Security Funding Management Bureau of Shenzhen Municipality	2019 (11)	

Appendix A: (Continued)

Types	*Cases*	*Case Number / Gazette Issue*	*In Total*
	Ma Shengzhong v The People's Government of Guyuan Municipality and the Housing and Urban-Rural Construction Bureau of Guyuan Municipality	2019 (12)	

Appendix B: List of J.Y. Interpretations (1999–2019)

Types	*Interpretations*	*In Total*
Constitutional Interpretation	498, 499, 520, 541, 601, 627, 632, 721, 735	9
Judicial review of statutes	472, 475, 476, 477, 483, 485, 486, 487, 488, 490, 491, 495, 502, 507, 509, 512, 515, 517, 518, 521, 522, 523, 524, 528, 531, 534, 535, 537, 544, 545, 549, 550, 551, 554, 558, 559, 560, 564, 567, 573, 575, 576, 577, 578, 579, 580, 583, 584, 585, 587, 588, 589, 591, 594, 596, 599, 602, 603, 604, 610, 613, 616, 617, 618, 623, 624, 630, 631, 633, 634, 636, 637, 639, 641, 642, 644, 645, 646, 647, 649, 653, 654, 655, 656, 659, 662, 663, 664, 665, 666, 667, 669, 670, 672, 673, 675, 677, 678, 680, 685, 687, 688, 689, 690, 694, 696, 697, 698, 699, 701, 702, 708, 709, 710, 711, 712, 714, 716, 718, 719, 721, 725, 727, 728, 731, 732, 733, 734, 736, 737, 739, 744, 745, 746, 747, 748, 749, 751, 752, 755, 756, 760, 761, 762, 763, 764, 766, 767, 768, 769, 770, 775, 777, 778, 779, 780, 781, 782, 783, 785, 786	161
Judicial review of regulations	473, 474, 478, 479, 480, 481, 482, 483, 484, 485, 488, 492, 493, 496, 497, 500, 501, 504, 505, 506, 508, 510, 511, 514, 516, 519, 524, 525, 526, 529, 530, 532, 536, 537, 538, 539, 542, 543, 547, 548, 555, 561, 562, 563, 565, 566, 567, 568, 569, 570, 571, 574, 575, 581, 582, 586, 587, 593, 597, 598, 600, 602, 605, 606, 607, 608, 609, 611, 612, 614, 615, 619, 620, 622, 624, 625, 626, 628, 629, 635, 638, 640, 642, 643, 648, 650, 651, 653, 657, 658, 660, 661, 665, 671, 674, 676, 681, 682, 683, 685, 692, 693, 696, 697, 698, 700, 703, 704, 705, 706, 707, 710, 711, 713, 715, 717, 722, 723, 724, 725, 730, 732, 734, 738, 739, 745, 746, 750, 753, 754, 755, 756, 765, 771, 776, 778, 779, 785	138

Appendix B: (Continued)

Types	*Interpretations*	*In Total*
Unifying interpretation of laws	489, 494, 513, 527, 533, 540, 556, 595, 621, 668, 691, 695, 726, 740, 743, 751, 758, 759, 772, 773, 787	21
Unifying interpretation of regulations	557	1
Complementary interpretation to the J.Y. Interpretations	503, 552, 556, 572, 590, 592, 610, 652, 679, 684, 686, 718, 720, 725, 729, 741, 742, 757, 774, 784	20
Judicial review of local self-governance matters	553	1

Note: The underlined interpretations involve two types of constitutional review. For example, the TCC scrutinised the constitutionality of the Civil Servant Election and Recall Act and interpreted Article 4 of the Amendment of the Constitution in J.Y. Interpretation No. 721.

Appendix C: List of the CFA Judicial Review Decisions (1999–2019)

Types	*Title*	*Series number*	*In total*
Judicial review of legislation	Ng Ka Ling & Others v Director of Immigration	(1999) 2 HKCFAR 4	33
	Chan Kam Nga & Others v Director of Immigration	(1999) 2 HKCFAR 82	
	Re Yung Kwan Lee & Others	(1999) 2 HKCFAR 245	
	HKSAR v Ng Kung Siu & Another	(1999) 2 HKCFAR 442	
	Director of Immigration v Chong Fung Yuen	2001 4 HKCFAR 211	
	Fateh Muhammad v Commissioner of Registration	2001 4 HKCFAR 278	
	Lau Cheong & Another v HKSAR	2002 5 HKCFAR 415	
	Gurung Kesh Bahadur v Director of Immigration	2002 5 HKCFAR 480	
	Director of Lands v Yin Shuen Enterprises Ltd and Another	2003 6 HKCFAR 1	
	Prem Singh v Director of Immigration	2003 6 HKCFAR 26	
	Solicitor and Law Society of Hong Kong v Secretary for Justice	2003 6 HKCFAR 570	

Appendix C: (Continued)

Types	*Title*	*Series number*	*In total*
	Tse Mui Chun v HKSAR	2003 6 HKCFAR 601	
	Leung Kwok Hung & Others v HKSAR	2005 8 HKCFAR 229	
	Secretary for Justice v Lau Kwok Fai & Another	2005 8 HKCFAR 304	
	Solicitor v Law Society of Hong Kong	2006 9 HKCFAR 175	
	So Wai Lun v HKSAR	2006 9 HKCFAR 530	
	Official Receiver & Trustee in Bankruptcy of Chan Wing Hing & Another v Chan Wing Hing & Another & (Third Party)	2006 9 HKCFAR 545	
	HKSAR v Lam Kwong Wai & Another	2006 9 HKCFAR 574	
	HKSAR v Hung Chan Wa & Another	2006 9 HKCFAR 614	
	Secretary for Justice v Yau Yuk Lung	2007 10 HKCFAR 335	
	HKSAR v Ng Po On	2008 11 HKCFAR 91	
	Koon Wing Yee v Insider Dealing Tribunal	2008 11 HKCFAR 170	
	Yeung Chung Ming v Commissioner of Police	2008 11 HKCFAR 513	
	Mok Charles v Tam Wai Ho	2010 13 HKCFAR 762	
	Catholic Diocese of Hong Kong v Secretary for Justice	2011 14 HKCFAR 754	
	Lee To Nei v HKSAR	2012 15 HKCFAR 162	
	Fu Kor Kuen Patrick v HKSAR	2012 15 HKCFAR 524	
	Ubamaka v Secretary for Security	2012 15 HKCFAR 743	
	Vallejos v Commissioner of Registration	2013 16 HKCFAR 45	
	W v Registrar of Marriages	2013 16 HKCFAR 112	
	Leung Chun Ying v Ho Chun Yan Albert	2013 16 HKCFAR 735	
	Official Receiver v Zhi Charles	2015 18 HKCFAR 467	
	Kwok Cheuk Kin v Secretary for Constitutional and Mainland Affairs	2017 20 HKCFAR 353	

Appendix C: (Continued)

Types	*Title*	*Series number*	*In total*
Judicial review administrative rules	Chow Shun Yung v Wei Pih & Another	(2003) 6 HKCFAR 299	8
	Lam Siu Po v Commissioner of Police	(2009) 12 HKCFAR 237	
	Medical Council of Hong Kong v Helen Chan	(2010) 13 HKCFAR 248	
	Fok Chun Wa v Hospital Authority	(2012) 15 HKCFAR 409	
	Kong Yun Ming v Director of Social Welfare	(2013) 16 HKCFAR 950	
	HKSAR v Fong Kwok Shan Christine	(2017) 20 HKCFAR 425	
	QT v Director of Immigration	(2018) 21 HKCFAR 324	
	Leung Chun Kwong v Secretary for Civil Service	(2019) 22 HKCFAR 127	
Judicial review of executive acts	Fu Kin Chi v Secretary for Justice	1997-98 1 HKCFAR 85	37
	Thang Thieu Quyen & Others v Director of Immigration & Another	1997-98 1 HKCFAR 167	
	Nomura International (Hong Kong) Ltd & Others v Securities and Futures Commission	1997-98 1 HKCFAR 250	
	Lau Kong Yung & Others v Director of Immigration	1999 2 HKCFAR 300	
	Secretary for Justice & Others v Chan Wah & Others	2000 3 HKCFAR 459	
	Tam Nga Yin & Others v Director of Immigration	2001 4 HKCFAR 251	
	Registrar of Births and Deaths v Syed Haider Yahya Hussain & Another	2001 4 HKCFAR 429	
	Ng Siu Tung & Others v Director of Immigration	2002 5 HKCFAR 1	
	Ng Siu Tung & Others v Director of Immigration (No 2)	2002 5 HKCFAR 499	
	Ng Siu Tung & Others v Director of Immigration (No 3)	2004 7 HKCFAR 24	
	Director of Immigration v Lau Fong	2004 7 HKCFAR 56	
	Secretary for Security v Sakthevel Prabakar	2004 7 HKCFAR 187	
	Noise Control Authority & Another v Step In Ltd	2005 8 HKCFAR 113	

Appendix C: (Continued)

Types	*Title*	*Series number*	*In total*
	PCCW-HKT Telephone Ltd v Telecommunications Authority	2005 8 HKCFAR 337	
	Lo Siu Lan v Hong Kong Housing Authority	2005 8 HKCFAR 363	
	Ho Choi Wan v Hong Kong Housing Authority	2005 8 HKCFAR 628	
	Ng Siu Tung & Others v Director of Immigration (No 4)	2006 9 HKCFAR 63	
	Stock Exchange of Hong Kong Ltd v New World Development Co Ltd & Others	2006 9 HKCFAR 234	
	Shiu Wing Steel Ltd v Director of Environmental Protection & (Third Party)	2006 9 HKCFAR 478	
	Lai Tak Shing v Secretary for Home Affairs	2007 10 HKCFAR 655	
	Solicitor v Law Society of Hong Kong	2008 11 HKCFAR 117	
	Chiang Lily v Secretary for Justice	2010 13 HKCFAR 208	
	Clarence Chan v Commissioner of Police	2010 13 HKCFAR 462	
	Ubamaka v Secretary for Security	2012 15 HKCFAR 743	
	Asif Ali v Director of Immigration	2013 16 HKCFAR 91	
	C v Director of Immigration & (Intervener)	2013 16 HKCFAR 280	
	HLB Hodgson Impey Cheng v Hong Kong Institute of Certified Public Accountants	2013 16 HKCFAR 460	
	Asia Television Ltd v Communications Authority	2013 16 HKCFAR 773	
	GA v Director of Immigration	2014 17 HKCFAR 60	
	Ghulam Rbani v Secretary for Justice	2014 17 HKCFAR 138	
	Ho Man Kong v Superintendent of Lai Chi Kok Reception Centre	2014 17 HKCFAR 179	
	Gutierrez v Commissioner of Registration	2014 17 HKCFAR 518	
	Hysan Development Co Ltd v Town Planning Board	2016 19 HKCFAR 372	

Appendix C: (Continued)

Types	*Title*	*Series number*	*In total*
	Yau Wai Ching v Chief Executive of HKSAR	2017 20 HKCFAR 390	
	Designing Hong Kong Ltd v Town Planning Board	2018 21 HKCFAR 237	
	Comilang Milagros Tecson v Director of Immigration	2019 22 HKCFAR 59	
	Au Nok Hin v Teng Yu Yan Anne	2019 22 HKCFAR 524	

Appendix D: List of the TUI Judicial Review Decisions (1999–2019)

Types	*Cases*	*In Total*
Review of legislation	2/2004, 5/2010, 25/2011, 33/2011; 9/2012, 19/2012, 27/2012, 33/2012, 23/3015, 88/2018, 90/2018, 102/2018, 112/2018	13
Review of administrative regulations and other normative instruments	7/2007, 2/2017	2
Review of executive decision	5/2000, 6/2000, 9/2000, 10/2000, 12/2000, 15/2000, 4/2001, 7/2001, 8/2001, 13/2002, 14/2002, 16/2002, 6/2003, 10/2003, 12/2003, 13/2003, 14/2003, 26/2003, 27/2003, 29/2003, 1/2004, 4/2004, 5/2004, 9/2004, 21/2004, 22/2004, 26/2004, 38/2004, 39/2004, 40/2004, 3/2005, 7/2005, 14/2005, 15/2005, 16/2005, 17/2005, 22/2005, 24/2005, 28/2005, 30/2005, 1/2006, 5/2006, 7/2006, 8/2006, 9/2006, 19/2006, 22/2006, 24/2006, 28/2006, 31/2006, 33/2006, 36/2006, 38/2006, 39/2006, 42/2006, 45/2006, 46/2006, 52/2006, 3/2007, 5/2007, 7/2007, 8/2007, 9/2007, 10/2007, 11/2007, 13/2007, 14/2007, 16/2007, 17/2007, 18/2007, 19/2007, 21/2007, 34/2007, 40/2007, 49/2007, 54/2007, 11/2008, 30/2008, 32/2008, 45/2008, 47/2008, 12/2009, 19/2009, 31/2009, 7/2010, 10/2010, 16/2010, 21/2010, 28/2010, 48/2010, 50/2010, 51/2010, 53/2010, 55/2010, 56/2010, 62/2010, 63/2010, 71/2010, 75/2010, 2/2011, 5/2011, 6/2011, 12/2011, 13/2011, 23/2011, 27/2011, 31/2011, 32/2011, 34/2011, 45/2011, 50/2011, 54/2011, 1/1012, 7/2012, 8/2012, 11/2012, 12/2012, 13/2012, 18/2012,	302

Appendix D: (Continued)

Types	*Cases*	*In Total*
	25/2012, 26/2012, 28/2012, 30/2012, 31/2012, 35/2012, 38/2012, 41/2012, 48/2012, 65/2012, 76/2012, 68/2012, 69/2012, 83/2012, 2/2013, 6/2013, 28/2013, 30/2013, 32/2013, 44/2013, 59/2013, 63/2013, 67/2013, 68/2013, 69/2013, 74/2013, 75/2013, 77/2013, 9/2014, 10/2014, 13/2014, 14/2014, 15/2014, 19/2014, 25/2014, 26/2014, 28/2014, 29/2014, 30/2014, 31/2014, 32/2014, 33/3014, 34/2014, 35/2014, 36/2014, 37/2014, 38/2014, 39/2014, 40/2014, 41/2014, 42/2014, 44/2014, 45/2014, 46/2014, 47/2014, 48/2014, 50/2014, 51/2014, 52/2014, 53/2014, 54/2014, 55/2014, 56/2014, 57/2014, 58/2014, 59/2014, 60/2014, 61/2014, 62/2014, 63/2014, 82/2014, 95/2014, 97/2014, 100/2014, 103/2014, 104/2014, 110/2014, 112/2014, 115/2014, 123/2014, 127/2014, 5/2015, 13/2015, 43/2015, 46/2015, 62/2015, 71/2015, 75/2015, 79/2015, 85/2015, 1/2016, 2/2016, 9/2016, 14/2016, 15/2016, 20/2016, 28/2016, 32/2016, 39/2016, 45/2016, 53/2016, 57/2016, 69/2016, 71/2016, 72/2016, 74/2016, 81/2016, 83/2016, 1/2017, 10/2017, 14/2017, 17/2017, 18/2017, 22/2017, 28/2017, 34/2017, 35/2017, 38/2017, 39/2017, 41/2017, 42/2017, 49/2017, 54/2017, 55/2017, 56/2017, 57/2017, 62/2017, 69/2017, 77/2017, 81/2017, 1/2018, 7/2018, 13/2018, 21/2018, 22/2018, 24/2018, 25/2018, 26/2018, 29/2018, 30/2018, 35/2018, 37/2018, 40/2018, 42/2018, 43/2018, 62/2018, 64/2018, 65/2018, 66/2018, 70/2018, 79/2018, 88/2018, 89/2018, 91/2018, 95/2018, 96/2018, 98/2018, 101/2018, 103/2018, 104/2018, 107/2018, 111/2018, 113/2018, 2/2019, 6/2019, 12/2019, 13/2019, 16/2019, 20/2019, 23/2019, 26/2019, 36/2019, 66/2019, 72/2019, 74/2019, 75/2019, 78/2019, 85/2019, 94/2019, 101/2019, 103/2019, 106/2019, 118/2019	

Bibliography

BOOKS AND ARTICLES

Ahl, Björn, 'Judicialization in Authoritarian Regimes: The Expansion of Powers of the Chinese Supreme People's Court' (2019) 17 *International Journal of Constitutional Law* 252.

Alexy, Robert, 'The Construction of Constitutional Rights' (2010) 4 *Law and Ethics of Human Rights* 20.

Alexy, Robert, "Constitutional Rights and Proportionality" (2014) 22 *Journal for Constitutional Theory and Philosophy of Law* 51.

Alexy, Robert, 'Proportionality and Rationality' in Vicki C. Jackson and Mark Tushnet (eds), *Proportionality: New Frontiers, New Challenges* (CUP 2017).

Aoyagi Koichi, 'Infringements on Basic Rights and the Principle of Proportionality' 基本权利的侵犯和比例原则 (1988) *Journal of Comparative Law* 比较法研究 34.

Barak, Aharon, 'A Judge on Judging: The Role of a Supreme Court in a Democracy' (2002) 116 *Harvard Law Review* 19.

Barak, Aharon, *Proportionality: Constitutional Rights and Their Limitation* (CUP 2012).

Beatty, David M., *The Ultimate Rule of Law* (OUP 2003).

Bingham, Tom, *The Rule of Law* (Penguin 2011).

Boer, Roland, *Socialism with Chinese Characteristics: A Guide for Foreigners* (Springer 2021).

Brooker, Paul, *Non-Democratic Regimes* (3rd edn, Palgrave Macmillan 2014).

Buhi, Jason, *Global Constitutional Narratives of Autonomous Regions: The Constitutional History of Macau* (Routledge 2020).

Calvão da Silva, 'The Administrative Litigation of the MASAR' in Manual Trigo (ed) *Report on Macau Law* (LexisNexis 2014).

Canas, Vitalino, 'The General Regime of Fundamental Rights in the Basic Law and in the International Instruments' in Jorge Oliveira and Paulo Cardinal (eds) *One Country Two Systems, Three Legal Orders - Perspectives of Evolution* (Springer 2009).

Cane, Peter, *Controlling Administrative Power: An Historical Comparison* (CUP 2016).

Cardinal, Paulo, 'Fundamental rights in Macau: From Territory Under Portuguese Administration to Special Administrative Region of the PRC' in Jorge A. F. Godinho (ed) *Study on Macau Civil, Commercial, Constitutional and Criminal Law* (LexisNexis 2011).

Carnwath, Robert, "From Rationality to Proportionality in the Modern Law" (2014) 44 *Hong Kong Law Journal* 447.

Castellucci, Ignazio, 'Legal Hybridity in Hong Kong and Macau' (2012) *McGill Law Journal* 665.

Chan, Cora, "Proportionality and Invariable Baseline Intensity of Review" (2013) 33 *Legal Studies* 1.

Chan, Cora, 'A Preliminary Framework for Measuring Deference in Rights Reasoning' (2016) 14 *International Journal of Constitutional Law* 851.

Chan, Cora, 'Rights, Proportionality and Deference: A Study of Post-Handover Judgments in Hong Kong' (2018) *Hong Kong Law Journal* 51.

Chan, Johannes M. M., 'Administrative Law' in Simon N. M. Young and Yash Ghai (eds) *Hong Kong's Court of Final Appeal: The Development of the Law in China's Hong Kong* (CUP 2014).

Chan, Johannes M. M., 'Proportionality after Hysan: Fair Balance, Manifestly without Reasonable Foundation and Wednesbury Unreasonableness' (2019) 49 *Hong Kong Law Journal* 265.

Chang, Wen-Chen, 'Back into the Political? Rethinking Judicial, Legal, and Transnational Constitutionalism' (2019) *International Journal of Constitutional Law* 453.

Chang, Wen-Chen張文貞, 'An Empirical Study on the Reference of Foreign Laws and Precedents by Constitutional Court Interpretations: The Study-abroad Backgrounds as the Key' 司法院大法官解釋引用外國法及判決之實證研究—大法官留學背景作為引用的關鍵因素 in Yun-Chien Chang 張永健 (ed) *Empirical Studies of the Judicial System 2011 2011*司法制度實證研究 (The Institutum Iurisprudentiae Academia Sinica 2013).

Chang, Wen-Chen 張文貞, 'Judicial Review of Administrative Rules and Regulations: Focusing on Reviewing Decisions of the Supreme Administrative Court" 行政命令的司法審查—以最高行政法院判決為中心 in Yen-Tu Su 蘇彥圖 (ed) *Constitutional Interpretation: Theory and Practice Volume 10* 憲法解釋之理論與實務第十輯 (Institutum Iurisprudentiae Academic Sinica 2020).

Chavez, Rebecca Bill, 'The Rule of Law and Courts in Democratising Regimes' in Keith E. Whittington, R. Daniel Kelemen, and Gregory A. Caldeira (eds) *The Oxford Handbook of Law and Politics* (OUP 2008).

Chen, Albert H. Y., 'Conclusion: Reflections on Administrative Law and Judicialised Governance in East and Southeast Asia' in Tom Ginsburg and Albert H. Y. Chen (eds) *Administrative Law and Governance in Asia* (Routledge 2009).

Chen, Albert H. Y., 'Pathways of Western Liberal Constitutional Development in Asia: A Comparative Study of Five Major Nations' (2010) 8 *International Journal of Constitutional Law* 849.

Chen, Albert H. Y., *An Introduction to the Legal System of the People's Republic of China* (4th edn, LexisNexis 2011).

Chen, Albert H. Y., 'The Global Expansion of Constitutional Judicial Review: Some Historical and Comparative Perspectives' 9 (1 January 2013), Available at SSRN: https://ssrn.com/abstract=2210340 or http://dx.doi.org/10.2139/ssrn.2210340

Chen, Albert H. Y., 'Constitutional Courts in Asia: Western Origins and Asian Practice' in Albert H. Y. Chen and Andrew Harding (eds) *Constitutional Courts in Asia: A Comparative Perspective* (CUP 2018).

Chen, Albert H. Y., 'Constitutions, Constitutional Practice and Constitutionalism in East Asia' in Christoph Antons (ed) *Routledge Handbook of Asian Law* (Routledge 2019).

Chen, Albert H. Y., and Lo, P. Y., 'The Constitutional Orders of 'One Country, Two Systems': A Comparative Study of the Visible and Invisible Bases of Constitutional Review and Proportionality Analysis in the Chinese Special Administrative Regions of Hong Kong and Macau' in Rosalind Dixon and Adrienne Stone (eds) *The Invisible Constitution in Comparative Perspective* (CUP 2018).

Chen, Benjamin M., Li, Zhiyu, Cai, David, and Ash, Elliott, 'Detecting the Influence of the Chinese Guiding Cases: A Text Reuse Approach' (2024) 32 *Artificial Intelligence and Law* 463.

Chen, Jianfu, *Chinese Law: Context and Transformation* (Brill 2008).

Chen, Weitseng, 'Twins of Opposites: Why China Will Not Follow Taiwan's Model of Rule of Law Transition toward Democracy' (2018) 66 *American Journal of Comparative Law* 481, 497.

Chen, Yunsheng 陈运生, 'The Initiation Requirements of Incidental Review of Normative Documents – An Empirical Examination Based on 1738 Judicial Decisions' 规范性文件附带审查的启动要件 – 基于1738份裁判文书样本的实证考察 (2019) *Legal Science* 法学 165.

Cheng, Hu 程琥, 'A New Approach to the Principle of Legality in Administrative Litigation' 行政诉讼合法性审查原则新探 (2019) 9 *Journal of Law Application* 法律适用 75.

Chou, Bill K. P., 'Politics and Social Organisations in Macao: A Historical Institutionalist Analysis' (2015) 13 *China: An International Journal* 22.

Cohn, Margit, 'Legal Transplant Chronicles: The Evolution of Unreasonableness and Proportionality Review of the Administration in the United Kingdom' (2010) 58 *American Journal of Comparative Law* 583.

Cormacain, Ronan, 'Legislation, Legislative Drafting and the Rule of Law' (2017) 5 *The Theory and Practice of Legislation* 115.

Coutinho, Francisco Pereira, and Piçarra, Nuno, 'Portugal: The Impact of European Integration and the Economic Crisis on the Identity of the Constitution' in Anneli Albi and Samo Bardutzky (eds) *National Constitutions in European and Global Governance: Democracy, Rights, the Rule of Law* (Routledge 2019).

Craig, Paul, "The Nature of Reasonableness Review" (2013) 66 *Current Legal Problems* 131.

Croissant, Aurel, 'From Transition to Defective Democracy: Mapping Asian Democratization' (2004) 11 *Democratization* 156.

Cui, Wei, Cheng, Jie, and Wiesner, Dominika, 'Judicial Review of Government Actions in China' (2019) 1 *China Perspectives* 35.

Diamond, Larry, 'Elections Without Democracy: Thinking About Hybrid Regimes' (2002) 13 *Journal of Democracy* 21.

Dong, Hao 董浩, *Judicial Interpretation* 司法解释论 (Chinese University of Political Science and Law Press 1999).

Dressel, Björn (ed), *The Judicialization of Politics in Asia* (Routledge 2012).

Epp, Charles R., *The Rights Revolution: Lawyers, Activists, and Supreme Courts in Comparative Perspective* (University of Chicago Press 1998).

Forsyth, Christopher, and Williams, Rebecca, 'Closing Chapter in the Immigration Children Saga: Substantive Legitimate Expectation and Administrative Justice in Hong Kong' (2002) 10 *Asia Pacific Law Review* 29.

Fu, Hualing, 'Putting China's Judiciary into Perspective: Is It Independent, Competent, and Fair?' in Erik G. Jensen and Thomas C. Heller (eds) *Beyond Common Knowledge: Empirical Approaches to the Rule of Law* (Stanford University Press 2003).

Fu, Hualing, 'Re-education through Labour in Historical Perspective' (2005) 184 *China Quarterly* 811.

Fu, Hualing, 'Duality and China's Struggle for Legal Autonomy' (2019) 1 *China Perspectives* 1.

Gardbaum, Stephen, 'Separation of Power and the Growth of Judicial Review in Established Democracies (or Why Has the Model of Legislative Supremacy Mostly Been Withdrawn From Sale?' (2014) 62 *The American Journal Comparative Law* 613.

Ghai, Yash, 'The Basic Law of the Special Administrative Region of Macau: Some Reflections' (2000) 49 *International and Comparative Law Quarterly* 183.

Ghai, Yash, 'Litigating the Basic Law: Jurisdiction, Interpretation and Procedure' in Johannes Chan, Hualing Fu, and Yash Ghai (eds) *Hong Kong's Constitutional Debate: Conflict Over Interpretation* (HKU Press 2000).

Ghai, Yash, 'The NPC Interpretation and Its Consequence' in Johannes Cham, Hualing Fu, and Yash Ghai (eds) *Hong Kong's Constitutional Debate: Conflict Over Interpretation* (HKU Press 2000).

Ginsburg, Tom, *Judicial Review in New Democracies: Constitutional Courts in Asian Cases* (CUP 2003).

Ginsburg, Tom, 'The Global Spread of Constitutional Review' in Keith E. Whittington, R. Daniel Kelemen, and Gregory A. Caldeira (eds) *The Oxford Handbook of Law and Politics* (OUP 2008).

Ginsburg, Tom, 'Administrative Law and the Judicial Control of Agents in Authoritarian Regimes' in Tom Ginsburg and Tamir Moustafa (eds) *Rule by Law: The Politics of Courts in Authoritarian Regimes* (CUP 2008).

Ginsburg, Tom, 'The Judicialization of Administrative Governance: Causes, Consequence and limits' in Tom Ginsburg and Albert H. Y. Chen (eds) *Administrative Law and Governance in Asia* (Routledge 2009).

Ginsburg, Tom, and Moustafa, Tamir (eds), *Rule by Law: The Politics of Courts in Authoritarian Regimes* (CUP 2008).

Ginsburg, Tom and Simpser Alberto, 'Introduction: Constitutions in Authoritarian Regimes' in Tom Ginsburg and Alberto Simpser (eds) *Constitutions in Authoritarian Regimes* (CUP 2014).

Gittings, Danny, *Introduction to the Hong Kong Basic Law* (2nd edn, HKU Press 2016).

Godinho, Jorge, A. F., *Macau Business Law and Legal System* (LexisNexis 2007).

Godinho, Jorge, and Cardinal Paulo, 'Macau's Court of Final Appeal' in Simon N. M. Young and Yash Ghai (eds), *Hong Kong's Court of Final Appeal: The Development of the Law in China's Hong Kong* (CUP 2014).

Goldstein, Leslie Friedman, 'Judicial Review' in Bertrand Badie and others (eds), *International Encyclopedia of Political Science* (SAGE 2011).

Graber, Mark A., 'The Nonmajoritarian Difficulty: Legislative Deference to the Judiciary' (1993) 7 *Studies in American Political Development* 35.

Grimm, Dieter, 'Canadian and German Constitutional Jurisprudence' (2007) 57 *University of Toronto Law Journal* 383.

Grote, Rainer, 'Judicial Review', *Max Planck Encyclopedia of Comparative Constitutional Law* (2018).

Gu, Yu, *Hong Kong's Legislature under China's Sovereignty: 1998–2013* (Brill Nijhoff 2016).

Hand, Keith, 'Resolving Constitutional Dispute in Contemporary China' (2011) 7 *University of Pennsylvania East Asia Law Review* 51.
Han, Dayuan 韓大元, 'The Issue of the Effectiveness of the Constitution in Macau Special Administrative Region' 憲法在澳門特別行政區的效力問題 (2016) 1 *Academic Journal of "One Country Two Systems"* "一國兩制"研究 1.
Han, Dayuan 韩大元, 'From NPC Law Committee to NPC Constitution and Law Committee: The Transformation of System and Function' 从法律委员会到宪法和法律委员会:体制与功能的转型 (2018) 4 *Journal of Eastern University of Political Science and Law* 华东政法大学学报 6.
Hao, Zhidong, *Macau: History and Society* (2nd edn, HKU Press 2020).
He, Haibo 何海波, 'The Principle of Due Process in Judicial Decisions' 司法判决中的正当程序原则 (2009) 1 Chinese Journal of Law 法学研究 124.
He, Haibo 何海波, 'Obvious Improperness of Administrative Actions' 论行政行为"明显不当" (2016) 3 *Chinese Journal of Law* 法学研究 70.
He, Xin, 'The party's leadership as a Living Constitution in China', in Tom Ginsburg and Alberto Simpser (eds), *Constitutions in Authoritarian Regimes* (CUP 2013).
He, Xin, 'Administrative Reconsideration's Erosion of Administrative Litigation in China' (2014) 2 *Chinese Journal of Comparative Law* 252.
Hirschl, Ran, *Towards Juristocracy: The Origins and Consequences of the New Constitutionalism* (Harvard University Press 2004).
Hirschl, Ran, 'The Judicialization of Politics' in Keith E. Whittington, R. Daniel Kelemen, and Gregory A. Caldeira (eds) *The Oxford Handbook of Law and Politics* (OUP 2008).
Hirschl, Ran, *Comparative Matters: The Renaissance of Comparative Constitutional Law* (OUP 2014).
Hirschl, Ran, 'Opting Out of "Global Constitutionalism"' (2018) 12 *Law & Ethics of Human Rights* 2.
Huang, Cheng-Yi, 'Judicial Deference to Legislative Delegation and Administrative Discretion in New Democracies: Recent Evidence from Poland, Taiwan, and South Africa' in Susan Rose-Auckerman and Peter L. Lindseth (eds) *Comparative Administrative Law* (Edward Elgar 2010).
Huang, Cheng-Y and Law David S., 'Proportionality Review of Administrative Action in Japan, Korea, Taiwan, and China' in Francesca Bignami and David Zaring (eds) *Research Handbook in Comparative Law and Regulation* (Edward Elgar 2014) 317, 320–321.
Huang, Songyou 黄松有, Talking about the Justiciability of Constitution and Its Significance from the Point of View of Today's Reply of the People's Supreme Court 宪法司法化及其意义——从最高人民法院今天的一个《批复》谈起, (2001) *People's Court Daily Legal Times* 人民法院报报法制时代周刊 (Aug. 13).
Hus, Tzong-Li 許宗力, *Law and State Power* 法與國家權力 (Angle Publishing 1999).
Hwang, Jau-Yuan 黃昭元, 'Choosing the Standard of Scrutiny for the Equality Right Cases: Questioning the Applicability of the Proportionality Principle' 平等權審查標準的選擇問題：兼論比例原則在平等權審查上的適用可能 (2008) 12 *National Taiwan University Law Journal* 台大法律論叢 253.
Hwang, Jau-Yuan 黃昭元, 'Development of Standards of Review by the Constitutional Court (1996 – 2011): Reception and Localisation of the Proportionality Principle' 大法官解釋審查標準之發展 (1996–2011)：比例原則的繼受與在地化 (2013) 42 *National Taiwan University Law Journal* 台大法律論叢 215.
Hwang, Jau-Yuan 黃昭元, 'Evolution of Equality Theory and Difficulties Concerning the Constitutional Application of the Conception of Substantive Equality'

從平等理論的演進檢討實質平等觀在憲法適用上的難題 in Chien-Liang Lee (李建良) (ed) *Theory and Practice of Constitutional Interpretation* 憲法解釋之理論與實務 (San Min Book 2017).

Hwang, Shu-Perng 黃舒芃, 'The Principle of Proportionality in the Trend of "Hierarchicalisation": Critical Remarks on the Current Developments in Constitutional Review' 比例原則及其階層化操作：一個著眼於司法院釋憲實務發展趨勢的反思 (2016) 19 *Academia Sinica Law Journal* 中研院法學期刊 1.

Ip, Eric C., 'The Evolution of Constitutional Adjudication in Chinese Special Administrative Regions: Theory and Evidence' (2013) 61 *American Journal of Comparative Law* 799.

Ip, Eric C., 'The Democratic Foundations of Judicial Review under Authoritarianism: Theory and Evidence from Hong Kong' (2014) 12 *International Journal of Constitutional Law* 330.

Ip, Eric C., *Hybrid Constitutionalism: The Politics of Constitutional Review in the Chinese Special Administrative Regions* (CUP 2019).

Ip, Eric C. and Yap Po Jen, 'Substantive Review of Administrative Discretion in Hong Kong: Divergence between Judicial Rhetoric and Practice' (2019) 7 *Chinese Journal of Comparative Law* 190.

Jackson, Vicki C., 'Constitutional Law in An Age of Proportionality' (2015) 124 *Yale Law Journal* 3094.

Jhaveri, Swati, 'Transforming "Fairness" as a Ground of Judicial Review in Hong Kong' (2013) 11 *International Journal of Constitutional Law* 358.

Jiang, Bixin 江必新, 'Judicial Review of the Justifiability of Administrative Procedure' 行政程序正当性的司法审查 (2012) 7 *Social Sciences in China* 中国社会科学 123.

Jiang, Bixin 江必新, *Understanding and Applying the Articles the Administrative Litigation Law of the People's Republic of China and Its Judicial Interpretation* 中华人民共和国行政诉讼法及其司法解释条文理解与适用 (People's Court Press 2015) 469–470.

Jiang, Hongzhen 蒋红珍, 'The Globalisation and Localisation of the Principle of Proportionality' 比例原则的全球化与本土化 (2017) 4 *Shanghai Jiaotong University Law Review* 交大法学 5.

Kwan, Martin, 'Is the Hong Kong Courts' Ability to Refer to Foreign Authorities Unrestrained?' (2022) 4 *Amicus Curiae* 71.

Kwong, Ying-Ho, 'Ruling Coalition Restructuring under Macao's Hybrid Regime' (2017) 17 *China Review* 111.

Leong, Angela V. M., 'The "Bate-Ficha" Business and Triads in Macau Casinos' (2002) 2 *Queensland University of Technology Law and Justice Journal* 83.

Levitsky, Steven, and Way, Lucan A., *Competitive Authoritarianism: Hybrid Regimes After the Cold War* (CUP 2010).

Li, Buyun 李步云 (ed), *Chinese Jurisprudence: Past, Present and Future* 中国法学——过去、现在与未来 (Nanjing University Press 1988).

Li, Cheng 李成, 'Judicial Construction of the Approach to Normative Documents Incidental Review' 行政规范性文件附带审查进路的司法构建 (2018) 2 *The Jurist* 法学家 61.

Li, Yanping 李燕萍, 'Study on the Legal Control over Macau Administrative Regulation' 澳門行政法規的法律控制問題研究 (2009) 1 *Academic Journal of "One Country Two Systems"* "一國兩制"研究 87.

Li, Yougen 李友根, 'Why Leading Cases Are Not Binding' 指导案例为何没有约束力 (2010) 4 *Law and Social Development* 法制与社会发展 86.

Liang, Ying 梁鹰, 'Comments on File and Check Work Report 2020' 2020年备案审查工作情况报告评述 (2021) 2 *China Law Review* 中国法律评论 171.

Lin, Chien-Chih, 'The Judicialization of Politics in Taiwan' (2016) *3 Asian Journal of Law and Society* 299.

Lin, Chien-Chih, 'Proportionality in Taiwan: American-German Fusion" in Po Jen Yap (ed), *Proportionality in Asia* (CUP 2020).

Lin, Chien-Chih, 'Global Constitutionalism in Taiwan' (2021) 10 *Global Constitutionalism* 275.

Lin, Yan 林彦, 'Two Dilemmas of the Operation of the Review System of Regulation' 法规审查制度运行的双重悖论, (2018) 4 *Peking University Law Journal* 中外法学 937.

Lin, Tzu-Yi 林子儀, *Freedom of Speech and Freedom of Press* 言論自由與新聞自由 (Angle Publishing 1999).

Liu, Dan 刘丹, 'The Principle of Good Faith in Administrative Law' 论行政法上的诚实信用原则 (2004) 1 *China Legal Science* 中国法学 32.

Liu, Quan 刘权, 'The Legitimacy of Aims and Reconstructing the Principle of Proportionality' 目的正当性与比例原则的重构, (2014) 4 *China Legal Science* 中国法学 133.

Lo, Sonny S. H. and Chong, Eric K. M., 'Casino Interests, Fujian Tongxianghui and Electoral Politics in Macao' (2016) 46 *Journal of Contemporary Asia* 286.

Lu, Chao 卢超, 'Judicial Predicament and Cohesive Function of Normative Documents Incidental Review' 规范性文件附带审查的司法困境及其枢纽功能 (2020) *Journal of Comparative Law* 比较法研究127.

Ma, Chao马超 and Yu, Xiaohong于晓虹, 'Application of Principle of Proportionality in Administrative Litigation – An Empirical Study Based in Published Judicial Decisions' 行政审判中比例原则的适用—基于公开裁判文书的实证研究 (2022) 4 *Journal of Shandong University* 山东大学学报（哲学社会科学版）58.

Mazmanyan, Armen, 'Judicialization of Politics: The Post-Soviet Way' (2015) 13 *International Journal of Constitutional Law* 200.

McMann, Kelly M., *Economic Autonomy and Democracy Hybrid Regimes in Russia and Kyrgyzstan* (CUP 2006).

Miners, Norman, *The Government and Politics of Hong Kong* (5th edn, OUP 1995).

Möller, Kai, *The Global Model of Constitutional Rights* (OUP 2012).

Morris, Robert J., 'China's Marbury: Qi Yuling v. Chen Xiaoqi – The Once and Future Trial of Both Education' (2010) 2 *Tsinghua China Law Review* 274.

Morse, Yonatan L., 'The Era of Electoral Authoritarianism" (2012) 64 *World Politics* 161.

Mustafa, Tamir, 'Law and Courts in Authoritarian Regimes' (2014) 10 *Annual Review of law and Social Science* 281.

Mustafa, Tamir, and Ginsburg, Tom, 'Introduction: The Functions of Courts in Authoritarian Politics' in Tom Ginsburg and Tamir Moustafa (eds), *Rule by Law: The Politics of Courts in Authoritarian Regimes* (CUP 2008).

Nachbar, Thomas B., 'The Rationality of Rational Basis Review' (2016) 102 *Virginia Law Review* 1627.

Ng, Kwai Hang and He, Xin, *Embedded Courts: Judicial Decision-Making in China* (CUP 2017).

Olley, Kate, 'Introduction of Judicial Review in Hong Kong' (2003) 8 *Judicial Review* 108.

Peerenboom, Randall, *China's Long March Toward Rule of Law* (CUP 2002).
Peerenboom, Randall, and Chen, Weitseng, 'Developing the Rule of Law' in Bruce Gilley and Larry Diamond (eds) *Political Change in China: Comparisons with Taiwan* (Lynne Rienner Publisher 2008).
Petersen, Niels, *Proportionality and Judicial Activism: Fundamental Rights Adjudication in Canada, Germany and South Africa* (CUP 2017).
Plattner, Marc F., 'Illiberal Democracy and the Struggle on the Right' (2019) 30 *Journal of Democracy* 5.
Pound, Roscoe, 'Common Law and Legislation' (1908) 21 *Harvard Law Review* 383.
Schedler, Andreas, 'The Logic of Electoral Authoritarianism' in Andreas Schedler (ed) *Electoral Authoritarianism: The Dynamics of Unfree Competition* (Lynne Rienner Publisher 2006).
Shapiro, Matin, 'United States' in C. Neal Tate and Torbjörn Vallinder (eds) *The Global Expansion of Judicial Power* (NYU Press 1995).
Shapiro, Matin, 'The Success of Judicial Review' in Sally J. Kenney, William M. Reisinger, and John C. Reitz (eds) *Constitutional Dialogues in Comparative Perspective* (Palgrave Macmillan 1999).
Shapiro, Matin, and Stone Sweet, Alex, 'The New Constitutional Politics of Europe' (1994) 26 *Comparative Political Studies* 397.
Stack, Kevin M., 'Rulemaking Regimes in the Modern State' in Peter Cane and others (eds), *The Oxford Handbook of Comparative Administrative Law* (OUP 2021).
Stone Sweet, Alex, *Governing with Judges: Constitutional Politics in Europe* (OUP 2000).
Stone Sweet, Alex, 'Judging Socialist Reform: The Politics of Coordinate Construction in France and Germany' (1994) 4 *Comparative Political Studies* 443, 446
Stone Sweet, Alex, 'Constitutions, Rights, and Judicial Power' in Daniele Caramani (ed) *Comparative Politics* (5th edn, OUP 2020).
Stone Sweet, Alex, 'The Necessity of Balancing: Hong Kong's Flawed Approach to Proportionality, and Why It Matters' (2020) *Hong Kong Law Journal* 541.
Stone Sweet, Alex and Mathews, Jud, 'Proportionality and Rights Protection in Asia: Hong Kong, Malaysia, South Korea, Taiwan – Whither Singapore?' (2017) 29 *Singapore Academy of Law Journal* 774.
Stone Sweet, Alex, and Mathews, Jud, *Proportionality Balancing and Constitutional Governance: A Comparative and Global Approach* (OUP 2019).
Sun, Xiangchen 孙向晨, 'Individual Rights in Modern Time and "Individual" in Confucian Tradition' 现代个体权利与儒家传统中的"个体" (2017) 3 *Journal of Chinese Humanities* 文史哲 90.
Su, Yeong-Chin, Law, David S. and Barak, Aharon, 'Forum: Constitutional Adjudication in Comparative Perspectives' in Su, Yen-Tu 蘇彥圖 (ed) *Constitutional Interpretation: Theory and Practice Volume. 10* 憲法解釋之理論與實務第十輯 (Institutum Iurisprudentiae Academic Sinica 2020).
Tai, Benny Y. T., 'Authoritarian Rule of Law in Hong Kong' in Brian Christopher Jones (ed) *Democracy and Rule of Law in China's Shadow* (Hart 2021).
Tan, Weijie 谭炜杰, 'Categorizing the Intensity of Administrative Reasonableness Review' 行政合理性原则审查强度之类型化 (2014) 12 *Journal of Law Application* 法律适用 49.
Tang, Te-Chung 湯德宗, 'A Primary Study on the Establishment of Intensity System of Constitutional Review – An Idea of Hierarchicalised Proportionality Principle'

違憲審查基準體系建構初探 ——"階層式比例原則"構想 in Liao Fu-Te廖福特 (ed) *Theory and Practice of Constitutional Interpretation* 憲法解釋之理論與實務 (San Min Book 2009).

Tate, C. Neil and Vallinder, Torbjörn (eds) *The Global Expansion of Judicial Power* (NYU Press 1995).

Thio, Li-ann, 'Varieties of Constitutionalism in Asia' (2021) 16 *Asia Journal of Comparative Law* 1.

Thio, Li-ann, 'Courts and Judicial Review' in Peter Cane and others (eds) *The Oxford Handbook of Comparative Administrative Law* (OUP 2021).

Thomson, Stephen, *Administrative Law in Hong Kong* (CUP 2018).

Tsai, Tzung-Jen 蔡宗珍, 'Examining the Related Institutional Factors of the Thoughts and Development of the Requirement of a Specially Enacted Statute' 法律保留思想及其發展的制度關聯要素探微 (2010) 39 *National Taiwan University Law Journal* 台大法律論叢 1.

Wade, William and Forsyth, Christopher, *Administrative Law* (9th edn, OUP 2004).

Wang, Chao 汪超, 'Judicial Review of Macau Courts as Protection of individual Rights and Implication after a comparison with Hong Kong's Judicial Review' 澳門法院的司法審查制度作為個人自由的保障及其與香港司法審查制度比較的啟示 (2021) 2 *Macau Law Review* 澳門法學 89.

Wang, Guohua 王国华 and Yi, Qingqing 易清清, 'Empirical Study of Judicial Review Administrative Normative Instrument: A Study Based on 947 Judgements' 行政规范性文件附带审查的实证分析 – 以947份裁判文书为样本 (2019) 5 *Law and Modernisation* 法治现代化研究 28.

Wang, Jing 王静, 'Application of the Principle of Proportionality in Chinese Administrative Litigation' 比例原则在中国行政判决中的适用 (2017) 4 *Shanghai Jiaotong University Law Review* 交大法学 22.

Wang, Yu 王禹, 'The Discussion of source of law in Macau Special Administrative Region' 澳門特別行政區的法律淵源探討 (2014) 20 *Academic Journal of "One Country Two Systems"* "一國兩制"研究 13.

Weinrib, Jacob, *Dimensions of Dignity: The Theory and Practice of Modern Constitutional Law* (CUP 2016).

Wesley-Smith, Peter, *Constitutional and Administrative Law in Hong Kong* (Longman Asia Ltd 1994).

Woolf, Harry and others, *De Smith's Judicial Review* (7th edn, Sweet and Maxwell 2013).

Wong, Mathew Y. H., 'Selectorate Theory in Hybrid Regimes: Comparing Hong Kong and Singapore' (2017) 53 *Government and Opposition* 707.

Wong, Mathew Y. H., Kwong, Ying-ho, and Chau, Venisa Yeuk Wah, 'Democracy, Constitutional Framework, and Human Rights: A Comparison of Monaco, Tonga, Hong Kong, and Singapore' (2021) 64 *International Journal of Law, Crime and Justice* 1.

Xiao, Shiling, 'State-centric Proportionality Analysis in Chinese Administrative Litigation' (2023) 21 *International Journal of Constitutional Law* 461.

Xiao, Weiyun, and Others, 'Why the Court of Final Appeal Was Wrong: Comments of the Mainland Scholars on the Judgment of the Court of Final Appeal' in Johannes Cham, Hualing Fu, and Yash Ghai (eds) *Hong Kong's Constitutional Debate: Conflict Over Interpretation* (HKU Press 2000).

Xin, Chunying 信春鹰, *Interpretation of the Administrative Litigation Law of the People's Republic of China* 《中华人民共和国行政诉讼法》释义 (Law Press 2014).

Xing, Bingwen 邢斌文, 'The Court's Role in Constitutional Review' 论法院在合宪性审查工作中的角色定位 (2021) 2 *People's Congress Study* 人大研究 17

Yam, Julius, 'Approaching the Legitimacy Paradox in Hong Kong: Lessons for Hybrid Regime Courts' (2020) 46 *Law and Society Inquiry* 153.

Yang, Xiaonan, 'Two Interpreters of the Basic Law: The Court of Final Appeal and the Standing Committee of the National People's Congress' in Simon N. M. Young and Yash Ghai (eds), *Hong Kong's Court of Final Appeal: The Development of the Law in China's Hong Kong* (CUP 2014).

Yao, Jianjun 姚建军, 'Judicial Review Against Administrative Abuses of Power' 对行政滥用职权的司法审查 (2011) 7 *People's Judicature* 人民司法 86.

Yap, Po Jen, *Courts and Democracies in Asia* (CUP 2017).

Yap, Po Jen, 'Authoritarian Regimes' in Peter Cane and others (eds), *Oxford Handbook of Comparative Administrative Law* (OUP 2020).

Yap, Po Jen, 'Democracy, courts and proportionality analysis in Asia' (2020) 37 *Global Constitutionalism* 531, 535.

Yap, Po Jen, 'Authoritarian Regimes' in Peter Cane, Herwig C H Hofmann, Eric C Ip, and Peter L Lindseth (eds), *Oxford Handbook of Comparative Administrative Law* (OUP 2020).

Yap, Po Jen and Lin, Chien-Chih, *Constitutional Convergence in East Asia* (CUP 2022).

Yeh, Jiunn-Rong, *The Constitution of Taiwan: A Contextual Analysis* (Hart 2016).

Yeh, Jiunn-Rong, 'Democracy-Driven Transformation to Regulatory State' in Tom Ginsburg and Albert H. Y. Chen (eds) *Administrative Law and Governance in Asia: Comparative Perspectives* (Routledge 2008).

Yeh, Jiunn-Rong, and Chang, Wen-Chen, 'The Emergence of East Asian Constitutionalism: Features in Comparison' (2011) 59 *American Journal of Comparative Law* 805.

Yeh, Jiunn-Rong and Chang, Wen-Chen, 'A Decade of Changing Constitutionalism in Taiwan: Transitional and Transnational Perspectives' in Albert H. Y. Chen (ed) *Constitutionalism in Asia in the Early Twenty-First Century* (CUP 2014).

Yeh, Jiunn-Rong and Chang, Wen-Chen, 'An Evolving Court with Changing Functions: The Constitutional Court and Judicial Review in Taiwan' in Albert H.Y. Chen and Andrew Harding (eds) *Constitutional Courts in Asia: A Comparative Perspective* (CUP 2018).

Young, Simon N. M., 'Fundamental Rights and the Basic Laws of the Hong Kong and Macau Special Administrative Regions' in Jorge Oliveira and Paulo Cardinal (eds) *One Country Two Systems, Three Legal Orders - Perspectives of Evolution* (Springer 2009).

Young, Simon N. M., 'Constitutional Rights in Hong Kong's Court of Final Appeal' (2012) *Chinese (Taiwan) Yearbook of International Law and Affairs* 67.

Young, Simon N. M., 'Does it Matter if Restrictions on the Right to Social Welfare in Hong Kong are Prescribed by Law or Policy' (2014) *HKLJ* 25.

Young, Simon N. M., 'Human Rights' in Simon N. M. Young and Yash Ghai (eds), *Hong Kong's Court of Final Appeal: The Development of the Law in China's Hong Kong* (CUP 2014).

Young, Simon N. M., 'Criminal Law' in Simon N. M. Young and Yash Ghai (eds) *Hong Kong's Court of Final Appeal: The Development of the Law in China's Hong Kong* (CUP 2014).

Young, Simon N. M., and Law, Anthony, 'Privileged to Vote: Inequalities and Anomalies of the FC System' in Christine Loh and Civic Exchange (eds), *Functional*

Constituencies: A Unique Feature of the Hong Kong Legislative Council (HKU Press 2006).
Yu, Eilo Wing-yat, and Chin, Natalie Ka-man, 'The Political Opposition and Democracy in Macao: Revolutionaries or Loyalists?' (2012) 47 *Government and Opposition* 97.
Yu, Jun 于军 and Zhang, Wen 张文, 'A Survey of the Effectiveness of Power of Judicial Review of Administrative Normative Documents' 行政规范性文件司法审查权的实效性分析 (2016) 2 *Chinese Journal of Law* 法学研究 42.
Yu, Lingyun 余凌云, 'Reasonableness Review in Administrative Proceedings' 论行政诉讼上的合理性审查 (2022) 1 *Journal of Comparative Law* 比较法研究 145.
Yu, Qi 余祺, 'Authority of Normative Document and Various Levels of Intensity of Judicial Review' 规范性文件的权威性与司法审查的不同层次 (2016) 6 *Administrative Law Review* 行政法学研究 51.
Yu, Wenhao 于文豪, 'The Implementation of Constitutionality Review Duty by the Constitution and Law Committee' 宪法和法律委员会合宪性审查职责的展开 (2018) 6 *China Legal Science* 中国法学 43.
Zhang, Jiansheng 章剑生, 'Judicial Review on the Grounds of Violating Statutory Procedure: Based on the Typical Cases Issued by the People's Supreme Court (1985–2008)' 对违反法定程序的司法审查——以最高人民法院公布的典型案例(1985–2008) 为例 (2009) 2 *Chinese Journal of Law* 法学研究 150.
Zhang, Qianfan, 'A Constitution with Constitutionalism? The Paths of Constitutional Development in China' (2010) 8 *International Journal of Constitutional Law* 950.
Zhang, Ting 张婷, 'The Constitutional Propositions and Unfolding of Administrative Litigation Incidental Review' 行政诉讼附带审查的宪法命题及其展开 (2018) 3 *Legal Forum* 法学论坛 120.
Zheng, Lei 郑磊, 'Development and Evolution of Filing and Review and Rule of Law' 备案审查与法治体系的复调变迁 (2022) 6 *Journal of Chinese University of Political Science and Law* 中国政法大学学报 73.
Zheng, Zhihang 郑智航, 'Domestic Application of Foreign Laws and Precedents 外国法与案例在本国司法中的运用' (2014) 2 *Global Law Review* 环球法律评论 105.
Zhou, Youyong 周佑勇, 'Strengthening the Development of the Principle of Due Process through Judicial Decisions' 司法判决对正当程序原则的发展 (2019) 3 *China Legal Science* 中国法学 26.
Zhu, Guobin, 'Constitutional Review in China: An Unaccomplished Project or a Mirage' (2010) 43 *Suffolk University Law Review* 625.
Zhuang, Zhenzhen 庄真真, 'Study on the Issue of the Application of the Constitution in Macau Special Administrative Region' 憲法在澳門特別行政區的適用問題研究 (2015) 1 *Academic Journal of "One Country Two Systems"* "一國兩制"研究 41.

GOVERNMENT/ORGANIZATIONAL PUBLICATIONS AND SPEECHES

Commission Against Corruption of Macau 澳門廉政公署, Report on the Investigation of 74 Land Approval Files Declaring Provisional Land Leases Void 關於74個被宣告臨時性租賃批給失效之土地審批卷宗之調查報告.
Judicial Yuan Research Project on Introducing Constitutional Complaints to the Draft of the CIPC Amendment: Final Report (司法院大法官審理案件法修正草案引進裁判憲法訴願制度專題研究計劃：期末報告) (31 July 2018).

Leung, Elsie, 'The Continuity of Hong Kong's Legal System', Speech at the Asia-Pacific Society, Oxford University on 4 March 2001.

Li, Andrew, 'Speech by the Chief Justice at the Ceremonial Opening of the Legal Year 1999'.

The Administrative Tribunal of the SPC 最高人民法院行政审判庭 (ed), *Chinese Administrative Adjudication Cases (Volume I)* 中国行政审判案例（第*1*卷）(China Legal Publishing House 2010).

Index

Note: Page numbers followed by 'n' indicates note numbers; Page numbers in **bold** refers to tables; Page numbers in *italics* refers to figures.

FSC
www.fsc.org
MIX
Papier | Fördert gute Waldnutzung
FSC® C083411

Kolibri 360 GmbH
Ferdinand-Jühlke-Straße 7
99095 Erfurt, Deutschland
produktsicherheit@kolibri360.de